Nelson's Annual

Preacher's Sourcebook

2005 EDITION

Nelson's Annual Preacher's Sourcebook

2005 EDITION

ROBERT J. MORGAN, EDITOR

NELSON REFERENCE & ELECTRONIC
A Division of Thomas Nelson Publishers
Since 1798
www.thomasnelson.com

Published in Nashville, Tennessee, by Thomas Nelson, Inc.

Published in association with the literary agency of Alive Communications, 7680 Goddard Street, Suite 200, Colorado Springs, CO 80920.

Book design by Mark McGarry, Texas Type and Book Works, Dallas, Texas

Typesetting by A&W Publishing Electronic Services, Inc., Chicago, Illinois

Morgan, Robert J. (ed.)
Nelson's annual preacher's sourcebook, 2005 edition.

ISBN 0-7852-5200-2

Printed in the United States of America

1 2 3 4 5 6 7—09 08 07 06 05 04

Contents

Introduction

This book is designed to give you more time.

In his book *Why Leaders Can't Lead,* Warren Bennis warns of the danger of letting routine work drive out non-routine work, smothering to death all creative planning. We become so overwhelmed with regular daily demands that we have little time for solitude, conceptualizing, dreaming, and creative planning.

Here is a book to help you with the weekly routines of ministry. Chock full of sermon outlines, wedding and funeral ideas, illustrations, children's sermons, and worship planning helps, *Nelson's Annual Preacher's Sourcebook* is designed to take some of the burden off your schedule.

Please let us know if it's helpful. If you have comments, feedback, or suggestions for future volumes, please contact me at www.robertjmorgan.com.

This book would have been impossible without the oversight of Lee Hollaway of Thomas Nelson who gently nudges, nags, improves, suggests, corrects, inspires, and encourages me. Thanks, too, to Joshua D. Rowe and to Sherry Anderson, my assistants. I'm also grateful to Phil Stoner and Wayne Kinde of Thomas Nelson, and to Greg Johnson of Alive Communications.

My life and ministry was largely shaped through the influence of my pastor, Rev. Winford R. Floyd of Elizabethton, Tennessee. He is now in heaven after a lifetime of "preaching the gospel to the mountains of East Tennessee." This book is dedicated to his memory.

Editor's Preface

Looking to Jesus

I was in college when I memorized Psalm 123: "Unto You I lift up my eyes ... Behold, as the eyes of servants look to the hand of their masters, as the eyes of a maid to the hand of her mistress, so our eyes look to the LORD our God, until He has mercy on us (NKJV)."

In mulling over this Psalm, I've visualized the joy of beholding the Lord's face. I've thought of other, similar passages, such as Psalm 121 that tells us to lift our eyes to the hills from whence comes our help. And 2 Chronicles 20, where Jehoshaphat, encircled by enemies, prayed, "Our eyes are on you" (NASB).

I've thought of Peter treading the tempest, his eyes on the Savior's face; and of Hebrews 12 with its rousing admonition to look unto Jesus, the author and finisher of our faith. I've thought of the old hymn that says: "Turn your eyes upon Jesus. / Look full in His wonderful face."

It's now dawned on me that the writer of Psalm 123 wasn't looking at the Lord's face, but at His hand. "As the eyes of servants look to the hand of their masters, as the eyes of a maid to the hand of her mistress, so our eyes look to the LORD our God" (NKJV). What's the significance of looking at the Lord's hand?

His Hand Hides Us

The writer of Psalm 123 is distressed and needs help from God. He intends to look toward the Lord's hand, "until He have mercy on us" (NKJV). The problem, according to verses 3, 4, is the opposition and disdain he is encountering. Here is a man who needs love, reassurance, and courage. He needs God's mercy. He needs what Fanny Crosby wrote about:

He hideth my soul in the cleft of the rock
That shadows a dry, thirsty land;
He hideth my life with the depths of His love,
And covers me there with His hand.

Ever feel that way? Four years ago, I was hit by a problem I never expected, one resulting in prolonged distress. The months stretched into years, and I struggled to cope with galloping anxiety. At times, I wondered if Satan wasn't intent on destroying my work and me.

Then one Sunday night I heard a man speak from Colossians 3:3: "For you died, and your life is hidden with Christ in God" (NKJV). The power of that verse instantly brought a peace to my heart that has never faltered and never left me. I knew I had to die to my problem, to my anxiety, and to everything in my world except Christ. I had to leave it all in the all-sufficient hand of my Savior.

The Lord conveys His love for us through His hands, for they absorbed the nails for us. It's those nail-pierced hands that tightly hold us and safely hide us. The devil looks for every opportunity to attack God's servants. Before, during, and after the sermon we're targets for every trial and temptation his smarmy brain can devise. We're subject to discouragement, to criticism, to thoughts of failure, to church problems, to illness, to opposition. But His nail-scarred hands hide us and keep us safe. As Frances Havergal put it:

Hidden in the hollow of His blessed hand,
Never foe can follow, never traitor stand.
Not a surge of worry, not a shade of care,
Not a blast of hurry touch the spirit there.

Are you facing issues that only His hands can resolve? Perhaps stresses with your children, your finances, or your church? Lift up your eyes to the nail-pierced hand of the Lord Jesus who hides us in His love.

His Hand Guides Us

A hundred years ago, the Syrian culture was similar to that of biblical days. A writer in Spurgeon's *Treasury of David,* while traveling in Damascus, tells of being entertained by a wealthy man. The traveler noticed that the lord of the house issued no verbal commands to his servants. It was all done by hand signals. "As soon as we were introduced and seated on the divan," wrote the man, "a wave of the master's hand indicated that sherbet was to be served. Another wave brought coffee and pipes. Another brought sweetmeats. At another signal dinner was made ready. The attendants watched their master's eye and hand, to know his will and do it instantly."

The lesson here is clear and wonderful. We need to keep our eyes on the hands of our Heavenly Father, ready in an instant to do His will. Just a flick of His finger or a wave of His hand should send us this way or that. There's an old hymn that says: "He leadeth me, He leadeth me, / By His own hand He leadeth me."

Psalm 139:9, 10 says: "If I take the wings of the morning, and dwell in the uttermost parts of the sea, even there Your hand shall lead me, and Your right hand shall hold me" (NKJV).

Vance Havner, the North Carolina evangelist, put it this way in a book he wrote at age eighty: "I thank God for the Unseen Hand, sometimes urging me onward, sometimes holding me back; sometimes with a caress of approval, sometimes with a stroke of reproof; sometimes correcting, sometimes comforting. My times are in His hand. I am graven on the palms of His hands. No one can pluck me out of His hand. I call that 'having the situation well in hand!'"[1]

His Hand Provides

Finally, His hand provides the power of our ministry. We need His hand on our preaching and on our ministry. The old-timers talked about the "unction of the Spirit," but no one needs it more badly than we do now.

Outside Boston's Trinity Episcopal Church is a statue of its illustrious former pastor, Phillips Brooks. He is shown preaching. Behind him stands Christ with His hand on the preacher's shoulder. Do you ever stand in the pulpit visualizing the hand of Christ on your shoulder, empowering you with divine unction as you preach?

We're called to do hard things. The ministry has never been easy, but it's never been harder. If you're discouraged, take your focus off yourself. Look to the Lord. Look full in His wonderful hands. As the eyes of servants look to the hand of their Master, let your eyes drift heavenward. See those torn but triumphant hands, and let them hide and guide and provide for you.

1. Vance Havner, *Forescore* (Old Tappen, N.J.: Revell, 1982), p. 23.

Create a Sermon Series!

If you would like to publicize and preach a series of messages, you can assemble your own by mixing and matching various sermons and sermon outlines in this *Sourcebook*. Here are some suggestions:

Sharing the Good News

- News Too Good to Keep Quiet (January 16)
- How to Win That Friend to Christ (March 20)
- Personal Magnetism (April 10)
- Effective Witnessing (August 7)
- Bringing a Friend to Jesus (September 25)
- Daring Determination (September 25)
- I Am Not Ashamed (October 30)

Praise and Worship

- The Year of Worship (January 2)
- The Beauty of His Holiness (April 17)
- The Graveyard Shift (May 22)
- Sing Praise! (June 5)
- Worthy Worship (August 21)
- Exuberant Praise (November 27)
- The Triune We Worship (December 18)

Overcoming Obstacles

- Overcoming Doubt (July 10)
- Overcoming Ambition (August 7)
- Overcoming Temptation (August 21)
- Overcoming Deception (September 4)
- Overcoming Prejudice (September 25)
- Overcoming Idleness (October 9)
- Overcoming Talkativeness (October 30)
- Overcoming Envy (November 13)
- Overcoming Division (December 4)
- Overcoming Greed (December 18)

Biblical Heroes

- A Man to Mimic (Stephen) (February 13)
- Trials and Troubles (Job) (February 13)
- Close Encounters of a Life-Changing Kind (The Disciples) (March 27)

- Noah's News (July 24)
- The Difference in Daniel (August 28)
- Enoch's Exit (October 2)
- Epaphras—The Man Who Prayed (October 16)

The Effective Church

- What's Right with the Church (April 24)
- The Perfect Church (November 20)
- Operation Restoration (February 20)
- The Sovereign's Standard (February 20)

The Life and Character of Our Lord

- Christ in Our Midst (January 30)
- Consider Him (March 20)
- Why I Preach the Literal Resurrection of Christ (March 27)
- The Christ of Easter (March 27)
- Serving a Magnificent Christ (June 26)
- Boast in the Cross (July 17)
- At His Appearing (August 21)
- Christ Is (November 6)
- A Third Opinion (November 20)
- Master in the Manger (December 11)
- What Christ Means to Me (December 11)

Contributors

Dr. Timothy K. Beougher

Billy Graham Professor of Evangelism and Associate Dean of the Billy Graham School of Missions, Evangelism and Church Growth, The Southern Baptist Theological Seminary, Louisville, Kentucky

Operation Restoration (February 20)
What's Right with the Church (April 24)
Parenting with Purpose (May 8)
Anchors During Adversity (June 12)
Effective Witnessing (August 7)
Worthy Worship (August 21)
Signposts (September 11)
Bringing a Friend to Jesus (September 25)
Daring Determination (September 25)
Four Types of People (October 16)
The Adventure of Faith (November 6)
A Third Opinion (November 20)
How Should We Then Give (December 4)
The Danger of Division (December 11)

Rev. Dan Chun

Senior Pastor, First Presbyterian Church of Honolulu, Co-Founder and Chairman of the Board of Hawaiian Island Ministries

Why We Deny (July 3)

Dr. Ed Dobson

Pastor, Calvary Church in Grand Rapids, Michigan, and Moody Bible Institute's 1993 Pastor of the Year

Practical Advice for Prayer Life (April 3)
As We Remember (September 11)

Rev. Michael Easley

Pastor and Teacher, Immanuel Bible Church, Springfield, Virginia

Strategic Planning (March 13)
Courage to Confront Sin (July 17)
Profaning What Is Holy (July 17)

Rev. Billy Friel
Pastor, First Baptist Church, Mt. Juliet, Tennessee

Trials and Troubles (February 13)
When Revival Comes (March 13)
Finding People for God (April 3)
Job's Trials and Ours (April 24)

Rev. Peter Grainger
Pastor, Charlotte Baptist Chapel, Edinburgh, Scotland

The Road to Salvation (January 2)
The Day of the Lord (January 23)
Who Rules? (March 6)
War and Peace (July 3)
The Vineyard of the Lord (July 31)
The Fear of the Lord (August 14)
Common Bond (September 4)
More Harm than Good (October 2)
The Sanctity of Marriage (October 23)
The Peril of Procrastination (November 6)
The Perfect Church (November 20)
Wrong on Two Counts (December 4)
The Call of the Lord (December 18)

Frances Ridley Havergal (1836–1879)
English hymn and devotional writer

Master in the Manger (December 11)

Dr. Rick Holland
Pastor, Student Ministries, Grace Community Church of Sun Valley, California

Conversations in a Pastor's Study: The Pastor and Today's Youth Culture

Rev. Mark Hollis
Former minister of 15 years and current freelance writer in Nashville, Tennessee. Master of Arts in Pastoral Counseling.

News Too Good to Keep Quiet (January 16)
Avoiding the Big Blowups (January 30)
In the Storms of Life, God Gives Mercy (February 13)
God Our Shepherd (March 6)
Close Encounters of a Life-Changing Kind (March 27)

Family Matters (April 17)
Resurrection Faith in ACTion (April 24)

T. C. Horton (1848–1932)
American evangelist, pastor, educator, and writer

Hungry? (May 15)

Dr. David Jeremiah
Senior Pastor of Shadow Mountain Community Church, El Cajon, California, and chancellor of Christian Heritage College

The Year of Worship (January 2)
A Man to Mimic (February 13)
The Lifestyle of the Righteous and Faithful (April 10)
The Gospel According to You (May 29)
Epaphras—The Man Who Prayed (October 16)
How to Celebrate Christmas (December 25)
What Is Christmas? (December 25)

Dr. D. James Kennedy
Pastor, Coral Ridge Presbyterian Church, Fort Lauderdale, Florida

The Rewards of Faithfulness (April 10)

Rev. Todd M. Kinde
Pastor of Grace Bible Church, Grandville, Michigan. Former pastor of North View Alliance Church, Grand Rapids Michigan.

Pray for Us (January 23)
Our Lord, the Merciful One (February 6)
Faith Amid Famine (March 6)
Overcoming Doubt (July 10)
Evidences of Genuine Christianity (July 24)
Overcoming Ambition (August 7)
Overcoming Temptation (August 21)
Overcoming Deception (September 4)
Overcoming Prejudice (September 25)
Overcoming Idleness (October 9)
Overcoming Talkativeness (October 30)
Overcoming Envy (November 13)
Overcoming Division (December 4)
Overcoming Greed (December 18)
Dead Center (Baptism Sermon)
Suitable for a Second Marriage (Wedding Sermon)

Dr. Woodrow Kroll
President and Senior Bible Teacher of Back to the Bible Broadcast

Ten Reasons for Family Devotions (February 27)
The Remolding Hand of God (August 14)

Dr. Denis Lyle
Pastor, Lurgan Baptist Church, Belfast, Northern Ireland

Praying for Your Life (January 9)
The Discipline of Disturbance (January 30)
Consider Him (March 20)
Turn Over the Controls (May 15)
The Spirit-Filled Soul (May 15)
Help, We're Surrounded (May 29)
An Anonymous Benefactor (June 26)
When God Crashes the Party (August 28)
The Difference in Daniel (August 28)
Divine Direction (October 2)
A Home with a Difference (November 13)
Requirements for Service (November 27)

Dr. F.B. Meyer (1847-1929)
Minister and Keswick Theologian

The Worldly Christian (May 29)
We Are His People (October 9)

Daniel Miles
Graduate of Columbia International University

The Characteristics of a Disciple (January 16)

Dr. Stephen Olford
Evangelist, Founder of the Stephen Olford Center for Biblical Preaching, Memphis, Tennessee

Conversations in a Pastor's Study: The Preacher's Spiritual and Physical Health

Rev. Kevin Riggs
Former Pastor, Franklin Community Church, Franklin, Tennesse
Praying With a Purpose (May 1)
Ordinary Greatness (May 22)

Joshua D. Rowe
Assistant Editor to Robert J. Morgan and Graduate of Columbia International University, with degrees in Bible and Biblical Languages

Expressing Our Faith (July 10)
Call to Service (July 24)
A Simple Message (September 18)
The Trap of Temptation (October 9)
True Commitment (October 23)
Caught Up Together in the Clouds (Funeral Sermon)
Why True Love Waits (Youth Sermon)

William Graham Scroggie (1877–1959)
Scottish minister and writer

God's Triune Benediction (January 2)
Christ in Our Midst (January 30)
One Thing I Know (February 20)
Boast in the Cross (July 17)
God's Guidance (July 31)
What Bethel Meant (August 28)

Rev. Richard Sharpe Jr.
Director of Small Church Ministries and President of Christian Home Crusade

Intimacy with God (January 9)
The Beauty of His Holiness (April 17)
Remember the Sacrifice (Communion Sermon)
It Is Well With the Child (Funeral Sermon)
Choices (Funeral Sermon)
Only One Unpardonable Sin (Funeral Sermon)

Rev. Charles Haddon Spurgeon (1834–1892)
Pastor, Metropolitan Tabernacle, London

The Power of Knowledge (January 16)
Forgiveness Made Easy (January 23)
Grace and Glory (August 14)
Christ Is (November 6)
Advice on the Voice

Dr. W. H. Griffith Thomas (1861–1924)
English minister, scholar, and teacher

What Christ Means to Me (December 11)

Dr. R. A. Torrey (1856–1928)
American evangelist, pastor, educator, and writer

Simple Directions (May 8)
When It Pays to Believe in Jesus Christ (May 22)
Eternal Life: What It Is and How to Get It (June 12)
Why I Am Glad I'm a Christian (July 10)
The Judgment Day (October 23)

John Wesley (1703–1791)
English preacher and minister

Good Angels (February 6)

Dr. Melvin Worthington
Executive Secretary, National Association of Free Will Baptists

The Sovereign's Standard (February 20)
At His Appearing (March 20)
The Apathetic Assembly (May 1)
The Danger of Discounting Doctrine (June 5)
The Faithful Father (June 19)
Noah's News (July 24)
The Viciousness of Slander (July 31)
The Profit of Persecution (August 7)
At His Appearing (August 21)
The Vice of Stealing (September 11)
Enoch's Exit (October 2)
The Horror of Hypocrisy (October 16)
Sinfulness of Selfishness (October 30)
The Creator's Character (November 13)
An Ambassador (November 27)
The Triune We Worship (December 18)
Thanksgiving Truths (Thanksgiving Sermon)
The Value of Human Life (Sanctity of Life Sermon)

All other outlines are from the pulpit ministry of the general editor, Rev. Robert J. Morgan, of The Donelson Fellowship in Nashville, Tennessee. Special appreciation goes to Jerry Carraway, worship leader of The Donelson Fellowship, for his invaluable assistance.

2005 Calendar

All boldface days are Sundays

January 1	New Year's Day
January 2	
January 6	Epiphany
January 9	
January 16	**Sanctity of Human Life Sunday**
January 17	Martin Luther King, Jr. Day
January 23	
January 26	Australia Day
January 30	
February 1-28	Black History Month
February 1	National Freedom Day
February 2	Groundhog Day
February 6	**Super Bowl Sunday**
February 9	Ash Wednesday
February 12	Lincoln's Birthday
February 13	**First Sunday of Lent**
February 14	Valentine's Day
February 20	**Second Sunday of Lent**
February 21	Presidents' Day
February 22	Washington's Birthday
February 27	**Third Sunday of Lent**
March 6	**Fourth Sunday of Lent**
March 13	**Fifth Sunday of Lent**
March 17	St. Patrick's Day
March 20	**Passion/Palm Sunday; Spring begins**
March 24	Holy Thursday
March 25	Good Friday; Purim
March 27	**Easter Sunday**

April 3	**Daylight Savings Time Begins**
April 10	
April 13	Jefferson's Birthday
April 17	
April 22	Earth Day
April 24	**Passover**
April 27	Administrative Professional's Day
May 1	
May 5	National Day of Prayer; Ascension Day; Holocaust Remembrance Day
May 8	**Mother's Day**
May 15	**Pentecost**
May 21	Armed Forces Day
May 22	**Trinity Sunday**
May 29	
May 30	Memorial Day
June 5	
June 12	
June 14	Flag Day
June 19	**Father's Day**
June 21	Summer begins
June 26	
July 1	Canada Day
July 3	
July 4	Independence Day
July 10	
July 17	
July 24	**Parent's Day**
July 31	
August 6	Transfiguration Day
August 7	**Friendship Day**
August 14	
August 21	

August 28	
September 4	
September 5	Labor Day
September 11	**Grandparent's Day**
September 18	
September 22	Autumn begins
September 23	Native American Day
September 25	
October 1-31	Pastor Appreciation Month
October 2	
October 4	Rosh Hashanah begins
October 9	**Clergy Appreciation Day; Children's Day**
October 10	Columbus Day
October 13	Yom Kippur begins
October 16	**National Boss Day**
October 23	
October 26	Mother-in-Law Day
October 27	Reformation Day
October 30	**Reformation Sunday; Daylight Savings Time ends**
October 31	Halloween
November 1	All Saints' Day
November 6	
November 8	Election Day
November 11	Veteran's Day
November 13	**International Day of Prayer for the Persecuted Church**
November 20	
November 24	Thanksgiving Day
November 27	**First Sunday of Advent**
December 4	**Second Sunday of Advent**
December 7	Pearl Harbor Remembrance Day
December 11	**Third Sunday of Advent**
December 18	**Fourth Sunday of Advent**
December 21	Winter begins

December 24	Christmas Eve
December 25	**Christmas Day**
December 26	Hanukkah begins; Kwanzaa begins
December 31	New Year's Eve

SERMONS AND WORSHIP SUGGESTIONS FOR 52 WEEKS

JANUARY 2, 2005

SUGGESTED SERMON *Date preached:*

The Year of Worship

By Dr. David Jeremiah

Scripture: Romans 11:33–36, especially verse 33
Oh, the depth of the riches both of the wisdom and the knowledge of God! How unsearchable are His judgments and His ways past finding out! (NKJV)

Introduction: As we begin a New Year, let's make it a year of worship, a year of exalting Jesus Christ, our Lord and God. In today's passage, Paul comes to the end of eleven chapters in Romans. He has systematically built a theological foundation for his readers. In Romans 1—3, he said the whole world was guilty before a righteous God. In Romans 3—5, he revealed God's remedy for sin's curse: justification through faith in Christ. In chapters 6—8, he gave us principles for effective Christian living. In chapters 9—11, we're brought face to face with the justice of God as we see how He deals with both Jews and Gentiles. When Paul finished verse 32, overwhelmed by everything he had said, he broke out in worship. He didn't see any difference between theology and doxology. To him, the great doctrines of God weren't subjects for a library or monastery. Theology was the fuel for the fire of his soul. He was like a traveler who had climbed up to the top of a mountain and, looking at all the area he had traversed, couldn't take it all in. So, he paused for worship.

1. **Worship Is Wondering After God (v. 33).** Worship is getting caught up in the things we know about God. You can never get your arms around God. If you could, He wouldn't be God. You just learn what you can about Him, and this causes you to step back in awe.

   A. **Wondering After God's Wealth.** Oh, the depth of the riches of God! One of Paul's favorite words about God is *rich*. He wrote about the riches of God's goodness, forbearance, longsuffering, glory, grace, and mercy. Trace that word in a concordance and ponder the infinite richness of the Almighty.

   B. **Wondering After God's Wisdom.** Wisdom is not merely God's grasp of information, it is His ability to integrate all the elements of the universe in a way that causes all things work for good.

C. **Wondering After God's Knowledge (see Col. 2:3).** God knows everything to be known—past, present, and future. He knows all things without having learned any of them. He is omniscient. He's perfectly acquainted with every detail in the life of every being in heaven, earth, and hell. Nothing escapes His notice, nothing can be hidden from Him, and He forgets nothing.

2. **Worship Is Waiting Before God (vv. 33–36).** Now Paul takes these truths about God and expounds them in reverse order.

   A. **The Knowledge of God Is Unsearchable. (See Is. 55:8–9).** C. S. Lewis said that trying to explain what God is like is similar to a shellfish trying to explain a human to another shellfish. God is incomprehensible, yet He has revealed Himself to us in His Son. We can know God, but we can never know Him exhaustively. He's not like anything else.

   B. **His Wisdom Is Untraceable.** Who has known the mind of the Lord? The phrase "past finding out" is sometimes translated "unfathomable," and the Greek word literally refers to footprints you can't track, like those of an animal a hunter can't follow (see Is. 40:13, Ps. 77:19, and Ps. 139:6).

   C. **His Wealth Is Unfathomable.** God has been wealthy forever, and He never is going to be wealthier than He is now. He is wholly self-sufficient. "For of Him and through Him and to Him are all things, to whom be glory forever. Amen." God is the source: "of Him." God is the means: "By Him." And God is the goal: "For Him." (Compare Col. 1:16, 17 NKJV).

Conclusion: At the end of verse 36, Paul simply says: "To whom [God] be glory forever. Amen." Sometimes we just need to fall down and say, "God, You're so wonderful! I don't even know how to pray. Lord, You're so incredible; I don't even know what to say. You're so vast; I don't know how to comprehend it." This should be our desire as God's people, to give glory to the One who is so wonderful. That's our desire for this new year of 2005, and for the rest of life. When you come to know the greatness of God, it changes everything about your life. All you want to do is bring glory to Him, to say: "Then sings my soul my Savior God to Thee, 'How great Thou art, how great Thou art!'"

STATS, STORIES, AND MORE

Great quotes about worship:

The world can be saved by one thing and that is worship. To worship is to quicken the conscience by the holiness of God, to feed the mind with the truth of God, to purge the imagination by the beauty of God, to open the heart to the love of God, to devote the will to the purpose of God.—William Temple

It behooves us to be careful what we worship, for what we are worshiping we are becoming.—Ralph Waldo Emerson

We tend by a secret law of the soul to move toward our mental image of God.—A. W. Tozer

Wash your face every morning in a bath of praise.—Charles Spurgeon

Christian worship is the most momentous, the most urgent, and the most glorious action that can take place in human life.—Karl Barth

Eyes Full of Wonder

The British actress Joan Winmill Brown once wrote: "Years ago John Ruskin, the English critic, wrote, 'I would sooner live in a cottage and wonder at everything, than live in a castle and wonder at nothing.' I have often thought of the statement that H. G. Wells made before his death, that the sight of the stars in the sky no longer moved his soul. The truth is, I cannot express to you all the wonder and joy that I have in my heart through Jesus Christ."

The Riches of God

A man once asked God, "What is time like to you?" God replied, "A thousand years to you is like one day to me." The man asked, "What is money to you?" God replied, "A million dollars to you is but a penny in my sight." The man boldly asked, "Well, God, could you give me just a penny?" God smiled and said, "Just a second."

FOR THE BULLETIN

❁ St. Basil the Great was a brilliant man from Caesarea of Cappadocia who might have been a statesman but for his sister's witness, which led him into the ministry. In 370, he became Bishop of Caesarea and archbishop of all Cappadocia. He fought Arianism by appointing orthodox bishops, and was active in mercy ministries, founding the first hospital in Christian history. He died on January 1, 379. News spread like wildfire; the next day he was mourned deeply. He is remembered every January 2, which is designated in western tradition as the Feast Day of St. Basil the Great. ❁ Aimee Semple McPherson, 19, was ordained into the ministry on this day in 1909 by an evangelist named William Durham in Chicago. She established her base in Los Angeles where, in 1923, the 5,500 seat Angelus Temple was dedicated and became the center of her revival, healing, and benevolent ministries. She was the first woman to receive a federal radio license and was a pioneer religious broadcaster. She later became the founder of the International Church of the Foursquare Gospel. She created international headlines when she disappeared off a California beach in 1926, and weeks later surfaced in the desert, saying she had been kidnapped. ❁ The first religious program heard over the radio was broadcast from Calvary Episcopal Church of Pittsburgh over local radio station KDKA on January 2, 1921. It wasn't considered a landmark event at the time. In fact, the senior pastor didn't speak, turning the responsibilities over to his associate.

APPROPRIATE SONGS AND HYMNS

Blessed Be the Name, Charles Wesley/Ralph E. Hudson; Public Domain.

Brethren, We Have Met to Worship, George Atkins/William Moore; Public Domain.

Bow Before the Lord, Terry Butler/Tom Osbrink; © 1993 Mercy/Vineyard Publishing.

The Heart of Worship, Matt Redman; © 1997 Kingsway's Thankyou Music; Admin. by EMI Christian Music Publishing.

Worthy of Worship, Terry W. York/Mark Blankenship; © 1988 McKinney Music, Inc., Van Ness Press, Inc.; Admin. by Genevox Music Group.

WORSHIP HELPS

Call to Worship:
Oh come, let us worship and bow down; Let us kneel before the LORD our Maker. For He is our God, and we are the people of His pasture, and the sheep of His hand. (Ps. 95:6, 7 NKJV)

Welcome:
I can't tell you how wonderful it is to begin a new year with this assembly of believers. I'm sure many of you are just beginning your New Year's resolutions—diets, exercise, spending more time with family, changing yourself for the better. I would ask you to make this morning a time of spiritual resolution and renewal. Paul said it best in 1 Timothy 4:8, "For bodily exercise profits a little, but godliness is profitable for all things, having promise of the life that now is and of that which is to come" (NKJV). Maybe you're a first-time visitor who has resolved to find a new church. Perhaps you've been here for years, but you haven't been involved or you have grown cold in your spiritual walk with the Lord. We as the Lord's church are to constantly grow together, to become more like Jesus Christ. Make that your resolution this year, and every day. Use this place of worship as a means to that end, and prepare your heart for this year's service to the Lord.

Benediction:
Therefore, I urge you, brothers, in view of God's mercy, to offer your bodies as living sacrifices, holy and pleasing to God—this is your spiritual act of worship. (Rom. 12:1 NIV)

Additional Sermons and Lesson Ideas

The Road to Salvation

Date preached:

By Rev. Peter Grainger

SCRIPTURE: Acts 8:26–40

INTRODUCTION: In every life won to Jesus, there are steps along the way. In most cases, there are three steps common on the "road to salvation":

1. In the Desert (vv. 26–31): A Meeting Arranged
   A. The Ethiopian: a man of status and wealth, and a seeker (Acts 17:26, 27).
   B. Philip: a man full of the Spirit and wisdom, and a gifted evangelist (Acts 8:4–8).
2. In the Chariot (vv. 32–35): A Message Explained
   A. The importance of the Scriptures (Is. 53).
   B. The need for understanding the focus: the gospel of Jesus Christ (Rom. 10:9–15).
3. In the Water (vv. 36–40): A Faith Proclaimed
   A. Trust in Jesus (Rom. 10:9).
   B. Public Witness (Acts 2:38, 39).

CONCLUSION: The Ethiopian went away rejoicing (v. 39). Do you have the joy of Christ? If not, I invite you to accept Jesus as your Savior and Lord today! If you have, follow Philip's example: Share your faith with confidence!

God's Triune Benediction

Date preached:

By W. Graham Scroggie

SCRIPTURE: 2 Corinthians 13:14

INTRODUCTION: There are many benedictions in Paul's letters, but this one is pre-eminently the Apostolic Benediction. From early times, it was adopted into the liturgy of the church. Notice:

1. The Ground of this Benediction. This is found in the Triune God. The truth of the Trinity is the foundation of revelation and the ground of Christian faith.
2. The Substance of this Benediction. It ascribes to each Person of the Trinity a special work in redemption: the grace of Christ, the love of God, the communion of the Spirit.
3. The Inclusiveness of this Benediction. Paul prays that these blessings may be "with you all." Paul included everyone—even those who had been critical of him.

CONCLUSION: What a difference it would make in our church if we claimed the richness of this Benediction as our own.

JANUARY 9, 2005

SUGGESTED SERMON *Date preached:*

Mountain Dew and Sweet Perfume

Scripture: Psalm 133

Behold, how good and how pleasant it is for brethren to dwell together in unity. It is like the precious oil upon the head .... It is like the dew of Hermon. (NKJV)

Introduction: We live in a fractured world. Many churches are divided; and even in a unified church like this one, none of us knows how many marriages are troubled, how many homes are tense, or how many friendships are strained. God wants us to be one, and Christ prayed for our unity in John 17:11. Psalm 133 gives three helpful truths about unity.

1. **Unity Is Well-Pleasing (v. 1):** Behold, how good and how pleasant it is for brethren to dwell together in unity. The word *behold* draws our attention to this. "Hey, look! Check this out! When people get along with each other it's both good and pleasant." Many things are good, but not pleasant. Other things are pleasant, but not good. Here is something morally good and emotionally pleasant about getting along with others. Suppose two families invited you to supper on the same night. One was fighting among itself. The other was happy and loving, and mealtime there was a joy. Which invitation would you accept? Suppose you could attend one of two churches. The first was fragmented and the other was loving. Which would you attend? It is good and pleasant to dwell together in unity.

2. **Unity Is Sweet-Smelling (v. 2),** like precious oil upon the head, running down on the beard of Aaron. In the Old Testament, God used the act of anointing with oil to signify the setting apart of certain people for divine service. The oil represented the Holy Spirit coming upon someone, sanctifying that person for holy use. God instructed Moses, for example, to appoint Aaron as High Priest, using oil (Lev. 8:30). Exodus 30 gives a unique recipe for this perfumed oil. It was made from four ingredients: olive oil, liquid myrrh, cinnamon, and cassia (Ex. 30:22–33). It was a sweet-smelling perfume. As Aaron knelt before the Lord, Moses slowly poured this oil over his head. It ran down his beard, saturating his clothing, down to the fringes of his garments. It covered him with a unique, wonderful fragrance. According to Psalm 133, that's what the unity of the body of Christ

is like. It's something the Holy Spirit does as He is poured upon the church, saturating and drenching the people of God, making them one and bestowing on them a wonderful fragrance. With that in mind, read Ephesians 4:30–32. We're told not to grieve the Holy Spirit with whom we've been sealed (that is, anointed). We're to get rid of bitterness, rage, and anger. We're to be kind, forgiving each other. Many people feel they've been mistreated in some way, by parents, by a bully, by an employer. God gives us the Holy Spirit to enable us to trust Him with those people who are making us angry. There comes a point when you say, "Lord, you know what my parents did to me. You know what my ex-wife is saying. You know how I was treated in school. But Jesus loved me enough to die for me, and I know He's big enough to settle things up. I'm going to leave it with Him." One of the best remedies to anger is faith in Christ; and one of the functions of the Spirit is to give us the wisdom needed to trust Him with things that would otherwise drive us to rage.

3. **Unity Is Life-Giving (v. 3).** Unity is also like the dew of Hermon. This is the highest mountain in Israel. Its moisture runs into steams and rivulets that flow into the Jordan River, which runs north to south through Israel, irrigating and giving life to all the land. That's the way of the unity of the Spirit—it gives life. A united marriage, friendship, ball team, or church gives life to others; one that is divided has no life to give.

Conclusion: Does someone here have a bitter, angry, critical spirit? You need the Holy Spirit's help as you seek to trust God with whatever has caused this. The Holy Spirit is powerful enough to help you. I believe Jesus Christ is real enough to give you an overcoming attitude. Bring your frustrations to Him and trust Him to do what He alone can do. And may He heal our homes, restore our relationships, give us patience, and make us one.

STATS, STORIES, AND MORE

Years ago, I had a man in my church who was always angry with me. After every service, he would tell me something that was wrong with the music or with my sermon or with the church. He was negative and critical all the time. Finally I said, "You know, we're not a perfect church and I'm not a perfect pastor, but the real problem is your negative, critical, angry attitude. What are you so mad about?" We had a blow-up over it, and he left the church. Years later he came back and said, "You know, you were right. I was getting shafted at work, and I was angry. It came out toward my wife. It came out toward my church. It poisoned my relationships. It just made me an angry, irritable, unpleasant person." *—Robert J. Morgan*

Angry Driver

I was driving along a narrow, country road when someone barreled around the curve, swerved into my lane, crashed into my car, and sped off. I tried to chase him, but he was long gone; and I was stuck with the repair bills. Everyday for the next week I went looking for that man's car so I could confront him. I finally realized that God knew who that person was and that He would settle the score in His own way and time. I also realized the Lord had protected me from being hurt or killed, and He could provide for my car to be repaired. I had to let go of the anger and trust the situation into God's hands. When I did, the fragrance of the Holy Spirit came back into my heart and life.
—Robert J. Morgan

FOR THE BULLETIN

❁ The Dutch theologian, Jacob Arminius, was born on January 9, 1560. ❁ It was on this day, January 9, 1793, that the Baptist Missionary Society ("The Particular Baptist Society for the Propagation of the Gospel Amongst the Heathen") voted to send William Carey to India as its first missionary. ❁ "Uncle" Bob Sheffey, 19, was converted on January 9, 1839, at a store in Abingdon, Virginia. Feeling the call to preach, he dropped out of college and started through the Virginia hills as a Methodist circuit rider preaching the gospel. His unorthodox prayers and sermons ushered many mountaineers into the kingdom and earned him the title *Peculiar Preacher*. ❁ Today is the birthday of Rees Howells, famous for his intercessory prayer life. He was born in 1879. ❁ On January 9, 1896, former baseball player, Billy Sunday, preached in Garner, Iowa, where the town's three Protestant churches rented an opera house for a week of evangelistic meetings. The choir was made up of twenty people, and Billy led the singing himself. It was Sunday's first attempt at an evangelistic campaign, and it resulted in nearly 100 conversions, launching Sunday's career as a mass evangelist. ❁ God called Baptist missionary Bertha Smith into missionary service on January 9, 1910. She served many years as a missionary to China, and spent the remaining years of her life traveling, speaking, and inspiring audiences across North America. Her autobiography, *Go Home and Tell*, is a missionary classic.

APPROPRIATE SONGS AND HYMNS

Called as Partners in Christ's Service, Jane Parker Huber/John Zundel; © 1982 Jane Parker Huber; Admin. by Westminster John Knox Press.

Blest Be the Tie that Binds, John Fawcett/Johann G. Nageli; Public Domain.

Help Us Accept Each Other, Fred Kaan/Doreen Potter/Sameul S. Wesley; © 1975 Hope Publishing Co.

Make Us One, Carol Cymbala; © 1991 Word Music, Inc./Carol Joy Music; Admin. by Integrated Copyright Group, Inc.

Reach Out and Take a Hand, Graham Kendrick; © 1996 Make Way Music; Admin. by Music Services.

WORSHIP HELPS

Call to Worship:
O praise our God today,
His constant mercy bless,
Whose love hath helped us on our way,
And granted us success.

—*Henry W. Baker*

Scripture:
If I speak with the eloquence of men and of angels, but have no love, I become no more than blaring brass or crashing cymbal. If I have the gift of foretelling the future and hold in my mind not only all human knowledge but the very secrets of God, and if I also have that absolute faith which can move mountains, but have no love, I amount to nothing at all. If I dispose of all that I possess, yes, even if I give my own body to be burned, but have no love, I achieve precisely nothing. This love of which I speak is slow to lose patience—it looks for a way of being constructive. It is not possessive: it is neither anxious to impress nor does it cherish inflated ideas of its own importance. Love has good manners and does not pursue selfish advantage. It is not touchy. It does not keep account of evil or gloat over the wickedness of other people. On the contrary, it is glad with all good men when truth prevails. Love knows no limit to its endurance, no end to its trust, no fading of its hope; it can outlast anything. (1 Cor. 13 PHILLIPS)

Benediction:
Lord, may it be our choice
This blessèd rule to keep,
"Rejoice with them that do rejoice,
And weep with them that weep."

—*Henry W. Baker*

Additional Sermons and Lesson Ideas

Praying for Your Life

Date preached:

By Dr. Dennis Lyle

SCRIPTURE: Daniel 6:10

INTRODUCTION: When it came to choosing prayer and death or no prayer and life, Daniel chose prayer and death. He:

1. Loves the Usual Place. Daniel prayed at his window facing Jerusalem. Where is your place of daily prayer? (see Matt. 6:6).
2. Pleads the Usual Promise. God made specific promises to Israel if they prayed toward Jerusalem (see 2 Chr. 6:36). In prayer, do you plead the promises?
3. Adopts the Usual Posture. Daniel kneeled. Sometimes it helps to humble the position of the body in order to humble the heart.
4. Continues the Usual Plan. Three times a day Daniel prayed (See Ps. 55:17).
5. Offers the Usual Petitions. Daniel gave thanks. Where did he learn that? He grew up in a home that served the Lord. Never underestimate your influence on the spiritual lives of your children.

CONCLUSION: You may never have to choose between prayer and life, but each day, prayer is a choice between spiritual life and complacency.

Intimacy with God

Date preached:

By Dr. Richard Sharpe Jr.

SCRIPTURE: Isaiah 6:1–8

INTRODUCTION: Imagine what a vision of God would look like. Would it strike fear in your heart, or love in your soul, or maybe both?

1. Vision of Individual God (vv. 1–4). Isaiah sees the Lord (Adonai) and seraphim singing: "Holy, Holy, Holy." A second name is used, LORD (Jehovah), meaning covenant-keeping God. Jehovah is a personal God.
2. Vision of Individual Self (vv. 5–7). Isaiah realized he was a sinner in need of cleansing. We must have a vision of God's holiness versus our own sin before repentance and forgiveness can occur.
3. Vision of Individual's Responsibility (v. 8). Isaiah heard the Lord ask, "Who will go?" Isaiah immediately volunteered his service.

CONCLUSION: The ultimate result of interaction with our intimate God is cleansing and forgiveness on God's part, and surrender and service on ours.

CONVERSATIONS IN A PASTOR'S STUDY

The Preacher's Spiritual and Physical Health

An Interview With Dr. Stephen Olford

Let's talk about the minister's spiritual and physical health, beginning with private prayer and daily devotions.

I make a distinction which some of my pastor friends will not agree with. I feel there is a difference between my devotional life and my professional life. My quiet time is different from my study time. And I have a very simple procedure. I read from Genesis to Revelation. When I reach Revelation I go back to Genesis. Even though I have read the Bible—over and over again—there is never a morning with God that He does not reveal something new to me. I actually wrote a page of reflections on what God had said to me. "Impression without expression brings depression." Something depressed in one's soul can actually create a blockage. Truth has to be expressed. I read the passage three times: First time generally, second time critically, third time personally. I wait for the Lord speak to me, showing me in His Word a promise to keep, a prayer to echo, a command to obey, a sin to confess, etc. I personalize it entirely and write that form using one page only. And then I like to take what I have written and turn what God has said to me into prayer so that my prayers are not mechanical. They are not a Chinese wheel I can just put on and watch TV while it plays. It is a prayer that comes right out of my quiet time before I go into thanksgiving, intercessions, etc.

Do you keep a prayer list?

Yes. My prayer list is a very interesting one. Mondays-Missions. Tuesdays-Thanksgiving. Wednesdays-Workers, staff, etc. Thursdays-Tasks. Fridays-Family. Saturdays-Saints (so much of Paul's praying was for the saints). And Sundays-Sinners. On the list of sinners for this present period of my life is a famous golfing figure that I'm praying for earnestly, because I believe if he were converted it would turn my young people to Christ. Anyway, I do have a prayer list, and under those headings. Now, it isn't the length of timc I spend in my quiet time, though I usually take an hour, but there is a carry-over of the activity of prayer into the attitude of prayer that marks the rest of the day. I never pick up a telephone without a prayer. I never dictate a letter to my secretary without a prayer. I never let anybody into my study or out of my study without a prayer, and as my beloved workers know, any time we get together we say, "Let's pray." And so, prayer is literally "praying without ceasing." Before we finish this interview we'll pray, and so I feel I live in that atmosphere of perpetual prayer.

Would you say just a word about the minister and exercise?

I've exercised all my life. Paul says so much about the physical body and its use, e.g., dedication (Rom. 12:1–4), discipline (1 Cor. 9:26–29), and exercise (1 Tim. 4:7). I believe that taking care of the temple of the Holy Spirit is one of the most sacred stewardships of a pastor. Over 400,000 people die each year from obesity alone (as I read in the paper today). It's a shame and a sin. I know a personal doctor who works with pastors and he laments the shape many of them are in. He says that many of them are almost past redemption physically; and, according to him, it bodes very unfavorably for the life of our pastors in the years to come. Yes, I believe in tip-top fitness. In spite of the afflictions the Lord has allowed—four bypasses, a bout with cancer from which I recovered—I continue to exercise within the boundaries of my limitations.

Do you walk? Is that your favorite exercise?

Yes. I think that is the cheapest, most effective. In fact, Ike's doctor came and lectured us as pastors in New York while I was at Calvary Baptist Church. No question, running is hard on your limbs, especially the older you get. Heel-to-toe, heel-to-toe walking is the best possible exercise you could have. What more comprehensive and sanctifying prayer could we offer to our God than the words that conclude Paul's first letter to the Thessalonians: "Now may the God of peace Himself sanctify you completely; and may your whole spirit, soul, and body be preserved blameless at the coming of our Lord Jesus Christ. He who calls you is faithful, who also will do it" (1 Thess. 5:23, 24 NKJV).

JANUARY 16, 2005

SUGGESTED SERMON *Date preached:*

News Too Good to Keep Quiet

By Rev. Mark Hollis

Scripture: 2 Kings 6:24–30; 7:3–11, especially 7:9
This day is a day of good news, and we remain silent. (NKJV)

Introduction: The lesson in this Bible story is so obvious we cannot help but suspect that God must have placed it here on purpose, to give us a vivid example of our obligation to share the gospel. The nation of Samaria was under siege, and within the city, an awful famine was stalking the residents. Outside the city were the mighty armies of Aramea. Just beyond the city's gates were four lepers about to experience the best day of their lives.

1. **The Bad News (2 Kin. 6:24–30).** Our story begins after the nation of Israel had been divided by civil war. The northern portion of the nation, which retained the name *Israel*, was suffering the siege of its capital city. The mighty armies of the nation of Aramea held the city in a death grip. Their siege was so effective that the city, Samaria, was facing a deadly famine. A donkey's head sold for two pounds of silver and a cup of dove dung cost two ounces of silver (2 Kin. 6:25). This siege and famine had come as a direct result of Israel's rebellion against God. In words recorded hundreds of years before, God had warned the nation of what would happen if they rebelled against Him (Lev. 26:27–29). As a result, people were so hungry they turned on their own children (2 Kin. 6:26–29). It's one of the most horrible scenes in Scripture. The bad news for Samaria was that death was certain. There was no hope. The bad news for us is that death is certain (Rom. 6:23) and afterward the judgment (Heb. 9:27).

2. **The Good News (2 Kin. 7:3–20).** While these atrocities were occurring within the walls of Samaria, at the gate of the city sat four lepers, outcasts of society. Since leprosy was considered extremely contagious they were forced to live outside the city walls, quarantined from normal society. Their disease forced them to live apart from wives and children, and there was a social stigma—they were despised and rejected by others. In normal circumstances, these four might have received scraps from residents of the city or spoiled vegetable or fruit from a merchant. Since the Arameans

had arrived there was nothing. Sitting outside the gates, they began reasoning that they had nothing to lose. The only place where there was food was in the camp of the Arameans, so they decided to go there. To their surprise, the camp was abandoned. Entering a tent, the lepers ate, drank, and carted off silver, gold, and clothes. They entered another tent to take what they wanted. But then, they had a serious bout of conscience. They knew they had to share the news. Here are four of society's outcasts, rejected, avoided, ridiculed by the people of their culture. Yet, when they received good news they didn't want everyone else to be left out. In the middle of the night, they went to the city gate and got the attention of the gatekeeper who sent the news to the palace. When the word got out it caused a stampede at the city gate in which one of the king's officials was trampled to death. The news was so good that the lepers could not keep it to themselves. The city that faced death without food now had plenty to eat. Those of us who know Christ as Savior have entered a camp of hope. We have discovered the life-giving promises. We now have life, and we have it more abundantly! Jesus is the greatest discovery of life!

Conclusion: The good news and bad news can be summed up simply. All of us will one day die and after death, we are destined to face judgment. The many wrong things I have done stack up against me to make an awful looking record. The good news is that Jesus died on the Cross to pay the penalty for all those wrong things. He offers forgiveness simply for the asking. How about you? Have you received the good news that Jesus is willing to forgive those who place their trust in him? If you have not done this, today is a great day to do it. If you still have questions, ask them, but don't put it off. The news is too good to refuse. If you have received the good news of Jesus' forgiveness and have placed your trust in Him, are you sharing it with others?

STATS, STORIES, AND MORE

A Survey:

The Institute for American Church Growth asked 10,000 people what led them to the church where they had an opportunity to enter into a relationship with Jesus Christ.

2%—Special need
3%—Walk-in
6%—Pastor's influence
1%—Home visit
5%—Sunday school
5%—Evangelistic crusade
3%—Special Program
79%—Influence of a friend or relative

What are you doing to communicate the Good News?

According to *The Bradford (Pennsylvania) Era*, Preacher George Lane spent $5,000 advertising the first service of what he hoped would become a newly formed church. Two thousand people signed up for a $1,000 giveaway as part of his promotion. The only requirement to win was to be present at the first service. Lane rented the Central Columbia Elementary School cafeteria expecting to preach to thousands. The large crowd, he reasoned, would put about $1,000 in the collection plate that first Sunday. He, in turn, would give that money away to the lucky winner. He prepared an hour-long service featuring songs and a humor-filled sermon and waited for the crowds to come. He was disappointed when only about 30 people showed up. The offering was only about $100. The prizewinner told him to keep the $1,000. He probably needed it more than she did. Lane was undaunted, "I'll be back next week," he promised, reporting that next week the drawing would be for a shopping spree. We may question Lane's methods; but his willingness to do something raises a question: "What are we doing to communicate the message of Jesus Christ to others?"

FOR THE BULLETIN

✽ At the Hampton Court Conference on January 16, 1604, John Rainolds proposed to King James that the Bible be newly translated into English. This resulted in the creation of the King James (Authorized) Version of the Old and New Testaments. ✽ Today is the birthday of two famous missionaries to China. Maria Dyer was born on this day in 1837. In China, she fell in love with J. Hudson Taylor. The two became one of the most famous couples in modern missionary history. Together they formed the China Inland Mission. ✽ This is also the birth of another famous missionary to China, Bertha Smith, whose autobiography, *Go Home and Tell*, gives a fascinating glimpse into the joys and struggles of missionary service. She was born in 1888. ✽ On this day, January 16, 1890, the Moody Bible Institute of Chicago was dedicated to God's service. ✽ On January 16, 1892, the mother of missionary Amy Carmichael wrote to her, giving her permission to follow Christ into the world of missions. She wrote: "Dearest Amy, He has lent you to me all these years. He only knows what a strength, comfort, and joy you have been to me ... So, darling, when He asks you now to go away from within my reach, can I say nay? No, no, Amy, He is yours—you are His—to take you where He pleases and to use you as He pleases. I can trust you to Him, and I do."

APPROPRIATE SONGS AND HYMNS

Bringing in the Sheaves, Knowles Shaw/George A. Minor; Public Domain.
Christ Receiveth Sinful Men, Erdmann Neumeister/James McGranahan; Public Domain.
Covered, David Byerley/Renee Byerley; © 1994 +2DB; Admin. by Music Services.
Grace Greater than Our Sin, Julia H. Johnston/Daniel Brink Towner; Public Domain.
I Will Dance, Kirk Williams; © 1996 Integrity's Hosanna! Music.
Sweet Forgiveness, Brent Helming; © 1998 Mercy/Vineyard Publishing.

WORSHIP HELPS

Call to Worship:
And He said to them, "Go into all the world and preach the gospel to every creature." (Mark 16:15 NKJV)

Hymn Story: "Bringing in the Sheaves"
"Sheaves" are bundles of harvested grain. This hymn speaks of our joy in bringing in the gospel harvest. Knowles Shaw, the "Singing Evangelist", wrote it in 1874. Four years later, Knowles and Kirk Baxter boarded a train in Dallas, en route to McKinney, Texas, where Shaw was beginning a revival. The train never made it. Baxter wrote: "I felt the car was off the track, bouncing over the ties. I saw Brother Shaw rise from his seat and realized at once the car was going over. All became dark as night. When I came to myself, the coach was at the bottom of the embankment. When I got out, I ran down to the wreck and saw a man's hand pointing out of the water. It was Brother Shaw's. I called for help, and in about fifteen minutes he was taken lifeless from the water." But his life proved his song. According to his diary, Shaw recorded over 11,400 conversions to Christ under his ministry. He entered heaven rejoicing, bringing in the sheaves.

Kids Talk

Show the children a picture of a loved one. Ask them if they can guess why you keep that person's picture on your desk. It's for two reasons: So you can think about that person often, and so you can brag about that person to others. We want to feel that way about the Lord, thinking about Him all the time and "bragging" about Him to others.

Additional Sermons and Lesson Ideas

The Characteristics of a Disciple

Date preached:

By Daniel Miles

SCRIPTURE: Luke 14:25–35

INTRODUCTION: Jesus gave His disciples a standard to live up to, and He gives us the same standards today:

1. A Disciple Has the Right Priorities (vv. 25–27).
   A. Jesus Is Above Family (v. 26).
   B. Jesus Is Above Life (v. 26; see also Ps. 39:4–6).
2. A Disciple Has the Right Perspective (vv. 27–33).
   A. He Bears His Cross (v. 27).
   B. He Counts the Cost (vv. 28–33).
3. A Disciple Has the Right Purpose (vv. 34, 35).
   A. To Be Salt in the World (v. 34).
   B. To Be Consistent in His Fruitful Walk and Ministry (v. 34).

CONCLUSION: Have you resolved to follow Jesus anywhere He leads? Have you counted the cost of being His disciple? Commit yourself to a life of discipleship, despite the cost, to Jesus Christ!

The Power of Knowledge

Date preached:

By Rev. Charles Haddon Spurgeon

SCRIPTURE: Daniel 11:32

INTRODUCTION: Knowing God is the highest and best form of knowledge. It is the Spirit's work to lead us into all truth and to foster our faith.

1. Knowledge Strengthens Love. It paints a portrait of Jesus, and when we see that portrait, we love Him. The more we know Him, the greater our love.
2. Knowledge Strengthens Hope. How can we hope for something if we do not know it exists? The more we know of the things of God, the more we will anticipate them.
3. Knowledge Supplies Reasons for Patience. How can we have patience unless we know something of the sympathy of Christ and understand the good that comes from trial?

CONCLUSION: Every Christian grace will be perfected by knowledge. How important it is to grow in the grace and in the knowledge of Christ Jesus.

A SANCTITY OF LIFE SERMON

The Value of Human Life

Date preached:

By Dr. Melvin Worthington

Scripture: Exodus 20:13

Introduction: This Commandment guards human life. The immensity of the issue of death is so great that there can be no sin against humanity or God greater than the taking of a life. Jesus came to defeat the final enemy—death. Death is never a friend. The Sixth Commandment is based on the proposition that God created and sanctified the principle of life.

Evolution, which became the misguided cornerstone of twentieth-century science, has caused us to lose all sense of life's value. In their book, *Darwin's Leap of Faith,* John Ankerberg and John Weldon say about the hypothesis of evolution: "Some ideas are so bad that it must be argued they should be rejected on the basis of their implications alone." They go on to say, "Evolution significantly impacts our views of both life and death in the logical development of its philosophical outlook." If we have simply descended from tadpoles and tapeworms, then life is cheap and expendable with no eternal significance. We're here today and gone tomorrow, and if we never cease to exist, what difference does it make? If, on the other hand, God has created us in His image and if He has a living plan for our lives both in time and eternity, then life is sacred and special. The Commandment prohibiting murder takes the view that life comes from God, therefore it is sacred and special.

1. **The Admonition in the Text.** The admonition here forbids the unlawful taking of life by suicide or homicide. It forbids all violence, passion, lust, intemperance in eating or drinking, and any other habit that tends to shorten life. It throws up a red flag at the mention of abortion, mercy killing, and euthanasia. It warns us that life is sacred, thus not to be deliberately taken by human will. This admonition includes the following truths:

   A. **The Source of Life (Gen. 1; 2; Ps. 139:4; Job 33:4; Col. 1:16; John 1:3).** The commencement of life embraces all and the cessation of life ends all. God gives human life and has reserved the right to take human life.

   B. **The Substance of Life (Gen. 1:26, 27; Gen. 2:7).** Human beings were made in the image of God. They are composed of soul (seat of affections,

emotions, and natural instincts); spirit (ability to know) and body (physical house).

C. **The Saving of Life.** God gives, guards, governs, grants, and guarantees life.

D. **The Sacredness of Life.** This admonition is simple, solemn, specific, sublime, and sufficient.

E. **The Sustaining of Life.** Human life is sustained by the laws of the Sovereign and the laws of society.

F. **The Stewardship of Life.** As God's stewards it is required that we be found faithful in exercise of our stewardship responsibilities. Paul said, "Or do you not know that your body is the temple of the Holy Spirit who is in you, whom you have from God, and you are not your own? For you were bought at a price; therefore glorify God in your body and in your spirit, which are God's" (1 Cor. 6:19, 20 NKJV).

G. **The Significance of Life.** If God made us, He did so for a purpose. We have significance on this earth, and in Christ we know that when He is finished with us, He will take us to glory. "For I know the thoughts that I think toward you, says the LORD, thoughts of peace and not of evil, to give you a future and a hope" (Jer. 29:11 NKJV). We can choose to live our lives sinfully and selfishly, or in obedience to the will of God, leading to holiness and happiness. In life we are responsible and in death we are accountable.

2. **The Analysis of the Text.** This passage—You shall not murder—a simple sentence of four words and five syllables, is easy to read and should be clear to all, though admittedly there are interpretive challenges.

All acts that are hurtful or injurious to the health and life of one's own body or any other person are forbidden. It further forbids all malice and hatred to any person and any personal revenge, rash anger upon sudden provocations and hurt said or done in passion (Matt. 5:22). It forbids slander, which is the destroying of another's name, and striking, which is the disfiguring of one's body. This Commandment goes deeper than just bodily harm against another. It includes attitudes as well as acts. Jesus condemned the act of murder and the attitudes and feelings that prompt the act (Matt. 15:19; 1 John 3:15). Life is precious and God sets this Commandment to guard it. Every sin that leads to murder is forbidden. The head, the hand, the pen may commit murder by suicide, by neglect, by abortion, by euthanasia, and by being unmerciful.

(Since Moses allowed for the death penalty, self-defense, and war in other places in Exodus and in the Pentateuch, it is widely accepted that this Commandment does not prohibit capital punishment, self-defense, and the taking of life in war, though there is no clear consensus on this among Christians.)

3. **The Application from the Text.** This commandment is valuable in regard to others and ourselves. Regarding others, it fosters a concern for the life, well-being, and longevity of other people. Regarding ourselves, it shows us that we are precious in God's sight, that He has a plan for our lives, and that any threat against our normal lifespan is contrary to His law. The protection, preciousness, and preservation of life are embedded in this Commandment.

Conclusion: Human beings are God's masterpieces of creation. He made us in His image and breathed into us the breath of life (Gen. 2:7). We are "His workmanship (lit: poems, compositions) created in Christ Jesus for good works, which God prepared beforehand that we should walk in them" (Eph. 2:10 NKJV). We are called and set apart for Him even from the womb (Jer. 1:5). Psalm 139 says that we are fearfully and wonderfully made, knit together in our mothers' wombs by the hand of God who has planned each day of our lives. Human life is precious to God. Though we have been degraded and disfigured by sin, this Commandment flings a fiery law around the life of every human being, which is reserved for Him alone.

HEROES FOR THE PASTOR'S HEART

Charles Haddon Spurgeon and the Case for Small Churches

Discouragement is the occupational hazard of ministry. Small crowds and meager results dishearten many of God's workers. Rev. Charles Haddon Spurgeon could teach them a lesson.

It isn't that Spurgeon ever struggled with small crowds. Almost from the beginning, multitudes flocked to his feet. When he assumed his London pastorate in 1854, the church had 232 members. Soon so many were crowding his auditoriums that he sometimes asked his members to stay away the next Sunday to accommodate newcomers. He seldom preached to fewer than 6,000, and on one occasion his audience numbered almost 24,000—all this before the day of microphones. During his lifetime, Spurgeon preached to approximately 10,000,000 people.

He also became history's most widely-read preacher. Today there is more material written by Spurgeon than by any other Christian author of any generation. The collection of his Sunday sermons stands as the largest set of books by a single author in the history of the church. He is called the "Prince of Preachers."

But ironically, Spurgeon himself is a testimony to the power of a *small* church. On Sunday, January 6, 1850, a blizzard hit England, and 15-year-old Charles was unable to reach the church he usually attended. He turned down Artillery Street and ducked into a Primitive Methodist Church, finding only a few people standing around the stove. Not even the preacher arrived.

At length, a thin-looking man stood and read from Isaiah 45:22—"Look unto me, and be ye saved, all the ends of the earth" (KJV). The speaker, groping for something to say, kept repeating his text. Finally, he paused and spied young Charles sitting in the back. Pointing his bony finger at the boy, he cried, "Look, young man! Look! Look to Christ!"

The young man did look, and Spurgeon later said, "As the snow fell on my road home from the little house of prayer, I thought every snowflake talked with me and told of the pardon I had found." Arriving home, his mother saw his expression and exclaimed, "Something wonderful has happened to you."

It had, proving that smaller ponds often yield the biggest fish.

So, don't be discouraged if you aren't pastoring a mega-church. Pray for conversions and work for souls. Think big, and dream bigger. See the world as your parish, as Wesley said. But, don't despair about a Sunday of lean attendance. Never despise the day of small things, for out of your ministry may come the next Moody, Graham, Livingstone, or Spurgeon. Our labor in the Lord is never in vain, and His Word never returns to Him void.

JANUARY 23, 2005

SUGGESTED SERMON *Date preached:*

Forgiveness Made Easy

By Rev. Charles Haddon Spurgeon

Scripture: Ephesians 4:32b
... forgiving one another, even as God in Christ forgave you. (NKJV)

Introduction: We shall take the text word-by-word to obtain the clearest divisions.

1. **For Christ's Sake.** All that God bestows on us comes "for Christ's sake," especially forgiveness of sin. We have been forgiven:

   A. **Because of the Great Atonement Christ Offered.** Sin is an attack on the moral government of God; it undermines the foundations of society. Were it permitted to have its way, it would reduce everything to anarchy. God's holiness compels Him to judgment. There must be a sacrifice for sin. It is a wondrous mystery, the way of salvation by an atoning sacrifice; but this much is clear: God for Christ's sake forgives us. The blotting out of sin seems hard till we see the Cross, then it appears easy. When I've seen Jesus die, I've not been able to understand how any sin could be difficult to remove. Let a person stand at Calvary and it becomes the simplest thing possible that his debt should be discharged now that it is paid. Because of what Christ suffered, God forgives us.

   B. **Because of the Representative Character of Christ.** We originally fell by a representative. Adam stood for us as our federal head. We did not fall personally at the first, but in our representative. Now Christ, having borne the penalty and fulfilled the law, is the representative of all in Him. God forgives us in Him.

   C. **Because of the Deep Love the Father Bears for Him.** Can you guess a little of the love the Father has toward the Son? We cannot pry into this mystery without being blinded by light; but this we know, that they are Three in One. The union between them is intense beyond conception. The Lord will do great things for a Son He loves as He loves Jesus. If you will say, "Lord, I don't ask You to forgive me for my own sake, but for the sake of Your dear Son," He will do it.

2. **God Has Forgiven You.**

   A. **God Forgives Certainly.** He has forgiven you. If you have believed in Jesus, your sin has been erased from the records of the past, never to be mentioned forever. Pardon is not a matter of hope but of fact.
   B. **God Forgives Us Continuously.** He not only forgave us at the first, but also continues daily to forgive. I have heard that we were so forgiven when we first believed there is no need to ask for further forgiveness; to which I reply—We were so completely forgiven when we first believed that we ought continually to ask for the perpetuity of that one far-reaching act. Pardon once given continues to be given.
   C. **God Forgives Freely and Eternally.** We did nothing to earn forgiveness. God forgave us for Christ's sake. The whole horrible list of our offenses He destroyed at once. He will never rake up our past sins a second time. There is now no condemnation to them in Christ Jesus.

3. **Forgiving One Another.** If anyone here finds difficulty in forgiveness, I'm going to give you three words that will help you: For Christ's Sake! It's true your son has behaved wrongly, and in a fit of anger, you spoke severely. I beg you to eat your words for Christ's sake. Come, you two who have fallen out, love each other for Christ's sake. Come, you two friends who have been alienated, get together, and end your ill feeling for Christ's sake. You must not keep a drop of malice in your soul, for Christ's sake.

Conclusion: Finally, if we are to forgive one another, we must do other things. Don't provoke each other. If I know a man doesn't like something, I will not push it his way. If someone has a diseased mind and is irritable, treat him gently, pity his infirmity, and do not irritate him. I blame the wood for burning, but what shall I say of the bellows? Often when a man is angry he may not be the only one to blame. And do not take offenses where they are intended. It's a splendid thing not to be offended. If you must be offended, don't exaggerate it. If you have a telescope, look through the large hole and minify instead of magnifying. And never avenge yourselves. The Master says, "Vengeance is mine. I will repay." Don't take into your hand what belongs to God; but as He for Christ's sake has forgiven you, so forgive those who do you wrong. Forgive one another, even as God for Christ's sake has forgiven you. Amen.

STATS, STORIES, AND MORE

More From Rev. Charles Haddon Spurgeon:

All our transgressions are swept away at once, carried off as by a flood and so completely removed that no guilty trace of them remains. They are all gone! O believers, think of this, for the all is no little thing: sins against a holy God, sins against His loving Son, sins against gospel as well as against law, sins against man as well as against God, sins of the body as well as sins of the mind, sins as numerous as the sands on the seashore, and as great as the sea itself: all, all are removed from us as far as the east is from the west. All this evil was rolled into one great mass, and laid upon Jesus, and having borne it all He has made an end of it forever. When the Lord forgave us, He forgave us the whole debt. He did not take the bill and say, "I strike out this item and that," but the pen went through it all;—PAID. It was a receipt in full of all demands. Jesus took the handwriting that was against us and nailed it to His Cross, to show before the entire universe that its power to condemn us had ceased forever. We have in Him a full forgiveness.

FOR THE BULLETIN

❁ Today marks the conversion of John Fletcher, 26, who was born again on January 23, 1755. He went on to become one of John Wesley's closest associates and one of Methodism's most powerful early leaders. ❁ Lott Carey, born into slavery on a Virginia Plantation, found Christ as his Savior in Richmond, Virginia. By hard work and frugality, he earned enough money to purchase his freedom in 1815, and was soon licensed to preach. On January 23, 1821, he and his family sailed for West Africa, becoming America's first black missionaries to Africa. ❁ January 23, 1837 marks the birthday of another African-American slave, Amanda Smith. Amanda grew up committed to Christ and became a Methodist holiness evangelist throughout the South. Her fame leaped the Atlantic, and she was called to England for meetings, then to India and Africa. She organized women's bands, young people's groups, temperance societies, and children's meetings. She adopted homeless youngsters and started an orphanage near Chicago. ❁ January 23, 1893 marks the death of Boston pastor, Phillips Brooks, author of "O Little Town of Bethlehem." ❁ During the Bolshevik Revolution in Russia, the Communists attacked Orthodox churches in the Ukraine. On the evening of January 23, 1918, they broke into the Petchersky Monastery and killed hundreds of Orthodox priests. The Orthodox Church later claimed that 2,000 priests and fifty bishops were slain or deported. ❁ Paul W. Fleming incorporated the New Tribes Mission in Los Angeles on January 23, 1943.

APPROPRIATE SONGS AND HYMNS

Though Your Sins Be as Scarlet, Wayne Goodine; © 1984 New Spring Publishing; Admin. by Brentwood/Benson Music Publishing, Inc.

Whiter than Snow, James Nicholson/William G. Fischer; Public Domain.

White as Snow, Leon Olguin; © 1990 Maranatha Praise, Inc./Sound Truth Publishing; Admin. by Maranatha! Music.

Wonderful, Merciful Savior, Dawn Rogers/Eric Wyse; © 1989 Word Music, Inc./Dayspring Music, Inc.; Admin. by Word Music Group, Inc.

Forgive One Another, Lenny LeBlanc/Kelly Willard/Rita Baloche/Bill Batstone; © 1990 Maranatha! Music/Doulos Publishing; Admin. by Maranatha! Music.

WORSHIP HELPS

Call to Worship:

Oh, the depth of the riches both of the wisdom and knowledge of God! How unsearchable are His judgments and His ways past finding out! (Rom. 11:33 NKJV)

Responsive Reading:

Worship Leader: And forgive us our debts, as we forgive our debtors

Congregation: Be kind to one another, tenderhearted, forgiving one another, even as God in Christ forgave you.

Worship Leader: Then Peter came to Him and said, "Lord, how often shall my brother sin against me, and I forgive him? Up to seven times?" Jesus said to him,

Congregation: "I do not say to you, up to seven times, but up to seventy times seven.

Worship Leader: "Take heed to yourselves. If your brother sins against you, rebuke him; and if he repents, forgive him. And if he sins against you seven times in a day, and seven times in a day returns to you, saying, 'I repent,' you shall forgive him."

Congregation: And the apostles said to the Lord, "Increase our faith."

Worship Leader: Even as Christ forgave you, so you also must do. But above all these things put on love, which is the bond of perfection. And let the peace of God rule in your hearts, to which also you were called in one body; and be thankful.

Congregation: Then Jesus said, "Father, forgive them, for they do not know what they do." (Matt. 6:12; Eph. 4:32; Matt. 18:21, 22; Luke 17:3–5; Col. 3:13–15; Luke 23:34 NKJV)

Benediction:
Dismiss us O Lord with Your extraordinary love that we may be Your extraordinary people, in Jesus' name. Amen.

Quotes for the Pastor's Wall

"The state of the pulpit may always be taken as an index of that of the church. Whenever the pulpit is evangelical, the piety of the people is in some degree healthy; a perversion of the pulpit is surely followed by spiritual apostasy in the church."

R. L. Dabncy

Additional Sermons and Lesson Ideas

Pray for Us

Date preached:

By Rev. Todd M. Kinde

SCRIPTURE: 2 Thessalonians 3:1–5

INTRODUCTION: Here is a guide for praying for one another and for our church.

1. Pray for the Propagation of the Gospel (v. 1). When we gather we are to pray that the gospel would go forth. The picture is of a runner carrying a message across a battlefield; we're to pray for rapid advance of the gospel.
2. Pray for the Protection of the Church (vv. 2, 3). Paul asked for boldness to speak the truth. Our fear in evangelism is normal, but we should pray for boldness and protection.
3. Pray for the Perseverance of the Saints (vv. 4, 5). We want to have a good start, but how important to finish well (1 Cor. 9:24)!

CONCLUSION: As we gather for our prayer meetings may they be characterized by these kinds of prayers.

The Day of the Lord

Date preached:

By Rev. Peter Grainger

SCRIPTURE: Malachi 4:1–6

INTRODUCTION: Jesus told us to be ready for the last days. The theme of the last chapter of the Old Testament is the Last Day.

1. The Day of the Lord: Separation (vv. 1–3). There will be a mixed reaction and effect of the Lord's coming:
   A. Like a Furnace. The wicked will be swallowed up as in flames.
   B. Like the Sun. The righteous will be restored and victorious over evil.
2. The Day of the Lord: Preparation (vv. 4–6). Two Old Testament prophets foreshadow what is to come.
   A. Moses: Holiness before God is stressed through the Law of Moses. (Mal. 3:1, 2; Gal. 3:19–24)
   B. Elijah: Repentance in preparation for the Lord's return is stressed through Elijah (Matt. 3:1–12).

CONCLUSION: The Sun of Righteousness has risen to make us ready for that Day. Are you ready?

JANUARY 30, 2005

SUGGESTED SERMON *Date preached:*

The Discipline of Disturbance

By Dr. Denis Lyle

Scripture: Deuteronomy 31:30—32:13, especially 32:11, 12
As an eagle stirs up its nest, hovers over its young, spreading out its wings, taking them up, carrying them on its wings, so the LORD alone led him, and there was no foreign god with him. (NKJV)

Introduction: Experts say that when the time has come for a young eaglet to learn to fly, the parent bird at first tries to coax the youngster into flight. If this method fails, the mother then resorts to what seems to be much harsher treatment. The mother bird will force her offspring off the nest out into the air. By this discipline of disturbance, she accomplishes her desire and design, the first flight of the eaglet. Now Moses, laying hold of this wonderful picture, shows that this is how God has acted toward His people. When they were settled down in Egypt, God stirred their nest through persecution until they were ready to leave for the Promised Land. Let's look together at this discipline of disturbance.

1. **The Reason for Divine Disturbance.** "As an eagle stirs up its nest ..." Why does God disturb our nest? Ultimately God uses the discipline of disturbance that we might fly. Moses is teaching us about this principle. "As an eagle ... so the LORD." The construction of the eagle's nest is quite interesting. The floor is laid with sharp thorns, this is then covered with down; the top layer is nice and soft. The young eagles are comfortable as they squat there waiting for mother to bring them food. But the time comes when the mother will no longer feed them. She will remove the soft down. Her young will be uncomfortable; the thorns will prick them. They will move around until they fall over the side of the nest. As the experience of falling overwhelms them, they literally get into a flap; they start to move their wings. This is the purpose behind their mother's harsh treatment. Moses is showing us that, in the same way, the Lord stirs up our nest for a purpose, to accomplish His will.

2. **The Resources in Divine Disturbance.** Our text is taken from a song of praise (31:30)! Why? In divine disturbance, there is:

A. **Knowledge of God's Plan.** God is working towards a plan: to bring us closer to Himself. Recall that it is God Himself who asks His people Israel to remember, "You have seen what I did to the Egyptians, and how I bore you on eagles' wings and brought you to Myself" (Ex. 19:4 NKJV). Is this not the plan that God is working out for us through the discipline of disturbance?
B. **Assurance of God's Presence.** Imagine that young eaglet, thinking "Here I am pushed out of my nest. I've never used my wings before. I panic. I'm falling through the air. All my security is gone. I long for it again. Oh, that I could get back to the nest" (see Num. 11:4–6). But there is another sound: the fluttering of mother bird's wings as she swoops around. For as the little chap steadily falls so she descends. Her eyes are always on him. Her presence is always near. Have you known the experience of spiritual panic? Most of us have. But oh, how close the Lord comes to the believer whose restfulness He has disturbed!
C. **Guarantee of God's Power.** Back to the falling little eagle: on his descent and seeming fate, the mother eagle swoops, she hovers right under her offspring, her majestic wings are spread out and the little fellow lands on them and regains his balance. Do you know what that is? Sustaining power! "As an eagle ... Spreading out its wings, taking them up, Carrying them on its wings, So the LORD alone led him ..." (Deut. 32:11, 12 NKJV).

Conclusion: Finally, Moses teaches us that the result of the discipline of disturbance is a higher life, "He made him ride in the heights of the earth, that he might eat the produce of the fields" (v. 13). My friends, Moses has taught us a life lesson, "As the eagle ... so the LORD." He stirs up the nests of our complacent lives whether through trials, persecutions, or struggles, but he does not let us fall. He is always watching us to accomplish His will: to teach us, to conform us into His image, and to ultimately bless us beyond all imagination.

STATS, STORIES, AND MORE

Moody's Voyage

After a year of work in Great Britain, D. L. Moody sailed home in 1892, eager to return to his family. About three days into the voyage, the ship ground to a halt with a broken shaft and before long, it began to take water. No one was sure whether the vessel would sink or not, and there were no known rescue ships in the area. After two days of anxiety, Moody asked permission to hold a meeting, and nearly every passenger attended. He opened to Psalm 91. Holding a pillar to steady himself he read, "He that dwelleth in the secret place of the most High shall abide under the shadow of the Almighty" (Ps. 91:1, KJV). Moody later wrote, "It was the darkest hour of my life ... but relief came in prayer. God heard me cry, and enabled me to say from the depth of my soul, 'Thy will be done.' I went to bed and fell asleep almost immediately." Psalm 91 became a vibrant new Scripture to Moody from that day, and he discovered the safest place in the world is in the shadow of the Almighty.

Someone Once Said:

Theodore Cuyler wrote: "God sees that you and I are all the time determined to nestle down among our creature comforts. We build these earthly nests for ourselves, and fix our affections on them: then settle down in them."

George Matheson, the poet-preacher of Scotland wrote, "What a startling thought ... that the breaking up of the nest is an act of God's benevolence."

FOR THE BULLETIN

❁ England's King Charles I was beheaded on January 30, 1649, during the Puritan Revolution led by Oliver Cromwell. ❁ On January 30, 1877, a delegation of three missionaries from the Church Missionary Society reached the court of King Mutesa of Uganda. Tribal insurgents soon killed two, leaving the survivor, C. T. Wilson, to begin Sunday services alone. Scottish missionary Alexander Mackay soon joined him, and the two labored for years before baptizing their first convert. Just as their work was accelerating, Mutesa was succeeded by his son. This cruel teenager promptly tortured and burned a group of Mackay's converts for refusing his homosexual demands. Many others were mutilated and slain. Mackay, 40, survived the tyrant's threats only to die of malaria while translating the Gospel of John. But his efforts were not wasted. The church grew faster than it perished, and the Ugandan church became one of Africa's strongest. ❁ After attending a military academy in Richmond, Virginia, and serving in the Civil War, George Minor devoted himself to the expansion of gospel music in America. He taught in singing schools across the South and helped found the Hume-Minor Company which manufactured pianos and organs. He's best remembered as the composer for the music for "Bringing in the Sheaves." He died on January 30, 1904. ❁ January 30, 1912 marks the birthday of Francis Schaeffer, Presbyterian philosopher and missionary to Switzerland who became best known for his evangelistic work among college students and as the author of *He is Here and He is Not Silent* and many other books.

APPROPRIATE SONGS AND HYMNS

All the Way My Savior Leads Me, Fanny J. Crosby/Robert Lowry; Public Domain.
God Leads Us Along, G. A. Young; Public Domain.
Jesus You Are Changing Me, Marilyn Baker; © 1980 Word's Spirit of Praise Music; Admin. by Maranatha! Music.
Refiner's Fire, Brian Doerkson; © 1990 Mercy/Vineyard Publishing.
We Give You Thanks, George T. Searcy; © 1994 Integrity's Praise! Music.

WORSHIP HELPS

Call to Worship:

He who dwells in the secret place of the Most High shall abide under the shadow of the Almighty. I will say of the LORD, "He is my refuge and my fortress; My God, in Him I will trust." (Ps. 91:1, 2 NKJV)

Pastoral Prayer:

Lord, we thank You for the way You push us out of the nest. You don't allow us to remain complacent or immature. Despite the pain or difficulty, we ask that You continue to disturb us when we're comfortable, and comfort us when we're disturbed. We ask that in it all, You work out Your plan for our lives. Remind us that all things work together for good in the lives of those who love You, and that, when committed to You, all these things happen for the furtherance of the gospel. Give us eyes to see Your will, hearts to trust Your grace, and joy to swallow our sorrows. We pray in Jesus' name. Amen.

Offertory Word:

What if every Christian tithed? According to a new report by Empty Tomb, a Champaign, Illinois-based nonprofit research organization, if U. S. Christians were giving their churches the biblical tithe, the churches would have $143 billion more to spread the gospel and aid the world's poor. That's $143 billion—with a B! It could begin with you today. May the Lord give us a tither's heart.

Benediction:

Lord, at this closing hour establish every heart / upon Thy word of truth and power to keep us when we part. —Eleanor Fitch.

Additional Sermons and Lesson Ideas

Avoiding the Big Blowups

Date preached:

By Rev. Mark Hollis

SCRIPTURE: James 1:19–21

INTRODUCTION: James offers five steps toward overcoming anger.

1. Be slow to speak (v. 19). Weigh your words carefully (Prov. 17:28 and 29:20).
2. Be quick to listen (v. 19). Avoid erupting into anger. Assume the posture of a listener (Prov. 18:13).
3. Be slow to anger (vv. 19, 20). No amount of yelling at my children will turn them into the righteous young people I long for them to be.
4. Get rid of all moral filth and evil (v. 21). When distracted by sin we cannot dedicate ourselves to controlling our anger.
5. Humbly accept the Word of God (v. 21). Submit to the Word as the final authority and guide for your life.

CONCLUSION: What if I do blow up? Admit it, ask for God's help, confess to the people you hurt, and continue.

Christ in Our Midst

Date preached:

Adapted from a message by W. Graham Scroggie

SCRIPTURE: John 20:19

INTRODUCTION: One of the great expressions in the gospels is the phrase "in the midst." It tells us that Christ is among us as our Immanuel. He is:

1. In the Midst of Our Questions—Luke 2:46. As a child, He stood among the questioning rabbis.
2. In the Midst of Our Persecution—Luke 4:40; John 8:59. He walked through the midst of His enemies.
3. In the Midst of Our Worship—Matthew 18:20.
4. In the Midst of Our Need—John 19:18 (KJV), crucified in the midst of thieves.
5. In the Midst of Our Victory—Luke 24:36 and John 20:19.
6. In the Midst of Our Church—Revelation 1:13, walking in the midst of the candlesticks.
7. In the Midst of Heaven—Revelation 5:6 and 7:17

CONCLUSION: Is He in the midst of your life, your business, your home, and your friendships?

CLASSICS FOR THE PASTOR'S LIBRARY

The Didache

How'd you like to peek through the shutters of a local church in the second century? Worship alongside ancient Christians? Ever wondered how church services were conducted 1,900 years ago?

Then you might want to read a short but precious document called the *Didache*.

"Didache" (did'-a-key) is a Greek word, frequently found in the New Testament, meaning, *teaching* or *instruction*. It serves as the title of this rare document discovered in 1873 that may be the oldest surviving piece of non-canonical literature in Christian history. In other words, apart from the New Testament itself, the *Didache* is the oldest church document we have. Some experts believe it was in existence (at least in an early form) within fifty years of the Lord's Resurrection, though most scholars give it a second-century date.

Archbishop Philotheos Bryennios, an Eastern Church theologian, discovered the Didache in a cache of manuscripts at the Jerusalem Monastery of the Holy Sepulchre in Istanbul in 1873. He published it in 1883.

You don't have to go to Istanbul—or even to a bookshop—to find a copy (though several excellent versions are available from major publishers). Just search the Internet and you'll find it verbatim on multiple sites. The most common English translations are those done by Lightfoot and Hoole, but more up-to-date versions get away from the Elizabethan "thou shalts" and are easier to read.

Who wrote the *Didache*? Though its longer title is *The Teaching of the Twelve Apostles*, we don't believe it was actually written by any of our Lord's disciples, but it is based in part on their teachings as handed down to the second and third generation of Christians. It was probably written in Syria for use in a local church, perhaps for the training of new converts.

It is short—sixteen very brief chapters or segments, just over 3,000 words total—falling into four sections.

Chapters 1—6 sound like the Sermon on the Mount—ethical instructions in short, pithy bites. Moral proverbs such as:

- There are two ways, one of life and one of death, and there is a great difference between the two.
- The way of life is this. First of all, love the God that made you. Second, your neighbor as yourself.

- If a man impress you to go with him one mile, go with him two. Be meek, for the meek shall inherit the earth.

The next four segments (7—10) discuss the early church's worship patterns and formulas. Certain liturgical practices such as corporate prayer, fasting, and communion are discussed. For example, here are the *Didache's* instructions regarding baptism:

> *"Baptize in the name of the Father and of the Son and of the Holy Spirit in living [running] water. But if you have no running water, then baptize in other water; and if you are not able to baptize in cold, then in warm. But if you have neither, then pour water on the head three times in the name of the Father and of the Son and of the Holy Spirit."*

Part three (segments 11—15) tells how to distinguish false prophets from true ones, and how to find good leaders for the church. For example:

- Let every apostle, when he comes to you, be received as the Lord ... but if he asks for money, he is a false prophet.
- And every prophet teaching the truth, if he does not do what he teaches, is a false prophet.
- Appoint for yourselves, therefore, bishops and deacons worthy of the Lord, men who are meek and not lovers of money, and true and approved; for to you they shall perform the service of the prophets and teachers.

To me, the most interesting part of the book is the final chapter. Segment 16 deals with the coming of the Antichrist and the approaching return of our Lord Jesus to earth:

- Be watchful for your life. Let your lamps not be quenched ... but be ready, for you know not at what hour your Lord comes.
- And then shall the signs appear; first, a sign of a rift in the heaven, then a sign of a voice of a trumpet, and thirdly a resurrection of the dead ... Then shall the world see the Lord coming on the clouds of heaven.

If you'd like to ride a time machine back to the second century and worship with a local congregation somewhere in ancient Syria, take time to study the *Didache*. We're always better equipped for the future when we appreciate our past.

FEBRUARY 6, 2005

SUGGESTED SERMON *Date preached:*

Our Lord, the Merciful One

By Rev. Todd M. Kinde

Scripture: Matthew 20:29–34, especially 30 and 34
And behold, two blind men sitting by the road, when they heard that Jesus was passing by, cried out, saying, "Have mercy on us, O Lord, Son of David!"... So Jesus had compassion and touched their eyes. And immediately their eyes received sight, and they followed Him. (NKJV)

Introduction: Do you need mercy in your life? Do you need it from your boss or your family? Do you find it hard to be merciful? We will find today that our God is the merciful One. In our text, we find Jesus traveling the old route Joshua took during the conquest of the Promised Land as He came up on two blind men who cried out for mercy from their painful existence.

1. **The Crowd (Matt. 20:29–31).** Jericho was the home of Jesus' ancestor, Rahab (1:5), and was just a day's journey from Jerusalem. The air was filled with excitement about the Messiah as the multitudes gathered, making pilgrimage to Jerusalem for the Feast of the Passover. The region was known for producing balsam, believed to be beneficial in treating eye defects, so it isn't surprising to find two blind men along the road begging for money or bread. The crowds, however, were filled with excitement and wanted everything to be positively perfect and uplifting in the festal procession. They rebuked the blind men who were crying out for help. Their motives may have been diverse just as our own are when we hinder people in one way or another from coming to Christ. The crowd following Jesus is often the biggest roadblock to others crying out to Him for mercy (Matt. 13:4–7, 18–22, 28, 41; 15:23; 16:22; 26:8). The crowds, like the disciples in Matthew 19:13–15, wanted to bask in His glory but not practice His compassion.

2. **The Confession (Matt. 20:30b, 31b).** Jericho was one of the wealthier cities of the region and as a result attracted both beggars and robbers. This cry for mercy was heard repeatedly in the streets as an appeal for physical help in times of need. These two men, though blind, saw Jesus as both Lord and Son of David. They understood that the Messianic Age was to be one

in which the blind would receive sight (cf. Is. 35:5, 6). Their cry for mercy was a confession of faith in Jesus as the Christ. The rebuke of the crowds served to test the faith of these men. These men cried out again, a mark of the reality of their faith. They made a true confession of faith in Jesus in the face of opposition. "Have mercy" was the typical cry of the beggar. It was a confession of lowliness, dependence, and poverty. This cry for mercy is the confession of the church. We are beggars crying out of our blindness and spiritual destitution for mercy. Jesus gives sight to those who know they cannot see.

3. **The Compassion (Matt. 20:32–34).**

   A. **Our Lord Stands Still for Us.** Jesus acknowledged the two men. He did not instantly heal but He did stand still and begin a conversation with them. He seeks a personal relationship with people. Jesus is not impersonal; He stands still for us.
   B. **Our Lord Calls Us.** Jesus asked, "What do you want?" Remember that the main cry of the beggar was for money. Jesus wanted to find out if their cry for mercy is a cry that trusted Him with their deepest needs.
   C. **Our Lord Aches for Us.** "Jesus had compassion." The word compassion originally indicated the moving of the inner parts of the body, like your stomach turning. In the Gospels when Jesus responded with compassion, it was often the turning point in someone's life. Jesus aches with you and for you. He has compassion on you in your need and pain.
   D. **Our Lord Touches Us.** The physical touch of Jesus came to these men. Jesus comes close where others keep away. Jesus heals by touching. Jesus saved these two men not only from their physical blindness but also from their spiritual blindness. They responded by following Him.

Conclusion: The two men joined the crowds in the festive pilgrimage. They received their sight and followed Jesus to Jerusalem and the place of the Cross. When we receive spiritual sight we are to keep our eyes fixed on Jesus the author and finisher of our faith who endured the Cross for us (Heb. 12:2 NKJV).

STATS, STORIES, AND MORE

What the World Needs Now Is ... Compassion

The University of Michigan published a new report on the subject of compassion in the workplace recently. News accounts of the report said: "Small interpersonal acts of compassion in the workplace have significant, far-reaching effects on coworkers, according to a new University of Michigan Business School study. In their report, 'What Good is Compassion at Work?' researcher Jane Dutton and colleagues identify a 'cascading effect,' whereby experiencing compassion at work generates positive emotion and, in turn, shapes employees' long-term attitudes and behaviors. 'Our findings suggest that compassion among coworkers is more than simply a momentary, humane response to pain,' said Dutton, professor of organizational behavior and human resource management at the Michigan Business School and professor of psychology at the College of Literature, Science, and the Arts. 'It fosters important organizational outcomes and leaves its imprint on the organizational landscape.' The research, conducted by Dutton, Jacoba Lilius and Jason Kanov of the U-M, Monica Worline of Emory University and Peter Frost and Sally Maitlis of the University of British Columbia, documents compassion's effects on daily work meanings, attitudes, and behaviors ... Their research comes at a time—in the aftermath of 9/11—when more attention is being focused on how individuals and organizations cope with loss and grief and promote emotional healing. According to one estimate, firms lose $75 billion annually from employees' grief-related incidences, which impacts bottom-line profitability."

Savior, Hear My Cry

Fanny Crosby wrote a hymn based on the blind men at Jericho: "Son of David! Hear my cry; / Savior, do not pass me by; / Touch these eyelids veiled in night, / Turn their darkness into light."

FOR THE BULLETIN

❁ Julius I was installed as Bishop of Rome on February 6, 337, during the days when Arius was teaching that Jesus, though the God the Son, could not be coeternal with the Father. Julius became a strong supporter of orthodoxy and one of the reasons for the eventual defeat of Arianism. ❁ On February 6, 1812, Adoniram Judson was commissioned as America's first foreign missionary. He sailed for Burma on February 18. ❁ Charles M. Alexander left home on this day in 1912 for his fourth journey around the world, preaching the gospel and leading music in evangelistic campaigns of Dr. Wilbur Chapman. Chapman and Alexander were the first to circle the globe in an evangelistic endeavor. ❁ Dr. Martyn Lloyd-Jones became pastor of the Forward Movement Mission Church of Wales in Sandfields, Aberavon. He announced on his first Sunday: "Young men and women, my one great attempt here at Aberavon, as long as God gives me strength to do so, will be to try to prove to you not merely that Christianity is reasonable, but that ultimately, faced as we all are at some time or other with the stupendous fact of life and death, nothing else is reasonable." Lloyd-Jones went on to become the pastor of London's Westminster Chapel, and one of the world's most respected preachers. On February 6, 1977, exactly fifty years after the start of his ministry at Sandfields, Dr. Lloyd-Jones returned and preached from 1 Corinthians 2:2—the very text he had used on his first Sunday at Sandfields.

APPROPRIATE SONGS AND HYMNS

According to Thy Lovingkindness, Robert C. Savage; © 1958 Singspiration Music; Admin. by Brentwood-Benson Music Publishing, Inc.
Give Me Jesus, Fanny Crosby/John R. Sweney; Public Domain.
Have Mercy on Me, Andy Park; © 1998 Mercy/Vineyard Publishing.
Jesus Has Lifted Me, Avis B. Christiansen/Haldor Lillenas; Public Domain.
Your Everlasting Love, Bill Batstone; © 1993 Maranatha Praise, Inc.; Admin. by The Copyright Company.

WORSHIP HELPS

Call to Worship:
Unto You I lift up my eyes, O You who dwell in the heavens .... Our eyes look to the LORD our God until He has mercy on us. (Ps. 123:1, 2 NKJV)

Word of Welcome:
Today we're talking about the wonderful compassion of Jesus. Charles Wesley wrote: "Jesus, Thou art all compassion, pure unbounded love Thou art; / Visit us with Thy salvation; enter every trembling heart." Our prayer is that the wonderful compassion of our wonderful Jesus will warm your heart today.

Scripture:
I will extol You, my God, O King; and I will bless Your name forever and ever. Every day I will bless You, and I will praise Your name forever and ever. Great is the LORD, and greatly to be praised; and His greatness is unsearchable. One generation shall praise Your works to another, and shall declare Your mighty acts. I will meditate on the glorious splendor of Your majesty, and on Your wondrous works. Men shall speak of the might of Your awesome acts, and I will declare Your greatness. They shall utter the memory of Your great goodness, and shall sing of Your righteousness. The LORD is gracious and full of compassion, slow to anger and great in mercy. The LORD is good to all, and His tender mercies are over all His works. (Ps. 145:1–9 NKJV)

Benediction:
You have been merciful to us this morning, O Lord; may we be merciful this week. You have given us joy today, Lord; may we convey that joy to others. May we praise You every day and hour until we meet again.

Additional Sermons and Lesson Ideas

Good Angels

Date preached:

Adapted from a sermon by John Wesley

SCRIPTURE: Hebrews 1:14

INTRODUCTION: An ancient poet wrote: "Millions of spiritual creatures walk the earth unseen." People have always believed in angels, but only God's Word gives us a clear, consistant account of those whom our eyes have not seen.

1. The Essence of Angels: They are spirits, not material beings, not clogged with flesh and bone like us. See Psalm 104:4.
2. The Office of Angels: They are sent to serve. Many of God's ministries of mercy to us are conveyed by angels. They minister to us in a thousand ways we do not now understand.
3. The Beneficiary of Angels: Their ministry is for us who are heirs of salvation.

CONCLUSION: "O everlasting God who ordains and constitutes the services of angels and men in a wonderful manner; grant that as your holy angels serve You always in heaven, so by Your appointment they may strengten and defend us on earth, through Jesus Christ our Lord."

Hiding in God

Date preached:

SCRIPTURE: Psalm 74

INTRODUCTION: When the troubles of life threaten to engulf us, we can find great strength in this Psalm. The writer, Asaph, is a fellow sufferer who can give us guidance.

1. Opposed (vv. 1–11). "The enemy has damaged everything," Asaph says in verse 3; and we feel as though God has cast us off forever (v. 1).
2. Enclosed (vv. 12–17). Even now, we are enclosed within the care of the one who works salvation in the midst of the earth.
3. Composed (vv. 18–23). How wonderful to regain our composure, knowing that the poor and needy will praise His Name.

CONCLUSION: Life is difficult, but God is greater than the difficulities. He overcomes the tumult of those who rise up against us.

FEBRUARY 13, 2005

SUGGESTED SERMON *Date preached:*

In the Storms of Life, God Gives Mercy

By Rev. Mark Hollis

Scripture: Jonah 1:1—3:4, especially 2:9

But I will sacrifice to You with the voice of thanksgiving; I will pay what I have vowed. Salvation is of the LORD. (NKJV)

Introduction: Tornados rip through towns, uprooting trees and destroying buildings. Hurricanes devastate seaports and surrounding cities. The storms of life can be like that. We may not have weathered a tornado, hurricane, or earthquake; but most of us have faced life's storms. Sometimes we make those storms worse by our reaction. Sometimes we even bring such storms upon ourselves. The prophet Jonah did.

1. **A Disobedient Prophet (Jon. 1:1–16).** Thunder raged and lightening flashed as waves battered the ship. On deck was a crew of veteran seamen. Curses turned to pleadings as they called on their gods for deliverance from the fury of the storm. In the hold of the ship was a sleeping Hebrew. Thunder, lightening, and the rolling of the sea did not wake him until the captain of the ship urged him to call on his God for mercy.

Jonah was running from the Lord. He was in the middle of a storm of his own making. His ministry came after the time that Israel had split into two kingdoms and before the Babylonian captivity. Jonah was a patriotic, God-fearing Israelite. He shared with his countrymen a love for Israel and a hatred for her enemies, the worst of whom was Assyria. God spoke to Jonah telling him to go directly to the capital city of the hated Assyrians and warn them of God's coming judgment. The Assyrians were a feared and hated people. They loved to torture their enemies. Sometimes they blinded their captives and made sport of them. Sometimes they tortured an enemy by pulling chunks of his skin off until he died. Sometimes a hook was pulled through the nose and the victim made the slave of a merciless master. Jonah had every reason to fear the Assyrians. Why should he care if God judged these wicked enemies? They deserved it anyway. Perhaps some of his kin had suffered at their hands. Jonah said what many of us have said at some point in our lives: "No way, Lord!" And he got in a boat headed in the opposite direction. As the sea grew rougher and all appeared lost, Jonah said, "Throw me in!" He knew he was running from the very God who made the sea and the heaven. The sailors did their best to make it to land, but the sea grew wilder and rougher. Devoid of options, they took Jonah at his word and threw him overboard. Immediately, the sea grew calm. The sailors turned to God and worshiped. The story of Jonah is about more than a disobedient prophet and a big fish. It is a story of mercy. In the storm, God gave mercy. The first act of mercy is the mercy God gave these pagan sailors. In the storms of life, God gives mercy.

2. **A Drowning Prophet (Jon. 1:17—2:9).** Thrown into the depths of the Mediterranean Sea, Jonah was swept away. Engulfed by the waters, he thought he would drown. Yet, in mercy, God sent along a living submarine to carry him to safety. Jonah sat in the steaming belly of that whale for three days and three nights. He had plenty of time to reconsider the hardness of his heart. He recognized the mercy of God who allowed him to be carried along by the whale. The entire second chapter of Jonah's Book is a psalm of praise to God for His mercy. In the storms of life, God gives mercy.

3. **A Delivered Prophet (Jon. 2:10—3:4).** God prompted the whale and it vomited Jonah onto dry land. Seasick, bleached white from the gases in the whale's stomach, and smelling of whale vomit, Jonah heard the voice of the Lord a second time (Jon. 3:2). This time he decided to obey. He preached the prescribed message. Nineveh repented and God again demonstrated His mercy by sparing the city. In the storms of life, God gives mercy.

Conclusion: Are you in the middle of one of life's storms? Do you feel you've made it worse by your own action? Do you worry because you brought the storm upon yourself? Jonah brought his storm upon himself. What did he find? Mercy! What do we find when we are in the middle of a storm of our own making? Mercy! In the storms of life, even the storms of our own making, God gives mercy.

STATS, STORIES AND MORE

Robber Holds Up Bank to Make Bail

The *Bradford* (Pennsylvania) *Era* reported about a thief named Donald Guthrie. He was out on bail for robbing a coin-operated laundry, but when he couldn't make the payment to his bondsman, he wrote a postdated check and robbed a bank to cover it. Hopping in his car for the getaway, he crashed at a turn. A passerby named Dale Shields stopped at the scene to help. Guthrie, who had suffered severe facial injuries, refused to go to the hospital. He gave Shields a false name and took several things from the crashed car. When Shield's saw Guthrie's real name in a newspaper story, he called police, and the star-crossed thief found himself back in to lockup. When we run from the storms of our own making we are likely to go from bad to worse. Jonah did.

Role Model

As famed baseball player Mickey Mantle neared the time of his death, he acknowledged the feelings of those who find themselves in a storm of their own making. He said, "God gave me a body and the ability to play baseball. He gave me everything. I just wasted it. Now I'm a role model. Don't be like me."

Guilty With an Exclamation!

Reader's Digest (April 1997) reported on a courtroom where those charged were instructed to respond in one of three ways: "Guilty," "Not guilty," or "Guilty with an explanation." Halfway through the roll call the assistant district attorney read off the next name. The man sharply answered, "Guilty with an exclamation!" Whether we are guilty with an explanation or guilty with an exclamation, all of us are guilty.

FOR THE BULLETIN

❁ In 1632, Galileo was called before the Inquisition to answer charges that his writings violated church teaching. Despite being 70 years old and infirm, he was forced to travel from Florence during the winter, arriving in Rome on a litter on February 13, 1633. Historians are unsure whether Galileo, during his trial, was tortured or simply threatened. In any event, the old scientist was forced to read a statement renouncing his views—especially his observation that the earth moves around the sun—confessing them as "errors and heresies." A legend persists that having read his recantation, Galileo muttered, *E pur si muove*—"But it moves after all." ❁ The American Temperance Society (later renamed the American Temperance Union) was organized in Boston on this day in 1826. ❁ After the death of London's great preacher Charles Spurgeon, the leadership of the church fell to his son, Thomas Spurgeon, who followed in his father's footsteps. On February 13, 1907, Thomas resigned from the pastorate, citing ill health. Writing to the congregation, he said, "I have long felt my powers overtaxed, and have many a time been on the point of resigning, but have struggled on again ... I am perfectly persuaded that the cause with its by no means diminishing difficulties stands in urgent need of a leader who is not handicapped by physical weakness." ❁ Rufus Henry McDaniel died on this day in 1940. A preacher in the Midwest, he wrote more than one hundred hymns, of which the best known is "Since Jesus Came Into My Heart."

APPROPRIATE SONGS AND HYMNS

Mercy Saw Me, Geron Davis/Becky Davis; © 1994 Integrity's Hosanna! Music/DaviShop; Admin. by Integrity Music.

Hide Me in the Cleft of the Rock, Dennis Jernigan; © 1987 Shepherd's Heart Music, Inc.; Admin. by Word Music Group, Inc.

I Gave My Life for Thee, Frances R. Havergal/Philip P. Bliss; Public Domain.

Tell It to Jesus, Jeremiah E. Rankin/Edmund S. Lorenz; Public Domain.

Trust His Heart, Eddie Carswell/Babbie Mason; © 1989 Dayspring Music, Inc./May Sun Music/Word Music, Inc./Causing Change Music; Admin. by Word Music Group, Inc.

WORSHIP HELPS

Call to Worship:
I will praise You, O Lord, among the peoples; I will sing to You among the nations. For Your mercy reaches unto the heavens, and Your truth unto the clouds.
(Ps. 57:9, 10 NKJV)

Suggested Scripture Readings on God's Mercy:
Psalm 118:1–9
Romans 11:30–36
Titus 3:3–7

Offertory Comment:
During World War II, a national radio broadcast interviewed the executives of Pillsbury and a Colorado farmer who had won first prize among farmers in eight states for his wheat production. The executives asked, "Mr. Lindstrum, have you any reason to offer as to why you won this honor?" The farmer replied, "Yes, I do. My wife and I have always been faithful tithers. In the Book of Malachi in the Bible, God promises people who faithfully [give their tithes and offerings] that He will not only "rebuke the devourer," but will also open His windows and pour out a blessing. We had a drought in our area, but we received showers when we needed them. Hail destroyed the grain of our neighbors, but our crop was saved. Besides tithing our increase, we have for years planted one acre for God and have given to Him the entire proceeds of that acre as a special thank offering. It may interest you gentlemen to know that it was wheat from God's acre that won us this national honor."

Benediction:
Grace, mercy, and peace be with you all from the Father of Mercies and from His Son, our Lord Jesus Christ. Amen.

Additional Sermons and Lesson Ideas

A Man to Mimic

Date preached:

By Dr. David Jeremiah

SCRIPTURE: Acts 7:54—8:1

INTRODUCTION: If you want a hero to mimic, consider Stephen.

1. His Conviction (v. 54)
2. His Confidence (v. 55)
3. His Courage (vv. 56–59)
   A. His Final Testimony (v. 56)
   B. His Final Trial (vv. 57, 58)
   C. His Final Triumph (v. 59)
4. His Coronation (v. 60)
5. His Contribution (v. 1) that led to Paul's conversion.

CONCLUSION: Sometimes God allows persecution to motivate His church to do its rightful work. Let Stephen's example be your motivation and model for ministry.

Trials and Troubles

Date preached:

By Rev. Billy Friel

SCRIPTURE: Job 1

INTRODUCTION: The story of Job can be brought into the year 2005 without problem. Each of us faces trials and troubles in our lives. We can learn some lessons from Job by noticing these things in chapter 1 of his Book:

1. Piety (vv. 1, 8). Job was upright and shunned evil.
2. Parent (v. 2). He was blessed with a large, happy family.
3. Prosperous (v. 3). He was a wealthy man.
4. Priest (v. 5). As head of his home, Job was like a concerned priest for his children.
5. Protected by God (vv. 9, 10). Whatever came to Job came only through God's permissive will.
6. Provoked by Satan (vv. 9–19). Behind the trials was the Accuser of the Brethren
7. Preserved by Faith (vv. 20–22). Job was still under God's protective wing.

CONCLUSION: There's no safer place than the center of God's will.

CONVERSATIONS IN A PASTOR'S STUDY

An Interview with D. L. Moody

Why do you think God has used you so greatly?

I am the most overestimated man in this country. For some reason the people look upon me as a great man, but I am only a lay preacher and have little learning. I don't know what will become of me if the newspapers continue to print all my sermons. My stock will be exhausted by and by, and I must repeat old ideas. I cannot get up sermons as many others who preach week after week.

What accounts for your incredible drive in ministry?

I have a work to do, laid out for me in the secret counsels of eternity; no other can do it. If I neglect it, it is not true that some other will do it; it will remain undone. If I know my own heart today, I would rather die than not be used by God in building up His kingdom.

You've been criticized for a lack of training in homiletics. Some make fun of your speaking style. Does that bother you?

We have too many orators. I am tired and sick of silver-tongued orators. I used to mourn because I couldn't be an orator. I thought, "Oh, if I could only have the gift of speech like some!" I have heard men with a smooth flow of language take the audience captive, but they came and they went, their voice was like the air, there wasn't any power back of it. Paul wrote, "My speech and my preaching was not with enticing words of man's wisdom, but in demonstration of the Spirit and of power." I tell you when the Spirit of God is on us for service, resting on us, we can do great things.

But wouldn't it be a good idea to study elocution and public speaking?

Yes and no. These studied gestures in the pulpit—my word, I am sick and tired of them! Some men remind me of a windmill, with their practiced gestures. How would Moses have succeeded if he had gone down into Egypt and tried elocution on Pharaoh?

Have you ever had trouble connecting with an audience?

Once, in Paris. I got up into a little box of a pulpit with the interpreter—there was hardly room enough for one. I said a sentence while he leaned away over to one side, and then I leaned over while he repeated it in the French. Can you conceive of a more stupid thing? If there is a stupid thing in the world, it is to talk through an interpreter.

Your ministry has attracted great crowds, but you've also had disappointing audiences, too, haven't you?

Very true. But if you want to kindle a fire you collect a handful of pine whittlings, light them with a match, and keep blowing them until they blaze. Then you pile on the wood.

What would you say to a minister whose crowd was small?

If I expected 5,000 people and found only five, I would give them the best I could.

What if someone goes to sleep in the audience?

It is good to stop and say, "Won't you open the window and let in a little air? Here is a gentleman who has gone to sleep." That'll wake up every one of them. You can't reach a man when he is asleep.

What's the secret of your sermon preparation?

I have no secret. I study more by subjects than I do by texts. If, when I am reading, I meet a good thing on any of these subjects, I slip it into the right envelope and let it lie there. When I want a new sermon, I take everything that has been accumulating. Between what I find there and the results of my own study I have material enough.

How can a person overcome nervousness in the pulpit?

Get so full of your subject that you forget yourself. Be occupied with the subject. Let me say right here that I like to say "to speak"' better than "to preach" because if I can only get people to think I am talking with them, and not preaching, it is so much easer to hold their attention. I think sometimes we almost preach the people to death.

Do you ever get discouraged?

I remember during the War, I was in a prayer meeting. We were all very dark and gloomy. Things had been going against us for some time. At last, an old man got up, and said, "What is the matter with us, that we are downhearted and sad? It is simply our lack of faith. Moses, Joshua, and David were men strong in faith. They believed, and therefore God honored them. God is not dead. He is as powerful, as willing, to help today as ever. He was. Why, then, are we not full of faith in Him? It is God-dishonoring to forget that He still has power, although our armies are defeated, and all seems dark and gloomy."

FEBRUARY 20, 2005

SUGGESTED SERMON *Date preached:*

Operation Restoration

By Dr. Timothy Beougher

Scripture: James 5:19, 20

Brethren, if anyone among you wanders from the truth, and someone turns him back, let him know that he who turns a sinner from the error of his way will save a soul from death and cover a multitude of sins. (NKJV)

Introduction: One of the most rewarding sights in the world is to see something that has fallen into neglect be restored to usefulness. Some of you in this congregation may be in the restoration business, and surely, all of us have had something restored whether it is furniture, an old car, or any other item. Seeing anything brought back to its original beauty and its designed usefulness is a wonderful sight. This morning the focus of our two verses is an appeal for believers in the church to restore those who have wandered.

1. **The Need for Restoration (v. 19a).** James begins verse 19 with this phrase that he has used fifteen times already in this letter. It's a reminder that the church is a family. Because of what Christ has done for us, we're part of the same spiritual family. He then says, "if anyone among you ..." Whom is he talking about? I think the best explanation is that he is referring to those who have professed faith, but are not evidencing the fruits of faith (James 2). However one may interpret this phrase, the fact is that restoration is essential within the church body. Restoration must take place when anyone within the church body "wanders from the truth." Remember John 17:17, "... Your word is truth."

James is addressing people who do not follow Scripture, who receive the Word, but do not live it out (cf. Matt. 13). So, James tells us there's a need for restoration. Secondly there is:

2. **The Process of Restoration (v. 19b; Gal. 6:1).** If a believer wanders, James continues, "someone turns him back ..." Notice that "someone" is mentioned, not a minister or elder or teacher; all of us should be in the restoration business. This process has two components, both of which are vitally important.

A. **Attitude (Gal. 6:1 NKJV).** "Brethren, if a man is overtaken in any trespass, you who are spiritual restore such a one in a spirit of gentleness, considering yourself lest you also be tempted." In dependence on the Spirit, we are to gently and humbly restore, not grudgingly or judgmentally criticize.

B. **Action (James 5:19b).** We are to "turn him back." This verse emphasizes the goal, to restore and not to prove a point.

3. **The Result of Restoration (v. 20).** Remember this, "he who turns a sinner from the error of his way will save a soul from death and cover a multitude of sins." Turning is an issue of repentance; that's our goal. Not to get an apology to us, but to encourage repentance to God Himself. The phrase, "from the error of his way" teaches us that there is absolute right and wrong. Scripture is the authority, and is very clear about sin. Sin is not subjective, and thus we are to support its teachings. Turning someone from sin introduces them to the forgiveness of God, which is salvation from the punishment of sin and the grace that covers a multitude of sins (cf. 1 Cor. 11:30, Ps. 32:1; 103:12; Mic. 7:18).

Application: Do you know how many people are on the membership roll in this church? In almost every church, the roll includes many more people than actually attend. What about those who have come to our church and, for whatever reason, have left? Sometimes they move or switch churches, but often they need restoration. What about those in your family who do not follow the Lord closely? Who better to approach them in love than you?

Conclusion: If you are here and have never trusted Jesus Christ, He has given you all these you see in this congregation today to help restore you. Come speak with me, or with one of our staff, or with someone here whom you know is living a different life marked by dedication to the Lord. Perhaps you know of someone who needs restoring today. My challenge is that we all commit ourselves to this ministry of restoration, for Jesus Christ has restored so many of us here this morning, and He is asking us to carry out His work.

STATS, STORIES, AND MORE

More from Dr. Timothy Beougher:

Here's an approach to restoring others that I've found helpful. I learned it long ago from a man named Brad Waggoner. I can't remember if it was because he shared it with me or practiced it on me, but I learned it nevertheless.

1. Pray for wisdom, boldness, and sensitivity.
2. Confront gently and lovingly.
3. Listen to the person's perspective.
4. Inform and give guidance.
5. Pray that God will continue to work in the situation.

The Apostle John and the Bandit

According to Clement of Alexandria, the aged apostle John entrusted a promising youth to a local bishop for discipleship. The bishop took the young man home, raised him, and finally baptized him. But after all this, the boy fell into the wrong crowd and eventually became the chief of a band of thieves. When John next visited the area, he asked for the young man. The bishop replied sadly, "He is dead. He is dead to God. He has taken possession of the mountain in front of the church with his bandits." Tearing his clothes, the apostle cried for a horse and rode into the mountains, seeking the youth. Being stopped by the robbers' detachment, he shouted, "It was for this I came. Lead me to your captain." The young bandit, recognizing John, turned to flee in shame. But John followed, forgetting his age, and crying, "Why, my son, do you flee from me your unarmed, old father? Have pity on me. I will willingly endure death for you, as the Lord did for us. Believe that Christ has sent me." Hearing this, the youth wept bitterly and was eventually restored to Christ.

FOR THE BULLETIN

✿ February 20, 1496 is the birthday of Johan Friis, Danish statesman who helped establish Lutheranism in Denmark. ✿ On February 20, 1547, the young and sickly Edward VI was crowned King of England following death of Henry VIII. Edward's early death led to the ascension of Mary I (1516–1558), known as "Bloody Mary," who unleashed a period of violent persecution against Protestants in England. ✿ February 20, 1656 marks the death of James Usher, Archbishop of Armagh. He is best known for establishing a biblical chronology for the King James Version of the Bible. ✿ On February 20, 1863, E. M. Bounds was given passage through the war lines to make his way into the South. He became a chaplain during the Civil War, and went on to write classic books on prayer. ✿ February 20, 1867, is the birthday of Barney Elliott Warren, author of the song, "Joy Unspeakable and Full of Glory." ✿ German-born Frederick M. Lehman immigrated to America, where his family settled down in Iowa. He came to Christ at age eleven while walking through a crabapple orchard, and eventually entered the ministry and pastored churches in the Midwest. But Frederick's greatest love was gospel music, and during his lifetime, he compiled five songbooks and published hundreds of songs. His best-known hymn is "The Love of God," written in a packinghouse in Pasadena, California, in 1917. Frederick died on February 20, 1953, and is buried at Forest Lawn Memorial Cemetery in Glendale.

APPROPRIATE SONGS AND HYMNS

Joy Unspeakable, Barney E. Warren; Public Domain.

Forgive Our Sins as We Forgive, Rosamond E. Herklots; © R.E. Herklots; Admin. by Hope Publishing Company.

Oh Lord, You're Beautiful, Keith Green; © 1980 Birdwing Music/BMG Songs, Inc.; Admin. by EMI Christian Music Publishing/BMG Music Publishing.

Then Jesus Came, Oswald J. Smith/Homer A. Rodeheaver; © 1940 Renewed 1968 Word Music, Inc.; Admin. by Word Music Group, Inc.

Wash Me Lord, Ed Kerr/Jerry Williams; © 1987 Singspiration Music; Admin. by Brentwood-Benson Music Publishing, Inc.

WORSHIP HELPS

Call to Worship:

Christ be with us, Christ within us,
Christ behind us, Christ before us,
Christ beside us, Christ to win us,
Christ to comfort and restore us!
—Adapted from "St. Patrick's Breastplate"

Scripture Reading Medley:

Let us consider one another in order to stir up love and good works, not forsaking the assembling of ourselves together, as is the manner of some, but exhorting one another, and so much the more as you see the Day approaching. We, being many, are one body in Christ, and individually members of one another. If a man is overtaken in any trespass, you who are spiritual restore such a one in a spirit of gentleness, considering yourself lest you also be tempted. Bear one another's burdens, and so fulfill the law of Christ. Be kindly affectionate to one another with brotherly love, in honor giving preference to one another; not lagging in diligence, fervent in spirit, serving the Lord; rejoicing in hope, patient in tribulation, continuing steadfastly in prayer; distributing to the needs of the saints, given to hospitality. Bless those who persecute you; bless and do not curse. Rejoice with those who rejoice, and weep with those who weep. Be of the same mind toward one another. Be kind to one another, tenderhearted, forgiving one another, even as God in Christ forgave you. (Heb. 10:24, 25; Rom. 12:5; Gal. 6:1, 2; Rom. 12:10–16; Eph. 4:32 NKJV)

Children's Story:

Today's theme lends itself to talking to the children about being kind to one another. Tell them a story of a time from your childhood when you acted in a kind or cruel way, or when someone was kind or cruel to you.

Additional Sermons and Lesson Ideas

One Thing I Know

Date preached:

Adapted from a sermon by W. Graham Scroggie

SCRIPTURE: John 9:25

INTRODUCTION: It is sad to see someone born blind; but what if we all were born blind? What if blind leaders, blind merchants, and blind artisans peopled this world? What if blindness were universal? Spiritually, is it not so? But here was a man who received his sight.

1. His Unanswerable Argument. In meeting his critics, he used the irrefutable argument of experience. His was a definite, conclusive, life-changing experience.
2. His Unimpeachable Knowledge. "One thing I know." His knowledge was limited to one thing, but it was certain and undeniable.
3. His Unsolicited Testimony. Immediately upon his healing, he began publicly declaring what had happened to him.

CONCLUSION: If you are a Christian, why should you mind if others know it. If Christ is worth having, surely He is worth confessing.

The Sovereign's Standard

Date preached:

By Dr. Melvin Worthington

SCRIPTURE: Revelation 3:7–13

INTRODUCTION: God's standard for Christians and churches is faithfulness. The Philadelphia church furnishes a great example.

1. The Inscription (v. 7). The inscription includes the angel, the assembly, the area, the authority, the address, and the Almighty—the holy one, the honest one and the head one.
2. The Inventory (v. 8). The inventory includes the deeds, the door, the durability, the doctrine, and the distinctiveness.
3. The Inspiration (v. 9). The inspiration includes the identified adversary and the intended adoration.
4. The Instruction (vv. 11b, 13). The instruction includes the duty prescribed—the Lord's challenge, the danger presented—the lost crown, and the divine proclamation—the lasting charge.
5. The Incentive (vv. 10, 11a, 12). The incentive includes the noted hour, the noted hope, and the noted honor.

CONCLUSION: Christ, in His message, supplies the comfort this church needs and corrects the error of its self-judgment. What would he say to us as a congregation?

FEBRUARY 27, 2005

SUGGESTED SERMON *Date preached:*

Ten Reasons for Family Devotions

By Dr. Woodrow Kroll

Scripture: Psalm 119:9–11, especially verse 9
How can a young man cleanse his way? By taking heed according to Your word. (NKJV)

Introduction: I'd like to deal with a once-popular subject that has fallen on hard times—family devotions. This old phrase simply means praying together as a family. I believe we can still find a formula for having the "family altar" if we realize how important it is. Today I'd like to share ten reasons for family devotions.

1. **Devotions Provide Communication with God.** They are the easiest, best way for your family to get together and talk to God (see Ps. 25:4, 5). When we have family devotions, we're communicating with God. Communication in business today is so important that 90% of U.S. companies provide communication skills training in the workplace. Subscribers to the *Harvard Business Review* rated the ability to communicate as more important than ambition, education, and the capacity for hard work. We teach our children how to communicate with their playmates. When do you teach them how to communicate with God? (see Ps. 119:145–152).

2. **Devotions Quench Spiritual Thirst.** We're all thirsty for something (see Ps. 42:1, 2). Blaise Pascal (1623–1662), the seventeenth-century French philosopher, wrote that we all have a God-shaped vacuum that only God can fill. That's true for our children, grandchildren, and spouse. Family devotions allow the opportunity to quench our spiritual thirst (see Ps. 84:2).

3. **Devotions Advance Personal Spiritual Growth.** Yes, I know we can grow with private devotions. praying with other members of the family helps all the family do the same (see 1 Pet. 2:2; 2 Pet. 3:18). If you're growing in God's Word but your spouse isn't, it makes for an unbalanced couple.

4. **Family Devotions Bring Us Together.** Sitting down and talking about spiritual things provides a safeguard against carnality in our homes (see

1 Corinthians 3:1–3). If you want to put a hedge against worldly activity in your family, the best way is to get together each day to discuss how we relate God's Word to our lives in the world. It's a tradition your child will treasure later in life.

5. **Devotions Provide Insight for Daily Life.** Take Proverbs 10:4, for example: "Lazy hands make a man poor, but diligent hands bring wealth" (NIV). It's important for kids to know that. The Book of Proverbs gives specific advice on how to treat a mean neighbor, what to do when your wife is mad at you, how to invest properly, when to speak and when to be silent, how to know when you've angered someone, and what to do about it. And that's just one book.

6. **Family Devotions Prevent Schizophrenic Faith.** It seems to me that some Christians who believe in God and come to church also believe some of the wildest, wackiest things. They've mixed truth and error. They sing praise choruses at church, yet hold beliefs that don't square with Scripture. Family devotions counter that. Consistent time before the Lord enables us to grow.

7. **Devotions Provide Daily Comfort and Encouragement.** If I didn't have a Bible, I don't know what I'd do. If I didn't have it open, I don't know what I'd do. And if I didn't have it open every day, I don't know how I'd face life's challenges (see Ps. 119:81).

8. **Devotions Prepare Us to Share Our Faith.** The more we're in God's Word, the more familiar with it we become and the more apt we are to share it (see 1 Pet. 3:15).

9. **Devotions Provide Daily Marching Orders.** When you get into Scripture, you find things that tell you what God wants you to do each day (see Deut. 5:27 and Ps. 119:105). God's will is revealed in His Word.

10. **Family Devotions Show Respect for the Author of the Bible.** The greatest compliment to pay an author is to say, "I read your book." I wonder what we'll say to God when we meet Him face to face, and He asks, "Did you read My book?" (see Ps. 119:127, 128).

Conclusion: How do you start? Well, everybody does it differently. In our family, we read a chapter every night and take a moment to discuss it. We take requests and pray, and it's a simple thing. It doesn't take long, but we never allow anything to disrupt that time. If the phone rings, we let it ring. If the doorbell rings, we don't answer it. My friend, when I'm spending time with my family, and we're spending time with God, there's nothing more vital. Having family devotions is important!

STATS, STORIES, AND MORE

More from Dr. Woodrow Kroll:

Carla Crumley-Forest said in a recent article in *Today's Christian Woman:* Shortly after our family began having nightly devotions (which isn't easy with a precocious four-year-old daughter and an impish two-year-old son) my daughter asked, 'Mommy, when are we gonna get together with Daddy and Austin to talk about God and have family commotions?'"

People with schizophrenic faith have not grown up because they're not getting the Word directly from God. They're getting it second-handedly. Maybe they've been a part of a chatroom on the Internet, and they thought that they were a part of a discussion about God's Word. Sometimes chatrooms are little more than pooled ignorance. If you want strong faith, get into the Word of God yourself, and get your family into the Scripture.

Examples:

Your children often see you reading the newspaper, watching a movie, or settling down for a long ballgame. It's important for them to see you pouring over God's Word. Ruth Bell Graham recalled the example of her own parents, Dr. and Mrs. L. Nelson Bell, missionaries to China. "Each morning," Ruth said, "when I went downstairs to breakfast, my father—a busy missionary surgeon—would be sitting reading his Bible. At night, her work behind her, my mother would be doing the same. Anything that could so capture the interest and devotion of those I admired and loved the most, I reasoned, must be worth investigating. So at an early age I began reading my Bible and found it to be, in the words of an old Scotsman, 'sweet pasturage.'"

FOR THE BULLETIN

❁ February 27, 272 marks the birthday of Constantine the Great, the first Roman Emperor to adopt Christianity. ❁ Scottish Reformer George Wishart was placed on trial on this day in 1546 for his Protestant beliefs. During the trial one of his accusers cursed and spat on him. Wishart responded that this action was worse than anything he was ever accused of doing. Wishart was burned at the stake at St. Andrews on March 1. ❁ John Wesley preached that Methodist people should die well. When he realized that he himself was dying, he asked everyone to leave the room for a half hour so he could be alone with God. Shortly thereafter, on Sunday, February 27, 1791, he rose from his deathbed, sat in his chair with a cheerful expression on his face, and repeated a hymn his brother Charles had written. Returning to bed, he lingered two days more before saying his last words: "The best of all is, God is with us. Farewell." ❁ February 27, 1807 is the birthday of Henry Wadsworth Longfellow, born in Portland, Maine. Henry became one of the most distinguished American poets. His brother, Samuel, became a famous hymn writer. Henry himself is remembered for his Christmas carol, "I Heard the Bells on Christmas Day," published in 1864. ❁ February 27, 1838 marks the birth of William J. Kirkpatrick, American Methodist sacred composer, best known for such melodies as: "He Hideth My Soul," "'Tis So Sweet to Trust in Jesus," "Redeemed, How I Love to Proclaim It," and "Lord, I'm Coming Home."

APPROPRIATE SONGS AND HYMNS

My Faith Looks Up to Thee, Ray Palmer/Lowell Mason; Public Domain.

Ah Lord God, Kay Chance; © 1976 Kay Chance.

God of Grace and God of Glory, John Purifoy; © 1985 Purifoy Publishing Company; Admin. by The Lorenze Corporation.

To Him Who Sits on the Throne, Debbye Graafsma; © 1984 Integrity's Hosanna! Music; Admin. by Integrity Music Inc.

WORSHIP HELPS

Call to Worship:
Hear, O Israel: The LORD our God, the LORD is one! You shall love the LORD your God with all your heart, with all your soul, and with all your strength. And these words which I command you today shall be in your heart. You shall teach them diligently to your children. (Deut. 6:4–7a NKJV)

A Practical Suggestion:
Before preaching on this subject, research the products that are available to assist family devotions. Check your local Christian bookstore and search your favorite websites. You might hold up some sample products. It would encourage parents to know they don't have to start from scratch in planning meaningful devotions for their children.

Scripture Reading:
I remember you in my prayers night and day, greatly desiring to see you, being mindful of your tears, that I may be filled with joy, when I call to remembrance the genuine faith that is in you, which dwelt first in your grandmother Lois and your mother Eunice, and I am persuaded is in you also ... (for) from childhood you have known the Holy Scriptures which are able to make you wise for salvation through faith which is in Christ Jesus. (2 Tim. 1:3–5 and 3:15 NKJV)

Kids Talk

Show the children a remote control device and ask them which button is the most important. It's the off button. Tell them you've been having some trouble with your remote control and you think the batteries are low. Remove the back cover and pull out a little paper with Psalm 119:37 written on it: "Turn away my eyes from looking at worthless things." You might give each child a copy of that verse to paste to their television sets.

Additional Sermons and Lesson Ideas

How God Spells Peace

Date preached:

SCRIPTURE: John 14:27

INTRODUCTION: An advertiser has told us how we should spell R-E-L-I-E-F, but how does God spell P-E-A-C-E?

P – Perfect (Is. 26:3)
E – Ease of Heart (John 14:27)
A – And
C – Confidence (Is. 30:15)
E – Every Day (Ps. 68:19)

CONCLUSION: Is this possible? Yes. Because it comes from Jesus, who said, "*My* peace I give unto you."

What Pleases God

Date preached:

SCRIPTURE: Proverbs 16:7

INTRODUCTION: Did you ever have a parent, teacher, or coach whom you especially wanted to please? How about pleasing God? Proverbs 16 contains some God-pleasing ideas:

1. Commit everything to the Lord (v. 3).
2. Fear God and depart from evil (v. 6).
3. Live honestly (v. 11).
4. Don't let money be the most important thing in your life (v. 16).
5. Trust Him (v. 20).
6. Age gracefully (v. 31).
7. Anger slowly (v. 32).

CONCLUSION: Gifts or ability do not please God, but attitudes and habits do.

HELPS FOR THE PASTOR'S FAMILY

Having Devotions with Your Spouse

Many pastors are not very good about having devotions with their spouses, given the demands, pressures, schedules, and expectations of family, friends, and church. Here's a simple, workable idea that's very enriching but doesn't take much time. Find an *old* devotional book. Begin or end the day by reading the day's entry together and then praying. Simple as that. But it needs to be an *old* devotional.

Why?

Because we're bombarded by the contemporary. We, who are always giving out, need to be nourished by an older, wiser saint who lived when people still had time to think. We need the depth of the ages. If you aren't sure where to start, I have some suggestions. A few of these books are still in print, but others will have to be sought out. Perhaps you have your own tried-and-true favorites, but let me offer a few of mine:

- The devotional books of Frances Ridley Havergal. These are the best. Most are divided into 31 segments instead of 365 segments, but they provide a rich month of nourishment. Havergal was a British hymnist and devotional writer who gave us such great hymns as "Like a River Glorious" and her signature song, "Take My Life and Let it Be." Try her little book *Royal Bounty: Evening Thoughts for the King's Guests,* published in 1878. The companion volume is *Royal Commandments: Morning Thoughts for the King's Servants.* She also has several books of poetry and her all-time favorite, *Kept for the Master's Use,* though the latter is not divided into daily readings. Even her children's devotional books like *Morning Bells* and *Morning Stars* are unusually rich and provide adult-level encouragement.

- *Daily Strength for Daily Needs,* a series of 365 readings, was compiled by Mary W. Tileston in 1913. Each day provides a selected Bible verse, along with great quotes or poems. This is the volume I'm currently using, and it's here that I found this jewel by Anna Waring which has become a daily prayer of mine recently:

  I love to think that God appoints
  My portion day by day;
  Events of life are in His hand,
  And I would only say,

Appoint them in Thine own good time,
And in Thine own best way.

- *Daily Light.* This classic of daily scripture medleys took three generations to compile, and Christians—especially missionaries—around the world have found just the right words for life's daily demands.
- *Thoughts for the Quiet Hour.* Evangelist D. L. Moody compiled this assortment of spiritual delicacies, some of which are very short.
- *Streams in the Desert* and *Springs in the Valley.* These two classic volumes by missionary and author, Mrs. Charles E. Cowman, are timeless sources of comfort for those who are troubled. Many people don't know there is a third volume as well, entitled, *Consolation.*
- *Edges of His Ways.* Though not as old, this devotional by Amy Carmichael has ministered to me when nothing else could get through the fog and pain. Her several devotional volumes are well underlined on my shelves.
- *Cheque Book of the Bank of Faith: Daily Readings by C. H. Spurgeon.* I'm a big Spurgeon fan, but I've never gotten a great deal out of his famous *Morning and Evening.* Don't ask me why. But this little checkbook-sized devotional is different. Give it a try.
- *The Moravian Daily Texts.* Since the early 1700s, the Moravians have been compiling Scriptures and hymns for each day. This is probably the most widely read daily devotional guide in the world, next to the Bible. One and a half million copies are now published in 51 languages and dialects. The verses for each morning are chosen by lot, but somehow they often seem strikingly appropriate.

These are just a few examples. If nothing else will do, of course, you can always turn to Oswald Chambers or to one of the more modern compilations. Or, if you're especially wise, deep, and brave-hearted, you can plunge into *The Imitation of Christ* by Thomas à Kempis, which is arguably Christianity's all-time greatest devotional classic. On the other hand, sometimes I just like to dip into something as simple as one of Vance Havner's books of daily devotions, such as *Peace in the Valley* or *Day by Day.*

Whatever you choose, take a moment each day with your husband or wife to ponder the wisdom of God's Word. Let an older saint be your mentor. Invite Moody or Spurgeon or Cowman or Havergal to share your bedside table or your breakfast nook. They make enriching guests and lead to a healthier marriage and ministry.

MARCH 6, 2005

SUGGESTED SERMON *Date preached:*

Faith Amid Famine

By Rev. Todd M. Kinde

Scripture: 1 Kings 17:7–24, especially v. 24
Now by this I know that you are a man of God, and that the word of the LORD in your mouth is the truth. (NKJV)

Introduction: This morning we are going to be learning quite an object lesson through a bin of flour and a jar of oil. I realize that talking about flour, oil, bread, and food can make your mouth water. I hope today we all came into this building hungry—at least spiritually hungry. Do you have a financial problem? Are your relationships hurting? Do you need a fresh encounter with the Lord? Jesus said, "I am the bread of life. He who comes to Me shall never hunger, and he who believes in Me shall never thirst" (John 6:35 NKJV).

1. **A Parchedness of Faith (1 Kin. 17:7–9).** The Word of the Lord came to Elijah instructing him to go to the town of Zarephath where a widow would supply him with food. The drought was an object lesson of the dryness of the nation's relationship with God (cf. Amos 8 and Ps. 42). Now that the brook had run dry, the Lord placed Elijah in Zarephath, a suburb of the capital city where the wicked Jezebel's father was king!

2. **A Preview of Faith (1 Kin. 17:10–15a).** In Zarephath, Elijah found a certain widow. Elijah and asked for a flask of water. He tested her willingness and obedience. When she agreed, Elijah added a request for bread. She told Elijah she had only enough for her and her son to have a last meal before starvation. Most of us would have reacted harshly, but this woman said, "As surely as the Lord your God lives ..." She knew Yahweh was the Living God, but He was not her God ("your God lives"). The gentle hand of God was leading her into progressive faith. Elijah said, "Can I have a drink? Can I have a slice of bread? Make me a pancake." As we respond to God's Word with trusting obedience in each step, so He will lead us to greater understanding of Himself and the blessing of His promise of salvation.

3. **A Provision of Faith (1 Kin. 17:15b, 16).** It's safe to assume that neither the flour jar nor the oil jug were large. At the end of each day, her jug and jar

looked to be just as nearly empty as they did that first evening when she met Elijah. God gave her and Elijah only their daily bread (Matt. 6:11). Faith is progressive, not a one-time commitment. Elijah and the widow did not respond with faith just once and then receive a warehouse full of flour and oil. At the end of each day, they had to acknowledge their complete dependence upon the Lord and trust Him for enough grace for the next day (see Lam. 3:22, 23).

4. **A Prayer of Faith (1 Kin. 17:17–23).** We don't know how long this way of life continued, but some time later the son of the woman became ill and died. Then her faith was tested in a new dimension. The woman faced death yet again, saying to Elijah, "What have I to do with you, O man of God? Have you come to me to bring my sin to remembrance, and to kill my son?" (v. 18). Did not God promise life when He gave the promise of food? On the basis of the promise of God's Word, Elijah prayed to the Lord to revive the boy. We should pray with such awareness of the Word of the Lord that our prayers are built on the foundation of God's promises.

5. **A Profession of Faith (1 Kin. 17:24).** The woman's response was a deeper and more personal profession of faith in the one true living God. She understood that there was more to this than simply the death of her son's body. It had to do with her sinfulness and spiritual death. Her confession is seen in verse 24. She comprehends the truth. God's Word can be trusted beyond doubt. You can trust the Word of the Lord for all your needs in life and death.

Conclusion: We don't live by bread alone but by every word that comes from the mouth of God (Deut. 8:3). Do not seek to satisfy the longing of your soul with bread, but trust the Lord of life who gives living water and the Bread of Life. Cling to the Cross of Christ. Through it you have the forgiveness of sin and the promise of life eternal. May we say, "Now we know that the Word of the Lord is the truth" and make that truth into a living faith.

STATS, STORIES, AND MORE

Walk of Faith

Many people get the wrong idea about the Christian life. In our excitement about Jesus, we expect never to have to deal with our same old habits, problems, or temptations. Often, more mature Christians advance this notion, hiding their own personal struggles and dilemmas. Many believe they should live a flawless life. How often do we say, "Oh, I just can't get it right! Am I really saved at all? Don't you hate me by now God?" The truth of God's grace throughout life is one that is difficult for humans to understand because we naturally rely on our works. We must understand that the walk of faith is just that—a walk. It is a progressive journey with Jesus as our guide. The late singer/songwriter Rich Mullins beautifully captured this truth in one of his most famous songs:

And on this road to righteousness
Sometimes the climb can be so steep
I may falter in my steps
But never beyond Your reach ...
I will seek You in the morning
And I will learn to walk in Your ways
And step-by-step You lead me
And I will follow You all of my days.

Growing in Faith

The following statistics indicate that we should take a much more active role in our Christian walk:

About three out of every five Christians have read from the Bible in the past week.

About 20% of Christians are involved in discipleship.

Only about 60% of Christians attend church each week.

FOR THE BULLETIN

✿ March 6, 1475 is the birthday of Michelangelo, famed Italian church painter and sculptor. He dominated the High Renaissance period, his most famous works being his statue of the David, and his fresco in the Sistine Chapel at the Vatican. ✿ After the Diet of Worms, Martin Luther was taken into hiding at Wartburg Castle where he occupied himself with translating the Bible into German. Increasingly restless, however, he refused to be shut, emerging on March 6, 1522 to face the world and lead the Reformation. ✿ March 6, 1806 is the birthday of Elizabeth Barrett Browning. Among her poems are several hymns including one that says: "The little cares which fretted me, / I lost them yesterday / Among the fields, above the sea, / Among the winds at play ..." ✿ Dr. A. T. Pierson, the American pastor, writer, missionary statesman, and author, was born on this day in 1837. When Charles Spurgeon became ill, he turned to Pierson to fill the pulpit in his absence. ✿ March 6, 1839 is the date of George Muller's last sermon. ✿ On March 6, 1901, Amy Carmichael began her work of rescuing temple children. She "kidnapped" [rescued] a temple runaway, a young girl dedicated to the Hindu gods and forced into prostitution to earn money for the priests. ✿ Julia H. Johnston died on this day in 1919 at the age of 70. She wrote about 500 hymns during her lifetime, the best known being "Grace Greater Than Our Sin."

APPROPRIATE SONGS AND HYMNS

'Tis So Sweet to Trust in Jesus, Louisa Stead/William J. Kirkpatrick; Public Domain.

All Things, Chris Christensen; © 1990 Integrity's Hosanna! Music.

Faith, Geoff Bullock; © 1994 Word Music, Inc./Maranatha Music; Admin. by Word Music Group, Inc.

Faith Is the Victory, John H. Yates/Ira D. Sankey; Public Domain.

Grace, Greater than Our Sin, Julia H. Johnston/Daniel Brink Towner; Public Domain.

WORSHIP HELPS

Call to Worship:
The LORD reigns; let the peoples tremble! He dwells between the cherubim; let the earth be moved! The LORD is great in Zion, and He is high above all the peoples. Let them praise Your great and awesome name— He is holy. (Ps. 99:1–3 NKJV)

Words of Welcome:
This morning, we're going to learn quite an object lesson, through food. Our message, "Faith Amid Famine," is going to paint a portrait of faith for us. Now I realize the risks of using food as an illustration in any sermon. I hope you all came today with a full stomach, otherwise I might not get through my first point without most of you making a beeline for the door. In all seriousness, I hope today we all came into this building spiritually hungry. What are you hungry for this morning? Do you have a financial problem? Are your relationships hurting? Do you need a fresh encounter with the Lord? Jesus said, "... I am the bread of life. He who comes to Me shall never hunger, and he who believes in Me shall never thirst" (John 6:35 NKJV).

Suggested Scripture Readings:
Proverbs 3:5, 6, 13–15
Luke 4:23–26
Hebrews 11:32–35

Benediction:
May God grant you, according to the riches of His glory, to be strengthened with might through His Spirit in the inner man, that Christ may dwell in your hearts through faith ... that you may be filled with all the fullness of God. (Eph. 3:14–19 NKJV)

Additional Sermons and Lesson Ideas

God Our Shepherd

Date preached:

By Rev. Mark Hollis

SCRIPTURE: Psalm 23

INTRODUCTION: This psalm points to how God meets six basic needs of our lives:

1. Provision (v. 1). Do you have a need? We can depend on our Shepherd to meet the most basic needs of our lives.
2. Rest (v. 2). Weary? Your Shepherd promises to provide rest (see Matt. 11:28–30).
3. Restoration (v. 3a). Does your battery need a recharge? Disconnect from our busy world and let God restore you.
4. Guidance (v. 3b). Uncertain? He guides in paths of righteousness (Ps. 37:4, 5, and Prov. 3:5, 6).
5. Safety (v. 4) Frightened? Run to your Father (Prov. 18:10).
6. Comfort (vv. 5, 6). In need of comfort? He has the weapons to care for any enemy as well as the means to comfort us in our greatest need.

CONCLUSION: Think of the three most worrisome needs in your life today. Trust your Shepherd to meet them!

Who Rules?

Date preached:

By Rev. Peter Grainger

SCRIPTURE: Daniel 4

INTRODUCTION: Nebuchadnezzar thought he was the supreme ruler, but this chapter tells of his encounter with the King of kings.

1. Nebuchadnezzar Rules. Nebuchadnezzar ruled the kingdom, but his pride became too strong (vv. 28–32). Like us, he was guilty of:
   A. Ignoring God (cf. Luke 12:16–21). Although Daniel warned him (v. 27), he allowed his pride to destroy his reign.
   B. Marginalizing God (cf. Mark 10:17–31). Nebuchadnezzar gloried in his own majesty (v. 30) rather than the Lord's.
2. The Lord Rules. Daniel prophesied that the king must learn that the Lord rules (v. 26). Nebuchadnezzar had to learn the hard way.
   A. The Fiery Furnace (Dan. 3).
   B. The Disturbing Dream (Dan. 4:19–27).
   C. The Painful Process (Dan. 4:28–33).

CONCLUSION: Nebuchadnezzar learned that the Lord rules. It resulted in his conversion (vv. 34–37). How are you dealing with successes and difficulties? May we recognize the Lord rules and attribute to Him the majesty due His name!

MARCH 13, 2005

SUGGESTED SERMON *Date preached:*

Strategic Planning

By Rev. Michael Easley

Scripture: Nehemiah 2:9–20, especially verse 18
And I told them of the hand of my God which had been good upon me, and also of the king's words that he had spoken to me. So they said, "Let us rise up and build." Then they set their hands to this good work. (NKJV)

Introduction: God is calling us to be spiritual leaders. Whether it is in our home, church, workplace, or anywhere else, we are called to lead our lives in such a way that others want to follow. As leaders, we are called to be strategic planners, with God as our focus. Our passage today relays the story of Nehemiah and his leadership. Through his example, we can learn how to be God-centered, prepared leaders.

1. **The Welcome (vv. 9, 10).** Nehemiah and a small band of associates traveled under military escort. The entourage wasn't as much for protection as it was to impress onlookers with the obvious credentials and backing of the king. Nehemiah was welcomed with harsh opposition from Sanballat and Tobiah. Both these men were powerful and were related to the high priest's family (Neh. 13:4ff., 28). Extra-biblical sources confirm Sanballat was governor of Samaria and Tobiah was likely governor of Ammon. They were disturbed (v. 10) that Jerusalem might be restored, so these neighboring nations were hostile toward them. Hostility is a real part of leading a Godly life and leading others in His ways. Are you facing hostility? At school, do others make fun of you for being in the youth group or for holding prayer meetings? To your fellow workers scowl when you speak of the Lord? Has the enemy interfered with your daily time with the Lord? We are all faced with opposition when we follow the Lord. How do you face opposition?

2. **The Survey (vv. 11–16).** Upon arrival, Nehemiah did not rush into action, but rested for three days. Then, he covertly inspected the situation. Nehemiah said in these verses that he did not disclose his plans to anyone, not to the enemies nor to his fellow workers, until he had accurate information. His route is traced in these verses. If seen on a map, this trek

proved to be a thorough assessment of the city's condition. How often we as Christians run blindly into ministry, as if it is random or mindless! Jesus, when speaking about ministry, said, "What king, going to make war against another king, does not sit down first and consider whether he is able with ten thousand to meet him who comes against him with twenty thousand?" (Luke 14:31 NKJV). We are to be, "... wise as serpents and harmless as doves" (Matt. 10:16 NKJV).

3. **The Report (vv. 17, 18).** Nehemiah exposed the negative situation: the land was desolate and the gates were burned. Then he reported the positive, "And I told them of the hand of my God which had been good upon me, and also of the king's words that he had spoken to me..." (v. 18). After the reminder of God's goodness, the people responded positively. Do we as God's people get discouraged too easily? We're to focus on God's promises and believe.

4. **The Opposition (vv. 19, 20).** Now a third enemy entered the picture, Geshem. Some scholars feel he was the most powerful of all the opponents. He and his son ruled a confederacy of Arabian tribes that were in control of Moab and Edom. Surrounded with opposition, Nehemiah's answer was, "The God of heaven Himself will prosper us; therefore we His servants will arise and build ... " (v. 20). Notice he did not say "King Artaxerxes will wipe you out if you mess with us." No, his faith was in the God of heaven! He continued, telling them, "... you have no heritage or right or memorial in Jerusalem" (v. 20). Imagine, Jerusalem was in rubble and yet he boasted that the Lord would fulfill His promise!

Conclusion: It's been said that God never gives His people tasks they can fulfill on their own. We will find ourselves in positions to glorify the Lord in such incredible ways that we don't believe they are possible. However, these are the very plans the Lord has for us. We will encounter hostility, we will have to survey and plan, and we will have to persuade others to continue in faith. If we, like Nehemiah, have an unshakable faith and commitment to God's promises, we will see incredible fulfillment, not only rebuilding a wall or a city, but also bringing nations to faith in Jesus Christ!

STATS, STORIES, AND MORE

More from Rev. Michael Easley:

Nehemiah did not believe in a one-man ministry; he challenged the leaders of the remnant to work with him (not for him) in repairing the walls. What was the motive? "That we may no longer be a reproach" (v. 17). He was concerned with the glory of God as well as the good of the nation. However, as a leader in this ministry, certainly he faced battles as we will. At least four battles face every leader:

1. Battle with self: doubt, fear, impatience, etc.
2. Battle with the mission: concerns about impossibility, timetables, cost, etc.
3. Battle with those you will lead.
4. Battle with the enemy.

I often wonder if there is a sequential connection. The better I can overcome the battle with myself and my mission, the better I'll lead others and face the enemy. Or perhaps it is reversed: the better I lead others and face the enemy, the easier it will be to overcome my insecurities or doubts about God's mission for me. In any case, we should be ready for these battles and face them with faith. As we face opposition, as did Nehemiah, there is an important principle to remember: never forget God's faithfulness in your life. Nehemiah reported the tragedy (v. 17) but he quickly informed the leaders how God had made Him successful up to that point (v. 18).

My wife has reminded me of this more vividly than anyone has. She says, "Sure, we're going to struggle. Sure, we'll have sickness. Sure, we're going to watch our kids do some things we wish they wouldn't, but we must look back and remember the good hand of God in our lives and go forward in faith."

FOR THE BULLETIN

❁ On March 13, 1464, the Bible was printed for the first time as Johannes Gutenberg began printing the Gutenberg Bible with his moveable type printing process. ❁ Because of their Anabaptist beliefs, Balthasar Hubmaier and his wife were arrested in Moravia. When they refused to recant, Hubmaier was burned in the public square in Vienna. His wife was drowned in the Danube River on March 13, 1528. ❁ On March 13, 1639, the college at Cambridge, Massachusetts, was named for John Harvard, who had left England to escape persecution because of his Puritan beliefs. The school had been founded by the Puritans in 1636 for the training of clergy with this admonition: "Let every student be plainly instructed, and earnestly pressed to consider well, the main end of his life and studies is, to know God and Jesus Christ which is eternal life, John 17:3." When Harvard University later took a liberal turn, Yale was established as a Calvinistic alternative. ❁ Today is the birthday of missionary Charles Cowman (1868), a telegraph operator who, following his conversion, felt called into missions. He and his wife, Lettie, sailed for Japan in 1901, and eventually founded the Oriental Missionary Society. Cowman continued in missionary service until 1917, when his health broke from complete exhaustion. During his last six years, his wife cared for him and wrote the devotional classic, *Streams in the Desert*. ❁ After seizing power in Cuba, Fidel Castro openly attacked what he called "Protestant sects" for the first time on this day in 1964, signaling an era of persecution that continues to this day.

APPROPRIATE SONGS AND HYMNS

God Can Do Anything But Fail, Ira Stanphill; © 1946 Singspiration Music; Admin. by Brentwood-Benson Music Publishing, Inc.

God Will Make a Way, Don Moen; © 1990 Integrity's Hosanna! Music.

I Call You Faithful, Bobby Price/Kevin Walker; © 1990 Dawn Treader Music/Shepherd's Fold Music; Admin. by EMI Christian Music Publishing.

The Solid Rock, Edward Mote/William B. Bradbury; Public Domain.

We Say Yes, Tommy Walker; © 1996 Doulos Publishing; Admin. by Maranatha! Music.

WORSHIP HELPS

Call to Worship:
Stand up and bless the LORD your God forever and ever!
(Neh. 9:5 NKJV)

Scripture Medley on Leadership:
These things I write to you, though I hope to come to you shortly; but if I am delayed, I write so that you may know how you ought to conduct yourself in the house of God, which is the church of the living God. Be blameless, as a steward of God, not self-willed, not quick-tempered, not given to wine, not violent, not greedy for money, but hospitable, a lover of what is good, sober-minded, just, holy, self-controlled, holding fast the faithful word. Now therefore, go, lead the people to the place of which I have spoken to you. Behold, My Angel shall go before you. Now thanks be to God who always leads us. (1 Tim. 3:14, 15; Titus 1:7–9; Ex. 32:34; Acts 20:28; Ex. 32:34; 2 Cor. 2:14 NKJV)

Benediction:
Remember us, today, O Lord, for good. And may we remember to praise You continually this week; in Jesus' name. Amen.
(Based on Neh. 13:31)

Additional Sermons and Lesson Ideas

When Revival Comes

Date preached:

By Rev. Billy Friel

SCRIPTURE: John 9

INTRODUCTION: What does revival look like? What happens to us when revival comes? We can answer that question by looking at this story.

1. Revival Is to See People and Become Sensitive to Their Needs (v. 1). Jesus "saw a man." The disciples saw him as a puzzle, not as a person.
2. Revival Enables Us to Recognize Opportunities (v. 4).
3. Revival is to Believe God Is Able to Work Miracles (v. 5).
4. Revival Produces Changed People (vv. 8–10).
5. Revival Sharpens Our Focus on Results, Not Procedures (vv. 10, 13–16, 26).
6. Revival Gives Us Courage to Share Our Testimony (vv. 25, 30–33).
7. Revival Makes the Presence of Jesus Precious to Us (vv. 34–38).

CONCLUSION: Jesus is passing by. He wants us to experience revival.

Why Should I Give God Ten Percent?

Date preached:

SCRIPTURE: 2 Corinthians 8:1–9

INTRODUCTION: Tithing is a practice followed by many of the heroes of Scripture, but why should we give God ten percent of our hard-earned money?

1. The Motivation of Example (vv. 1–7). Paul used the motivating example of the Macedonian churches.
2. The Motivation of Love (v. 8).
3. The Motivation of Grace (v. 9).

CONCLUSION: So let each one give as he purposes in his heart, not grudgingly or of necessity; for God loves a cheerful giver (2 Cor. 9:7 NKJV).

CLASSICS FOR THE PASTOR'S LIBRARY

The Shield of Patrick

One of the earliest hymns in Christian history—the Shield (Breastplate) of Patrick—is attributed to Saint Patrick of Ireland, one of history's premier missionaries. Born at the end of the fourth century in Britain, son of a local politician, Patrick was brought up in a Christian home. At age 16, he was seized by pirates, bundled away on a ship, and spirited across the Irish Sea into slavery.

For six years, Patrick tended goats among the green hills of Ireland. But nothing happens to the Lord's people by accident. In Ireland, God awakened Patrick's heart and began planting within him the seeds of an evangelistic burden. Patrick finally escaped his captivity and returned home, but he could never escape his burden for the Irish. After a period of training, he returned to Ireland with a Bible in his hand where he eventually baptized over 100,000 converts.

Patrick left us an autobiographical account of his life, *Patrick's Confessions*. He's also the likely author of this great Celtic hymn that bears his name, though it's impossible to authenticate. One legend claims Patrick wrote this hymn as a prayer for safety while traveling through Druid territory, fearful of an ambush.

Nearly 1,500 years passed before the "Shield of Patrick" was adapted for singing. H. H. Dickinson, Dean of the Chapel Royal at Dublin Castle, wrote to the poet, Ms. Cecil Alexander, suggesting she "fill a gap in our Irish Church Hymnal by giving us a metrical version of St. Patrick's [Shield], and I sent her a carefully collated copy of the best prose translations of it. Within a week she sent me that exquisitely beautiful ... version which appears in ... our Church Hymnal." Irish-born organist, Charles Villagers Stanford, composed the music.

While "Patrick's Breastplate" isn't widely sung today, it remains one of the classics of Christian history and shouldn't be missed.

My favorite part of this hymn speaks of the all-encompassing presence of Christ around His children.

Christ be with me, Christ within me,
Christ behind me, Christ before me,
Christ beside me, Christ to win me,
Christ to comfort and restore me.

Christ beneath me, Christ above me,
Christ in quiet, Christ in danger,
Christ in hearts of all that love me,
Christ in mouth of friend and stranger.

Quotes for the Pastor's Wall

"As the years go by, we think less about preaching a good sermon, and more about preaching a sermon that will do good."

Clarence Macartney

"I have but one passion, and I have lived for it—the absorbingly arduous yet glorious work of proclaiming the grace and love of our Lord and Savior Jesus Christ."

John Henry Jowett

MARCH 20, 2005

SUGGESTED SERMON

Date preached:

Consider Him

By Rev. Dennis Lyle

Scripture: Matthew 26:36–46, especially verse 39b
Not as I will, but as You will. (NKJV)

Introduction: Imagine yourself facing the most crucial moment of your life. We might go to great lengths to deal with our problems. Matthew uses a phrase that summarizes our study this morning about Jesus in the Garden of Gethsemane, "He went a little farther" (v. 39). Today I'd like to suggest four reasons our Savior went a little farther.

1. **To Expose the Place of Submission (vv. 36–39).** Our scene is set in the Garden of Gethsemane, the unforgettable scene of our Lord's travail. Notice here:

   A. **The Quietness of the Spot.** The clamor of the crowd that had so often filled the ears of the Master died away in the distance. At the entrance to the Garden He left the disciples, taking with Him the three, and then He left even them and went a little farther, until He was all alone, at the spot where the sound of a falling leaf might have been heard.

   B. **The Loneliness of the Hour.** That hour (see John 31:31) that the Savior had often spoken of, had now come and the Master was alone, "He began to be sorrowful and deeply distressed" (v. 37). His disciples were sleeping, one was betraying, and all would soon desert Him. Imagine the loneliness of that moment!

2. **To Experience the Price of Submission.** Spurgeon once said of the Lord approaching the cross, "He was bowed down as if an enormous weight rested on His soul as indeed it did." The Savior experienced:

   A. **Physical Agony.** Luke, the doctor, tells us, "... His sweat became like great drops of blood falling down to the ground" (Luke 22:44). A rare physical phenomenon caused by great stress, known as hematidrosis, in which the tiny blood vessels rupture in the sweat glands and produce a mixture of blood and sweat. Can you see your Savior bowed in agony on your behalf?

B. **Spiritual Agony (v. 39).** Jesus cries to allow the cup to pass from Him if possible. What was the cup that Christ spoke of here (see also Mark 10:38, 39; John 18:11)? Our Lord looked deeply into the cup of human sin and groaned as He smelled its foul odor and viewed the rising poisonous fumes. This cup was a cup full of sin; this cup was a cup full of wrath. Christ drank a cup of wrath without mercy, that we might drink a cup of mercy without wrath. Christ drank a cup of suffering that we might drink a cup of salvation (see Ps. 116:12, 13).

3. **To Express the Prayer of Submission (vv. 39–42).** Jesus, King of kings, who could have had it any way He desired, chose to pray in submission:

A. **Christ's Determined Supplication.** Before He faced His mock trial, a merciless environment, and the terror of the Cross, He entered the Garden to pray. He was determined to pray. He prayed reverently, submissively, earnestly, and obediently. Does the same determination mark you when you come to pray?

B. **Christ's Devoted Supplication.** In no way did Jesus shrink before the task before Him. Rather, as our Example, He fully complied with the perfect will of God. In prayer, He yielded Himself to the will to which He had always been submitted. Tell me, have you ever prayed the prayer of submission? It is a renunciation of our own will and a resignation to God's will.

4. **To Exhibit the Peace of Submission.** As we look into the Garden, finally the voice of prayer is silent.

A. **The Battle Has Stopped.** The kneeling figure of the Master rises quietly. He comes forth with peace in His heart and serenity on His face. He has experienced turmoil and now manifests peace. His heart is not troubled anymore. He catches a glimpse of the torches and wakes the sleeping disciples, saying "let us be going" (v. 46). He was going forward to do the Father's will with peace in His heart.

B. **The Blessing Has Started.** The stream of blessing that flowed from Golgotha began to flow in Gethsemane.

Conclusion: Is the Lord calling you to go a little farther than you have ever been before to the place of submission, to pay the price of submission, to express the prayer of submission, and to find the peace of submission? Has the time come for you to tell the Lord, "Not as I will, but as You will"? Will you tell Him now? Will you go a little bit farther now?

STATS, STORIES, AND MORE

More on Gethsemane

It is certainly interesting to note that history began in a Garden (Gen. 2:8), that history for the redeemed will end in a Garden (Rev. 22:1), and that history was transformed by two Gardens: the Garden of Gethsemane and the Garden Tomb, "Now in the place where He was crucified there was a garden, and in the garden a new tomb in which no one had yet been laid" (John 19:41)

The name "Gethsemane" means, "an oil, or olive press." Usually, the press was a hewn out rock into which the olives were poured. Another large stone was used to crush and press them, forcing the juice to run out through a bored opening near the bottom. Certainly this illustrates the anguish and difficulty of this place for Jesus. J. C. Ryle says, "The experience in the Garden is a knot which nothing can untie but the old doctrine of our sin being imputed to Christ, and Christ being made sin and a curse for us."

Why was the Lord Jesus filled with sorrow and anguish in that garden? Was it because of what was about to happen: Judas' betrayal (v. 47), Peter's denial (v. 70), the disciples' forsaking Him (v. 56), the Sanhedrin condemning Him (27:1), Pilate's sentencing Him (27:26), His enemies ridiculing Him (27:39–41), the soldiers crucifying Him (27:35)? No doubt, this was all included, but He was filled with sorrow because He, being of a most sensitive, tender nature was being driven more and more into isolation. Many of the people had already left Him, (John 6:66), the disciples were going to forsake Him (26:56), and worst of all on the Cross, there would be the cry of separation, "My God, My God, why have You forsaken Me?" (v. 46).

FOR THE BULLETIN

❁ March 20, 687 is the traditional date for the death of Cuthbert, the English monk who energetically evangelized the British Isles. ❁ On March 20, 1415, Pope John XXIII fled Constance dressed as a groom. ❁ "Bloody" Queen Mary planned for old Thomas Cranmer to publicly read a confession recanting his reformation beliefs. On the eve of the event, March 20, 1556, as Thomas sat at a small desk in Oxford jail reading the speech planned for the next morning, he started writing a second version. The next day he boldly declared that his recantations had been signed under duress, and he embraced the pure gospel. Thomas was pulled from the pulpit and hustled to the stake. ❁ Sir Isaac Newton died on this day in 1727. ❁ David Brainerd, American colonial missionary to Native Americans, was forced to resign from his ministry on this day in 1747 due to failing health. ❁ On March 20, 1793, William Carey was set apart for missionary work. ❁ *Uncle Tom's Cabin* was published on this day in 1852. The book sold a million copies and helped precipitate the Civil War. ❁ March 20, 1870 is the birthday of May Whittle Moody, daughter of famed hymnist Daniel Webster Whittle and the wife of D. L. Moody's son, William. She assisted her father and Moody in their evangelism efforts, and wrote the music for her father's hymn, "Moment by Moment." ❁ March 20, 1957 marks the death of missionary/author Isobel Kuhn.

APPROPRIATE SONGS AND HYMNS

All He Wants Is You, Audrey Mieir; © 1967 Manna Music, Inc.

Ceaseless Praise, Tom Fettke/Frances R. Havergal; © 1982 Pilot Point Music; Admin. by The Copyright Company.

Here's My Heart, Julie Morrow; © 1997 Blond Strawberry Music.

Not My Will, But Thine, Hugh C. Benner; © 1951. Renewed 1979 Lillenas Publishing Company; Admin. by The Copyright Company.

Not My Will, Ron Hamilton; © 1983. 1985 Musical Ministries, Inc.; Admin. by Majesty Music, Inc.

WORSHIP HELPS

Call to Worship:
Rejoice the soul of Your servant, for to You, O Lord, I lift up my soul. For You, Lord, are good, and ready to forgive, and abundant in mercy to all those who call upon You (Ps. 86:4, 5 NKJV).

Welcome:
Today I would like to ask you to come with us. As we enter this place, we should come to the Lord as hungry people: hungry to worship Him, hungry to fellowship with His people, and hungry to learn more about Him. We will journey today in Scripture to learn. In the words of James Montgomery, who wrote this hymn:
Go to dark Gethsemane, ye that feel the tempter's power;
Your Redeemer's conflict see, watch with Him one bitter hour,
Turn not from His grief away; learn of Jesus Christ to pray.

Suggested Scripture Reading:
Esther 4:13–16
Acts 21:8–14

Kids Talk

Gather the children around you and ask, "Do any of you have a favorite hiding place?" Allow some of them to answer. Ask them what they do there. Then read Matthew 6:6, "When you pray, go into your room, and when you have shut your door, pray to your Father who is in the secret place; and your Father who sees in secret will reward you openly." Explain that the Lord Jesus was often alone to pray, and we need to find a good time and a good place to spend time with Him each day alone. Ask them where and when they think they should do this, and praise their ideas.

Additional Sermons and Lesson Ideas

At His Appearing

Date preached:

By Dr. Melvin Worthington

SCRIPTURE: 2 Timothy 4:1, 8

INTRODUCTION: The anticipation of the Second Coming of our Lord Jesus Christ gives cleansing hope, comforting hope, and compelling hope to this world.

1. Look for His Appearing (Heb. 9:28)
2. Loyal Until His Appearing (John 2:28)
3. Labor Till His Appearing (2 Tim. 4:2)
4. Love His Appearing (2 Tim. 4:8)
5. Listen for His Appearing (1 Thess. 4:16)
6. Long for His Appearing (Titus 2; 1 Thess. 1)

CONCLUSION: Anticipation of Christ's return gives hope to every believer. Our prayer should be that of the apostle John: "Even so, Come Lord Jesus" (Rev. 22:20).

How to Win That Friend to Christ

Date preached:

SCRIPTURE: Proverbs 11:30

INTRODUCTION: How can we win our friends, relatives, and neighbors to Christ? We must do it by deliberate design.

1. Pray. Develop a daily personal prayer list of those for whom you're concerned.
2. Build Bridges. Begin working on being their friend. Develop a relationship.
3. Live a Consistent Christian Life Before Them. Jesus called it letting your light shine.
4. Share the Gospel. Look for opportunities to encourage them with Bible verses and to share the plan of salvation.
5. Invite Them to Church. Most people come to church for the first time at the invitation of a friend.

CONCLUSION: Sanctify the Lord God in your hearts, and always be ready to give a defense to everyone who asks you a reason for the hope that is in you (1 Pet. 3:15).

COMMUNION SERMON

Remember the Sacrifice

Date preached:

By Rev. Richard Sharpe Jr.

Scripture: 1 Corinthians 11:23–32

Introduction: The Corinthian church had many problems. All churches have problems because they have people in them. The people in this particular church had no problem putting up with sin among other church members. They had no reservations against treating some better than others. They had no qualms about withholding food from those who were less fortunate. In the early church there was a fellowship dinner called a love feast that was followed by Communion. Everyone was to bring something to this feast and share what he or she brought with everyone who attended, much like our modern potluck dinners. Imagine someone withholding their potluck stew from certain members of our congregation! That's what was happening in Corinth. Paul opposed this behavior and warned that they were not honoring the memory of Christ's death for their sins. They were sinning at the Communion table.

1. **Proper Elements for the Lord's Supper (vv. 23–26).** Paul used to persecute the church and was saved in a miraculous manner. He withdrew for three years to be instructed by Christ, and one of the things he was instructed in was the Lord's Supper. So he shared what he had learned with the Corinthians. They were instructed in the proper way to celebrate the Lord's death.

   A. **The Bread.** The bread represents the body of Christ who died on the Cross for our sins. He suffered many abuses on His way to the Cross. He gave His all for us.

   B. **The Cup.** The cup represents the blood of Christ that was shed on the Cross for our sins. Without the shedding of blood there is no forgiveness of sin (Heb. 9:22). Christ had to shed His blood for us. The animal sacrifices in the Old Testament were made looking forward to the time when Christ would shed His blood for the sins of the world. His sacrifice was the final one, and His blood was enough for all those who accept Him as Savior. Paul tells us that these elements remind the church of Christ's sacrifice. We so often and so easily forget this. We often complain about small sacrifices we must make, ignoring the incredible sacrifice of Jesus' body and blood!

2. **Proper Attitude for the Lord's Supper (vv. 27–29).** Paul makes it clear that there are two ways someone could take the Lord's Supper.

   A. **Those Who Examine Themselves Before Taking the Supper.** These people take it in a worthy manner. We are to examine ourselves for sin; sin keeps us from a right relationship with the Lord. When we examine ourselves, we are to confess sin. God has promised to forgive us and restore us to a proper fellowship with Him (1 John 1:9).

   B. **Those Who Are Judged for Not Examining Themselves.** This group is made up of individuals who come to church flippantly, not taking seriously any sin that may be plaguing their lives. They might be people who have accepted Christ as their Savior but are living an uncommitted life. They may be those that we sometimes call Sunday Christians. Those outside the church call these people "hypocrites." The pastor knows this group as individuals who sit, soak, and sour in the pews. They are usually the ones who find fault in everything in the church. Often they're not involved in daily Bible reading.

   This type of person should reflect and repent before taking the Lord's Supper, for the Lord will not tolerate this behavior; there are consequences: "For this reason many are weak and sick among you, and many sleep. For if we would judge ourselves, we would not be judged. But when we are judged, we are chastened by the Lord, that we may not be condemned with the world" (vv. 30–32). He warns that:

   (1) Many Become Weak and Sickly. This type of judgment is called "chastening." The Lord will judge those individuals who have accepted Christ as their Savior, but are not living for the Lord. If any of you is living a life of sin, but is not being chastened or disciplined, check yourself to be sure you are a true believer. The Bible says, "For whom the Lord loves He chastens, and scourges every son whom He receives" (Heb. 12:6).

   I once visited a hospital room where a woman was having a health issue. She said to me privately that she knew she was having this problem because she was involved in an affair. She confessed the sin to the Lord and was healed. Before you involve yourself in the remembrance of Christ's sacrifice, repent, be restored and renewed.

   (2) Many Die. This judgment is terminal. The Bible uses the term *sleep* when it talks about a Christian's death. Here we find that some Christians die prematurely because of sin in their lives. I had a teenager in one of my churches that had a problem with drinking. He came to the parsonage on a regularly basis wondering what to do with this problem. I gave him some suggestions, which he never followed. One night his friends challenged him to drink a bottle of whiskey after he had consumed a lot of beer. He died of the combination. He knew what needed to be done, but he didn't want to give up his friends. Don't let it go this far. Cut sin off at its roots, for Scripture tells us, "When desire has conceived, it gives birth to sin; and sin, when it is full-grown, brings forth death" (James 1:15 NKJV).

Conclusion: The Corinthian church had some real problems. The church today has many of the same problems. There are Christians who come to the Lord's Table without examining their lives. They are challenging God's Word; they will lose. God is going to deal with His children. If you are here today and have not been examining your life for sin, I would challenge you today to examine your relationship with the Lord. Are you in fellowship with Him? Are you keeping short accounts with Him? If there is sin in your life, and are you willing to confess it, turn from it, and follow the Lord more closely? Only you can make that decision. The Lord's Supper can be an experience of worship and worthiness, a time of repentance and remembrance, or it can be a time of disobedience that will result in God's ultimate discipline.

Now, let's spend some time in prayer and self-examination before we partake in the Lord's Supper.

HEROES FOR THE PASTOR'S HEART

James Chalmers

You might as well know the end of the story now. Cannibals on Goaribari Island in the South Seas ate James Chalmers on April 8 of 1901. But his death matched his life—both were invested in passionately inviting benighted souls to come freely to Christ.

Chalmers heard God's call to missionary service as a teen. His Scottish pastor read a letter one Sunday from the Fiji Islands, telling of the gospel's power to transform cannibals, followed by an appeal for more workers. James resolved then and there to go.

James conversion occurred three years later, at age eighteen, when a couple of Irish evangelists came into the area to preach. He later wrote:

> It was raining hard, but I started; and on arriving at the bottom of the stairs I listened whilst they sang "All People That On Earth Do Dwell" to the tune "Old Hundreth," and I thought I had never heard such singing before—so solemn, yet so joyful. I ascended the steps and entered. There was a large congregation intensely in earnest. The younger of the

evangelists was the first to speak. He announced as his text these words: "Then the Spirit and the bride say, 'Come!' And let him who hears say, 'Come!' And let him who thirsts come. Whoever desires, let him take the water of life freely." He spoke directly to me. I felt it much; but at the close, I hurried away back to town.

James agonized over his spiritual condition for several days, describing himself as "pierced through and through, and lost beyond all hope of salvation." The next morning, his minister, Rev. Gilbert Meikle, spoke to him of Christ's blood, assured him of God's love, and led him to the Water of Life.

Almost instantly, James began preparing for the South Seas, never doubting his earlier call to missions. In 1866, he sailed for the South Pacific as a Presbyterian missionary.

Chalmers had a way with people. "It was in his presence, his carriage, his eye, his voice," a friend wrote. "There was something almost hypnotic about him. His perfect composure, his judgment and tact and fearlessness brought him through a hundred difficulties." Robert Louis Stevenson, who didn't like missionaries until he met Chalmers, said, "He is a rowdy, but he is a hero. You can't weary me of that fellow. He took me fairly by storm."

In 1877, Chalmers sailed on to New Guinea. His ministry was successful there. Packed churches replaced feasts of human flesh. But as the years passed, he grew lonely. He was delighted when young Oliver Tomkins came to join him in 1901. The two men decided to explore a new part of the islands, and on Easter Sunday they sailed alongside a new village. The next morning, Chalmers and Tomkins went ashore. They were never seen again. A rescue party soon learned that the men had been clubbed to death, chopped to pieces, cooked, and eaten.

News flashed around the world. "I cannot believe it!" exclaimed Dr. Joseph Parker from the pulpit of London's famous City Temple. "I do not want to believe it! Such a mystery of Providence makes it hard for our strained faith to recover. Yet, Jesus was murdered. Paul was murdered. Many missionaries have been murdered. When I think of that side of the case, I cannot but feel that our honored and noble-minded friend has joined a great assembly."

In all, James Chalmers established 130 mission stations throughout New Guinea, and thousands came to Christ, including 64 men who became pastors, preachers, and missionaries.

MARCH 27, 2005

SUGGESTED SERMON *Date preached:*

Why I Preach the Literal Resurrection of Christ

Scripture: 1 Corinthians 15:1–20, especially verse 4
He rose again the third day. (NKJV)

Introduction: Easter is our greatest celebration as Christians, because it focuses our minds on the highlight of the Christian faith—the Resurrection of our Lord Jesus Christ, His rising physically, visibly, bodily from the tomb, His remarkable return to life following His torturous death. This isn't just another wonderful gospel story or another in a series of amazing miracles. This is *the* story and *the* miracle of Christianity. It ties together all the other strands of our faith. As scientist Henry Morris put it, "The bodily resurrection of Jesus Christ from the dead is the crowning proof of Christianity. If the resurrection did not take place, then Christianity is a false religion. If it did take place, then Christ is God and the Christian faith is absolute truth." According to Acts 1:3, Jesus presented Himself alive by "many infallible proofs." Notice those three words: *Many*—not just one or two indications. *Infallible*—this means irrefutable, certain, convincing. *Proofs*—these are solid evidence, admissible in a court of law. In the first part of 1 Corinthians 15 (the Bible's Resurrection chapter), Paul lists some of these proofs:

1. **Fulfilled Prophecy (v. 4).** The Resurrection of Christ was predicted in advance. Verse 4 says, "He rose again the third day according to the Scriptures."

   A. **Old Testament Predictions**: See Isaiah 53:9–11 (NIV), Psalm 16:9–11, and Zechariah 12:10. See also Psalm 2:7–9; Psalm 30; Psalm 40:1–3; Psalm 110:1; Psalm 118:21–24; Hosea 5:15—6:3. There's also the example of Jonah, whose departure from his "grave" in the fish foreshadowed our Lord's emergence from the tomb.

   B. **Jesus' Own Predictions**: His enemies did us the favor of pulling out His resurrection predictions and reinforcing them for all history. How? They used them in His trial and afterward (Matt. 26:61, 27:63). See also John 2:19, Matt. 12:40, and Matt. 17:22, 23.

2. **The Eyewitnesses (vv. 5–8).** Following his Resurrection, Jesus remained on earth for forty days, appearing at least ten times to various individuals

and groups. The genuineness and historical reliability of these accounts are well attested. Some people assume that Christ only appeared to His hardcore believers. That isn't true. First, all the disciples were skeptics; none imagined that He would rise from the dead (Matt. 16:21, 22). Second, Thomas was a vocal and determined doubter (John 20:24–29). Third, James, the Lord's half-brother, had ridiculed and rejected Christ (John 7:1–5). And fourth, Saul of Tarsus was the greatest enemy to His movement (Acts 8:1; 9:3–5).

3. **The Power of the Resurrection to Change Lives (vv. 9–11).** How else can the transformation of Saul of Tarsus be explained? What about the change among the disciples? John Stott wrote: "Perhaps the transformation of the disciples of Jesus is the greatest evidence of all for the resurrection. It was the resurrection that transformed Peter's fear into courage and James' doubt into faith. It was the resurrection that changed the Sabbath into Sunday and the Jewish remnant into the Christian Church. It was the resurrection that changed Saul the Pharisee into Paul the apostle and turned his persecuting into preaching."

4. **The Absence of Alternatives (vv. 12–20).** There is no other truth discovered by humanity by which we can be both logically consistent in our thinking and spiritually happy in our souls. Francis Schaeffer wrote in *He is There and He is Not Silent*: "There is no other sufficient philosophical answer. You can search through university philosophy, underground philosophy, filling station philosophy—it doesn't matter which—there is no other sufficient philosophical answer to existence." Only Christianity provides a comprehensive explanation for the reality of death and a satisfying answer for the problem of death; and only Christianity has authenticated its message by providing a Leader who actually arose from the tomb.

5. **The Theological Fit (vv. 1–4).** The Resurrection completes the gospel and fits into the entire structure of biblical theology. It is so woven into the warp and woof of the biblical plan of salvation that the entire Bible is held together by it, and the entire plan of salvation depends on it. Without the Resurrection of Jesus Christ, nothing in the Bible makes sense.

Conclusion: He is alive! He is alive indeed! He showed Himself alive by many infallible proofs, and we can preach the literal Resurrection of Christ with intellectual integrity and spiritual joy. He is alive today! He wants to touch your life. He wants to save you, to give you hope, to bring peace into your heart. Will you come to Him now, while there's still time and while you still can?

STATS, QUOTES, AND MORE

Albert L. Roper

Albert L. Roper was a prominent Virginia attorney, a graduate of the University of Virginia and its law school, who eventually became mayor of the city of Norfolk. He once began a thorough legal investigation into the evidence for the Resurrection of Christ, asking himself the question: "Can any intelligent person accept the Resurrection story?" After examining the evidence at length, he came away asking a different question: "Can any intelligent person deny the weight of this evidence?"

Frank Morison

Frank Morison was an English journalist who viewed Christianity with disfavor and set out to disprove the Resurrection of Christ. He poured over the evidence, absorbing all the information he could, marshalling his arguments. Not only was he unable to disprove the Resurrection, but also he was compelled on the weight of the evidence to become a Christian himself. His book became a powerful argument in support of the historicity of the Easter event, entitled *Who Moved the Stone?*

Josh McDowell

Josh McDowell was a young university student looking for a good time. He found religion unsatisfying and lived for parties and popularity. One day he noticed a group of students engaged in Bible study, and he became intrigued by the radiance of one of the young ladies. He asked her a reason for it, and she replied, "Jesus Christ." He scoffed at her, but she challenged him to intellectually examine the claims of Christianity. After much research, he admitted that he could not refute the historical reality of the Resurrection of Jesus Christ. He became a Christian and the author of *Evidence that Demands a Verdict*.

FOR THE BULLETIN

✽ March 27, 1592 marks the birth of the "Polish Luther," Georgius Tranovsky. ✽ James I of England is well known among Christians for having authorized the translation of the Bible that bears his name. He issued the order in 1604, and the "King James Version" was published in 1611. He died "of gout and senility" at age 58 on March 27, 1625. He was among England's best-educated kings, but his bi-sexual immorality kept London scandalmongers busy. ✽ On March 27, 1667, the English poet John Milton published *Paradise Lost*. ✽ The shoelace was invented on this day in 1790. ✽ March 27, 1816 marks the birthday of hymnist George Job Elvey, the English organist who devoted his life's work to Saint George's Chapel in Windsor, home church of the royal family. He's best known today as the composer of the tunes to "Crown Him with Many Crowns," and "Come, Ye Thankful People Come." ✽ Another great hymnist was born on this day—George Matheson (1842). He become blind while studying for the ministry, and his fiancée broke her engagement to him as a result. Consoling himself with God's love, Matheson wrote the hymn, "O Love That Wilt Not Let Me Go." For many years, he was the beloved pastor of St. Bernard's Church in Edinburgh. ✽ Housewife and homemaker Carrie E. Breck, author of the hymn "Face to Face with Christ My Savior," died on this day in 1934.

APPROPRIATE SONGS AND HYMNS

Christ Arose, Robert Lowry; Public Domain.
Christ, the Lord Is Risen Today, Charles Wesley; Public Domain.
Rejoice the Lord Is King, Charles Wesley/John Darwall; Public Domain.
Joyful, Joyful We Adore Thee, Henry Van Dyke/Ludwig von Beethoven; Public Domain.
Celebrate Jesus, Gary Oliver; © 1988 Integrity's Hosanna! Music.
Lord, I Lift Your Name on High, Rick Founds; © 1989 Maranatha Praise, Inc.; Admin. by The Copyright Company.

WORSHIP HELPS

Call to Worship:
Moreover, brethren, I declare to you the gospel which I preached to you, which also you received and in which you stand, by which also you are saved … that Christ died for our sins according to the Scriptures, and that He was buried, and that He rose again the third day according to the Scriptures. (1 Cor. 15:1–4 NKJV)

Welcome:
Welcome, all of you! Today's message is "Why I Preach the Literal Resurrection of Christ." This is the day—Easter Sunday—when we focus on our greatest truth, we rejoice in our greatest hope, and we preach our greatest message. I'm glad you're here to say with me: "He is risen! He is risen indeed!"

Hymn Story—Christ Arose!
Robert Lowry, a native Pennsylvanian, pastored churches in New York, New Jersey, and Pennsylvania, gaining a reputation for keen biblical scholarship and powerful, picturesque preaching. He's best known, however, for his gospel songs, including: "Nothing but the Blood" (words and music), "Shall We Gather at the River?" (words and music), "All the Way My Savior Leads Me" (music), and "I Need Thee Every Hour" (music).

"Christ Arose" was written one evening during the Easter season of 1874 while Lowry was in his devotions. He became deeply impressed with Luke 24:5, 6–8, especially the words of the angel at the tomb of Christ: "Why do you seek the living among the dead? He is not here, but is risen!" (NKJV) The words and music formed together in his mind. Going to the little pump organ in his home, Lowry soon completed what was to become one of our greatest Resurrection hymns.

Additional Sermons and Lesson Ideas

The Christ of Easter

Date preached:

SCRIPTURE: Revelation 1:13–17

INTRODUCTION: What the church needs today is a new awareness of Christ and His glory. We need to see Him "high and lifted up." The apostle John, who had seen Jesus resurrected in the gospels, saw Him glorified in Revelation 1. Notice the awesome sight:

1. The Resurrected Christ (v. 13: standing; also v. 18)
2. The Reigning Christ (v. 13: girded with a golden band)
3. The Righteous Christ (v. 14: white like wool, snow)
4. The Revealing Christ (v. 14: His eyes were as a flame of fire, like an X-Ray)
5. The Relentless Christ (v. 15: His feet were like brass, a symbol of judgment)
6. The Regal Christ (v. 15: His voice was as the sound of many waters)
7. The Regulating Christ (v. 16: His hand held seven stars, signifying His sovereignty)
8. The Revenging Christ (v. 16: the two-edged sword)
9. The Resplendent Christ (v. 16: like the sun shining)

CONCLUSION: Oh, see Him as the Christ we worship today!

Close Encounters of a Life-Changing Kind

Date preached:

By Rev. Mark Hollis

SCRIPTURE: John 20:19–29

INTRODUCTION: The disciples were not who you'd expect to begin a great movement. They were a simple band chosen by Jesus. What transformed them into heroes willing to lay down their lives for Christ?

1. They were Fleeing Disciples: running scared (Matt. 26:56)
2. They were Fearful Disciples: not running, just scared (John 20:19–23). They had an encounter with Jesus (vv. 19, 20) and a commissioning by Jesus (v. 21–23).
3. They were Fearless Disciples: turning the world upside down (Acts 2)

CONCLUSION: Two simple factors brought about the transformation from frightened to fleeing to fearless: They had a genuine encounter with the living Christ, and they were empowered by the Holy Spirit.

APRIL 3, 2005

SUGGESTED SERMON *Date preached:*

Practical Advice for Prayer Life

By Dr. Ed Dobson

Scripture: Daniel 6:6–11; 1 Thessalonians 5:16–18; Matthew 15:36, 26:39 especially 1 Thessalonians 5:17

Pray without ceasing. (NKJV)

Introduction: A pastor was planning to preach about prayer one night when a young man asked, "What are you speaking about tonight?" He replied, "Practical advice on your personal prayer life." The young man said, "As opposed to impractical advice about your prayer life?" Humorous as his response was, I believe we are often misguided with impractical advice. I would like to discuss with you different aspects of prayer and how to apply them to our lives.

1. **Types of Prayer.**

   A. **Organized Prayer (Dan. 6:6–11).** Suppose you had been Daniel, a slave in a foreign land with a powerful king. A decree is passed that for the next thirty days you may only pray to the king, not to God. Do we pray so much that this would have been a problem? Daniel prayed three times a day in his room, facing Jerusalem (v. 10). He set an example for us to have daily, consistent times with the Lord in prayer.

   B. **Conversational Prayer (1 Thess. 5:16–18).** Paul does not give us a simple command in these verses. He tells us to always rejoice, to pray without ceasing, and to give thanks in everything. I think the idea here is to cultivate the habit of continually praying throughout the day, to change our mindset to be in constant communication with God.

   C. **Event Prayer (Matt. 15:36).** Notice that Jesus gave thanks to the Lord before the crowds ate. We should pray for events throughout daily life: before a drive, before an exam, before a meeting, etc. We should condition ourselves to rely upon God for every event.

   D. **Emergency Prayer (Matt. 26:39).** In the great events of life, at the crisis moments of life, the most appropriate thing we can do is pray. In this prayer, we begin to discover the heart of all prayer. Jesus displayed this concept beautifully in the Garden of Gethsemane when He said, "Not as I will, but as You will" (Matt. 26:39 NKJV). In our darkest hour, we must learn to submit ourselves fully to the Lord's will.

2. **Tools of Prayer.**

   A. **A Bible.** One of the most essential parts of communication with God is receiving His Word. Before we approach God with our needs, it is helpful to focus on Him through the divine revelation of Scripture.
   B. **A Journal.** We should have a means of remembering the Lord's work in our lives; a journal is a great way to do this.
   C. **A Devotional.** This resource is not necessary, but it certainly helps. Devotional books can be a very inspiring and thought-provoking method to help us along in a time of prayer.

3. **Time of Prayer.** There are several elements involved in a personal time of prayer with the Lord. The following are some of the most important.

   A. **Preparing Our Hearts.** After a busy day at the office, or a hectic day with the children or at school, we must have some time to simply focus. We can rest in God's presence and begin to think about and meditate on Him.
   B. **Listen to His Words.** After re-focusing on the Lord, we must take time to listen to what He might say to us. Our Bible and our devotional book will help us to focus on what He has to say.
   C. **Praise and Thanksgiving.** Someone very wise once said, "If you think about it, all we really deserve, apart from Christ, is hell. Anything and everything above that is something to praise God for." Our time of prayer should certainly include thanking God for what He's done and praising Him for who He is.
   D. **Forgiveness.** We must continually come to the Lord in repentance, asking forgiveness for our failures. As Jesus told His disciples to pray, we should ask forgiveness, forgive others, and ask God to lead us not into temptation.
   E. **Petition.** Jesus commands us to pray for others and especially for His workers (Matt. 9:37, 38).
   F. **Writing.** We can see the change in David's heart as he writes out prayers to the Lord on so many occasions. When we write out our prayers, it helps us slow down and think about our communication with God.

Conclusion: We are to pray consistently, continually, during events or emergencies, in all circumstances! We must cultivate the habit of continual prayer.

STATS, STORIES, AND MORE

Four More Practical Suggestions about Prayer:

1. Have a quiet place and go there every day. Perhaps there's a spare room in your house. Perhaps it is in the basement. Perhaps there is a secluded spot in the yard or a nearby park. Maybe you can pray at the kitchen table early in the morning before anyone else is up. Perhaps there is time to pray in your office with a do-not-disturb sign on the door. Perhaps you can pray in your car. Jesus didn't have a house of His own during His earthly ministry. He stayed with Peter's family when He was in Galilee, and with friends like Lazarus when He was in Jerusalem. But every day, early in the morning, He'd leave and walk to a secluded spot to pray. In Galilee, He hiked into the mountains above the Sea of Galilee. In Jerusalem, He'd go to a private garden on the western slope of the Mount of Olives.
2. Maintain an alert posture. People in the Bible assumed many different postures when they prayed. Sometimes they knelt. Sometimes they fell facedown on the ground. Sometimes they were standing or walking. Sometimes their faces were turned toward heaven.
3. When you get to your private spot and assume an alert posture, spend a few moments thinking about the fact that you're drawing near to God's very presence. Don't primarily think about your prayer list or the things you need to ask for. Think about the fact that the next few minutes will be spent in fellowship and conversation with your heavenly Father.
4. Pray out loud, even if it's just in a whispered voice. Very few of the prayers in the Bible were silent prayers. Hannah prayed silently in 1 Samuel, but even then, her lips formed her words. We do so much mental praying that our voices are seldom heard.

FOR THE BULLETIN

❁ Ambrose, the bishop of Milan, died the night of April 3. After practicing law in the Roman courts, Ambrose had been named governor of an Italian province and headquartered in Milan. When Bishop Auxentius died in 374, the city became divided over who should replace him. Assembling the people, Ambrose used his oratorical powers to plead for unity. While he was speaking, a child reportedly cried: "Let Ambrose be bishop!" The crowd joined the chant, and the thirty-five-year-old governor, to his dismay, was elected the city's pastor. He became one of the great leaders of the early church. ❁ Bishop John of Lasphe ordained Martin Luther a priest on this day in 1507. ❁ The evangelical poet, George Herbert, was born in Wales on April 3, 1593. He seemed destined for a political career until quitting politics to become the pastor of a rural British congregation. His religious poetry is among the finest in the English world. ❁ Reginald Heber, English clergyman, died in Trichinopoly, India on this day in 1826. In 1823 he had been consecrated as the Anglican bishop of Calcutta with oversight for all of India and Ceylon. He is best known, however, for his 60 hymns, including "Holy, Holy, Holy." ❁ Ten years to the day after Heber's death, another hymnist was born. April 3, 1836 marks the birthday of Rigdon M. McIntosh of Tennessee. In 1875, he became head of the Music Department at Vanderbilt University in Nashville. He later started his own music publishing business. He wrote the music to "On Jordan's Stormy Banks" and "How Firm a Foundation."

APPROPRIATE SONGS AND HYMNS

Write Your Blessed Name, Thomas A. Kempis/K. Lee Scott; © 1989 Hope Publishing Company.

When We Talk to Him, Ken Bible; © 1980 Pilot Point Music; Admin. by The Copyright Company.

To Commune with You, Patsy Hilton Kline; © 1992 Maranatha Praise, Inc.; Admin. by The Copyright Company.

Tell It to Jesus, Jeremiah E. Rankin/Edmund S. Lorenz; Public Domain.

Spirit Divine, Hear Our Prayer, Andrew Reed/Bill Wolaver; © 1986 Word Music, Inc.; Admin. by Word Music Group, Inc.

WORSHIP HELPS

Call to Worship:
As for me, I will call upon God, and the LORD shall save me. Evening and morning and at noon, I will pray, and cry aloud, and He shall hear my voice. (Ps. 55:16, 17)

Reader's Theater or Responsive Reading:

First speaker:	And when you pray ...
Second speaker:	You shall not be like the hypocrites. For they love to pray standing in the synagogues and on the corners of the streets, that they may be seen by men. Assuredly, I say to you, they have their reward.
First speaker:	But you, when you pray ...
Second speaker:	Go into your room, and when you have shut your door, pray to your Father who is in the secret place; and your Father who sees in secret will reward you openly.
First speaker:	And when you pray ...
Second Speaker:	Do not use vain repetitions as the heathen do. For they think they will be heard for their many words ... Therefore I say to you, whatever things you ask ...
First Speaker:	... when you pray, believe that you receive them, and you will have them. So He said to them, "When you pray, say ...
All Speakers:	Our Father in heaven, hallowed be Your name. Your kingdom come. Your will be done on earth as it is in heaven. Give us day by day our daily bread. And forgive us our sins, for we also forgive everyone who is indebted to us. And do not lead us into temptation, but deliver us from the evil one.

(Matt. 6:1–7; Mark 11:24; Luke 11:2–4 NKJV)

Additional Sermons and Lesson Ideas

Finding People for God

Date preached:

By Rev. Billy Friel

SCRIPTURE: Acts 11:19–26

INTRODUCTION: Baseball scouts are always looking for a "blue chipper" who can make it to the big leagues. Barnabas hit it big when he discovered and developed a Christian named Paul. But Paul may have been lost to history if Barnabas had not cherished these positive beliefs about people:

1. Barnabas Believed Everyone Needs a Friend (Acts 9:26, 27). When no one wanted Paul, Barnabas befriended him.
2. Barnabas Believed Everyone Wants to Feel Needed (Acts 11:25, 26). Barnabas needed help in the work and recruited Paul. Everyone needs to feel useful and significant.
3. Barnabas Believed Everyone Needs Encouragement (Acts 11:23). His very name meant "Son of Encouragement."

CONCLUSION: Someone has said that people tend to become what the most important people in their lives think they will become. Who discovered and developed you? Your positive belief about a person may make a significant impact on his/her life.

How to Cultivate Friendships

Date preached:

SCRIPTURE: Proverbs 18:24

INTRODUCTION: The Bible says that those who would have friends must "show themselves friendly." How do we do that?

1. Understand the Friendship Hierarchy. Your three closest friends should be your Savior, your spouse (if you're married), and yourself. When your primary needs are met here, you'll be free to minister generously to others.
2. Take the Initiative and Make the Effort.
3. Become a Servant.
4. Learn to Listen (James 1:19).
5. Spread Cheerfulness (Proverbs 15:13, 15, 30, NIV).
6. Stay in Touch.
7. Pray for Your Friends.

CONCLUSION: The greatest secret to having friends is not looking for one, but being one.

APRIL 10, 2005

SUGGESTED SERMON

Date preached:

The Rewards of Faithfulness

By Dr. D. James Kennedy

Scripture: 1 Corinthians 3:14
If anyone's work which he has built on it endures, he will receive a reward. (NKJV)

Introduction: Well, the dear fellow had thoroughly and most completely died, and now he had been pumped, primped, and painted and laid out for all his friends to see. One lady who came by to pay her last respects daubed her eyes and said with great emotion, "Dear Harry has gone to his just reward."

If that lady really meant what she said, it was no compliment. Heaven is not anyone's just reward. Every Christian ought to know that. We do not seek our just reward; rather, we seek divine grace. Heaven is not earned by anyone, but hell is earned and deserved by everyone. I have often said there are two things I know: I am going to heaven, and I deserve to go to hell. It is faith in Christ Jesus and His atoning death that alone gains for us eternal life. However, on top of that, God tells us that by our faithfulness we can receive rewards in heaven. So, heaven is a gift; rewards are given according to our faithful service for Christ in this world (see Matt. 6:19, 20; Col. 3:23, 24; 2 John 1:8; Rev. 11:18b; 22:12; and 1 Cor. 3:14).

1. **The Question Is Important.** There are two classes of Christians, and there's no more important question, if you are God's child, than which category you fall into. In 1 Corinthians 3, Paul distinguishes between these two groups. Both have built their lives on the foundation of Christ, but one class has built with gold, silver, and precious stones. Their work will abide. The others, who have built with wood, hay, and stubble will find their work burned up. This reminds us that there are two great tragedies in life. The first is to lose your eternal soul. The second is to lose an entire life's work.

Just suppose you didn't trust banks, and you invested everything in your house. There you hid your money and business interests. One day it catches fire and burns to the ground and you're left with nothing but the pajamas on your back. It's possible for all our life's work to be burned up like that, leaving us with no rewards in heaven. On the other hand, great rewards are possible for us. The Bible doesn't clearly state the exact nature of those rewards but there seem to be degrees of reward in heaven even as there are degrees of penalty in hell. God is willing for Christ's sake to accept the works which are done out of sincere hearts in faith for the glory of God, and to reward us for them.

2. **The Rewards Are Eternal.** These rewards will go on forever and ever. Isn't it amazing how many people have gone through great pains and made elaborate preparations to prepare for their retirement years. They have seen to their pension and make plans to enjoy themselves without realizing that the average person only lives two years after retirement. But we give so little thought to preparing for a hundred trillion quadrillion eons of centuries in eternity.

3. **The Key Is Faithfulness.** The world would be astonished at the faithfulness of some Christians. Here at our church, I've known some people for decades. They volunteer for everything they can and put their hearts into their service for the Lord. They give of themselves sacrificially. They give of their treasure sacrificially. They have a great passion for souls and take every opportunity to witness for Him. But as it has always been said: the 80-20 principle applies. Twenty percent of the church members do eighty percent of the work. Ah, dear friend, how about you? The hymnist says, "Only one life and soon 'tis past, / Only what's done for Christ will last."

Conclusion: A faithful missionary was returning from overseas on the same boat on which Teddy Roosevelt was traveling. Hundreds were there to greet Roosevelt, but no one was there to meet the missionary. He almost felt sorry for himself. Then he heard an almost audible voice that said: "But you're not home yet."

One day you will be home. What a wonderful day it will be if you are a faithful Christian for you will hear Him say, "Well done, thou good and faithful servant ... Enter thou into the joy of thy Lord."

STATS, STORIES, AND MORE

More from Dr. D. James Kennedy:

Years ago, I came across a tract that had this intriguing title: "What must you do to go to hell?" Like most people, I guess, I opened it to see, and it was blank. You see, my friend, you don''t have to do anything to go to hell. You have already done quite sufficiently. In fact, one sinful thought would be enough. Lucifer, the angel of light, had one proud thought and was transformed into Satan and cast out of heaven. Now, we have already done enough.

Years ago, I came across another tract entitled, "What must you do to go to heaven?" Again, opening the tract, I discovered that it, too, was blank. You see, there is nothing you can do to go to heaven, for the same reason. It has already been done. But Christ did it. Christ accomplished redemption on the Cross. But I think it is fascinating to note that whether we are talking about going to heaven or hell, everything has already been done. In the one case, we did it, earning a ticket to hell; and in the other case, Christ did it, earning us a ticket to heaven.

Of course, we have things that must be done in this life. We all have our responsibilities. But beyond those, there is a greater kingdom than the kingdom of this earth. There is the kingdom of our Lord and Savior Jesus Christ. Am I living for Christ's kingdom or am I living merely for this world and the things that are passing away?

FOR THE BULLETIN

❁ The Geneva Bible was published on April 10, 1560. It was the first English version of the Bible to contain verse numbers. Its popularity was due in part to its Calvinistic study notes. It was the primary Bible in England until the Authorized (King James) Version in 1611. The Geneva Bible is called the "Breeches Bible" because of its translation of Genesis 3:7: "They ... made themselves breeches." ❁ William Brewster, principal founder of Plymouth Colony, died on this day in 1644. A dedicated Christian separatist, Brewster served as the spiritual leader for the Pilgrims in the absence of an ordained pastor.
❁ Christmas Evans, born on December 25, 1766, grew up running with rough gangs, fighting and drinking heavily. He came to Christ under the preaching of the Welsh evangelist David Davies, and soon became an itinerant evangelist himself. In the early 1800s, his faith grew cold and his passion died. On April 10, 1802, Evans climbed into the Welsh mountains and made a covenant of rededication with God that day, writing down thirteen items and initialing each one. He went on to shake Wales with the gospel until his death thirty-six years later. ❁ On April 10, 1802, Richard Allen became the first elected bishop of the new African Methodist Episcopal (A.M.E.) Church. ❁ William Booth, founder of the Salvation Army, was born in Nottingham, England, on April 10, 1829. ❁ Chinese evangelist Watchman Nee was arrested on April 10, 1952. He died in prison, a martyr for Christ, under the tyranny of the Chinese Communists.

APPROPRIATE SONGS AND HYMNS

You're Worthy of My Praise, David Ruis; © 1986 Maranatha Praise, Inc./Shade Tree Music; Admin. by Maranatha! Music.
God Is in the House, Darlene Zschech/Russell Fragar; © 1995 Darlene Zschech (Hillsong)/Russell Fragar (Hillsong); Admin. by Integrity Music, Inc.
My Wonderful Lord, Haldor Lillenas; © 1938. Renewed 1965 Lillenas Publishing Company; Admin. by The Copyright Company.
Raise Up the Standard, Kevin Prosch; © 1993 7th Time Music.
There's No One Like You, Eddie Espinosa; © 1987 Mercy/Vineyard Publishing.

WORSHIP HELPS

Call to Worship:
Beloved, now we are children of God; and it has not yet been revealed what we shall be, but we know that when He is revealed, we shall be like Him, for we shall see Him as He is. (1 John 3:2 NKJV)

Pastoral Prayer:
Our Father, we confess our sins today—our unfaithfulness. We are not always concerned with that which concerns You. We become enamored with our own cares, crises, concerns, and ambitions. We go for days without remembering Your passion for a lost world. We go for months without witnessing actively for You. We go for years without building an eternal foundation of gold, silver, and precious stones, as the Scripture puts it. We're too busy with our wood, hay, and stubble. Oh, Lord, redirect us. Revive us. Restore our passion for Your passions. Restore our concern for Your heart cries. And use us mightily for Your glory that we might be found, in the end, faithful in all things; in Jesus' name. Amen.

Hymn Story: Be Firm and Be Faithful
Some of our great hymns come from the pens of anonymous authors. Either the writers wished to remain unknown, or their identity has been lost. One such hymn is the little known "Be Firm and Be Faithful." It was sung in the 1800s, but the date and source of its composition is unknown. Sing it to the tune "Immoral, Invisible, God Only Wise."

Be firm and be faithful; desert not the right;
The brave become bolder the darker the night.
Then up and be doing, though cowards may fail;
Thy duty pursuing, dare all and prevail.

Additional Sermons and Lesson Ideas

The Lifestyle of the Righteous and Faithful *Date preached:*

By Dr. David Jeremiah

SCRIPTURE: Ephesians 4:25–32

INTRODUCTION: This section of Ephesians is a litmus test for all of us who say we are believers. Our walk with God is pictured outwardly by the things we do. In these verses, Paul spells out five areas where Christians are to be distinctive from the world.

1. Our Morality (v. 25)
2. Our Moods (vv. 26, 27)
3. Our Money (v. 28)
4. Our Mouths (vv. 29, 30)
5. Our Manners (vv. 31, 32)
   A. Put off Meanness (v. 31)
   B. Put on Kindness (v. 32)

CONCLUSION: Can you imagine the impact we would have on our city if we lived like that? Every day when you wake up, say, "Holy Spirit, take control of my life. Make me the kind of person You want me to be." Then watch God work in your life to make you someone with the lifestyle of the righteous and faithful.

Personal Magnetism *Date preached:*

SCRIPTURE: Matthew 10:5–31

INTRODUCTION: In this chapter, Jesus gave His disciples instructions for winning the world around them. He wants us to be personal magnets, attracting others to Himself. That means we must be:

1. As Harmless as Sheep (v. 16)
2. As Shrewd as Snakes (v. 16)
3. As Innocent as Doves (v. 16)
4. As Bold as Lions (vv. 17–26)
5. As Precious as Sparrows (vv. 27–31)

CONCLUSION: When we abide in Christ, we must let Him radiate through us the power that draws all people to Him. How are you doing with that assignment?

HEROES FOR THE PASTOR'S HEART

Paul Gerhardt

I'd like to introduce you to a "friend" of mine, a man who might be called the "Charles Wesley of Germany." He was a prolific hymnist who gave Lutheranism some of its warmest hymns. Paul Gerhardt (1607–1676) grew up in Grafenhaynichen, Germany, where his father was mayor. This village near Wittenberg was devastated by the Thirty Years' War, and Paul's childhood was marked by scenes of bloodshed and death. But he had a good mind and heart, and he was able to enroll at the University of Wittenberg at age 21.

After graduation, Paul found a job in Berlin tutoring children. During this time, encouraged by Johann Crüger, choirmaster at Berlin's St. Nicholas' Church, he began writing hymns. When Crüger published a hymnbook in 1648, Paul was delighted to find his hymns in it. Others were added to later editions. In all, Gerhardt wrote 123 hymns. His hymnody reflects the shift from the rugged theological hymns of Luther to the more subjective, devotional songs of German Pietistic revival.

Paul was ordained into the ministry at age 44 and began preaching in and around Berlin. In 1651 he became chief pastor at Mittenwalde, just outside Berlin, and later he returned to Berlin to labor in St. Nicholas' Church alongside his mentor, Johann Crüger.

At that point, however, Paul became embroiled in a conflict with the Elector Friedrich Wilhelm, who wanted Lutheran clergymen to sign an edict limiting their freedom of speech on theological matters. Refusing, Paul was deposed from his pulpit in February of 1666. He was even forbidden to lead in private worship in his home. During this time four of his five children died; and in 1668, his wife also passed away.

Late that year, 1668, Paul assumed the pastorate of the Lutheran church in Lübben an der Spree, where he ministered faithfully until his death on May 27, 1676. In my opinion, Paul Gerhardt was privileged to pen some of Christendom's richest hymns. Here, for example, is his great Easter hymn, *Auf, Auf, Mein Herz, Mit Freuden:*

Awake, my heart, with gladness,
See what today is done;
Now, after gloom and sadness,
Comes forth the glorious Sun.
My Savior there was laid
Where our bed must be made
When to the realms of light
Our spirit wings its flight.

The foe in triumph shouted
When Christ lay in the tomb;
But, lo, he now is routed,
His boast is turned to gloom.
For Christ again is free;
In glorious victory
He Who is strong to save
Has triumphed o'er the grave.
This is a sight that gladdens;
What peace it doth impart!
Now nothing ever saddens
The joy within my heart.
No gloom shall ever shake,
No foe shall ever take,
The hope which God's own Son
In love for me hath won.
The world against me rages
Its fury I disdain;
Though bitter war it wages
Its work is all in vain.
My heart from care is free,
No trouble troubles me.
Misfortune now is play
And night is bright as day.
Now I will cling forever
To Christ, my Savior true;
My Lord will leave me never,
Whate'er He passes through.
He rends Death's iron chain,
He breaks through sin and pain,
He shatters hell's dark thrall,
I follow Him through all.
To halls of heavenly splendor
With Him I penetrate;
And trouble ne'er may hinder
Nor make me hesitate.
Let tempests rage at will,
My Savior shields me still;
He grants abiding peace
And bids all tumult cease.

APRIL 17, 2005

SUGGESTED SERMON *Date preached:*

The Beauty of His Holiness

By Rev. Richard Sharpe Jr.

Scripture: 1 Chronicles 16:29

Give to the LORD the glory due His name; bring an offering, and come before Him. Oh, worship the LORD in the beauty of holiness! (NKJV)

Introduction: In our church and in every church, a trap is set for us. We often come in tired from our week, thinking about other things, and go through the worship service in a daze, singing without taking the words to heart, or closing our eyes without really praying. Today we will look at five reminders from Scripture of how the Lord wants us to worship.

1. **Bring Glory to His Name.** When we bring glory to the name of the Lord, we are bringing honor to His name. The Hebrew word for *glory* connotes "weight." When we worship, we are giving Him weight in our lives. Many things are important to us: family, possessions, jobs, etc. God wants us to put more weight to our relationship with Him than in any other relationship. The word *glory* also carries the meaning of giving God splendor. We should imagine the Lord in heaven with all the splendor of that place.

We must remember that His name is *the LORD* or Jehovah. This name emphasizes that He is our personal, covenant-keeping God. We worship a personal God, who wants to have a personal relationship with us.

2. **Bring an Offering.** This word "offering" carries with it the idea of bringing a donation, a gift, or a present to our meeting with the Lord. When we come to a worship service, we bring our monetary offering to Him. This gift is a portion of what He has allowed us to earn on a weekly basis. It is an offering that gives glory to His name. The Bible indicates that this should be at least ten percent of our paycheck. Remember that He gave the greatest gift of His Son to us. Therefore, we should give gratefully and graciously.

3. **Bring Ourselves to the Person.** When we come into the presence of a person, we see that person. How is that possible with God? The Bible says we can't see God face to face on earth (Ex. 33:20). So, what does this verse mean? It means we must get into the presence of God spiritually. Our lives need to be marked by closeness to God. We have to confess our sins and ask to be filled with the presence of the Holy Spirit. When we are filled with the Holy Spirit, we can listen to God talk with us through His servants, His Word, and our prayer. Then we are truly worshiping the Lord.

4. **Bring Fear.** Study of the Bible's original languages enhances our worship of the Lord. The word "fear" means *hope, tremble, trust, wait carefully, rest, shake, twist,* or *whirl.* In fear we shake, twist, and whirl in our amazement of His glory. There is also the idea of trembling at His presence. Furthermore we wait carefully for Him to work. God is working in His time and His way for our good (Rom. 8:28).

5. **Practice the Beauty of His Holiness.** The word *beauty* carries with it the idea of adornment or decoration. When the Lord allowed Moses to see the back end of His glory, Moses' face glowed for many days afterwards (Ex. 33:19ff.). Our God is adorned with the same glory today. When we are in His presence in worship, our faces glow from His presence. In this way, we show the beauty of His holiness. Here we see that the holiness of God causes others to be afraid, to be in awe of the Lord's glory.

Conclusion: Our lives should be full of worship. This affects those around us in a real way. When people see God in us, they want to know more about the God we worship.

STATS, STORIES, AND MORE

Someone once said:

All human activity is to be doxological in nature.—David L. Larson

The most acceptable service we can do and show unto God, and which alone He desires of us, is, that He be praised of us.—Martin Luther

One of the greatest evidences for the existence of God is His beauty. Have you ever snorkeled off the coast of a tropical island? Or have you peered into the saltwater acquarium of your local pet store? Have you ever visited a botanical garden and soaked in the beauty of a thousand varieties of flowering shrubs and plants? Ever stood on the edge of a vast chasm, gazing into rugged rocks and hills and valleys and canyons? Ever visited the zoo and noticed the colors of the animals, the richness of their fur, the patterns adorning their hides, the shape of their bodies, the tenderness of their young? Ever peered through a microscope at the hidden world contained in waterdrops from a pond? Or through a telescope at the mind-boggling array of endless galaxies?

Is this all-encompassing splendor the blind product of random accidents? Well, ask this: If we visited an art museum to view a painting of a beautiful landscape with trees and a river, fluffy white clouds and a pasture dotted by flowers, would we assume the artwork was an accident? Did a delivery truck wreck, spilling cans of paint onto a canvas? Or would we assume that an artist of fabulous skill had created the beauty and signed his name at the bottom? The beauty of the cosmos is God's signature. He could have made an ugly world and a loathsome universe. But He is a God of beauty, and we must worship Him in the beauty of His holiness.

FOR THE BULLETIN

✲ Alexander, the bishop of Alexandria, Egypt, died on April 17, 328. He is remembered for his excommunication of the heretic Arius and for his active roll at the Council of Nicaea. Athanasius, the great defender of the faith, succeeded him. ✲ The death of Theobald, Archbishop of Canterbury, on April 17, 1161, led to the appointment of Thomas Becket by King Henry II. ✲ On April 17, 1492, King Ferdinand and Queen Isabella of Spain authorized Christopher Columbus to sail westward, seeking an ocean route to Asia. ✲ Martin Luther appeared before the Diet of Worms on this day in 1521, to defend his doctrine. He was admitted into the assembly at about six o'clock in the evening as thousands assembled outside the building. Speaking in a low voice, Luther seemed near collapse. He asked for a recess overnight, and during the night, the Lord strengthened him. The next morning, April 18, he appeared again before the Diet, this time bold, heroic, and undaunted. ✲ Pioneer missionary to Japan, Lettie Cowman, died on this day in 1960. She had gone to Tokyo with her husband, Charles, in 1902, to establish a Bible Institute. This led to the founding of the Oriental Missionary Society (O.M.S.) in 1907. She is best known, however for her devotional books, *Streams in the Desert* and *Springs in the Valley*.

APPROPRIATE SONGS AND HYMNS

Give Unto the Lord, Tim Jines; © 1987 Dayspring Music; Admin. by Word Music Group, Inc.

Oh, Worship the Lord, Robert C. Clatterbuck; © 1985 Hope Publishing Company.

Worship the Lord in the Beauty of Holiness, Jacquelyn Gouche; © 1992 J.A.A.G. Music/Doulos Music Publishing; Admin. by Maranatha! Music.

Glorious Things of Thee Are Spoken, Franz Joseph Haydn/John Newton; Public Domain.

Great Redeemer, We Adore Thee, Paolo Conte/John Roy Harris; © 1940. Renewal 1968 Broadman Press; Admin. by Genevox Music Group.

WORSHIP HELPS

Call to Worship:
Give to the LORD, O families of the peoples, give to the LORD glory and strength. Give to the LORD the glory due His name.
(1 Chr. 16:28, 29 NKJV)

Responsive Reading:

Worship Leader:	Oh, give thanks to the LORD! Call upon His name; make known His deeds among the peoples!
All:	Sing to Him, sing psalms to Him.
Worship Leader:	Talk of all His wondrous works! Glory in His holy name. Let the hearts of those rejoice who seek the LORD.
All:	Sing to Him, sing psalms to Him.
Worship Leader:	He is the LORD our God; His judgments are in all the earth.
All:	Sing to the LORD, all the earth; proclaim the good news of His salvation from day to day.
Worship Leader:	Declare His glory among the nations, His wonders among all peoples.
All:	Give to the LORD glory and strength. Give to the LORD the glory due His name.

(1 Chr. 16 NKJV)

Kids Talk

Since this is the springtime of the year, bring a beautiful arrangement of seasonal flowers to show the children. See if they can identify each blossom. Tell the children that all of nature is full of praise to the Lord. The flowers praise Him by blooming as beautifully as they possibly can. The birds praise Him by whistling their sweet songs. The sun praises Him by shining and the moon by glowing. We praise the Lord by coming to church, singing about Him, talking about Him, giving our offerings to Him, and talking about all His great works.

Additional Sermons and Lesson Ideas

Family Matters

Date preached:

By Rev. Mark Hollis

SCRIPTURE: Ephesians 5:21–33 and 6:1–4

INTRODUCTION: The Bible provides clear instructions for each member of the family.

1. Everyone (5:21). Our responsibility is to submit to one another. Our model: Reverence for Christ.
2. Wives (5:22–24). Our responsibility is to respect our husbands. Our model: Submission to Christ.
3. Husbands (5:25–33). Our responsibility is to love our wives. Our model: Christ's love for the church. That love is sacrificial (vv. 25, 26), purifying (v. 27), and caring (vv. 28–30).
4. Children (6:1–3). Our responsibility is to obey our parents. Our model: Christ's obedience to His Father (John 6:38).
5. Parents (6:4). Our responsibility is to not exasperate our children. Our model: The training and instruction of the Lord.

CONCLUSION: Are you willing to make this commitment? I will seek to serve the other members of my family. I recognize that true greatness in a family comes through service to others.

Never Give In

Date preached:

SCRIPTURE: 1 Corinthians 15:58

INTRODUCTION: Discouragement is the great enemy of small group leaders, ushers, musicians, pastors, teachers, nursery workers, and everyone else involved in our ministries. But listen to this verse:

1. *Therefore* ... Because of the resurrection truth described in this chapter.
2. *Be steadfast* ... Stand firm, like a fencepost imbedded in concrete.
3. *Immovable* ... Don't be moved by adversity or disappointment.
4. *Always abounding in the work of the Lord* (NIV) ...: Always give yourselves fully to it.
5. *For you know* ... Indicates a solid fact.
6. *That your labor is not in vain in the Lord.*

CONCLUSION: Not the slightest service we do humbly in Christ's name will be futile. God will use you in ways greater than you realize. Don't give up.

APRIL 24, 2005

SUGGESTED SERMON *Date preached:*

What's Right with the Church

By Dr. Timothy Beougher

Scripture: Acts 9:31
Then the churches throughout all Judea, Galilee, and Samaria had peace and were edified. And walking in the fear of the Lord and in the comfort of the Holy Spirit, they were multiplied. (NKJV)

Introduction: How often we hear news coverage of scandals or crimes in the church! More often, we hear people complain or give reasons not to attend church. In any case, a tremendous focus is placed upon problems in the church. This morning I want to look at a different picture, a picture of a church that was doing it right. Throughout history, Christians have looked to the church in the Book of Acts as a model of what Christ wants in His body. Our verse for the morning sets forth five evidences of a healthy church.

1. **Climate of Peace.** Notice that the verse begins with the word *then*. The context of this verse is the conversion of Saul and the resulting decrease of external persecution on the church. However, peace involves much more than the absence of persecution. A church can have peace outwardly and not inwardly. Peace involves absence of conflict, both outwardly and inwardly, and the presence of harmony. A church filled with division will not see multiplication. The climate of peace naturally produces an atmosphere of unity. Are you helping to unify your congregation or do you create divisions?

2. **Consistent Spiritual Growth.** Notice the verse says, "... and were edified." This word literally means, "to build a house" referring to us, the household of God! It's a reference to spiritual growth. A healthy church is one blossoming with spiritual growth in its members. We grow spiritually through spiritual food and spiritual exercise. Our spiritual food is the regular intake of God's Word, and our spiritual exercise is our ministry and service. If you are going to grow spiritually, it will cost you time and effort (see Col. 2:6, 7).

3. **Compelling Spiritual Vitality.** Acts 9:31 tells us the New Testament church was, "walking ... in the comfort of the Holy Spirit." This church was alive! A clear spiritual dynamic was at work! Distinct characteristics identify a dynamic church. The church must live by faith (Heb. 11:6; 2 Cor. 5:7). The church must commit to holiness (Eph. 4:30). The church must depend on prayer (Eph. 6:18). Without these components, our church would be dead! Are we making progress in these areas?

4. **Consistent Numerical Growth.** The New Testament church was multiplied. A healthy church will experience consistent numerical growth. Not numbers for numbers' sake, but because numbers represent people and people matter to God! We need to reach people for Christ! A healthy church is a church where lives are changed by the gospel, a church that sees consistent numerical growth. Now there are settings where a church is reaching people and not growing numerically. In areas of rapidly declining population, a church may reach many for Christ and not see a numerical increase. For most churches, however, this is simply not the case.

5. **Consuming God-Focus.** A key phrase in our verse is, "walking in the fear of the Lord." Walking involves a way of life. The fear of the Lord portrays an idea of being afraid to offend God in any way. A healthy church seeks God's will above all else. A church that pleases God is a church where the people honor Christ in their daily conduct, in their thoughts (Phil. 4:8), deeds (2 Cor. 7:1), and words (Eph. 4:29).

Conclusion: In the face of all the problems in the church, we can become part of the solution. We need to follow the model of the New Testament church, cultivating the lifestyle of peace, spiritual growth and vitality, numerical growth, and Godliness. Will you commit yourself to help build that type of church here? It has been said there are three kinds of people: those who make it happen, those who watch it happen, and those who wonder what happened. Will you commit to be a part of that first group, those who make it happen?

STATS, STORIES, AND MORE

More from Dr. Timothy Beougher:

An article in Dr. Thom Rainer's newsletter, "The Rainer Report" of March, 2003, was titled "Ten Reasons Many Churches Do not Grow." Under reason number two, "Conflict in the Church," Rainer wrote: "I wish I could say that conflict in the American church has abated, but that just does not seem to be the case. The reasons behind the conflicts are as innumerable as one could imagine: Leadership style, facility differences, power and control, worship style, programming, times of services, and the list goes on and on. It seems that for many the church has become the place to have 'my needs and desires met,' rather than seeking to serve God and others through the local congregation."

Have you ever noticed that the words "unite" and "untie" use the same five letters? The difference is where you put the letter "I".

There are two mottos that churches can adopt: (1) "We've never done it that way before!" or (2) "We can do all things through Christ who strengthens us" (Phil. 4:13 NKJV).

Vance Havner said, "If the Holy Spirit were to leave all the churches in America, 95% of them could continue on with no interruption of activity."

The House of Many Lamps

There is a legend of a village in Southern Europe that boasted of a church called "The House of Many Lamps." When it was built in the sixteenth century, the architect provided for no light except for a receptacle at every seat for the placing of a lamp. Each Sunday night, as the people gathered, they would bring their lanterns and slip them into the bracket at their seat. When someone stayed away, his place would be dark; and if very many stayed away, the darkness became greater for the whole. The regular presence of each person lit up the church.

FOR THE BULLETIN

❁ On April 24, 387, Augustine was baptized. He had been a wild youth, but the prayers of his mother coupled with the preaching of Bishop Ambrose of Milan brought him to Christ. He became Bishop of Hippo, a great theologian, and one of the primary figures in Christian history. ❁ On April 24, 1547, Protestant forces trying to stave off destruction by the Roman Catholic armies of Charles V were crushed in the Battle of Muehlberg. ❁ Johann Walther, the "Father of Lutheran church music" died on this day in 1570. ❁ On April 24, 1649, the Toleration Acts were passed in Maryland under the administration of Protestant deputy governor William Stone. They provided for religious freedom for all Christians. ❁ Eliza E. Hewitt died on this day in 1920. In 1887, while teaching at the Northern Home for Friendless Children, an unruly student struck Eliza. She was 35 years old. The doctor placed her in a heavy cast for six months, but Eliza's injuries plagued her for the rest of her life. She went on to write such hymns as "My Faith Has Found a Resting Place," "Victory in Jesus," "When We All Get to Heaven," and "Will There Be Any Stars in My Crown?" ❁ "Uncle" Cameron Townsend, founder of Wycliffe Bible Translators, died on this day in 1982.

APPROPRIATE SONGS AND HYMNS

A Glorious Church, Ralph E. Hudson; Public Domain.

Break Out, O Church of God, Wesley L. Forbis/Aaron Williams; © 1990 Broadman Press; Admin. by Genevox Music Group.

For Zion's Sake, Graham Kendrick; © 1981 King'sway Thankyou Music; Admin. by EMI Christian Music Publishing.

I Love Thy Kingdom Lord, Aaron Williams/Timothy Dwight; Public Domain.

I Was Glad, John Chisum/George T. Searcy; © 1990 Ariose Music/Tourmaline Music, Inc.; Admin. by Tourmaline Music, Inc.

WORSHIP HELPS

Call to Worship:
O praise ye the Lord and sing a new song,
Amid all His saints His praises prolong;
The praise of their Maker His people shall sing,
And children of Zion rejoice in their King.

—*Henry W. Baker*

Offertory Comments:
This story, entitled "God Kept the Family Together," appeared years ago in a little book called *I Tithe Joyfully*, published by Moody Press Colportage Library. The story was simply signed Mrs. R. H., Iowa. "When my husband died in 1935, during the Depression, I was left with four little boys ... I was expecting another baby. We were so poor that the county had to pay my husband's funeral expenses. In spite of these circumstances, I trusted in my Savior. Every time anyone gave me money, I took out a tenth for the Lord, regardless of how small or how large. I kept my children together, and we never did suffer lack of something to eat or something to wear. God looked after us in a wonderful way. Now my children are grown, married, and have families of their own. I am married again and am still living for God and paying my tithes. God is taking care of us. We are getting up in years and are tithing and praising God for His goodness to us."

Benediction:
And now, O Lord, give us peace. May we remain edified. And walking in the fear of the Lord and in the comfort of the Holy Spirit, may we see Your numbers multiplied and Your work blessed; for Jesus' sake. Amen.

Additional Sermons and Lesson Ideas

Job's Trials and Ours

Date preached:

By Rev. Billy Friel

SCRIPTURE: Job 1

INTRODUCTION: The story of Job can be brought into the year 2005 without any problem. Each of us struggles with problems of varying levels of severity. Notice these things about Job:

1. Piety (vv. 1, 8). He was blameless, upright, feared God, and shunned evil.
2. Parent (v. 2). His family was large and happy.
3. Prosperity (v. 3).
4. Priest (v. 5). As head of his home, he exercised priestly concern for his children.
5. Protected (vv. 9, 10). God had put a hedge of protection around him.
6. Provoked (vv. 9–19). Satan strikes hardest at those who are walking with God.
7. Preserved (vv. 20–22). Job lost the physical things of life, but not his faith in God.

CONCLUSION: All of us have trials and troubles. These are faith-tests. Cast your cares on Him.

Resurrection Faith in ACTion

Date preached:

By Rev. Mark Hollis

SCRIPTURE: James 1:26, 27

INTRODUCTION: Genuine faith is demonstrated in transformed lives.

1. Watch your tongue (James 1:26). **ACT**ion Steps:
   Assess the problem: When do your words hurt others?
   Commit to change: What will you do about it?
   Tell a friend: Who can help you change?
2. Look after the needy (James 1:27). **ACT**ion Steps:
   Assess the problem: Who are the needy around you?
   Commit to change: What will you do to help?
   Tell a friend: Who can help you make a difference?
3. Keep yourselves pure (James 1:27). **ACT**ion Steps:
   Assess the problem: How does your life reflect the character of Christ?
   Commit to change: What will you do to reflect Him?
   Tell a friend: Who can help you keep yourself pure?

CONCLUSION: True faith is a matter of heart, head, and hands. It is demonstrated in action.

MAY 1, 2005

SUGGESTED SERMON *Date preached:*

The Apathetic Assembly

By Dr. Melvin Worthington

Scripture: Revelation 3:14–21, especially verses 15, 16
I know your works, that you are neither cold nor hot. I could wish you were cold or hot. So then, because you are lukewarm, and neither cold nor hot, I will vomit you out of My mouth. (NKJV)

Introduction: The letter to the church at Ephesus is the final letter of the seven we find in Revelation 1—3. It is addressed to an affluent and apathetic church. Christ charged this church with being lukewarm. Beneath this condemnation, there is an even more heart-searching lesson. The result of self-complacency is a lukewarm condition. It is impossible for self-complacent people to be anything other than lukewarm. Christ would rather that His church is cold or hot, but He cannot tolerate a lukewarm state. This is the crowning indictment of all of the seven letters.

1. **The Inscription (v. 14).** The inscription includes the angel, the assembly, the area, the authority, the address, and the Almighty. The Almighty is presented as the "Amen, the faithful and true witness; the beginning of the creation of God." The "Amen" describes Jesus' way of speaking. He is the one whose statements are true and whose promises can be trusted. Jesus is the "faithful and true witness." Everything He says is true. There is never any minimizing or exaggeration. As He speaks of the church, He speaks the whole truth. Jesus is the "beginning of the creation of God." This statement reminds us that He is the King of Creation. He was the moving cause of all creation.

2. **The Inventory (v. 15a).** The inventory includes the appraisal, the activities, and the actuality. The Lord does not offer any compliments to this church and yet He reminds them that He is aware of their works.

3. **The Indictment (vv. 15b, 16, 17).** The indictment includes the desired state, the disgusting state, and the destitute state. Christ condemned their attitude of indifference. Indifference is one of the hardest feelings to combat. The basic problem of modern evangelism is not hostile opposition but

complete indifference. It is impossible for the Christian to be neutral. Those who will not help Christ are a hindrance to Christ. It is better not to start on the Christian way than to start and then slip and drift into a Christianity of respectability. No leader finds any value in a loyalty that has turned to indifference. This church was convinced of its wealth and blind to its poverty. By human standards, there was not a more prosperous city in Asia. Yet, by spiritual standards, there was not a more poverty-stricken community. Laodicea prided itself in its financial wealth, clothing trade, and famous eye salve. The church claimed it was rich, increased with goods and had need of nothing. This was not the evaluation of Christ. He declared that they were wretched, miserable, poor, blind, and naked. They were proud of themselves, but the Lord felt sorry for them. This poor rich church was blind to its own spiritual condition.

4. **The Instruction (vv. 18, 19, 20, 22).** The instruction includes the counsel, the chastisement, the condensation, and the challenge. Jesus exhorted them to repent and reminded them that He chastens those He loves. Many are living close enough to the world to be chilled by it and close enough to the church to be warmed by it. Christ stands at the door of the church and knocks. This means that Christ pleads with us and that we have the responsibility to open the door and allow Christ inside. His pleading and offering are of no avail if men will not open the door.

5. **The Incentive (v. 21).** The incentive includes the triumph, the throne, and the thrill. Christ promises the overcomers that they will reside with Him in Heaven. John declares, "To him who overcomes I will grant to sit with Me on My throne, as I also overcame and sat down with My Father on His throne" (Rev. 3:21 NKJV).

Conclusion: This letter addresses the dangers faced by a lukewarm church that is self-sufficient and unconscious of its spiritual needs. The Laodicean church was a self-complacent church. Complacency leads to a lukewarm condition. Lukewarm believers are self-complacent. This truth reveals the source of the grave and conspicuous evil in churches. When one is self-centered, the heart is hopeless. Christ prefers His church to be either cold or hot but not lukewarm. The lukewarm church makes Christ sick.

STATS, STORIES, AND MORE

The dictionary defines "lukewarm" as: (1) moderately warm, tepid; (2) lacking conviction, half-hearted. It's a word that frequently shows up in newspaper headlines: *Voters Lukewarm on Proposition 39, Wall Street Lukewarm on Proposed Tax Cuts, Lukewarm Support for President's Initiative, 49ers Put On Lukewarm Performance*. This word never paints a positive picture.

From Vance Havner:

Worldliness is rampant in the church. The devil is not fighting churches, he is joining them! He is not persecuting Christianity, he is professing it. When many think the world is becoming more Christian, Christians are becoming worldlier. The friend of the world is the enemy of God and if we love the world the love of the Father is not in us.

Someone Once Said . . .

Let us not hold aloof from our church meetings, as some do. —Hebrews 10:25 (PHILLIPS)

There is something wrong with our Christianity when we have to beg most of our crowd to come to church to hear about it. —Vance Havner

Eighty percent of life is just showing up. —Woody Allen

The great task of the church is not only to get sinners into heaven, but to get saints out of bed. —Anonymous

Silver and Gold

The medieval theologian John Duns Scotus was visiting Rome and the Pope took him into the Vatican treasuries. Running his hands through the silver, the Pope said, "No longer does the church have to say, `Silver and gold have I none.'" The theologian replied, "That's true, but no longer can we say, "In the name of Jesus Christ of Nazareth, rise up and walk."

FOR THE BULLETIN

❁ On May 1, 305, the Roman Emperor Diocletian abdicated. He had assumed power with enormous gifts of organization and energy, and he sought to stabilize the reform the empire. For most of his reign, Christians lived in relative peace, but in 303, Diocletian unleashed the "Great Persecution" in which countless churches were destroyed and believers were martyred. ❁ The Second Period of the Council of Trent began on this day in 1551, furthering the Counter-Reformation. ❁ Today is the birthday of hymnist A. J. Showalter, who was born in Chattanooga, Tennessee, in 1858. He wrote the music to "Leaning on the Everlasting Arms." ❁ David Livingstone, Scottish missionary and African explorer, died on this day in 1873. He was found dead in East Africa, on his knees in a posture of prayer. His heart was buried in Africa, and his body taken to England and buried in Westminster Abbey. ❁ May 1, 1939 marks the first broadcast of "Back to the Bible," the radio program begun by Theodore Epp. ❁ On May 1, 1945, Amy Carmichael of Dohnavur, India, sent a message to her workers, giving them a poem she had written following a period in which she had felt unusually helpless. The poem was entitled, "Leave it to Me, child, leave it to Me."

APPROPRIATE SONGS AND HYMNS

Blow On Us, O Wind of God, Warren Hastings; © 1987 Master Song Music.
Come, Holy Spirit, John W. Peterson ; © 1971 John W. Peterson Music Company.
God's Gonna Do It Again, David Baroni/Niles Borop; © 1994 Niles Borop Music/Integrity's Praise! Music; Admin. by Integrity Music, Inc.
Sing Praise to God Who Reigns Above, Johann J. Schutz; Public Domain.
Stir My Spirit, Darrell Dement; © 1986 ZionSong Music.
Revive Us Again, William P. MacKay/John J. Husband; Public Domain.

WORSHIP HELPS

Call to Worship:
Sing hallelujah, praise the Lord! Sing with a cheerful voice;
Exalt our God with one accord, and in His Name rejoice.

—John C. Bechler, 1789

Pastoral Prayer:
Almighty God, we exalt in Your name, we extol Your greatness, and we express our adoration. We acknowledge You Creator of the universe and Redeemer of the world. You are our Maker, Redeemer, Defender, and Friend. But we, O Lord, are frail children of dust and feeble as frail. We're often distracted and seldom committed. Thinking ourselves rich and blessed, we do not always know when we are spiritually wretched, miserable, poor, blind, naked, and lukewarm. Forgive us our sins, and send a great revival, O Lord, to the hearts of all gathered here. Strike us with new fire. Inflame us with new passion. Bless thus this hour, and bless thus Your church; in Jesus' name. Amen.

Hymn Story: Sing Praise to God Who Reigns Above
Lutheranism lost steam after Luther's death, and by the 1600s, it tended to be formal and shallow. That's when Philip Spener began pastoring in Frankfort-on-Main. Rather than preaching from prescribed texts, he began preaching through the entire Bible, calling for repentance. In 1669, revival broke out in the church. No one was more excited than Johann Schütz, a life-long resident of Frankfort. He suggested Spener take these converts and disciple them in small, home prayer and Bible study groups. Spener did so, and it became the talk of the town. These people were called "Pietists" in derision, but the revival spread throughout Germany and is known to history as the "Pietistic Movement." Out of his joy for what was happening, Johann Schütz wrote a hymn in 1675: "Sing praise to God Who reigns above, the God of all creation."

Additional Sermons and Lesson Ideas

How Firm a Foundation: A Hymn Sermon

Date preached:

INTRODUCTION: The great hymn, "How Firm a Foundation" is based on the trustworthiness of some of the greatest promises in the Bible. Each stanza is based on a different verse.

1. Isaiah 41:10—"Fear not, I am with thee; O be not dismayed ..."
2. Deuteronomy 33:23—"As your days may demand shall your strength ever be."
3. 1 Peter 1:7 and 5:12—"When through fiery trials ..."
4. Isaiah 43:2—"When through the deep waters I call thee to go ..."
5. Hebrews 13:5—"I'll never, no never, no never forsake ..."

CONCLUSION: Do you need a special promise for today? Do you need a "firm foundation"? What more could He say than to you He hath said / to you who for refuge to Jesus have fled?

Praying With a Purpose

Date preached:

By Rev. Kevin Riggs

SCRIPTURE: Philippians 1:1–11

INTRODUCTION: A person can withstand almost anything if he or she knows they are not alone. Each local church is a community of believers. We have God as our Father, and each of us as brothers and sisters. One of the best ways we can build relationships with each other is by praying for one another.

1. Pray for love to increase (v. 9): The word translated *abound* was also used to describe a flower going from a bud to full bloom.
2. Pray for wisdom (v. 10)
3. Pray for fruit (v. 11). The "fruit of righteousness" refers to good works, living a life that is consistent with what you say you believe.

CONCLUSION: Apply this message to your lives this week by partnering with another believer. As you pray, pray their love will increase, pray they will receive wisdom, and pray their lives will produce fruit.

TECHNIQUES FOR THE PASTOR'S DELIVERY

Should We Repeat Our Sermons?

By R. W. Dale

One advantage on the side of writing and reading sermons is rarely mentioned. Extemporaneous sermons, as Hooker says, "spend their life in their birth, and may have public audience but once." If a man writes and reads, he can preach his old sermons over again, and preach them effectively.

When ministers remove to a new congregation, I suppose that they have no scruples about preaching sermons which they have preached before; but I can see no sufficient reason for not preaching sermons a second or a third time to the same congregation. Many of the people have died; some have removed to other churches or to other parts of the country; new people have taken their places; children have become young men and women; young men and women who were uninterested in the sermon when it was first preached have had their moral and intellectual interest in religious truth awakened, and will listen to it with eager attention.

If you write a sermon on any of those great topics to which you are bound to recur frequently—on the divinity of our Lord Jesus Christ, for instance, or on the personality of the Holy Spirit, or on the nature of Regeneration, or on the Protestant doctrine of Justification, or on the principles which will determine the judgment of men at the Last Day—if the substance of the sermon is the result of reading and thought extending over many months, if you think that the statement of the scriptural proof of the doctrine is clear and full and strong; if the arrangement satisfies you; if the whole discussion is as complete and effective as you can make it—I think that you will waste a good piece of work if you use it only once and then throw it aside.

Some of the people—perhaps many of them—will recognize it as an old sermon; but your congregation will be a very remarkable one if there are more than a very few persons who will remember the contents of it so perfectly that it will not do them good to hear the sermon again.

Not only sermons that contain an elaborate proof and illustration of the great central doctrines of the Christian faith may be preached over again. Ten years ago, certain aspects of ethical and religious truth and duty exerted exceptional power over my own moral and spiritual life: five years earlier, certain other aspects of truth had the same ascendancy and ruled me with the same authority. These particular truths or particular aspects of truth do not seem to me less important now than they were when they haunted me day and night. Their practical value to my congregation does not seem to me less that it was then. But they have been so incorporated into the very substance of my faith and life that the intense intellectual interest that they once excited has gone by. I could not state them now with the same energy with which I stated them when they absorbed my whole thought and fired me with enthusiastic ardor. And yet when I take up an old sermon in which these aspects of truth or duty are illustrated and enforced, the flame burst out again. I am ten, fifteen years younger; I can preach the sermon with the same vehement moral interest with which I first preached it. Sometimes, indeed, I think I preach an old sermon of this kind with even stronger emotion than I felt when it was fresh, for the experience of subsequent years has deepened my sense of the value of the truth or the sacredness of the duty which it was intended to illustrate. If, however, I had to write a new sermon on the same subject, I should not be able to write with the same force and fire.

Do not misunderstand my meaning. The sermons which we have a right to repeat are sermons to which we have given so much time and strength that they contain the very best that we can say on some great subject; or sermons which, though of permanent interest and value, derived their force from the special intellectual and moral experiences which we were passing through when they were written.

When you preach an old sermon, be frank about it. There are people who keep a record of our sermons; the margins of their Bibles are enriched with dates placed against the texts we have preached from. Do not try to cheat these keepers of homiletical chronicles. The old sermon may sometimes require a great deal of revision; you may have to cancel some passages and replace them with others; you may have to strike out many superfluous epithets, to improve the form of an illustration, to strengthen the foundations, or change the structure of an argument; but do not try to conceal the fact that the sermon is not a new one; let the old text stand.

Do you say that if you preach old sermons and people know it they will think that you are getting lazy? If there is any chance of your people thinking that you are lazy, you have no right to preach at all. A man who is doing his work as he ought to do it, will be quite safe from imputations of that sort.

(Excerpted from Lecture 6, "Extemporaneous Preaching and Style," from *The Yale Lectures on Preaching*, 1877–78, by R. W. Dale)

MAY 8, 2005

MOTHER'S DAY SUGGESTED SERMON *Date preached:*

Parenting with Purpose

By Dr. Timothy Beougher

Scripture: Psalm 78:1–8, especially verse 4

We will not hide them from their children, telling to the generation to come the praises of the LORD, and His strength and His wonderful works that He has done. (NKJV)

Introduction: Today is that wonderful Sunday we call Mother's Day, a day when we celebrate our moms and the priceless role they play in family and society. Moms, it's not my intention today to add to your struggles as a mom, because many of you already feel overwhelmed. It's never been harder to be a parent. But because parenting is so crucial and because God has called us to do certain things as moms and dads, I do want to share some truth from Scripture about raising children. Though this is Mother's Day, my message is specifically targeted to all parents; and in addition, I believe God has a word for all of us here this morning, whether we're parents or not. On Psalm 78, the Lord gives us four principles to follow in parenting with purpose.

1. **Teach our Children God's Greatness (vv. 1–4).** How does the Psalmist communicate to us in these verses? He first gets our attention, "Give ear, O my people, to my law; incline your ears to the words of my mouth" (v. 1). In modern terminology, he is shouting, "Don't touch that dial! Pay attention! This is important stuff!" Then he uses historical material to drive home his points. The first principle he emphasizes that we are to pass on to the next generation is God's greatness. He describes: "His praiseworthy deeds"—the awesome things God has done; "His power"—He is above all other powers—nothing is too difficult for Him. "His wonders"—He is a God of miracles! It's our responsibility to teach our children, our grandchildren, and our spiritual children God's greatness (cf. Ps. 145:3, 4).

2. **Teach Our Children God's Word (vv. 5, 6).** In the maze of moral confusion, God's Word serves to guide us. Notice the multi-generational aspect of these verses: forefathers, their children, the children yet to be born, and their children. The psalmist is talking about four generations! Grandparents, your spiritual assignment is not over when your children are grown. You are to influence your grandchildren spiritually as well! It's not always

easy to teach children of God's Word. Sometimes our own lack of knowledge and understanding hinders us, but remember that the teacher most always learns more than the student. Sometimes our supposed lack of time hinders our teaching of the Word to children. We can make time for what's important, and the psalmist puts utmost importance on this task! Why not share with each other what you are learning in God's Word? Your children can teach you, too, which excites them to learn.

3. **Teach Our Children to Trust God (v. 7a).** How can we teach our children to trust God? We do this by trusting God ourselves and by sharing stories about God's faithfulness with them. These verses tell of how Israel forgot about the Lord's work. How could they forget? God had done so many miracles (the parting of the Red Sea, the providing of manna, etc.) how could they forget? We do the same thing! When God parted the Jordan for Israel to pass through, Joshua set up stones to commemorate God's mighty acts so future generations would remember (Josh. 4:20–24). What are we doing to commemorate God's mighty work in our lives?

4. **Teach Our Children to Obey God (vv. 7b, 8).** We need to help our children build their own set of convictions. When our children leave home, we can't make their decisions for them! Remember Joseph when away from home and tempted said, "How then can I do this great wickedness, and sin against God?" (Gen. 39:9b NKJV). We must teach our children by example. Do you ever say when the phone rings, "Tell them I'm not home," but then get upset when your kids tell a lie? We must model obedience for our children.

Conclusion: Diana Allen nicely sums up the sentiment of many mothers in a poem called "I Quit." After explaining the hardships of parenthood, she concludes, "There will be days when I'll still hunt through the yellow pages for the number for the Mother's Resignation Hotline ... or my heart will feel as though it has been shattered into a thousand pieces. One thing is sure, however: I have to hang on, to stand firm, to fight the good fight. The souls of my children and the quality of the lives they live here on earth is at stake—and so is their eternity. My children are too precious for me to do anything but persevere."

STATS, STORIES, AND MORE

More from Dr. Timothy Beougher:

A man came home from work to find his house in chaos. His children were outside, still in their pajamas, playing in the mud. Inside the house, a lamp had been knocked over, the throw rug was wadded against a wall, and the living room was littered with toys and clothing. Dishes filled the kitchen sink, cereal was spilled on the counter, and a broken glass lay under the table. The man went up the stairs, stepping over toys and piles of clothes, looking for his wife. She was still in bed in her pajamas, reading a novel. She looked up at him, smiled, and asked how his day went. "Never mind *my* day," he said, "What happened *here* today?" She said, "You know every day when you come home from work and ask me what in the world I did today? Well today I didn't do it."

Someone sent me this e-mail: I had a "drug" problem when I was a young person and teenager. I was "drug" to church on Sunday morning. I was "drug" to church on Sunday night. I was "drug" to church on Wednesday night. I was "drug" to Sunday School every week. I was "drug" to Vacation Bible School. I was "drug" to the family altar to read the Bible and pray. I was "drug" to the woodshed when I disobeyed my parents. Those "drugs" are still in my veins, and I don't think I'll ever kick the habit.

FOR THE BULLETIN

✿ Julian of Norwich (c. 1342–c. 1413) was a British mystic and Benedictine nun about whose life little is known. On May 8, 1373, she claimed to have received fifteen revelations in a state of ecstasy, lasting five hours. Another came the next day. She later wrote *Revelations of Divine Love*, which was the first book written by a woman published in English. ✿ The Edict of Worms was issued on this day in 1521, outlawing the preaching of Martin Luther and attempting to call a halt to the growing Reformation movement in Germany. On the same day, a baby was born in Nijmegan, Netherlands. Peter Canisius later became a powerful Catholic theologian and a leader in the Counter-Reformation. ✿ On May 8, 1559, Queen Elizabeth ratified the Act of Uniformity mandating the use of the *Book of Common Prayer* among British churches. It also made the English monarch the head of the Church of England. ✿ Count Nicolaus Ludwig von Zinzendorf spoke his last words on this day in 1760. On his deathbed, Zinzendorf recalled the remarkable decades of Moravian missionary advance, telling David Nitschmann: "Did you suppose in the beginning that the Savior would do as much as we now really see, in the various Moravian settlements, amongst the children of God of other denominations, and amongst the heathen? I only entreated of him a few of the firstfruits of the latter, but there are now thousands of them!" The next day he died. ✿ The Southern Baptist Convention was organized on May 7, 1845, in Augusta, Georgia.

APPROPRIATE SONGS AND HYMNS

Would You Bless Our Homes and Families, Walter Farquharson/Ron Klusmeier; © 1974 Worship Arts.

When Love Is Found, Brian Wren; © 1983 Hope Publishing Company.

The Joy of Your Way, Jack Hayford; © 1978 Rocksmith Music; Admin. by Mandina/Rocksmith Music.

Prayer for Families, Claire Cloninger/Margaret Moody; © 1991 Word Music, Inc.; Admin. by Word Music Group, Inc.

Lord, Make Our Homes, Bob Burroughs/Esther Burroughs; © 1982 Broadman Press; Admin. by Genevox Music Group.

WORSHIP HELPS

Call to Worship:
Open to me the gates of righteousness; I will go through them, and I will praise the LORD. This is the gate of the LORD, through which the righteous shall enter. (Ps 118:19, 20 NKJV)

Responsive Scripture Reading:

Worship Leader:	And Hannah prayed and said: My heart rejoices in the LORD; my horn is exalted in the LORD. I smile at my enemies because I rejoice in Your salvation.
All:	No one is holy like the LORD, for there is none besides You, nor is there any rock like our God.
Worship Leader:	The LORD is the God of knowledge; and by Him actions are weighed. The bows of the mighty men are broken, and those who stumbled are girded with strength. The LORD makes poor and makes rich; He brings low and lifts up.
All:	He raises the poor from the dust and lifts the beggar from the ash heap to set them among princes and make them inherit the throne of glory.
Worship Leader:	He will guard the feet of His saints, but the wicked shall be silent in darkness. The LORD will judge the ends of the earth. He will give strength to His king, and exalt the horn of His anointed.

(A Mother's Prayer condensed from 1 Sam. 2 NKJV)

Kids Talk

We have to be aware that not all children live with mothers, so it might be best to speak generically. Ask them what they like best about a dad, mom, or grandparent. Tell them of a time from your own childhood when your mom or dad helped or encouraged you. End the time by praying with the children for their parents and guardians.

Additional Sermons and Lesson Ideas

Why All This Evil?

Date preached:

SCRIPTURE: Romans 5:17

INTRODUCTION: Many wonder why the world is in such a mess. And what is the solution to it all? The answer is found in the two Adams. Romans 5:14 says Adam was "a type of Him who was to come," meaning Christ.

1. Both Adams entered the world supernaturally. One was created in a special way and the other was conceived in a special way.
2. Both were tempted by the devil.
3. Both were sinless. The first Adam fell into sin when tempted, but no sin was found in Christ.
4. Both Adams were put into a deep sleep and their sides were wounded.
5. Both produced, from their wounded sides, a Bride (Eve and the church).
6. Both Adams became the head of a race. Adam was the head of the human race, and Christ is the Head of the redeemed.

CONCLUSION: 1 Corinthians 15:21, 22 says: "For since by man came death, by Man also came the resurrection of the dead. For as in Adam all die, even so in Christ all shall be made alive." (NKJV)

Simple Directions

Date preached:

Dr. R. A. Torrey

SCRIPTURE: Ephesians 4:15

INTRODUCTION: The reason so many Christian lives are comparative failures is because of the lack of simple directions about living the Christian life. There are six very simple things to do, and it is sure that any one who does these six things will make a success of the Christian life.

1. Confess Christ Before Others.—Matthew 10:32
2. Study the Word of God Regularly.—Psalm 119:11 and 1 Peter 2:2
3. Pray Without Ceasing.—1 Thessalonians 5:17
4. Surrender Your Will Absolutely to God and Obey Him in All Things.—Acts 5:32
5. Be a Constant and Continuous Giver.—2 Corinthians 9:6–8
6. Go to Work for Christ.—Matthew 25:14–30

CONCLUSION: Go over these six points again and again; write them down with the texts, and let Christ make you into one of His successes.

MAY 15, 2005

SUGGESTED SERMON *Date preached:*

Turn Over the Controls

By Dr. Denis Lyle

Scripture: Ephesians 5:15–21, especially verse 18
And do not be drunk with wine, in which is dissipation; but be filled with the Spirit. (NKJV)

Introduction: What does it mean to be filled with the Spirit? The filling or controlling of the Holy Spirit is a profound reality in the believer's life, and understanding it can change your life. I want us to focus on Ephesians 5:18 to explain how we can allow the Spirit to change our lives.

1. **Some Reasons for a Spirit Filled Life**

   A. **Our Obedience.** God has commanded us "be filled with the Spirit." This is not a suggestion nor a request, but a command. Dr. K. Wuest tells us that the verb here is in the imperative mood; it is imperative that we be filled with the Spirit. God commands it. Being continually filled with the Spirit is not an option for the believer but a biblical mandate. The idea "to be filled" is plural in this passage. The context of this passage is addressing husbands and wives, children and parents, employers and employees; the command is addressed to every believer. The verb is also present tense, indicating that it's an ongoing command: "Constantly, moment by moment, be controlled by and filled with the Spirit." Are you continually filled? Does the Spirit of God control you moment by moment?

   B. **Our Obligation.** Believers have tremendous responsibilities that they must fulfill. We should look at the obligation for our life of worship. It is to be alive with joy and the reality of Christ; this is the overflow of the Spirit-filled life (v. 19; John 4:24). We have an obligation in our marriage life (Eph. 5:21, 25). Love and submission cannot be displayed apart from the power of the Spirit. We have an obligation in our work life (Eph. 6:5, 6). When an employer goes to the employment agency looking for new workers, he ought to ask for Christians because they work the hardest and have the best attitudes. We have an obligation in our life of spiritual warfare (Eph. 6:12). The Christian is at war. Ours is a fight to the finish with a sinister foe, and there are no holds barred.

How can we withstand satanic opposition? Only by being filled with the Holy Spirit.

C. **Our Opportunities (5:16).** This verse is God's reminder that we are to use our time and opportunity wisely. What golden opportunities we let slip through our fingers because the Spirit is not in control! While Christians should want to be filled with the Spirit to have power in serving, they often want to be filled to have pleasure in living. They see the Spirit-filled life as a source for enjoyment rather than a force for employment. Acts 1:8 tells us that we are given the power of God to preach the gospel; our opportunities are a reason to be Spirit filled.

2. **Some Requirements for a Spirit-Filled Life**

A. **Surrendering Your Life to Christ.** We must abandon our will, intellect, and emotions, as well as our time, talents, and treasure to God's control. This involves restraint and getting rid of lusts (Rom. 6:13), and pro-active submission (Rom. 12:1).

B. **Studying the Word of Christ.** A parallel passage to Ephesians 5 is Colossians 3, which says "let the Word of Christ dwell in us richly" (3:16). Do you desire a Spirit-filled life? Feed yourself a steady diet of the Word of God.

C. **Standing in the Presence of Christ.** A person who is always full of wine keeps close to the source and supply of it. We need to be close to the Lord Jesus to be full of the Spirit (cf. Matt. 16:13; John 6:67, 68). Do you know what it is to stand in the presence of Christ? Do you take time to be holy? Do you speak often with your Lord?

3. **Some Results of a Spirit-Filled Life**

A. **Speaking:** Expressing God-Given Truth (v. 19; cf. John 4:29; Acts 2:14, 4:8, 31; 9:17; 13:9).

B. **Singing:** Expressing God-Given Joy (5:19; cf. Acts 4:31; 9:17; 13:9).

C. **Sacrificing:** Expressing God-Given Thanks (5:20).

D. **Submitting:** Expressing God-Given Love (5:21).

Conclusion: A Spirit-filled life is one that is completely surrendered to the Lord's control, and as a result produces undeniable spiritual fruit. Won't you come to the altar, physically or spiritually, and yield yourself fully to the Spirit's control?

STATS, STORIES, AND MORE

More from Dr. Denis Lyle:

Homer Lindsay tells the gripping story of an air tragedy which occurred in his seminary days in Forth Worth, Texas. One morning at breakfast, he was reading the *Fort Worth Star Telegram*. An article told of a tragic plane crash. A young student pilot was making one of his final training flights. Evidently, he froze at the controls. His instructor yelled at him, "Turn over the controls! Turn over the controls!" The student did not. Both were killed in the crash. Tragedy can occur when those who are in training don't turn over the controls to the wiser instructor.

On the day of Pentecost, the 120 who gathered in the Upper Room were all different. They were different in temperament, in sex, in gift, but they were all filled with the Holy Spirit. (Acts 2:4) Impetuous people like Peter were filled with the Spirit (Acts 4:8); courageous people like Stephen were filled with the Spirit, (Acts 6:3; 7:55); good people like Barnabas were filled with the Spirit (Acts 11:24); outstanding people like Saul were filled with the Spirit (Acts 9:17; 13:9); responsible people like those who served tables, were men "full of the Holy Ghost." (Acts 6:3). You see, Peter needed the filling to preach for Christ (Acts 4:8); Stephen needed the filling to suffer for Christ (Acts 7:55); Barnabas needed the filling to encourage for Christ (Acts 11:23); Paul needed the filling to rebuke for Christ (Acts 13:9). Don't you think that you and I need to be filled with the Holy Spirit, too?

FOR THE BULLETIN

✿ May 15, 710 marks the consecration of Bishop Boniface, English Benedictine missionary known as "The Apostle to the Germans." ✿ Today is the birthday of Dante, author of "The Divine Comedy. He was born in 1265. ✿ The Peasant's War came to an unhappy conclusion in Germany on this day in 1525. The radical reformer Thomas Muenzer was beheaded. ✿ On May 15, 1785, John Marrant was ordained into the ministry. He is sometimes called the first black preacher in America. He wrote, *A Narrative of the Lord's Wonderful Dealings With John Marrant, a Black*, which went through twenty editions over the next fifty years. ✿ On May 15, 1820, Florence Nightingale was born in Florence, Italy. ✿ "Uncle" John Vassar grew up in his family's brewery in Poughkeepsie, New York. Following his conversion to Christ, he abandoned beer making for soul winning, and on May 15, 1850, he was commissioned as an agent for the American Tract Society of New York. Vassar took off across the country, never resting in his mission of selling Christian literature and asking everyone he met about their relationship with Christ. He became one of the most powerful personal evangelists of the nineteenth century. ✿ Today is the birthday of Mel Trotter (b. 1870). He was a hopeless alcoholic who staggered into the Pacific Garden Mission of Chicago where he was converted and went on to become a powerful advocate for Union Missions in America.

APPROPRIATE SONGS AND HYMNS

Baptize Me, Dennis Jernigan; © 1992 Shepherd's Heart Music, Inc.; Admin. by Word Music Group, Inc.

Blessed Assurance, Fanny Crosby/Phoebe P. Knapp; Public Domain.

God Is Here, Don Moen/Paul Overstreet; © 1997 Integrity's Hosanna! Music/Scarlet Moon; Admin. by Copyright Management, Inc.

Wind of the Spirit, Handt Hanson/Paul Murakami; © 1991 Changing Church Forum, Inc.

Spirit of the Living God, Daniel Iverson; © 1935. Renewed 1963 Birdwing Music; Admin. by EMI Christian Music Publishing.

WORSHIP HELPS

Call to Worship:
How precious is Your lovingkindness, O God! Therefore the children of men put their trust under the shadow of Your wings. They are abundantly satisfied with the fullness of Your house, and You give them drink from the river of Your pleasures. For with You is the fountain of life; in Your light we see light. (Ps. 36:7–9)

Hymn Story: "The Breastplate of Patrick"
Born in the fourth century in Britain, Patrick was brought up in a Christian home. At age 16, he was seized by pirates, bundled away on a ship, and spirited across the Irish Sea into slavery. For six years, Patrick tended goats among the green hills of Ireland. But there, God awakened Patrick's heart and began planting within him the seeds of an evangelistic burden. He finally escaped his captivity and returned home, but after a period of training, he returned to Ireland with a Bible in his hand where he eventually baptized over 100,000 converts. Patrick left us an autobiographical account of his life, *Patrick's Confessions*. He's also the likely author of this great Celtic hymn that bears his name, though it's impossible to authenticate. One legend claims Patrick wrote this hymn as a prayer for safety while traveling through Druid territory, fearful of an ambush. It says, in part:
Christ be with me, Christ within me,
Christ behind me, Christ before me,
Christ beside me, Christ to win me,
Christ to comfort and restore me.
Christ beneath me, Christ above me,
Christ in quiet, Christ in danger,
Christ in hearts of all that love me,
Christ in mouth of friend and stranger.

Additional Sermons and Lesson Ideas

The Spirit-Filled Soul

Date preached:

By Dr. Denis Lyle

SCRIPTURE: Ephesians 5:18

INTRODUCTION: This is the Bible's most definitive text about being filled with the Holy Spirit. Notice the qualities of a Spirit-filled soul:

1. The Spirit-filled person is joyful. (Eph. 5:19)
2. The Spirit-filled wife is submissive. (v. 22)
3. The Spirit-filled husband is loving. (v. 25)
4. The Spirit-filled children are obedient. (Eph. 6:1)
5. The Spirit-filled father is winsome. (6:4)
6. The Spirit-filled employee is conscientious. (6:5)
7. The Spirit-filled employer is fair. (6:9)

CONCLUSION: Everyday our prayers should include a request for God to fill our hearts with the Holy Spirit.

Hungry?

Date preached:

By T. C. Horton

SCRIPTURE: Matthew 4:4 and John 6

INTRODUCTION: The world today is hungry, starving for the true bread of the soul.

1. Jesus is the bread from heaven (John 6:32). Moses, by God's power, bought daily bread from heaven, but Jesus is the true bread from heaven. He alone can satisfy our hunger.
2. Jesus is the bread of God (John 6:33). He is a heavenly gift who satisfies the longing souls and fills the hungry soul with goodness.
3. Jesus is the bread of life (John 6:35). He answers the world's cry: "Lord, evermore give us this bread."
4. Jesus is the living bread (John 6:51). We must feed on Him!

CONCLUSION: Many believers are not strong. Lord, make us strong through feeding upon Thyself.

MAY 22, 2005

SUGGESTED SERMON *Date preached:*

The Graveyard Shift

Scripture: Psalm 134

Behold, bless the LORD, all you servants of the LORD, who by night stand in the house of the LORD! Lift up your hands in the sanctuary, and bless the LORD. The LORD who made heaven and earth bless you from Zion! (NKJV)

Introduction: Psalm 134 is the last of the famous "Psalms of Ascents," and among the theories behind the compilation of this little psalm-book (Ps. 120—134) is the belief they were collected as a special hymnal for Jewish pilgrims going up to Jerusalem for the annual festivals. These are evidently Pilgrim Psalms. Since we're all pilgrims in the world, these Psalms are meaningful to us. Picture our travelers entering Jerusalem at the end of their journey. It's late in the day, but they want to visit the temple before settling down. Approaching the temple, they see the evening shift of priestly workers arriving to care for the house of God during the night. Filled with excitement, our travelers shout to them: "Behold! Bless the Lord, all you servants of the Lord, who by night stand in the house of the Lord! Lift up your hands in the sanctuary, and bless the Lord." The priests' reply: "The Lord who made heaven and earth bless you from Zion!" This Psalm is in the form of a reciprocal blessing. It's antiphonal. Verses 1 and 2 are an exhortation to the night workers at the temple, and verse 3 is their reply to us.

1. **We Can Apply This Psalm Literally.** We're to bless God through the night. A book published in the 1880s was entitled, *Night Scenes in the Bible.* Have you noticed how often the Lord met people at night when they couldn't sleep? Check it out in the Bible—many people had evening encounters with the Lord. On those nights when we can't sleep, we can either toss and turn in bed, we can get up and watch television, or we can grab our Bibles and say, "Well, Lord, I'm going to spend time with You until You let me get drowsy." Some of our greatest moments with God come when sleep eludes us.
2. **We Can Apply This Psalm Missiologically.** Like Levites on the graveyard shift, many of God's servants are working in darkened areas, away from our view and vision. They're on a spiritual graveyard shift. Some around the globe are literally working for Christ while we're sleeping in

bed. What can they do when darkness nearly overwhelms them, when fatigue grows, when they feel unnoticed and under-appreciated? They can lift up their hands in the sanctuary and bless the Lord. A life that learns to praise can bear the burdens of the night. A life that learns to praise can work through the darkness, shining a light that can never be quenched.

3. **We Can Apply This Psalm Personally.** Sometimes life seems very dark. Psalm 134 says we should praise God at life's darkest moments. We should bless and serve Him during life's graveyard shift. Wesley's great hymn, "O for a Thousand Tongues to Sing," was probably inspired by an earlier hymn entitled, "O That I Had a Thousand Voices," by Johann Mentzer who pastored a church in the village of Kemnitz, Germany. Most of his parishioners were poor serfs whose hard work benefited their wealthy masters. Mentzer's heart went out to his people, toiling in poverty and trouble, and he often counseled them to praise the Lord whatever the circumstances. One evening as Johann returned from a Bible study he grew alarmed at a frightening red glow in the sky. Hurrying onward, he found his own home ablaze. It had been set afire during his absence. As he later inspected the ruins, he was disturbed and downhearted. It was then that a serf reportedly tapped him on the shoulder, saying, "So, Pastor, are you still in the mood for praise and thanksgiving?" Johann offered a silent prayer, and at that moment, his whole attitude changed. It seemed to him that a Christian's praise to God should be louder than the sound of the tongues of flame that had just consumed his home. The next day, he composed this hymn: "O that I had a thousand voices / and with a thousand tongues could tell / of Him in whom the earth rejoices / who does all things wisely and well."

Conclusion: If you can't sleep at night, get up and bless the Lord. If you find yourself working for Christ in a benighted area, learn to praise the Lord in the darkness. If you're facing difficulty right now, try praise and thanksgiving.

STATS, STORIES, AND MORE

Since the invention of the light bulb, American factories have felt it was cost efficient to keep their equipment running all the time, but it isn't easy to work the graveyard shift. Some of you have worked all night, and you've come here this morning without yet going to bed. It isn't easy. The magazine *Business Week* recently carried an interesting story about the graveyard shift. It reported that a new study has discovered that graveyard shift workers make five times as many serious mistakes and are 20 percent more likely to suffer severe accidents than those who work during the day. They are less likely to get regular exercise, and more likely to eat unhealthy foods. All-night workers tend to have heart disorder rates 40 percent higher than those on dayside shifts. The divorce rate is 60 percent, and the study found that maintaining a graveyard shift was actually costing American companies over $200 billion a year in related costs. Psalm 134 is written for the graveyard shift.

O That I Had a Thousand Voices

By Johann Mentzer

O that I had a thousand voices
And with a thousand tongues could tell
Of Him in Whom the earth rejoices
Who all things wisely does and well!
My grateful heart would then be free
To tell what God has done for me.

FOR THE BULLETIN

✽ May 22, 337 marks the death of Constantine the Great, the first Christian Emperor of the Roman Empire. ✽ May 22, 1542: Pope Paul III called the Council of Trent to deal with the Reformation and renewal in the church. ✽ On May 22, 1789, the first American Presbyterian General Assembly convened in Philadelphia. ✽ Today is the birthday (1868) of William R. Newell. When Dr. R. A. Torrey was president of the Moody Bible Institute of Chicago, he received a letter from a distressed father. The man, a pastor, had a prodigal son named William who was breaking his heart. The young prodigal did come to Moody where he caused no end of trouble. But several years later, he himself was a beloved professor at Moody Bible Institute. In 1895, William Newell began putting his testimony into verse form, and the result was "At Calvary," with its opening lines, "Years I spent in vanity and pride ..." ✽ On May 22, 1883, baseball player Billy Sunday, 21, began his major league career with the Chicago White Stockings. He struck out. But he went on to play professional baseball for eight seasons before retiring to become a gospel evangelist who took the message of Christ to millions. He had been converted while in Chicago through the street preaching of Harry Monroe of the Pacific Garden Mission. Sunday's preaching style was bombastic and unconventional, but it's estimated that as many as 300,000 people came to Christ under his ministry.

APPROPRIATE SONGS AND HYMNS

All Creatures of Our God and King, St. Francis of Assisi/William H. Draper; Public Domain.

All Things Are Possible, Darlene Zschech; © 1997 Darlene Zschech (Hillsong); Admin. by Integrity Music, Inc.

Beautiful Savior, Stuart Townend; © 1998 Kingsway's Thankyou Music; Admin. by EMI Christian Music Publishing.

Clap Your Hands, Bill Batstone/Tom Howard; © 1986 Maranatha! Music.

Get All Excited, William J. Gaither/Gloria Gaither; © 1972 William J. Gaither, Inc.; Admin. by Gaither Copyright Management.

WORSHIP HELPS

Call to Worship:
Behold, bless the LORD, all you servants of the LORD!
(Ps. 134:1 NKJV)

Pastoral Prayer:
Lord of day and night, we know that we can never flee from Your presence, for if we ascend up to heaven, You are there. If we make our bed in hell, behold You are there as well. If we take the wings of the morning and dwell in the uttermost parts of the sea, even there Your hand will lead us, and Your right hand shall hold us. Indeed, the darkness shall not hide from You, but the night shines as the day; for day and night are both alike to You. You will not allow our feet to be moved; You who keep us will not slumber. Behold, You who keep us all will never slumber nor sleep. Lord of day and God of night, we rejoice in You this morning; in Jesus' name. Amen.

Suggested Scripture Readings:
Night Scenes in the Bible
Genesis 32:22–32—Jacob wrestles with the angel of the Lord
John 3:1–21—Nicodemus meeting with Jesus by night
Acts 16:16–24—Paul and Silas in the Philippian prison
Daniel 6—Daniel in the lion's den
Exodus 12—The first Passover and the death of the firstborn in Egypt
Judges 7—"The Sword of the Lord and of Gideon"
Matthew 26:36–46—Gethsemane

Benediction:
The LORD who made heaven and earth bless you from Zion—(Ps. 134:3 NKJV)

Additional Sermons and Lesson Ideas

When It Pays to Believe in Jesus Christ

Date preached:

By Dr. R. A. Torrey

SCRIPTURE: Philippians 4:19

INTRODUCTION: This text is a guarantee to the believer to have every need supplied, and that guarantee is good. It pays to believe in Jesus:

1. In Health and Strength. What's the benefit of having strength and health if not to serve the Lord?
2. In Sickness. Faith in Christ promotes restoration to health, and it brings joy and blessing in the midst of illness.
3. In Sorrow. Jesus heals our hurts and heartaches.
4. In Adversity. Romans 5:3, 4.
5. In Prosperity. Success will eternally ruin anyone who is not stayed on Christ.
6. In Death. Philippians 1:23 and 2 Timothy 4:6–8.
7. In Judgment. Romans 14:12
8. In Eternity. John 3:36

CONCLUSION: Our God will supply all your needs all the time when you're in Christ and Christ is in you.

Ordinary Greatness

Date preached:

By Rev. Kevin Riggs

SCRIPTURE: Matthew 4:18–20 & 10:1–4

INTRODUCTION: How many of us have forgotten how unique we are? Have you concluded you are common, everyday, and ordinary? Can God use ordinary people? Jesus was no ordinary person, but He did change the world through twelve ordinary men. The only thing remarkable about them was their ordinariness.

God looks for ordinary people He can use in extraordinary ways.

1. In order to be the best you can be, give your best to Jesus Christ.
2. It's not what you are but what you can become that matters.
3. Jesus looks for originals not copies.
4. A changed life is the greatest of all miracles.

CONCLUSION: God is looking for people just like you and me. We just have to leave our nets and follow Jesus.

MISSIONS SERMON

I'll Shout It From the Mountaintop

Date preached:

Scripture: Mathew 28:18–20

Introduction: A British writer named Derek Ratcliffe recently analyzed our television viewing habits. He spoke of "the mindless, shallow hedonism that seems to be the way our society is heading: a restless search for instant gratifications, trivial and ephemeral pleasures that leave no lasting satisfaction, let alone fulfillment." He described today's entertainment as "a decadent media culture of soap operas, docusoaps, quiz games, police action, cooking shows, home makeovers ... football, pornography, and other expressions of the current intellectual and aesthetic development of modern western society." Most of us want something more in life than what we see on television. We want to make a difference. We want to make a mark on our empty, mindless age. We want a cause bigger, purer, and nobler than we are. We want to change the world and to impact eternity. In the words of a popular book, we want to live a purpose-driven life. There's only one way to do this. We've got to rediscover the Great Commission. Everyone who is committed to Jesus Christ is by logical extension connected to His great purpose. In fact, perhaps the only reason He is leaving us on this planet is because we have a part in fulfilling His worldwide plan (Phil. 1:21–24). So let's look again at this familiar passage at the end of Matthew's Gospel, our Lord's final instructions to His church.

There are three aspects to Christ's words:

1. **The Authority Behind Us.** Jesus began the Great Commission by telling us that all authority had been given to Him. The implication is that we will be going, working, preaching, sharing, and ministering in the power of His name. Later, Jesus explained that this power is conveyed to us by means of the Holy Spirit (Acts 1:8). It's highly motivational to read through the Book of Acts and the Epistles, looking for the 95 occurrences of the word "power." Here's some of what you'll find:

> By what power or by what name have you done this? By the name of Jesus Christ of Nazareth. And with great power the apostles gave witness

> to the resurrection of the Lord Jesus. And great grace was upon them all. For I am not ashamed of the gospel of Christ, for it is the power of God to salvation for everyone who believes. My speech and my preaching were not with persuasive words of human wisdom, but in demonstration of the Spirit and of power. For our gospel did not come to you in word only, but also in power, and in the Holy Spirit and in much assurance. Therefore, most gladly I will rather boast in my infirmities, that the power of Christ may rest upon me.
>
> Christ, the power of God, and the wisdom of God. For the message of the cross is foolishness to those who are perishing, but to us who are being saved it is the power of God. For the word of God is living and powerful, and sharper than any two-edged sword, piercing even to the division of soul and spirit, and of joints and marrow, and is a discerner of the thoughts and intents of the heart.
>
> Finally, my brethren, be strong in the Lord and in the power of His might. For God has not given us a spirit of fear, but of power and of love and of a sound mind, according to the power that works in us. (Acts 4:7; Acts 4:10; Acts 4:33; Rom. 1:16; 1 Cor. 2:4; 1 Thess. 1:5; 2 Cor. 12:9; 1 Cor. 1:24: 1 Cor. 1:18; Heb. 4:12; Eph. 6:10; 1 Tim. 1:7; Eph. 3:2).

What does this mean to us? It means that as we work for Christ, as we lead prayer meetings and teach Bible classes, as we go as missionaries and send out others, as we sing and win souls and serve Him, we must do so prayerfully. We can't accomplish the task by the force of our own passion or personalities. We must do it in the name of the One to whom all power was given—Jesus Christ.

Sometimes this power comes like a bolt from the sky as it did for Elijah on Mt. Carmel. Other times, it's like the power of a seed. It slowly germinates and sends up a shoot that, though frail, breaks concrete. But whenever we labor for our Master, we are doing so under His authority and with His power.

2. **The Task Before Us.** Armed with that power, then, we go into all the world preaching, baptizing, teaching, and discipling. It's particularly encouraging to see how the gospel is spreading in our own day. Fifty percent of today's Christians and 70% of today's evangelicals now live in the Southern Hemisphere, and the church is exploding in growth in Latin America and Sub-Saharan Africa. South America is the largest continent of Christians, and Africa has the fastest growing church. In parts of Asia, there is tremendous growth in evangelism and missions. Meanwhile, Christianity in Europe and America is declining. These shifts have been taking place with accelerating speed since World War II, and by the mid-1980s the number of Christians in the non-Western world had outstripped those in the West.

Two billion people in the world now identify themselves as Christians, but nearly a billion (918 million) people worldwide profess to have no faith at all—to be nonreligious or atheistic. There are over a billion (1.2 billion) Muslims. The missionary task has never been more important, and I believe that one of the ways to revitalize our church here and churches throughout the Western World is missions—we've got to be revived in our evangelistic burden for the world. The keystone of church revival is missions. We must especially be burdened for the countries with the largest populations of non-Christians. Those countries are, in order: China, India, Pakistan, Indonesia, Bangladesh, Iran, Japan, Turkey, Vietnam, and Nigeria. We have our work cut out for us. We've got to love as Christ loves, preach as He preached, and go where He is going. He is going to the ends of the earth.[1]

3. **The Presence Beside Us.** Jesus ended His Great Commission by promising that He would be with us always, to the very end of the age. J. Sidlow Baxter suggested an interesting truth about this promise. He noticed that the Lord, following His Resurrection, kept appearing and disappearing, sometimes at surprising moments, during the forty days prior to His Ascension. Baxter suggested that Christ was weaning the disciples from depending on His physical presence, and teaching them to depend on His spiritual presence. Even when they could not see Him, He was there in their midst. This promise in Matthew 28:20 has strengthened many a missionary during times of intense loneliness. This verse kept David Livingstone from virtual insanity. He said he could depend on it as the "word of a Perfect Gentleman." Whether we go to the nations or to our neighbors, Jesus is there, beside us, near us, within us, around us.

Conclusion: Those who grew up in the 1970s probably remember the classic Christian folksong "Pass it On." It was very popular among student groups who were experiencing a wave of revival during The Jesus Movement. The final words expressed a passion that we must never lose:

I'll shout it from the mountaintop;
I want my world to know—
The Lord of love has come to me.
I want to pass it on.

---

1 The statistics in this message are gleaned from the excellent book, *Exploring World Mission: Context & Challenge* by Bryant L. Myers (Monrovia, CA: World Vision International, 2003).

HEROES FOR THE PASTOR'S HEART

Ebenezer Erskine

Among the lesser-known heroes of the church is a man with the unlikely name of Ebenezer Erskine (1680–1754), founder of the Scottish Secession Church. He was born in a Scottish village called Dryburgh, the son of Rev. Henry Erskine, who was among the pastors ejected from their pulpits in 1662 due to their nonconformity.

When Ebenezer was only ten, his father taught him the Shorter Catechism. The forty-third question of the Catechism asks: "What is the preface to the Ten Commandments?" The answer: "The preface to the Ten Commandments is: 'I am the Lord thy God which have brought thee out of the Land of Egypt.'"

Young Ebenezer learned the whole Catechism, but this question took central place in his thoughts.

Eighteen years later and now married, Ebenezer followed his father's footsteps into the pastorate. "But I began my ministry without much zeal, mechanically, being swallowed up in unbelief," he wrote. His ministry was unsatisfying to him, boring to his congregation, and a heavy burden on his godly, praying wife.

One-day Ebenezer's wife grew fevered, and in her delirium, she cried out about her husband's cold heart. Ebenezer, sitting by her, was pierced, and the old text came back to him: "I am the Lord your God." Shortly after, he offered himself up in full surrender, praying, "Soul and body, unto God the Father, Son, and Holy Ghost. I flee for shelter to the blood of Jesus. I will live to Him; I will die to Him."

His ministry took on new life, resulting in changed lives all around.

Ten years later, now a 38-year-old pastor, Ebenezer preached a powerful sermon on his old text: "I am the Lord thy God." It made a lasting impression on his congregation and swept over Scotland in printed form. Ebenezer's sermons became so powerful that he frequently had to dismiss his church out-of-doors because the building wouldn't contain all the worshipers. He lived a long and fruitful life, giving out at age 73.

One of his elders, visiting his bedside, said, "You have often given us good advice, Mr. Erskine, as to what we should do with our souls in death; may I ask what you are now doing with your own?"

"I am doing what I did forty years ago," replied the old preacher. "I am resting on that word, 'I am the Lord thy God.'"

MAY 29, 2005

SUGGESTED SERMON *Date preached:*

Help, We're Surrounded

By Dr. Denis Lyle

Scripture: 2 Kings 6:8–23, especially verse 16
Do not fear, for those who are with us are more than those who are with them. (NKJV)

Introduction: We believers should be like those old whistling kettles: still singing when we are up to our necks in hot water! Elisha and his servant, in our text today, seemed to be in hot water. His servant boiled under the pressure, saying in effect, "Help, we're surrounded!" Elisha, however teaches us how to react when we are surrounded.

1. **A Force to be Discerned.** The Syrian King Ben-hadad (Naaman's monarch, see 6:24) had proved a constant irritant to Israel. Frequent border raids were mounted on Jordan's territory in Northern Israel. From 5:18 we know that Ben-hadad regularly worshiped at the temple of Rimmon, the Syrian god of war. There's an old maxim that says we become like the gods we worship. We come to resemble what we most worship, as the power-hungry, war-driven King of Syria illustrates. The motive behind these acts of aggressive piracy was a diabolical lust for power over the people of God, and therefore over God! We can hear it in the Syrian king's words: "My camp will be in such and such a place" (6:8). We, like Elisha, must discern three things:

   A. **The Hostility of the Enemy.** Remember that the King of Syria was done a great service when Elisha healed Naaman (5:1–16), but the king rendered evil for good. We, too, are called to a great battlefield, to be aware of a war with an enemy who doesn't play fair.

   B. **The Strategy of the Enemy.** Ben-hadad avoided open attack. His plan was to set ambushes in unexpected places, cutting off his enemy by stratagems and wiles (6:8). Israel had a special "intelligent unit" in the person of Elisha, who was given supernatural "intelligence" concerning enemy positions and enemy maneuvers. Similarly, Paul says that believers "... are not ignorant of (Satan's) devices" (2 Cor. 2:11).

   C. **The Tendency of the Enemy.** Satan's aim and objective is to attack key people: people who are getting in Satan's way, people who are winning souls, people who are Spirit-filled, leaders who have influence (see Acts 12:1). Ben-hadad quickly realized that to subdue the nation he needed to silence the prophet! Did you know spiritually effective people have a reputation in hell? Jesus and Paul prove this principle (Luke 4:33, 34; Acts 19:15). With such an enemy there is also:

2. **A Fear that Is to Be Dispelled.** When we face a crisis, we have two choices. We can react as Elisha did in perfect calm, or we can choose the response of his servant and panic. The longer you gaze on a difficulty, the bigger it appears unless God enables you to see through it (v. 17). Fear is meditation on the lies of Satan; faith is meditating on the promises of God. The greatness of our fears shows us the weakness of our faith. Notice in our text:

   A. **The Cause of This Fear.** Facing the ranks of the enemy, this young servant was at a complete loss as to the way out. His imagination conjured up the worst and he cried out in panic (6:15). Is this not so like us in the hour of trial? Faced with the forces of evil or temptation we often cry out, "What shall we do?" Do you focus on your insecurities, your weaknesses, or your faults rather than the strength and power of God?

   B. **The Cure for This Fear.** Being around Elisha must have been like going to a plastic surgeon: you would walk away with a "faith lift." Elisha was totally undisturbed about the enemy and calmly replied, "Do not fear, for those who are with us are more than those who are with them" (6:16). Elisha had God's Word to sustain him and guardian angels to surround him (v. 16). How then did this end for Elisha?

3. **A Favor to Be Displayed.** The first time Elisha prayed, the eyes of his servant were opened, the second time Elisha prayed, the eyes of his enemies were blinded (6:18)! The man they had come to capture led them right into Jehoram's barracks and the clutches of the Israelite army (v. 20). Understandably, King Jehoram wanted to butcher the elite of Syria's military forces, but instead of force, there was favor and the Syrians returned home an impressed people! Elisha showed grace to the enemies (see Prov. 25:21; Ex. 23:4, 5; Matt. 5:44).

Conclusion: Elisha's servant said in effect "Help, we're surrounded." Do you feel like that? Are there pressures upon you, people against you, or problems before you? God is watching over you and saying to you, "Fear not."

STATS, STORIES, AND MORE

More from Dr. Denis Lyle

Guardian Angels

In June 1920, the people of Shansi, China were warned that bandits were coming. Villagers quickly made what preparation they could. A missionary within the village was responsible for a mission school for about forty girls. How was she going to protect them from these lawless men? She called all the girls together into the classroom, explained their danger, and calmly asked them all to kneel as she committed them into the care of the Lord. Well, the bandits did come that night and it seemed as if all hell had broken loose in that village. There was death, theft, girls carried away in the darkness by the bandits, but not one had attempted to enter the mission compound. The next morning, that missionary went out into the village to give what whatever help she could. She said, "The Lord in His mercy spared us and our school of girls." "No wonder," the villagers replied, "you see on the corners of your compound walls, standing on guard, we saw four angels with drawn swords in their hands."

Someone once said:

A good general must penetrate the brain of his enemy. —Victor Hugo
If you know yourself and your adversary clearly, then in a hundred battles you will win a hundred times. —Chinese proverb

FOR THE BULLETIN

✽ Hans Luther, the father of Reformer Martin Luther, died on this day in 1530. ✽ In the face of the mushrooming Reformation Movement in Germany, Pope Paul III called a counsel to begin May 12, 1538. The counsel sputtered at first, but finally got down to business in the city of Trent. The Counsel of Trent became a great force in the Roman Catholic Counter-Reformation. ✽ May 29, 1546, The Scottish Reformation had its violent beginning on this day with the assassination of Cardinal David Beaton, cruel foe of the fledging Reformers. He was shot and killed in St. Andrews in retaliation for the execution of Reformation preacher George Wishart. ✽ On May 29, 1765, American Patriot Patrick Henry reacted to the British Stamp Act with a powerful speech during which the cry of "Treason!" was raised against him. His famous reply: "If this be treason, make the most of it!" ✽ Reginald Heber wrote the missionary hymn, "From Greenland's Icy Mountains," on May 29, 1819. ✽ Today is the birthday (1874) of G. K. Chesterton. He was a huge man (400 pounds) with a huge mind and with enormous creativity. He converted to Roman Catholicism from the Church of England, and is chiefly remembered for his essays and poems, and for his fictional detective, Father Brown.

APPROPRIATE SONGS AND HYMNS

We Trust in the Name of the Lord Our God, Stephen Curtis Chapman; © 1994 Sparrow Song/Peach Hill Songs; Admin. by EMI Christian Music Publishing.

Put All Your Trust in Jesus Today, Carol Cymbala/Jim Hammerly; © 1992 Word Music, Inc./Carol Joy Music; Admin. by Integrated Copyright Group, Inc.

My Life Is in Your Hands, Kirk Franklin; © 1996 Lilly Mack Music.

The Rock that Is Higher than I, Erastus Johnson/William Gustavus Fischer; Public Domain.

Trusting Jesus, Edgar Page Stites/Ira D. Sankey; Public Domain.

WORSHIP HELPS

Call to Worship:
O come and sing to the God, the Lord,
To Him our voices raise;
Let us in our most joyful songs
The Lord, our Savior, praise.
(From the 1912 Psalter, Psalm 95)

Offertory Comments:
The reformer Martin Luther could be remarkably blunt. "You ungrateful beasts!" he once said to parishioners who were not giving to the church. "You're not worthy of the treasures of the gospel. If you don't improve, I will stop preaching rather than cast pearls before swine!" Well, a statement like that wouldn't go over very well today, even if it were true. For my part, I just want to continue to encourage us to express our love toward Jesus our Savior by rendering to Him our tithes and offerings, week by week, as a token of our submission to His Lordship. May God bless us as we give today.

Reader's Theater or Responsive Reading:

Reader 1:	To which of the angels did God ever say:
Reader 2:	"You are my Son. Today I have begotten You"?
Reader 1:	And again:
Reader 2:	"I will be to Him a Father, and He shall be to Me a Son"?
Reader 1:	But when He again brings the firstborn into the world, He says:
Reader 2:	"Let all the angels of God worship Him."
Both Readers:	Your throne, O God, is forever and ever; a scepter of righteousness is the scepter of Your kingdom.
Reader 1:	To which of the angels has He ever said:
Reader 2:	"Sit at My right hand, till I make Your enemies Your footstool"?
Both Readers:	Are they not all ministering spirits sent forth to minister for those who will inherit salvation?

(Heb. 1 NKJV)

Additional Sermons and Lesson Ideas

The Worldly Christian

Date preached:

Adapted from a sermon by Dr. F. B. Meyer

SCRIPTURE: 1 Corinthians 3:1–4

INTRODUCTION: The carnal person is a Christian who is a babe in Christ. Instead of Christ being predominant, the carnal element is predominant. This person has four characteristics:

1. The Carnal Life Is a Babe Life (v. 1).
2. The Carnal Life Lives on Milk Not Meat (v. 2).
3. The Carnal Life Is Sectarian (vv. 3, 4).
4. The Carnal Life Is Unable to Discern Good and Evil (see Heb. 5:14).

CONCLUSION: May God help us to reverse this, so that the carnal element is crowded out, and the Christ element becomes predominant.

The Gospel According to You

Date preached:

By Dr. David Jeremiah

SCRIPTURE: 1 Thessalonians 2:1–12

INTRODUCTION: This passage gives us lessons about ministering to others, a subject on which Paul the apostle was an expert.

1. We Must Be Courageous as Good Soldiers (vv. 1, 2). Paul was bold in his presentation of the gospel.
2. We Must Be Conscientious as Stewards (vv. 3–5). God has given us a sacred stewardship of the gospel, and we can never take our responsibility lightly. The gospel must be presented courageously, clearly, and convincingly.
3. We Must Be Cautious as Gracious Servants (v. 6). Notice what this verse says about the desire, duty, and delight of a servant.
4. We Must Be Comforting as a Godly Mother (vv. 7, 8).
5. We Must Be Careful as a Good Example (vv. 9, 10).
6. We Must Be Concerned as a Father (vv. 11, 12).

CONCLUSION: Our goal is to bring people to a place where they walk in a godly lifestyle. That isn't just the responsibility of pulpit and preacher; it's the responsibly of us all.

JUNE 5, 2005

SUGGESTED SERMON *Date preached:*

The Danger of Discounting Doctrine

By Dr. Melvin Worthington

Scripture: Revelation 2:12–17, especially verse 14
But I have a few things against you, because you have there those who hold the doctrine of Balaam. (NKJV)

Introduction: Why do we emphasize doctrine in an age in which it's disdained? Why do we hold tightly to our beliefs in a day in which everyone believes what they want? Revelation 2:11–17, the Lord's message to the church at Pergamos, deals with the danger of doctrinal compromise. This church was indifferent to subtle influences that corrupted its teachers and endangered the spiritual life of its membership.

1. **The Designation of Christ (v. 12).** The "angel" probably refers to the pastor or bishop of the church. The church in Pergamos was established early since it is one of the seven churches addressed by Christ. Antipas was martyred there, the first Christian put to death by the Roman state. Revelation 2 mentions Pergamos as the place "where Satan's throne is," probably referring to the temples in which the Roman emperors worshiped. This city was located in Mysia, an ancient province of Asia, in the Caicus valley. The city had a great library and four beautiful temples representing the gods Zeus, Dionysus, Athena, and Asklepios. In addressing this letter, Christ describes Himself as having a two-edged sword. The sword, a symbol of judgment, denotes the Lord's vengeance on the guilty world. To those who refuse to own His absolute authority, the sword must do its sure work in the execution of judgment.

2. **The Discernment of Christ (v. 13).** Jesus declares that He knows their works. Jesus knows where they live. He commends them for holding fast His name and their refusal to deny their faith in spite of the martyrdom of Antipas. Christ knows our temptations and takes into consideration our circumstances. The church is commended for holding fast His name in spite of its circumstances. They were not ashamed of their relationship to Christ.

3. **The Denunciation of Christ (vv.14, 15).** This church, however, tolerated the Nicolaitan sect and those who held the doctrine of Balaam. Although the Savior could approve their general course, He could not approve their toleration of these who held to a pernicious error that sapped the very foundation of morals. The church was indifferent to subtle inward influence that corrupted its teachers and endangered the spiritual life of its congregation. It was a church with devotion and yet lax in dealing with doctrinal error. The false teachers taught the same doctrine as Balaam and, therefore, deserved to be classed with him. The doctrine of Balaam permitted heathen religious rituals, which led to the doctrine of the Nicolaitans that sanctioned immoral practices. The essence of Balaamism is worldliness. It is a grave mistake for the church to make a union with the world. Satan seeks to nullify the power of the church by mixing Christianity with worldliness. Some churches today are seducing their members away from Christ by providing worldly amusements unworthy of Christ. The church must preach and practice sound doctrine. Doctrinal distortion, dilution, and defection lead to disaster.

4. **The Directive of Christ (v. 16).** Christ issued a sharp command to repent. Unless the church repents, judgment will be swift and decisive. In spite of their faithfulness, the evil character of those things that were tolerated in the church was so serious to the mind of Christ that He would judge the church with the sword of His mouth. The impending judgment, unless they repented, was designed for their edification and salvation. The church was condemned for its laxity. While all in the church did not practice the deeds or adhere to the deeds condemned by Christ, the church tolerated them in the assembly. The pastor of this church had not practiced or imbibed the reprobate deeds, but neither had he denounced them nor opposed their entrance into the church.

5. **The Disclosure of Christ (v. 17).** Christ admonished the church to hear, heed, hold, and honor the Spirit's words. He assured the church that overcomers would be given hidden manna to eat and a white stone with a new name written on it which no man would know without receiving it.

Conclusion: Doctrinal defection is a real danger for the church today. Every church must maintain doctrinal purity. The message to the church at Pergamos is valid for the church today. Diligence, discernment, and discipline are necessary to maintain doctrinal purity, for we are commanded to contend earnestly for the faith that has been once for all delivered to the saints (Jude 3)

STATS, STORIES, AND MORE

Research by George Barna:

Almost half of born again Christians (45%) agree that Satan is "not a living being but is a symbol of evil." (2001)

About one-third of born again Christians (34%) believe that if a person is good enough they can earn a place in heaven. (2001)

Fifteen percent of born again Christians claim that "after He was crucified and died, Jesus Christ did not return to life physically." (2000)

About one out of four (26%) born again Christians believe that it doesn't matter what faith you follow because they all teach the same lessons; a belief held by 56% of non-Christians. (2000)

Someone Once Said:

The chief need of the present age is great theology. —Dr. Loraine Boettner

Great saints have always been dogmatic. —A. W. Tozer

There can be no spiritual health without doctrinal knowledge. —J. I. Packer

We cannot have the benefits of Christianity if we shed its doctrines.
—D. Martyn Lloyd-Jones

The time will come when they will not endure sound doctrine. —2 Timothy 4:3

Doctrinal Maps:

In *Mere Christianity*, C. S. Lewis says that doctrines are like maps. They are not the reality and may not be as exciting as reality, but they chart reality for us in a vital way. Just as studying a map of the shore of the Atlantic is not as exciting as walking along the Atlantic coast itself, so studying the doctrine of Atonement is not exactly the same as the experiencing the Cross itself. But the purpose of a map is to represent, graph, and explain the reality. If you want to find your way, you need to have a reliable map and consult it frequently.

FOR THE BULLETIN

✽ On June 5, A.D. 404, the great preacher, John Chrysostom of Antioch, was deposed and exiled. An ancient biography states, "Chrysostom received it with calm submission, and after a final prayer in the cathedral with some of his faithful bishops ... he surrendered himself to the guards and was conveyed at night to the Asiatic shore. He had scarcely left the city, when the cathedral was consumed by fire." ✽ Boniface, the apostle to the Germans and perhaps the greatest missionary of the Dark Ages, was slain on this day in 754. Boniface was an Englishman, born in A.D. 680. He entered a monastery and at age 30 was ordained. He felt a strong missionary call, and in 718 traveled to Germany where he traveled from village to village, smashing idols, destroying temples, and preaching the gospel. On June 5, 755, a band of hostile pagans fell upon him as he camped by the River Borne. He was slain while clutching the Bible in his hand. ✽ June 5, 988, is the traditional date for the conversion of Russia to Christianity under Grand Prince Vladimir who personally oversaw the baptism of the majority of the population of Kiev, the capital of his realm. ✽ On June 5, 1414, the Bohemian reformer John Huss appeared before the Council of Constance. He was condemned and burned the next month. ✽ June 5, 1955 marks the founding of L'Abri Fellowship in Switzerland by Francis and Edith Schaeffer.

APPROPRIATE SONGS AND HYMNS

I Could Sing of Your Love Forever, Martin Smith; © 1994 Curious? Music UK; Admin. by EMI Christian Music Publishing.

Redeemed, James Rowe/S.A. Ganus; Public Domain.

We Believe, Todd Warren; © 1997 Doulos Publishing; Admin. by Maranatha! Music.

Your Ways Are Right, Dan Adler; © 1997 Heart of the City Music.

How Firm a Foundation, George Keith/Anne Steele/John Rippon/Joseph Funk; Public Domain.

WORSHIP HELPS

Call to Worship:
Oh, the depth of the riches both of the wisdom and knowledge of God! How unsearchable are His judgments and His ways past finding out! (Rom. 11:33 NKJV)

Scripture Reading Medley:
As I urged you when I went into Macedonia—remain in Ephesus that you may charge some that they teach no other doctrine, nor ... any other thing that is contrary to sound doctrine according to the glorious gospel ... the doctrine which accords with godliness. For the time will come when they will not endure sound doctrine, but according to their own desires, because they have itching ears, they will heap up for themselves teachers; and they will turn their ears away from the truth, and be turned aside to fables. The Spirit expressly says that in the latter times some will depart from the faith, giving heed to deceiving spirits and doctrines of demons, speaking lies in hypocrisy, having their own conscience seared with a hot iron ... Reject profane and old wives' fables, and exercise yourself toward godliness. All Scripture is given by inspiration of God, and is profitable for doctrine, for reproof, for correction, for instruction in righteousness, that the man of God may be complete, thoroughly equipped for every good work. (1 Tim. 1:3, 10, 11; 6:3; 2 Tim. 4:3, 4; 1 Tim. 4:1, 2, 7; 2 Tim. 3:16, 17 NKJV)

Benediction:
Lord, in Your truth we go forth. With Your gospel, we leave this place. With Your blessings, we bid one another farewell. May God be with us till we meet again. Amen.

Additional Sermons and Lesson Ideas

How in the World Will the World Know You're a Disciple?

Date preached:

SCRIPTURE: Selected verses from John's Gospel

INTRODUCTION: The world isn't going to be changed by our average style of Christianity. It is going to be changed by the presence of true disciples of our Lord. John Wesley wrote, "If I had 300 men who feared nothing but God, hated nothing but sin, and determined to know nothing among men but Christ, and Him crucified, I would set the world on fire." Jesus defined discipleship in three ways in the Gospel of John.

1. A Disciple Is Someone Who Continues in the Word—John 8:31
2. A Disciple Is Someone Who Demonstrates Christ's Love—John 13:35
3. A Disciple Is Someone Who Bears Much Fruit—John 15:8

CONCLUSION: Vance Havner once said, "Our Lord never put discipleship in fine print in the contract. He called on us to forsake all, take up our cross, deny self, and love him more than anything else. We are not our own, we are bought with a price, we are the personal property of Jesus Christ with no right to anything. Love so amazing, so divine, demands my soul, my life, my all."

Sing Praise!

Date preached:

SCRIPTURE: Psalm 108:1–4

INTRODUCTION: You don't need a beautiful voice to sing praise to God; you only need a melody in your heart.

1. Sing Praise to the Master (v. 1)
2. Sing Praise in the Morning (v. 2)
3. Sing Praise Among the Masses (v. 3)

CONCLUSION: Why? Because His mercy is great above the heavens and His truth reaches to the clouds.

THOUGHTS FOR THE PASTOR'S SOUL

"Pastor, We're Leaving the Church"

Another family left our church today. They called and asked if they could stop by for a moment, and I agreed despite back-to-back responsibilities and a half-finished sermon. For a solid hour, I listened as they bashed our church, listing all the things they were unhappy about—the clothing the teens wore, inadequate follow-up of Sunday school absentees, a perceived snub from another member, a children's event that they felt was too wild.

I tried to explain that churches aren't perfect places. "Not everyone is equally mature," I said. "Some who attend here aren't even Christians. We're trying to win them, but a church is made up of a wide variety of people from all sorts of backgrounds with all kinds of personalities. There will always be problems. We have to stay committed to each other, loving each other, even putting up with one another. We can't bail out whenever things don't go our way."

They were unimpressed, and I finally said a little too bluntly, "Well, do what you want. There are 750 other churches in this city for you to choose from."

During the 25 years I've been at my church, we've lost a lot of members. Fortunately we've gained considerably more than we've lost, but we'd be a mega-church now if it weren't for those who left. I've often wished I could keep everyone—and that I could keep them *gruntled*. But it isn't possible; through the years I've had to deal with my share of *dis*gruntled souls.

Every church faces this, and no pastor is exempt. In our highly mobile society, people move around a lot; and with a consumer-oriented generation that eschews loyalty and demands quality, we're going to lose some along the way. We're ministering to a generation of church-hoppers. Here are some things to remember as you try to cope with it:

1. Some losses are gains. God not only gives us wonderful additions, but blessed subtractions. Just as a fruit tree needs occasional pruning, God prunes His church. Those who are leaving may represent a blockage in the spiritual life of the congregation, and their removal will allow God to work in newer, fresher ways.

2. We can use departures as occasions for improvement. People often leave in search of a ministry that better meets their needs. We

can learn and improve from the loss. In the early days of my pastorate, a leading family left because we didn't have a strong youth program for their teen. Frankly, I couldn't blame them. Their troubled teen clearly needed more than we could provide. But I used the occasion to explain to church leaders why we needed to hire a Youth Pastor. "If we don't provide for our teens, we're going to keep losing families," I said. It worked, and within a year we had a staff member in place.

3. When families leave, ask God to keep you from taking it too personally. As objectively as possible, think through the reasons for their departure. The loss of one family may prompt changes that will keep others from leaving later.

4. Ask God to send two people for every one who leaves. "Lord, You know that Tyrone is leaving, and he's been a leader in our singles ministry. Please send us two people to take his place." Through the years this has been my practice, and the Lord has honored this prayer.

5. Don't succumb to discouragement. Jesus once preached a sermon that cost Him most of His congregation, but He knew how to persevere. In the end, our Lord had provided redemption for the whole world. Every church is going to lose people, but cast out self-pity. Persevere. Learn from the departures and determine to work harder than ever to build a magnetic ministry.

6. Remember that it's not your church. God has the right to move His people wherever He desires, and our job is just to be faithful. Blessed are those who don't complain about the way He does His business.

No one understands how hard it is to be a pastor. When families or individuals leave, it feels like having a tooth pulled without anesthetic. If this happens to you—and especially if the dear, departing saint gives you all the reasons for the exit—you might need to take a day off, play a round of golf, or plan your summer vacation.

You might also take a moment to pray for the poor pastor down the street who inherits your problems.

JUNE 12, 2005

SUGGESTED SERMON *Date preached:*

Anchors During Adversity

By Dr. Timothy Beougher

Scripture: Romans 5:1–11, especially verse 1

Therefore, having been justified by faith, we have peace with God through our Lord Jesus Christ. (NKJV)

Introduction: We are all familiar with storms such as hurricanes, tornadoes, thunderstorms, and floods. These are symbolic of other types of storms we face in life: physical storms, emotional storms, spiritual storms, financial storms, and family storms. We all face storms in life. Boats have anchors to keep them steady during storms. God has given us spiritual anchors, truths that can help us to remain steady during the storms of life we face.

1. **Realizing Our Present Position (vv. 1–2a).** This verse begins with *therefore,* which points us back to the preceding four chapters. In Romans 1—4, we have seen the reality of human sin and depravity, and the atoning work of Christ on the Cross for sinners. In Romans 5:1, Paul then reflects on our present position. What is our present position? Those justified through faith have:

   A. **Acceptance by God.** Paul tells us we have peace with God; what a concept! Chapters 1—4 make clear that God is not at peace with sinners, but is at war with them. The word Paul uses repeatedly is *wrath* (see Rom. 1:18). He then tells how Jesus has satisfied God's wrath against sin, taking our place and our punishment on the Cross.

   B. **Access to God (v. 2a).** We have the privilege of entering God's presence at any time (cf. Heb. 10:19, 22). We can approach Him by grace. Before our justification, we stood before God as condemned criminals; now we can stand before Him as sons and daughters!

2. **Reflecting on Our Future Hope (v. 2b).** The word *rejoice* does not indicate half-hearted smiles but a sense of jubilation. The word *hope* is not like our English word which conveys something uncertain; biblically, *hope* means that something that has not happened yet but will certainly come to pass and is reason for praise and thanksgiving. An equivalent English word is

confidence. We have hope and confidence in the glory of God (cf. Rom. 8:18).

3. **Recognizing God's Purposes (vv. 3, 4).** How many of you like to suffer? How many of you wish you could suffer more? None of us likes to suffer. An anchor during adversity is the recognition of God's purpose. These verses refer to the knowledge we have during adversity. What knowledge? It is the knowledge that all things work together for our good (Rom. 8:28). But how can this be? God doesn't always tell us but in Romans 5:3–5, God does give us at least a glimpse into one part of the answer. This passage doesn't attempt to explain everything we might want to know about suffering, but it does highlight the fact that sufferings work together to promote spiritual growth. A little poem beautifully illustrates this principle:

> *I walked a mile with pleasure, she chatted all the way*
> *But left me none the wiser, with all she had to say.*
> *I walked a mile with sorrow, and never a word said she,*
> *But, oh, the things I learned from her, when sorrow walked with me.*

Can we really have confidence in God through the worst of suffering? Verse 5 tells us, "Hope does not disappoint, because the love of God has been poured out in our hearts by the Holy Spirit who was given to us."

4. **Recalling God's Amazing Love (vv. 6–8).** We might be willing to die for a friend or family member, but for an enemy? Are you kidding? Humans without Christ are described as without strength, ungodly, sinners, and enemies (vv. 6, 8, 10). God's love was not motivated by anything in us. Because this love is unmerited and is not dependent on us, it will never change! God's love is the permanent possession of the child of God.

5. **Rejoicing in God's Person (vv. 9, 10).** Salvation involves justification: we have been saved from the penalty of sin. It involves sanctification: we are being saved from the power of sin. It involves glorification: we will be saved from the presence of sin. God has already pronounced His verdict!

Conclusion: All our anchors during adversity revolve around the truth given to us in verse 11: We can rejoice in the reconciled relationship we have with God through Jesus Christ. The storms of life are going to come. When they do, we can turn to the spiritual anchors that God has provided for us.

STATS, STORIES, AND MORE

More from Dr. Timothy Beougher:

God accomplishes certain things in our lives through suffering that He could not accomplish any other way!

God's love is unconditional. It's also invincible.

A Christian who was suffering under Communists once said, "We are like nails: the harder you hit us the deeper you drive us."

We have an anchor that keeps the soul / Steadfast and sure while the billows roll. / Fastened to the Rock which cannot move, / Grounded firm and deep in the Savior's love. —Priscilla Owens

These Strange Anchors

The late Dr. Thomas Lambie, missionary to Ethiopia, had to ford many streams and rivers during his years in Africa. The danger in swollen waters was great, for one can easily be swept off one's feet and carried down the stream to greater depths or hurled to death against hidden rocks. Dr. Lambie learned from the nationals the best way to make such a hazardous crossing. A local person would find a large stone, the heavier the better, lift it onto his shoulder, and carry it across the stream as "ballast." The extra weight of the stone kept his feet solid on the bed of the stream allowing him to cross safely without being swept away. Dr. Lambie said, "While crossing the dangerous stream of life, enemies constantly seek to overthrow us and rush us down to ruin. We need the ballast of burden bearing, a load of affliction, to keep us from being swept off our feet."

FOR THE BULLETIN

✽ This is the traditional date for the commemoration of Justin Martyr. ✽ On June 12, 1458, the College of Saint Mary Magdalene was founded at Oxford University in England. ✽ On June 12, 1833, George Muller of Bristol, England, took the first steps down a path that would lead to the establishing of world-famed orphanages in England. It occurred to him on that day to gather hungry children from the streets and give them breakfast, then to teach them to read by reading to them the Scriptures. He had about thirty children to begin with. In the end, he ministered to thousands. ✽ Sanford Bennett, pharmacist and the author of the hymn "The Sweet By and By" died June 12, 1898, in Illinois. On this day in 1919, John Sammis, author of "Trust and Obey" passed away. ✽ Today is the birthday of Charles Feinberg, Jewish scholar, born in 1909. He became a Christian and a leading defender of the faith during the fundamentalist/modernist controversy of the twentieth century, and an author of *The Fundamentals*. He taught at Dallas Theological Seminary, BIOLA University, and Talbott Theological Seminary. ✽ Southern Baptist missionary and missionary statesman, Bertha Smith, passed away on this day in 1988. She had been born in 1888. Her book, *Go Home and Tell*, describes her years in China, her mandatory retirement in 1958 at age seventy, and her widespread travels for the next thirty years as she advanced the cause of missions across America.

APPROPRIATE SONGS AND HYMNS

We Have an Anchor, Priscilla J. Owens/William J. Kirkpatrick; Public Domain.

A Shelter in the Time of Storm, Vernon J. Charlesworth/Ira D. Sankey; Public Domain.

You Will Be My Rock, Dennis Jernigan; © 1997 Shepherd's Heart Music; Admin. by Word Music, Inc.

The Earth Shakes, Chris Christensen; © 1988 Integrity's Hosanna! Music; Admin. by Integrity Music, Inc.

Now Unto Him, David Morris; © 1986 Integrity's Hosanna! Music; Admin. by Integrity Music, Inc.

WORSHIP HELPS

Call to Worship:
Blessed be the name of the LORD from this time forth and forevermore. (Ps. 113:2 NKJV)

Verses that Mention the Anchor:
Psalm 97:1, 2 MSG: GOD rules: there's something to shout over! On the double, mainlands and islands—celebrate! Bright clouds and storm clouds circle 'round him; Right and justice anchor his rule.
Psalm 119:61 NLT: Evil people try to drag me into sin, but I am firmly anchored to your law.
Mark 6:53 NKJV: When they had crossed over, they came to the land of Gennesaret and anchored there.
Acts 27:29 NKJV: Then, fearing lest we should run aground on the rocks, they dropped four anchors from the stern, and prayed for day to come.
Hebrews 6:19 NKJV: This hope we have as an anchor of the soul, both sure and steadfast, and which enters the Presence behind the veil.

Benediction by Dr. Timothy Beougher:
Father, the storms of life frighten us because they remind us that we are not in control. But we are thankful that You are always in control. Help us to trust in You and to hold on to Your anchors in stormy times. Amen.

Kids Talk

Romans 5:8 says that God demonstrated His love for us in that while we were yet sinners Christ died for us. Tell the children how wonderful it is to say, "I love you" to parents and grandparents. We should say those three words often. Then tell the children there's something even better—*showing* our love to parents and grandparents. Ask for some ideas about how to do this. For example, obeying, listening, picking up toys, doing chores, and giving gifts. God tells us that He loves us, but He also showed us His love by sending Jesus as our Savior.

Additional Sermons and Lesson Ideas

Confession Is Good for the Soul

Date preached:

SCRIPTURE: Psalm 32

INTRODUCTION:

1. David's Theme (vv. 1, 2). Blessed are those whose:
   A. Transgressions are forgiven.
   B. Sins are covered.
   C. Sins are not counted against them.
   D. Hearts harbor no deceit.
2. David's Experience (vv. 3–5). David was not such a man. He had sinned, and his sin was stealing his blessing. He confessed his guilt with a contrite heart.
3. David's Exhortation (vv. 6, 7). We should all approach God with contrition.
4. David's Word to the Repentant (vv. 8–10). God not only forgives us, He guides us and surrounds us with His love.

CONCLUSION: Verse 11 concludes this Psalm with rejoicing. When we learn to biblically confess our sins, it brings the joy back into our lives.

Eternal Life: What It Is and How to Get It

Date preached:

By Dr. R. A. Torrey

SCRIPTURE: Romans 6:23

INTRODUCTION: How wonderful to go to bed at night with the assurance of eternal life.

1. What Eternal Life Is:
   A. Eternal Life Is Real Life (1 Tim. 6:12, 19).
   B. Eternal Life Is Abundant Life (John 10:10).
   C. Eternal Life Is Joyous Life (1 Pet. 1:8).
   D. Eternal life Is a Life of True Knowledge (John 17:3).
   E. Eternal Life Is Endless Life (John 10:28).
2. Who Can Have It? Anybody Can (Rev. 22:17).
3. How to Get It:
   A. It Is a Gift.
   B. It Is in Jesus Christ. When you have Christ, you have eternal life (1 John 5:12).

CONCLUSION: Eternal Life is God's gift to you through Jesus Christ. Will you receive it?

THOUGHTS FOR THE PASTOR'S SOUL

Why Pastors Make Great Counselors

I love it, and I hate it. It's exhilarating, and it's exhausting. Pastoral counseling—it's part of who I am and what I do, yet it often feels as if it's an invasion into my life. Still, no one does pastoral counseling better than a pastor. Not a psychiatrist, a psychologist, or a psychotherapist.

Professional counselors, the good and the biblical ones, have an important role to fill. I don't understand much about schizophrenia, repressed memories, cyclothymic disorder, or the treatment of ADHD, OCD, or PTSD. Mental illnesses are complex, and I'm not equipped even to recognize some of them. My parishioners and I have benefited from good counselors, and I consider them my allies.

But they are not my replacements. I'm not prepared to yield to a society enamored with Sigmund Freud, B. F. Skinner, Carl Rogers, or Albert Ellis. Pastors can still do things that professional therapists can't. After all, the prefix psych means "soul," and pastors are tenders of the soul. That's our job.

Pastoral counseling, as I'm using the term, is helping people resolve their problems, facilitating positive changes in their lives, and helping them grow toward greater wholeness. No one does this better than pastors do. Here's why.

Pastors Care As Friends

When people come to me with problems, they come to someone who loves them. I'm not just a professional; I'm an extension of the love of Christ, a channel of His grace. Professional counselors exhibit genuine concern, even love, for their clients—but not as a pastor can.

When I began pastoring twenty years ago, I studied *shepherding* in the Bible. The Hebrew word is closely aligned to the Jewish word for *friend*. That's what people need. In its essence, Christianity is nothing more than personal relationships—with God and each other. Within these friendships comfort is best proffered, advice best taken, rebukes best accepted, and corrections best made.

I may not have all the answers, but I can love and listen. I may feel I'm doing little well, but I can pray. Recently I sat in my office absorbing the laments of a young couple. I felt a tide of frustration rising in me, and my inner voice muttered, "How in the world can I help them?" My outer voice took them to the Scriptures, shared an anecdote from my marriage, and prayed with them.

When they left, I sighed, feeling the session had been wasted. But the next week, the wife called. "Thanks for seeing us," she said. "John said he wouldn't talk to anyone else, but he likes you. He said you'd understand, and things have been a little better. He said he'd like to see you again."

Pastors Build On An Existing Relationship

Recently a Bible study leader called and said, "I'm about to leave my wife. I've gotten involved with a woman at work. But I want to talk to you about it." We met, and after several chin-quivering, heart-throbbing, plain-talking sessions, he repented.

I referred him and his wife to a trusted marriage counselor, but our friendship of years laid the cobblestone path he followed to my door. We had long joined in worship every Sunday. We had butted heads in meetings, prayed, planned, and consoled one another. I had baptized his children, buried his father, and visited his hospitalized sister at all hours. The connections were already in place.

A therapist recently told me, "You pastors have a real advantage because you're part of a person's life more than I can ever be. Counselors get intimate with people quickly; then we're gone. You are in a person's life consistently. My role is short-term; yours is long-term, and it's the long-term role that usually proves more valuable."

Who but pastors can do incisive, on-the-spot grief counseling at funerals, marriage counseling at weddings, bedside counseling in hospitals, and conflict resolution at committee meetings?

Pastors Preach Care Every Sunday

The apostle Paul said to his elders, "You know that I have not hesitated to preach anything that would be helpful to you but have taught you publicly and from house to house."

Our house-to-house, person-to-person ministry isn't stand-alone. It rests on a public role of preaching the Word, correcting, rebuking, and encouraging with great patience and careful instruction. One of the boons of a long pastorate is the accumulation of encouraging letters that testify to this, like this one:

"I wanted to let you know how much I appreciated your message Sunday morning ... I learned Saturday night that my younger brother in Idaho attempted suicide after drinking all night Friday. I badly needed your words about troubled loved ones. I want you to know I'm keeping two copies of the message in our file with important papers, one copy for each of our two sons so I can share it with them when they are older."

Pastors Give Biblical Solutions For Spiritual Issues

Most people who approach pastors expect us to speak of spiritual realities. Many would be disappointed if our Bibles remained closed and our knees straight. I can't reduce everything to an over-simplified, black-and-white, wave-the-Bible-at-it problem. Human complexities can be as impossible to untangle as a child's ball of string. Yet, I sometimes wonder if such an over-simplified reduction might, in the final analysis, prove more helpful than some of the counsel dispensed at $75 an hour.

Do you ever wonder what a psychoanalyst would have said to Cain? "Let's talk about your childhood. How did you feel when your father bragged on Abel's mutton stew instead of your vegetable soup? And your mom's apple pies—what was that problem all about?"

The Divine Counselor told him, "Sin is crouching at your door."

What would a modern therapist have said to the unraveling King Saul, the woman taken in adultery, shy young Timothy, the demoniac of Gadara, the intense apostle Paul?

There is no better tool than Scripture for penetrating soul and spirit, joints and marrow, thoughts and intents. It is the Bible in all its authority—specifically the promises in all their sufficiency—that revives the soul, makes wise the simple, gives joy to the heart, and light to the eyes.

Pastors Are More Accessible

I have the privilege of sacrificing more. Few professional therapists remain on call twenty-four hours a day. Maybe I don't either, for over the years I *have* learned to build some safeguards into my schedule and some hedges around my family. But I'm still generally more accessible than anyone listed in the Yellow Pages. I have the opportunity to hurt more, to care more, to weep with those who weep and mourn with those who mourn.

One More Reason

For these reasons, I think I am better at counseling than other professionals. The final reason is my fees. I'm free, so to speak. Even that counts for something.

TECHNIQUES FOR THE PASTOR'S DELIVERY

How to Speak

By Samuel Logan Brengle

I thank God for such preachers and such preaching as are spoken of in the Bible, where we read: "And it came to pass in Iconium, that they went both together into the synagogue of the Jews, and so spake that a great multitude both of the Jews and also of the Greeks believed" (Acts 14:1). How did they do it? What was their secret?

1. *Their manner.* They must have won the multitude by the sweetness, grace, persuasiveness, and earnestness of their manner. They certainly did not offend and shock them by coarse, vulgar, uncouth speech, or by a weak and vacillating, light and foolish, or boisterous and domineering manner. They wanted to win men, and they suited their manner to their purpose.

Solomon said, "He that loveth pureness of heart, for the grace of his lips, the king shall be his friend" (Prov. 22:11 KJV).

This "grace of the lips" is not a thing to be despised. It is rather something to be thought about, prayed over, and cultivated. It was said of Jesus: "They wondered at the gracious words which proceeded out of His mouth" (Luke 4:22 KJV), and a police officer said of Him, "Never man spake like this man" (John 7:46 KJV). Doubtless this graciousness was not only in what He said, but also in the way He said it. His manner was authoritative, yet gentle; strong, yet tender; dignified, yet popular and familiar. You can say to a little child, "Come here, you little rascal," in such a sweet manner as to win his confidence and draw him to you; or you can say, "Come here, you darling child," in such a rough, coarse way as to fill him with fear and drive him from you. It is largely a matter of manner.

A great actor was asked why he could so mightily move men by fiction, while preachers, speaking such awful and momentous truths, left them unmoved. He replied, "They speak truth as though it were fiction, while I speak fiction as though it were truth." It was a matter of manner. A woman so far away from Whitefield that she could not hear what he said, was weeping. A bystander asked her why she wept, since she knew not what he said. "Oh," said she, "can't you see the holy wag of his head?" His manner was matchless. Lawyers pleading before judges and juries, and political speakers seeking to win votes, cultivate an ingratiating manner. Why, then, should not men who are seeking to save souls and win men to Jesus Christ seek from God the best manner in which to do this?

2. *Their matter.* I judge that not only was their manner agreeable and attractive, but their subject matter was interesting, grave, and unspeakably important. They preached the Word; they reasoned out of the Scriptures; they declared that the prophecies were fulfilled; that Jesus Christ, the Son of God, of whom Moses and the prophets wrote and spake, had come, was crucified, was buried, but was risen again, and that through obedient faith in Him men might have their sins forgiven, their hearts purified, and their whole being sanctified and filled with God. It was not stale platitudes they preached, or vain babblings about the Seventh Day, about baptisms and feet-washings and incense and vestments, or harsh criticisms of authorities and powers that be, or divers and strange doctrines, but it was "repentance toward God, and faith toward our Lord Jesus Christ" (Acts 20:21 NKJV). This was the substance of their message.
   (a) It was a joyful message. It was good news; it was a declaration that God was so interested in men—"so loved the world that He gave His only begotten Son, that whosoever believeth on Him should not perish, but have everlasting life; for God sent not His Son into the world to condemn the world, but that the world through Him might be saved" (John 3:16, 17). This war-worn, sorrowful old world needs such a joyful message.
   (b) It was an illuminating message. It showed them how to be saved from sin and made acceptable to God. It also threw a flood of light into the grave and beyond, and "brought life and immortality to light" (2 Tim. 1:10 NKJV). Jesus was "the firstfruits of them that slept" (1 Cor. 15:20 KJV). It robbed earth of its loneliness, and the tomb of its terrors. It turned the world into a schoolroom and preparation place for the Father's house of many mansions, and made heaven real.
   (c) It was a solemn and a searching message. It called men to remember their sins and repent of them, forsake them, and surrender themselves no longer to the pleasures of ease, but to the service of God. They must take sides. If they would be saved, they must follow Christ crucified. Every road leads two ways. If they put away sin and followed Jesus, He would lead them to heaven; if they rejected Him, they would surely go their own way to damnation, to hell.

The best teacher of style in public speech is a heart filled to bursting with love to Jesus, and love and hope, and fear and faith for men. A love that makes a man feel that men must and shall be won from hell and turned to righteousness and heaven and God, will surely, in due time, make the manner effective.

And it will shape and control, if it does not make the message. It is marvelous the messages men get whose hearts are afire. Someone asked why Mr. Bramwell could say such wonderful things. The reply was, "He lives so near the heart of God and the Throne that he gets secret messages, and brings them down to us." It is pitiable, the flat, insipid, powerless, soulless messages men manufacture when their faith is feeble and their hearts are cold!

Can we not, then, sum up for ourselves the secret of these men in the words of Solomon, "Keep thy heart with all diligence, for out of it are the issues of life" (Prov. 4:23 KJV)?

Quotes for the Pastor's Wall

We dare not measure the quality of our sermons by the quantity of the statistics. If we do, we might become either too elated or too depressed; and both pride and discouragement are sins.”

Warren W. Wiersbe

JUNE 19, 2005

FATHER'S DAY SUGGESTED SERMON *Date preached:*

The Faithful Father

By Dr. Melvin Worthington

Scripture: Various, especially Joshua 24:15
As for me and my house, we will serve the LORD. (NKJV)

Introduction: Faithful fathers are necessary for stable families. Faithful fathers understand and undertake their role in the home as dictated in the Word of God. The moral breakdown in American society is due, in a large measure, to the failure of men to assume their God-ordained roles. There is no adequate substitute in the home for a strong and spiritual father. The father ought to do for his human family what our Heavenly Father does for His family.

1. **The Faithful Father Assumes His Duties.** The faithful father is aware of his duty to his Creator. The greatest commandment for a father is to love God with all of his being.

The faithful father fulfills his duty toward his companion. His first priority is to his Creator, the second to his companion. He loves his wife with an unselfish love. His leadership is godly, gracious, and gentle. Under God's decree, he provides all that is necessary for the well being of his companion.

The faithful father carries out his duty to his children. The responsibility of training depends greatly upon the father's role. The home is a place of instruction, interaction, interdependence, a place of instilling values, and a place of intimacy.

The father is a verbal teacher. That is, he instructs or speaks the truth to his children as he gives the precepts and principles of God's Word to them. The father is a visual teacher. What he teaches verbally he puts into practice. By his daily life, he becomes a model and pattern for his children to imitate. The father is a vital teacher. Faithful fathers teach their children with consistency and competency. His effective teaching must be coupled with compassion for the children and a comprehension of the children's needs. Fathers will give an account to God for the training and teaching of their children.

2. **The Faithful Father Avoids Hidden Dangers.** Selfishness is a danger that the faithful father faces. Quite often fathers push their children into

vocations or life styles which please them rather than freeing the child to do the will of God. Slackness is a similar danger. Eli's house was judged because he refused to restrain his sons from wickedness (1 Sam. 3:13). In today's permissive society, it is too easy to allow one's children to run with the crowd. Fathers must never be guilty of ignoring the lifestyle of their children. Every father must give biblical direction to his children. A child left to himself brings the parent to shame.

Slothfulness plagues the human race. Many fathers are just too lazy to fulfill their Scriptural duty. They neglect the responsibility until one day it is too late. The father who is too lazy to get involved with his children while they are young often lives to regret this fatal mistake.

Severity is another danger that fathers face. Colossians 3:21 declares, "Fathers, do not provoke your children, lest they become discouraged." (NKJV) Ephesians 6:4 warns, "And you, fathers, do not provoke your children to wrath, but bring them up in the training and admonition of the Lord." (NKJV) It seems clear from these passages that it is possible for a father to so impose regulations and restrictions on his children that they find it impossible to live up to his expectations. Caution must be exercised lest fathers lose sensitivity for their children.

Sinfulness stalks the best fathers. Fathers must never justify or condone sin in their lives while condemning it in the lives of their children. Fathers who would, effectively lead value personal discipline. A father must control his tongue, taste, and temper.

3. **The Faithful Father Anticipates Honorable Dividends.** Faithfulness produces a spirit of contentment. Another dividend is commendation. The Sovereign, the saints, and the society in which he resides will commend the father who by God's grace effectively leads his family in the ways of the Lord. Godly families are a standing tribute to the faithful father.

A final dividend of the faithful father is compensation. Money cannot buy what the faithful father enjoys as he views the godly life style of his wife and children. His is the altogether satisfying compensation of a job well done.

Conclusion: The motto of the faithful father is Joshua 25:15, "... as for me and my house, we will serve the LORD." (NKJV) Every father needs to ask himself the following questions: Am I the father I want to be? Am I the father God wants me to be? Am I the father my family expects me to be?

STATS, STORIES, AND MORE

The Perils of Parenting (Source Unknown)

What in the world is happening with our kids today? Let's see ... I think it started when Madalyn Murray O'Hair complained that she didn't want any prayer in our schools, and we said OK. Then someone said you'd better not read the Bible in school. And we said, OK. Remember Dr. Benjamin Spock, who said we shouldn't spank our children when they misbehave, because their little personalities would be warped and we might damage their self-esteem? And we said, OK, we wouldn't spank them. Then someone said that teachers and principals had better not discipline our children when they misbehave. And school administrators agreed, insisting that no one in their school could touch a child or else we'd all be sued. Then someone insisted we provide abortions to our daughters without parents' knowledge. And we said OK. Then someone else said, let's give our sons all the condoms they want without telling parents. And we thought it was another great idea. Then Hollywood decided to establish a new set of standards for our young people, taking our nation's morals to sodomic levels. Everyone said, "Well, I guess it's all right as long as we put letters on the advertisements, like PG, PG-13, and R. And in the process, everyone decided to ignore the old rule about reaping what you sow. And now we're wondering why it's so hard to raise kids.

FOR THE BULLETIN

❁ Today marks the closing session of the famous Council of Nicaea, which completed its work on June 19, 325. The council had produced the Nicene Creed to help establish Christian orthodoxy, especially as it related to the person of Christ, and had formulated the method for calculating the date of Easter. ❁ On June 19, 1535, Carthusian monks were butchered by Henry VIII at Tyburn for resisting Henry's plan to make himself head of the Church of England. ❁ King James I of England, who authorized the famous King James Version of the Bible, was born in Edinburgh on June 19, 1566. He became king of Scotland when his mother, Mary Queen of Scots, abdicated; and King of England upon the death of Queen Elizabeth in 1603. ❁ Today is the birthday of the great French philosopher, mathematician, and Christian, Blaise Pascal. He is credited with inventing a calculating machine that is considered the forerunner of modern computers. His unfinished book, the *Pensees*, is a classic in the area of Christian apologetics. ❁ Charles H. Spurgeon was born on June 15, 1834, in Essex, England. He became known as the "Prince of Preachers" and his sermons are still popular to this day. He also launched an ambitious ministry to London's orphans, and on this day in 1868, he celebrated his birthday by laying a foundation stone for his orphanage. ❁ The first observance of Father's Day occurred on July 19, 1910, in Spokane, Washington.

APPROPRIATE SONGS AND HYMNS

Faith of Our Fathers, Frederick W. Faber/Henri F. Hemy; Public Domain.

Find Us Faithful, Jon Mohr; © 1987 Jonathan Mark Music/Birdwing Music; Admin. by EMI Christian Music Publishing.

As for Me and My House, Tom Brooks/Don Harris/Martin J. Nystrom; © 1994 Integrity's Hosanna! Music; Admin. by Integrity Music, Inc.

Me and My House, Tim Shepperd; © 1981 Tim Shepperd Music Company.

We Will Serve the Lord, Tom Brooks/Tim Riso; © 1994 Integrity's Hosanna! Music; Admin. by Integrity Music, Inc.

WORSHIP HELPS

Call to Worship:
Glory be to the Father, and to the Son, and to the Holy Ghost;
As it was in the beginning, is now, and ever shall be,
world without end, Amen, Amen. (The Gloria Patri)

Word of Welcome:
Father's Day has become an awkward day for churches. Nowadays many families don't have fathers and many children don't have dads. We'd like to ask for God's blessings on your home today regardless of your circumstances. We'd like to encourage and pray for the well-being of your home, for Christ lives with us and abides among us. He provides fathering for the least of His children.

Offertory Comments:
In his book *Stott on Stewardship: Ten Principles of Christian Giving,* John Stott writes, "Our Christian giving can express our theology, because our gift symbolizes our support of the cause to which we are giving. For example, when we contribute to evangelistic enterprises, we are expressing our confidence that the gospel is God's power for salvation, and that everybody has a right to hear it. When we contribute to economic development, we express our belief that every man, woman, and child bears God's image and should not be obliged to live in dehumanizing circumstances. When we give to the maturing of the church we acknowledge its centrality in God's purpose and His desire for its maturity."

Kids Talk

For today's children's sermon, select an incident from your childhood to share with the children in which your father, grandfather, or other significant male role model encouraged you. Then offer a prayer for all the dads and moms in the audience.

Additional Sermons and Lesson Ideas

What's a Father?

Date preached:

SCRIPTURE: Colossians 3:21

INTRODUCTION

F—Friend
A—Affirmer
T—Teacher
H—Hero
E—Example
R—Rule/Giver

CONCLUSION: If any father lacks wisdom as to how to do these things, let him ask of God who gives wisdom freely, and it shall be given him (James 1:5).

Wheat, Fire, and Hammer

Date preached:

SCRIPTURE: Jeremiah 23:21–29

INTRODUCTION: The priests and people of Judah treated Jeremiah miserably. (Jer. 20 NKJV). Turning his attention to the political leadership of the land, he warned the people not to listen to the prophets and pundits. Speaking for God he pointed out:

1. The Presence of the Lord (vv. 23, 24). God's true men and women stand in His counsel and receive His message, for He is a God who is near.
2. The Perversion of the Prophets (vv. 25–27). How easily false dreamers deceive the modern mind!
3. The Power of the Word (vv. 28, 29). It is like:
   A. Wheat (v. 28). It feeds.
   B. Fire (v. 29). It burns.
   C. A Hammer (v. 29). It breaks rock to pieces.

CONCLUSION: Vance Havner said, "This old book has been buried many times, but the corpse has a habit of coming to life in the midst of the interment to outlive all the pallbearers."

JUNE 26, 2005

SUGGESTED SERMON *Date preached:*

An Anonymous Benefactor

By Dr. Denis Lyle

Scripture: 2 Kings 4:42–44, especially verse 43
Give it to the people, that they may eat; for thus says the LORD: "They shall eat and have some left over" (NKJV)

Introduction: Have you not discovered that God's provision always comes at the right time and often from an unexpected place? Try for a moment to put yourself in the position of Elisha and these trainee prophets at Gilgal. For seven long years, famine had plagued the land (8:1). No doubt, the faith of the sons of the prophets was being tested. This little community at Gilgal had been delivered from the danger of unwholesome stew but their troubles were not yet over. In a climate of economic deprivation and shortages the natural reaction is predictable: selfishness and covetousness!

1. **A Donation for Elisha (v. 42).** In verse 42, we read about a kind-hearted stranger, of whom we know nothing other than what is told us in these verses. There's enough to indicate that here was a man who had a heart for the Lord's servant in his time of need and who went to some trouble to minister to him in his season of distress. The Lord cares and provides for His people (see Phil. 4:19). Let's look at the gift that was brought. There was something:

   A. **Scriptural about It.** This man brought his firstfruits to Elisha (v. 42). Concerning firstfruits, we read in Exodus 23:19 (NKJV), "The first of the firstfruits of your land you shall bring into the house of the LORD your God" (see also Num. 18:8–13). Remember that during this time Baal worship and idolatry had been established in the land (1 Kin. 12:28, 16:31; 2 Kin. 3:3). This servant boycotted the corruption to bring his firstfruits to the servant of the Lord. Do we go against the tide, against our materialism and self-service to sacrifice for God's purposes?

   B. **Sacrificial about It.** The man also saw his responsibility to God despite the needs his family may have had, and the drought that had taken place. Surely, he had needs and could have hoarded this wealth.

2. **A Demand from Elisha (v. 43).** Elisha might have easily reasoned that he had no responsibility to share this gift. Many Christians have that reasoning, saying "I'll tithe after my loans are paid," or, "After my children leave the house, I'll have money to tithe." Elisha gave generously during such time of need. Notice the interaction between Elisha and his servant.

   A. **The Attitude Conveyed to His Servant.** What had been sacrificially given to Elisha was now sacrificially given to others. Why has God been so good to us? Paul tells us that we have provisions to do His good work (2 Cor. 9:8). Have you received a promotion at work? Have you prospered in business? The Lord blesses us so that we might bless others.

   B. **The Challenge Presented by His Servant (v. 43).** What Elisha was given would only feed ten people at the most. His servant surely thought there would be nothing left for himself. Do you believe that your tithe or offering will leave you with less than enough? The Bible opposes this teaching (see Prov. 11:24, 25). Small faith produces tight fists; people who clinch their money do not cling to faith.

   C. **The Scripture Was Confirmed for His Servant (v. 43).** Elisha shows us that his life was lived for the Lord and for others. He trusted God for the supernatural, to multiply the little food he was given. He anticipated not only sufficiency, but also surplus, and indeed there was. God is always liberal in His giving (James 1:5). What's your faith like in times of crisis? Are you fully persuaded that what God has promised He will provide?

3. **A Distribution by Elisha (v. 44).** Notice how the story ends. Elisha supplies the needs of the people. This story relays the Old Testament counterpart to the New Testament's feeding of the 5,000 (Matt. 14:16). Not one person went hungry. Everyone was satisfied. God can do this in us today (2 Cor. 9:8). Not only this, but the provision surpassed the needs of the people. God meets sacrificial giving with supernatural blessing (see Phil. 4:18). This farmer came to feed a prophet and fed 100 others! We never know how God will use what we give.

Conclusion: Will you give what you have to the Lord? He will take it, bless it, multiply it, and use it to the blessing of His people, for His kingdom's sake.

STATS, STORIES, AND MORE

More from Dr. Denis Lyle:

Today in Great Britain, Barnardo's Charities are the largest provider for needy children. It began in the nineteenth century, when Dr. Thomas Barnardo conceived of putting London's homeless and stray children into the safety and security of small cottages where they could be loved and cared for. Close friends tried to dissuade Barnardo because this was a pointless and well-nigh crazy idea. Barnardo wavered, unsure whether or not this was God's will. At that time, he attended a conference in Oxford, settling into a small hotel in that town. He had barely begun to unpack his cases when a knock came at his door. Opening the door, the doctor saw a total stranger who said, "Dr. Barnardo? You are thinking of building a village for orphan girls at Ilford, are you not? Well, put me down for the first cottage." The visitor placed a check for a large amount of money in Barnardo's hands, and promptly left, closing the door with a gentle click. The rest is history! Here was God's provision that came just at the right time from an unexpected quarter! Have you ever proven God like that?

What about Tithing?

Do you believe in giving ten percent of your income to the Lord? No? Well, that's all right. The widow in Mark 12:44 gave 100 percent. That's a good place to start. Zacchaeus gave fifty percent for a starter (Luke 19:10). The Macedonians gave "liberally out of their deep poverty" (2 Cor. 8:2 NKJV).

FOR THE BULLETIN

✽ Julian the Apostate, Emperor of Rome, received some Christian training as a young man, but turned from it and, as Emperor, attempted to reestablish paganism in the Empire. His reign of 18 months ended when he died in battle on June 26, 363. ✽ On June 26, 1520, Martin Luther published "The Papacy at Rome," presenting his views on the nature of the true church. ✽ After the Protestant Reformation, Roman Catholic leaders tried to re-catholicize Europe. This triggered the Thirty Years War. The king of Sweden, Gustavus Adolphus left Sweden to defend the Protestants in Germany, landing in northern Germany on June 26, 1630. The Catholic troops outnumbered the Swedish army 10 to 1, but Gustavus knelt before his men, praying, "Merciful and gracious God, both victory and defeat You hold in Your hand. Turn Your face to Your servants ... Grant us victory for Your holy name's sake, amen." Gustavus won an overwhelming victory. ✽ David Hackston, outlawed Scottish Presbyterian preacher, was placed on trial In Edinburgh on this day in 1679, and condemned three days later. His hands were stretched out and hacked off. He was pulled to the top of the gallows, allowed to choke a while, and then dropped with his whole weight. This was repeated twice. Then the hangman with a sharp knife sliced open his chest and pulled out his heart, still beating. His body was disemboweled, drawn, quartered, and burned. His head and hands were nailed to the top of a nearby bridge.

APPROPRIATE SONGS AND HYMNS

God Will Take Care of You, Civilla D. Martin/Walter Stillman Martin; Public Domain.

God Is Able, Bob Fitts ; © 1993 Integrity's Hosanna! Music; Admin. by Integrity Music, Inc.

Hope in God, Dennis Jernigan; © 1994 Shepherd's Heart Music; Admin. by Word Music Group, Inc.

May You Run and Not Be Weary, Handt Hanson/Paul Murakami; © 1991 Changing Church Forum, Inc.

WORSHIP HELPS

Call to Worship:
But He gives more grace. Therefore He says: "God resists the proud, but gives grace to the humble." Therefore submit to God ... Draw near to God and He will draw near to you. (James 4:6–8 NKJV)

Suggested Scripture Readings:
Genesis 14:18–24
Mark 12:38–44
2 Corinthians 9:6–15

Hymn Story: "We Give Thee But Thine Own"
William How, a nineteenth-century English pastor, put David's words in 1 Chronicles 29:14 into verse form in this great stewardship hymn. Bishop How had a burning desire to minister to the masses of London. This was the era of the Industrial Revolution, when multitudes had left the tranquility of the English countryside to work in the burgeoning factories and dockyards of London's East Side. It was like living in a Dickens novel.

How was called the "Poor Man's Bishop" as he visited, counseled, preached, evangelized, and provided for the needs of the desperate. Always in need of more funds for his ministry, How wrote this hymn from an understanding that our money is not ours at all, but God's. When we give, we're giving Him but His own. As one man put it, the real question of stewardship is not how much of our money we're going to give God, but how much of His money we're going to keep for ourselves.

Benediction:
Thanks be to God for His unspeakable gift!
(2 Cor. 9:15 KJV).

Additional Sermons and Lesson Ideas

The Rotten Figs

Date preached:

SCRIPTURE: Jeremiah 24:1–10

INTRODUCTION: The word *discipline* isn't very popular now, but the lack of it turns students into fools, children into culprits, athletes into losers, and gardens into weed patches. It's the subject of this passage.

1. The Setting (v. 1). Judah was a nation under occupation because the Lord was disciplining His people for their sins.
2. The Sign (vv. 1, 2). Two baskets of figs.
3. The Significance (vv. 4–10). The ripe figs are described in vv. 4–7 and the rotten ones in vv. 8–10. The ripe figs represented those who had already been carried away into exile. They were under the Lord's discipline. The rotten figs were those who had been left behind and were not under the Lord's discipline. They thought they were survivors, but they had it backward. The good figs had been exiled for their good (vv. 5, 6). Compare Hebrews 12:7–11. The rotten figs had rejected God's discipline on their lives. Though they seemed more fortunate, their future was precarious.

CONCLUSION: Perhaps like those carried into Babylon you feel God has forsaken you. Maybe He is simply disciplining you for your good.

Serving a Magnificent Christ

Date preached:

SCRIPTURE: Colossians 1:15–20

INTRODUCTION: How do we keep focused in life? We do this by focusing on our magnificent Christ.

1. Christ and God (vv. 15, 19)
   A. Christ is the image of the invisible God.
   B. Christ is the complete expression of God.
2. Christ and Creation (vv. 15–17)
   A. Christ is the Source of Creation.
   B. Christ is the Sustainer of Creation.
   C. Christ is the Goal of Creation.
3. Christ and Humanity (vv. 18–20). He is the Savior of the World.

CONCLUSION: Is He your Savior? Is your life focused on His magnificence?

JULY 3, 2005

SUGGESTED SERMON *Date preached:*

America's Need for Revival

Scripture: 2 Chronicles 7:14 and 2 Chronicles 34—35

Introduction: Christians should individually be involved in the political process and churches like ours should take biblical stands on the moral issues of our day. But the answer to our nation's problems is not the advancing of a particular political agenda or the dominance of a particular political party. Our root problems are spiritual and only a revival can reverse the moral tide of our country. The term revival refers to a special movement of God in which His church is dramatically refocused and revitalized with ensuing conviction and conversion among sinners. 2 Chronicles is the greatest book in the Bible on the subject of revival. It gives us a plan for revival and then it describes five different revivals under five different Old Testament kings.

1. **The Plan of Revival (2 Chr. 7:14).** At the dedication of the temple in 2 Chronicles 7, the Lord issued a seven-point plan for revival. There are four things for us to do, and three things God can do. As His people, we must (1) humble ourselves; (2) pray; (3) turn from our wicked ways; and (4) seek His face. If we obey those four commands, then God will fulfill these three promises. He will: (1) hear from heaven; (2) forgive our sins; and (3) heal our land.

2. **The Pattern for Revival.** The rest of 2 Chronicles describes a series of revivals that swept over Judah. Since we don't have time to study these in depth today, let's focus on the one that occurred under King Josiah in 2 Chronicles 34. Here we learn:

   A. **Biblical Revivals Come Just in the Nick of Time (v. 1).** "Josiah was eight years old when he became king." Why so young? Because his father and grandfather were among the wicked men in the Bible. His father was so evil that his own servants conspired to kill him. (See the conditions in chapter 33.) Our world and our nation are in nearly the same shape today, but at just such a time, God sends revival.

   B. **Revival Often Begins in the Heart of a Single Individual (vv.1, 2).** Josiah's father and grandfather were evil, and the royal court was corrupt. Josiah was eight years old and surrounded by wicked advisors, yet God gave him an upright heart. Even as a child, he sought the Lord. Verses 3–7 describe him as a sixteen-year-old. Teenagers have started many of the great revivals in history. When God gets hold of a group of teens, He can use them to change the world. Many revivals have started on college campuses. The eyes of the Lord range to and fro throughout the earth, seeking someone whose heart is loyal toward Him. He is looking for someone—perhaps a young person—to stand in the gap and build up the hedge against the land. Revival begins in the heart of one person fully devoted to the Lord. Will it be you?

C. **Revival Involves Pulling Down Idols (vv. 3–7).** This young man, Josiah, waged a one-man war against idolatry in his kingdom. Anything that comes before the Lord Jesus in our lives is an idol. Revival begins when we make up our minds we're going to wage war against the idols that are robbing us of our affection for the Lord.

D. **Revival Releases Renewed Resources (vv. 8–13).** The people began supporting the work of God financially; and the money was used to repair and renovate the temple, which had become dilapidated. In many places, today's Christians are the wealthiest generation of believers to live on earth. God has given us these resources to finance His evangelistic vision at the end of history. But according to the Barna Group, only 6 percent of born-again Christians in America tithe.

E. **Revival Unleashes the Power of the Word of God (vv. 14–28).** As they repaired the temple, they re-discovered the Scriptures, and the power of the Word of God was unleashed. The rediscovery of the Book of the Law sparked an awakening and a revival that changed the course of a nation and the story of history. (vv. 29–33.)

Conclusion: If we study the chronology carefully, we realize that it was during this revival that Daniel the prophet was saved. He was a product of the revival times of Josiah; and so were his compatriots, Shadrach, Meshach, and Abed-Nego. Revival is God's way of launching a new generation of workers into His kingdom. One man said that during a time of revival, the church can accomplish in a few weeks or a few months the work that otherwise would take years and years.

STATS, STORIES, AND MORE

We cannot organize revival, but we can set our sails to catch the wind from Heaven when God chooses to blow upon His people once again. —G. Campbell Morgan

Christopher Columbus in his *Book of Prophecies* (a compilation of studies on the Scriptures completed after his third voyage to the New World): "It was the Lord who put into my mind (I could feel His hand upon me) the fact that it would be possible to sail from here to the Indies. All who heard of my project rejected it with laughter, ridiculing me. There is no question that the inspiration was from the Holy Spirit, because He comforted me with the rays of marvelous inspiration from the Holy Scriptures ... I am a most unworthy sinner, but I have cried out to the Lord for grace and mercy, and they have covered me completely. I have found the sweetest consolation since I made it my whole purpose to enjoy His marvelous presence. For the execution of the journey to the Indies, I did not make use of intelligence, mathematics, or maps. It was simply the fulfillment of what Isaiah had prophesied ... No one should fear to undertake any task in the name of the Savior, if it is just and if the intention is purely for His holy service. The working out of all things has been assigned to each person by our Lord, but it all happens according to His sovereign will."

FOR THE BULLETIN

❁ On July 3, 1721, Hans Egede, Norway's "Apostle of Greenland," landed in Greenland with a party of 46 people. Egede had been born in 1686 in northern Norway and, after his university studies in Copenhagen, became a Lutheran pastor there. His great missionary burden led him to form the "Greenland Society." Buying a boat and naming it "Hope," his band of 46 missionaries tried to evangelize the Eskimos, but it proved a thankless task. Egede returned, broken in health, to Copenhagen to direct a newly founded school for missionaries. ❁ From George Muller's Journal: "In July, 1853, it pleased the Lord to try my faith in a way in which before it had not been tried. My beloved daughter and only child, and a believer since the commencement of the year 1846, was taken ill on June 20th. This illness, at first a low fever, turned to typhus. On July 3rd there seemed no hope of her recovery. Now was the trial of faith. But faith triumphed. My beloved wife and I were enabled to give her up into the hands of the Lord. He sustained us both exceedingly ..." The little girl later recovered. ❁ Today marks the death of Zionist Theodor Herzl, in 1904. His most important book was *The Jewish State*, published in 1896, calling for the re-establishment of the State of Israel. ❁ Bertha Smith was appointed as missionary to China on July 3, 1917. ❁ Alfred H. Ackley, composer of the music for the Easter hymn, "He Lives," died on this day in 1960.

APPROPRIATE SONGS AND HYMNS

Spirit of Revival, Darrell Patton Evans; © 1997 Integrity's Hosanna! Music; Admin. by Integrity Music, Inc.

Send Down the Fire, Keith Wilkerson; © 1995 Transformation Music.

Revive Us Again, Graham Kendrick; © 1989 Make Way Music; Admin. by Music Services.

Lord of My Salvation, Marsha Skidmore/David Hook; © 1993 Maranatha! Music/Doulos Publishing.

Send a Great Revival, B.B. McKinney; © 1925. Renewed 1952 Broadman Press; Admin. by Genevox Music Group.

WORSHIP HELPS

Call to Worship:
For thus says the High and Lofty One who inhabits eternity, whose name is Holy; I dwell in the high and holy place, with him who has a contrite and humble spirit, to revive the spirit of the humble, and to revive the heart of the contrite ones. (Is. 57:15 NKJV)

Pastoral Prayer:
Our Almighty Lord, today we pray for our nation and its leaders. We pray for our president, our governor, our mayor. We ask You to give wisdom to our legislators in our Statehouse and in Washington. We pray for our police officers, fire fighters, and emergency responders. We pray for the men and women of the Armed Forces. And we ask You to "bless America, land that we love. Stand beside her and guide her through the night with a light from above." We pray that You would lead Your people to pray, to humble themselves, to confess their sins, and to turn from their wicked ways. And we ask You to hear from heaven, forgive our sins, and heal our land. Send a great revival to our souls. O Lord, will You not revive our nation again, that we might rejoice in You? We pray in Jesus' name. Amen.

Suggested Scripture Readings:
Revival in the Psalms
Psalm 71:19–21
Psalm 80:14–19
Psalm 85:4–7
Psalm 119:25, 37, 40, 88, 107, 149, 154, 156, 159
Psalm 138:7, 8

Benediction:
May the blessings of God rest upon our hearts, enrich our homes, and heal our land.

Additional Sermons and Lesson Ideas

Why We Deny

Date preached:

By Rev. Dan Chun

SCRIPTURE: Luke 22:55–62

INTRODUCTION: Why do we, like Peter, sometimes deny or neglect our Lord?

1. We Don't Like Change.
2. We're Afraid of Getting Hurt.
3. We Don't Want to Be Called Zealots.
4. We Find More Value in Other Things.

CONCLUSION: Jesus calls us to follow Him. We should never deny Him, but instead deny ourselves daily and take up our cross to follow Him (Matt. 16:24).

War and Peace

Date preached:

By Rev. Peter Grainger

SCRIPTURE: Psalm 2

INTRODUCTION: This psalm shows us world events from heaven's vantage point (v. 4).

1. Man in Rebellion: The Nations Plot (vv. 1–3).
   A. Commencing with the Fall (Gen. 2—3).
   B. Culminating in the Death of Christ (Luke 23).
   C. Continuing Against the Church (Acts 4:23–27).
   D. Concluding with the Last Battle (Rev.).
2. God in Control: The Almighty Laughs (vv. 4–6).
   A. The Lord Reigns. He is enthroned in heaven.
   B. The Lord Speaks. His word terrifies (Rev. 1:8; 19:15).
   C. The Lord Plans. His King is already installed.
3. Jesus in Authority: The King Speaks (vv. 7–9).
   A. At His Baptism and Transfiguration (Luke 3:22; 9:35).
   B. In His Resurrection (Acts 13:32, 33; Rom. 1:4).
   C. In Heaven (Heb. 1:3–5).
   D. In Final Judgement (Rev. 19:11–16).
4. Bow in Worship: The Psalmist Warns (vv. 10–12). We have two choices:
   A. His Anger and Destruction.
   B. His Blessing and Security.

CONCLUSION: Whose side are you on?

A PATRIOTIC SERMON

The Soldier's Psalm

Date preached:

Note: This message was first delivered when welcoming home troops from Operation Iraqi Freedom. It has an evangelistic theme and can be adapted to any patriotic occasion.

Scripture: Psalm 144 (NKJV)

Introduction: It's our honor to welcome home soldiers from the 2nd Brigade of the 101st Airborne Division of the United States Army. We've gathered to honor these men and give them a heartfelt thank you for the service performed for our nation. One of the men of this Brigade, First Lieutenant Steven Pierce, said that on the eve of a terrible battle—one in which he was wounded—he claimed a passage of Scripture and read it to his men. It is the Soldier's Psalm. Psalm 144 has encouraged many servicemen and women throughout the history of the United States Armed Forces.

1. **The Basis of Life (vv. 1, 2)**.. The first paragraph of this psalm speaks of the basis of life: "Blessed be the Lord, my Rock." Sometimes life is overwhelming; perhaps you feel overwhelmed today. The Bible refers to God as our Rock. "When I am overwhelmed," the psalmist said elsewhere, "lead me to the Rock that is higher than I." Jesus ended His Sermon on the Mount by describing two men. Both saved their money, bought property, hired carpenters, and built dream homes. One built on bedrock. The other built on sand. Every night the men would go to bed in their respective houses feeling safe and secure, but one day a storm arose. The house on the rock stood firm; but the one on the sand collapsed. Jesus said it represented two types of people: "Whoever hears these sayings of mine and obeys them builds on a solid foundation; but the person who hears me but does not do the things that I say builds on sand" (Matt. 7:26).

Actor Matthew Perry once said, "I have all this money and fancy cars and beautiful girls, but it doesn't make me happy." Christ alone is the basis of life and happiness. He is the Rock of Ages and the Sure Foundation. He calls us to be His disciples and to build our lives on the foundation of Himself. In a Gideon publication, a soldier named Joe Paduano tells of being shot down over Vietnam in 1972. Expecting capture by the enemy, he put a gun to his head. Just then he heard sounds of approaching helicopters. An American chopper lowered a ladder. Joe said, "When I was pulled in, I threw my arms around the nearest soldier and said, 'Man, you just saved my life.'" The solider looked at him with compassion and said, "I didn't save you today; Jesus Christ did. Now you should live your life for Him." He handed Joe a New Testament. As he read it, he accepted Christ as Savior. That's a decision everyone needs to make. Jesus died to give us eternal life, and He bids us join His army and follow Him. He alone is the basis of life.

2. **The Brevity of Life (vv. 3, 4).** Here the Psalmist uses two pictures for brevity of life—a sigh and a shadow. There's a story having to do with King Xerxes who once reigned over the ancient land of Persia. At the height of his rule, he staged a review of his army. For hours he watched the soldiers march by. His general noticed signs of sadness on the king's face, and he finally reminded him that these men had conquered the world for him. "Yes," said the king, "but I've just been sitting here thinking that a hundred years from now, not one of these men will be alive." No army can withstand the enemy of time and death, but Jesus said, "I am the resurrection and the life. He who believes in Me, though he may die, he shall live" (John 11:25 NKJV). When these soldiers were in Iraq, not a day passed but they thought of home. They were willing to be there, but they were eager for their deployment to end. They looked forward to the end of their mission. That's the way it is with Christians. God has placed us here for a brief deployment. We're here to serve in His army and to spread His gospel, but it's a brief deployment and we long for the day when we'll go home.

3. **The Battles of Life (vv. 5–8).** The next refrain deals with the battles of life. Life is hard, and it gets harder all the time. I couldn't make it but for the Lord. Listen to these verses from various passages. If you know Christ as Lord, you can claim these verses during hard times.

> The Battle is the Lord's. Be strong in the Lord and in the power of His might. Today you are on the verge of battle. Do not let your heart faint, do not be afraid, and do not tremble or be terrified because of them; for the LORD your God is He who goes with you, to fight for you against your enemies. Do not be afraid nor dismayed because of this great multitude, for the battle is not yours, but God's. You will not need to fight in this battle. Position yourselves, stand still, and see the salvation of the LORD! The LORD your God Himself fights for you. You will not need to fight in this battle. The LORD is a man of war; the LORD is His name. With [our enemy] is an arm of flesh; but with us is the LORD our God, to help us and to fight our battles. Who is this King of glory? The

> LORD strong and mighty, the LORD mighty in battle. You are of God, little children, and have overcome them, because He who is in you is greater than he who is in the world. And this is the victory that has overcome the world—our faith. Not by might nor by power, but by My Spirit. (Eph. 6:12; Deut. 20:3, 4; 2 Chr. 20:15, 17; Deut. 3:22; Ex. 15:3; 2 Chr. 32:8; Ps. 24:8; 1 John 4:4, 5:4 NKJV).

If you're fighting some battles today, turn to Jesus Christ who alone gives victory.

4. **The Blessings of Life (vv. 9–15).** The psalm ends with a description of God's blessings on us: over our enemies, in our families, on our farms, and in our lives. "Happy are the people who are in such a state; happy are the people whose God is the LORD." Do you have a happiness the world can neither give nor take away? That kind of happiness comes through Jesus Christ our Lord. The Bible teaches that all have sinned and fallen short of the glory of God. But God, loving us, became the perfect, sinless Son of God who died on the Cross, taking on Himself our sins and failures. If we confess with our mouths Jesus as Lord and believe in our hearts that God has raised Him from the dead, we shall be saved.

During World War II, a Marine named James Colson was scheduled to sail from San Diego aboard the USS President Adams. Someone handed him a New Testament, which he stuffed in his gear. One day in the South Pacific, he opened his combat gear for rations and saw the little Bible. He began reading it and soon read these words: "If you confess with your mouth the Lord Jesus and believe in your heart that God has raised Him from the dead, you will be saved. (Rom. 10:9 NKJV)"

Shortly thereafter, at Guadalcanal, the Japanese began a three-day siege of round-the-clock shelling, and James had dug a foxhole under a tall tree. Suddenly he detected a missile coming straight toward them. James and his buddy leaped into their foxhole, but the shell landed just in front of them. They knew when the shell exploded, it would kill them both. James looked over at his friend and shouted, "Kenny, I want you to know that I'm confessing Jesus Christ as Lord!" His buddy looked back at him and said, "So am I!" The shell never exploded, but that was the turning point for James Colson. From that day on, he was a changed man.[1]

---

1. *Changed Lives: USA Testimonies* (Nashville: The Gideons International, 1995), pp. 10–12.

Today, you can be changed as well. "For if you confess with your mouth the Lord Jesus, and believe in your heart that God has raised Him from the dead, you shall be saved" (Rom. 10:9 NKJV). When you do this, you become heir of all the blessings of God. Happy are the people in such a state! Happy are the people whose God is the Lord!

Quotes for the Pastor's Wall

"Too many church services start at eleven o'clock sharp and end at twelve o'clock dull."

Vance Havner

"If you will stop preaching your own words and preach God's Word, He will make you a power for good."

Henry Moorhouse to D. L. Moody

JULY 10, 2005

SUGGESTED SERMON *Date preached:*

Expressing Our Faith

By Joshua D. Rowe

Scripture: John 12:1–8; Mark 14:3–9, especially Mark 14:9
Truly I say to you, wherever the gospel is preached in the whole world, what this woman has done will also be spoken of in memory of her. (NASB)

Introduction: In our lives we have a choice. We might respond to Jesus in a conventional way, "going through the motions," or we might surrender our lives to Him as an expression of our faith no matter how unconventional it may seem. Our lesson today contrasts these differing ways to respond to the Gospel.

1. **The Occasion (John 12:1, 2).**

   A. **An Honorary Meal.** Six days before Passover, Jesus and His disciples came to Bethany. They stopped to have a meal with Lazarus and his family. Lazarus was there, whom Jesus had raised from the dead. Martha was the host. To most, this seemed a normal occurrence. Jesus had blessed them and now they were hosting a dinner in His honor. This seems very sensible and conventional.

   B. **A Final Opportunity.** What the disciples and most of the dinner guests didn't realize was how close they were to the most important moment in history. Jesus had been prophesying His death to the disciples repeatedly (Matthew 16:21; Mark 8:31; 9:31; 10:33, 34; Luke 9:44). At this point, Jesus was traveling towards his Crucifixion in Jerusalem (Mark 10:33, 34). The beginning of the end, was upon them. No one except Mary seemed to understand the gravity of what was about to take place. Mary didn't see an ordinary occasion, but a final opportunity to express her faith to the Savior at the crux of His ministry.

2. **The Response (John 12:2b, 3).**

   A. **Lounging with Friends.** At this meal, the disciples, Lazarus, and Jesus were "reclining" (v. 2, NIV). The word comes from a root word meaning "to be laid up," or, "to lie." It emphasizes the relaxed atmosphere of being served at a table. We get the idea that, to most of the dinner guests, this was a typical and casual gathering to honor Jesus.

B. **Anointing the Savior.** Mary was far from a typical person. She knew the Lord would not be with them much longer. His days were numbered. Mary had invested over a year's worth of wages into a pint of pure nard, an incredibly expensive perfume (Mark 14:5, NIV). In those days, spices and perfumes were used in the burial process (see Mark 16:1). Mary recognized the occasion for what it really was and seized the opportunity in a tremendous act of faith: using the perfume, she anointed the Lord for burial, wiping it off with her own hair (John 12:7).

3. **The Reaction (John 12:4–8).**

A. **Judas' Reaction (vv. 4–6).** Judas asked, in effect, "Why waste a year's wages on one man's feet at dinner? We could have used that money to do all kinds of ministry!" That sounds logical, financially responsible, intelligent, and strategic. We might have elected him as chairperson of the financial committee; but our text says Judas' intent was to hoard the money for himself. His true motives should be described as selfish, deceitful, and criminal.

B. **Jesus' Reaction (vv. 7, 8).** We may have responded to Mary's expression of faith as irresponsible, emotion-driven, or foolish. How did Jesus respond?

During His ministry on earth, Jesus reacted strongly to several acts of faith (Matt. 8:10, 15:28; Luke 5:19, 20), but His reaction to Mary stands above them all. He said, "Truly I say to you, wherever the gospel is preached in the whole world, what this woman has done will also be spoken of in memory of her" (Mark 14:9 NASB). No wonder such an act should go hand in hand with the gospel, for this is how everyone should respond to Jesus! Mary either read the Old Testament or heard from Jesus' mouth that He was to die and she believed it. She knew His death was of such magnitude that she should be willing to do anything to express her faith in Him. She displayed submission of both her material possessions and her own body; she surrendered everything to Jesus.

Conclusion: Did you enter this worship service thinking that just going to church, doing good things, or praying occasionally are appropriate expressions of faith? While these things are good, Jesus deserves much more. We are to follow Mary's example in response to the Gospel. We must first believe that Jesus' Crucifixion is the key to our salvation and then be willing to lay down our pride, our material possessions, and anything that may be required to follow Him.

STATS, STORIES, AND MORE

More from Joshua D. Rowe:

My father once told me a story I've never forgotten. He was in a church service when a man came to the front to minister in music. He sat down in front of the piano and began to sing "Amazing Grace." The man was doing his best, but he was off key, and only hit enough notes to allow the audience to barely recognize the song. But as my father told me this story, he looked at me with intense sincerity and said, "The words of 'Amazing Grace' had never hit me as hard as they did coming from this man. The singer may have been lacking in voice, but he had tears streaming down his face. He was singing with his heart, for he knew Jesus had truly saved him and he was going to sing about it with all his soul." Perhaps many in the audience whispered to each other, saying, "Who let him sing?" or "What's his problem?" Others may have felt uncomfortable during the song. Many would have chosen the best singer in the choir for the job. But the most logical or conventional methods of expressing our faith are not always the right ones. Because of this man, my father and many others in the congregation walked away from that service with a deeper appreciation for the amazing grace of Jesus.

FOR THE BULLETIN

❁ Today is the birthday (1509) of the Geneva Reformer, John Calvin. Calvin grew up expecting to be a lawyer and a man of letters. It was after his "sudden conversion" in 1533 that the Lord turned his heart toward theology and Scripture. ❁ Puritan Joseph Alleine, ejected from his pulpit in 1662 for nonconformity, was arrested in 1663 for singing and preaching to his family in his own home. He was released a year later, but was arrested again on July 10, 1666. Though later released, his health failed and he died at age 34. Today he is chiefly remembered for his 1672 book, *An Alarm to the Unconverted*. ❁ Hymnist Clement C. Moore died on this day in 1863. He is mainly remembered for his greatest non-religious poem, "A Visit from St. Nicholas." ❁ Phoebe Palmer Knapp was a holiness leader and hymnist whose wealth allowed her to focus on her first love—Christian music. One of her friends was the blind hymnist, Fanny Crosby. Together the two wrote "Blessed Assurance." Phoebe may have been one of the first hymnists to hear her own song on a phonograph. In February, 1908, Edison's National Phonograph Company of Orange, New Jersey, released a wax cylinder recording of "Blessed Assurance." It's likely Phoebe heard the original recording prior to her death on this day, July 10, 1909. ❁ On July 10, 1925, jury selection took place in Dayton, Tennessee, in the trial of schoolteacher John T. Scopes, charged with violating the laws of the land by teaching Darwin's Theory of Evolution.

APPROPRIATE SONGS AND HYMNS

Burdens Are Lifted at Calvary, John M. Moore; © 1952 Singspiration Music; Admin. by Brentwood-Benson Music Publishing, Inc.

God Can Do Anything But Fail, Ira Stanphill; © 1946 Singspiration Music; Admin. by Brentwood-Benson Music Publishing, Inc.

Healer in the House, Randy Phillips; © 1990 Birdwing Music; Admin. by EMI Christian Music Publishing.

I Believe, Geoff Bullock; © 1992 Word Music/Maranatha! Music; Admin. by Word Music Group, Inc.

Broken and Spilled Out, Bill George/Gloria Gaither; © 1984 William J. Gaither, Inc./Yellow House Music; Admin. by Brentwood-Benson Music Publishing, Inc.

WORSHIP HELPS

Call to Worship:

All Your works shall praise You, O LORD, and Your saints shall bless You. They shall speak of the glory of Your kingdom, and talk of Your power, to make known to the sons of men His mighty acts, and the glorious majesty of His kingdom. Your kingdom is an everlasting kingdom, and Your dominion endures throughout all generations. (Ps. 145:10–13 NKJV)

Scripture Medley:

Give to the LORD, O families of the peoples, give to the LORD glory and strength. Give to the LORD the glory due His name; bring an offering, and come before Him. Oh, worship the LORD in the beauty of holiness...I beseech you therefore, brethren, by the mercies of God, that you present your bodies a living sacrifice, holy, acceptable to God, which is your reasonable service. And do not be conformed to this world, but be transformed by the renewing of your mind, that you may prove what is that good and acceptable and perfect will of God. (1 Chr. 16:28, 29; Rom. 12:1, 2 NKJV)

Offertory Comments:

The Scripture passage we'll be looking at today paints a beautiful picture of sacrifice. Mary knew Jesus was about to sacrifice His life for us, so she sacrificed her most costly possession, a pint of pure perfume. King David once asked to buy a threshing floor on which to build an altar. When the seller offered it to him free of charge, David replied that he would not "offer burnt offerings to the LORD my God with that which costs me nothing" (2 Sam. 24:24 NKJV). Should we not express our gratitude by giving to Him sacrificially? I encourage you this morning to give as He leads you, graciously, gratefully, and generously.

Additional Sermons and Lesson Ideas

Overcoming Doubt

Date preached:

By Rev. Todd M. Kinde

SCRIPTURE: James 1:1–8

INTRODUCTION: The testing of our faith brings mature growth and results in joy.

1. God Gives Us Patience through Trials (1:1–3).
2. God Gives Us Wisdom through Patience (1:4–7).

CONCLUSION: When you are assailed by doubt and held captive in a castle of doubting by the giant of despair then look to Jesus. See His hands; see His feet, and His side. Let the sacrifice of Christ dispel the doubt and darkness. The eternal wisdom of God gives you victory over the powers of darkness.

Why I Am Glad I'm a Christian

Date preached:

By Dr. R. A. Torrey

SCRIPTURE: 2 Corinthians 9:5

INTRODUCTION: My heart echoes the words of Paul—thank God for His unspeakable gift. I'm glad I'm a Christian because:

1. I know my sins are forgiven (1 John 1:7, 9).
2. Jesus has set me free from sin's power (Rom. 6:14).
3. I know I'm a child of God (John 1:12).
4. I have been delivered from anxiety and fear (Phil. 4:6, 7).
5. I have found an overflowing joy (1 Pet. 1:8).
6. I know I shall live forever (1 John 2:17).
7. I have an inheritance incorruptible (1 Pet. 1:4, 5).

CONCLUSION: Hallelujah!

THOUGHTS FOR THE PASTOR'S SOUL

The Need to Be Needed

I found my buddy drunk and dazed, parked on the shoulder of a Tennessee back road. It was 2:30 in the morning. His eyes, wild with cocaine and alcohol, darted toward me, then to his ignition. As he drove off, I jumped on the hood of his car and shouted at him through the windshield.

"Mark, we love you! I just want to talk."

"Get off the car, Rob!"

"Mark, listen to me. We love you."

"Rob, don't make me hurt you!" he shouted. "Get off the car!"

"Not till you talk to me," I yelled. "Stop the car and talk to me!"

"Rob, get off the car! Get off! Get off the car!"

I didn't think he'd hurt me, but I knew he wouldn't listen. I slid off his moving vehicle and watched the taillights vanish in the night. I felt the emptiness of the darkness swallow me.

Trail of Tears

I was Mark's pastor, but he had become more than a parishioner. My wife and I had taken him into our home to help him overcome his addictions, and for months, we watched him grow. He loved the Lord and devoured his Bible, memorizing key verses with the enthusiasm of a child. He became like a son to my wife and me, like a brother to our three daughters.

Then one Sunday he disappeared.

We weren't emotionally prepared for Mark's relapse, and when it came, it unearthed a problem in my life that lay buried like a leaking gas line—a tendency to become badly over-involved.

"I'm unsuccessfully struggling to retain—regain emotional perspective," I scribbled in my diary. "I spent hours yesterday searching for Mark in bars all over town. Last night I found him, but he wouldn't talk to me. I actually rode on the hood of his car clinging to the windshield wipers, trying to reason with him through the glass as he drove down the road. A throbbing depression has hit me."

My journal tracks the next several months:

December 19, 1990—Mark charged from his girlfriend's apartment last night so drunk, doped, and frightened that we feared for his life. Called police to be on the lookout. We knelt around the sofa and prayed through tears.

December 22, 1990—Mark came dragging in today, drunk and high. He's sitting in his car, trying to decide whether or not to let me check him into a treatment center. It's our daughter's thirteenth birthday, and my family is all here. It's a real mess.

January 15, 1991—Today is the deadline for peace in the Persian Gulf, and war seems at hand. My greater attention, however, is with Mark. I repeatedly awaken in a sweat through the night to pray for him. My heart literally hurts. Katrina and I feel he's probably going to leave, to run away, to relapse, perhaps to die a miserable, lonely death. I can't stop him.

February 4, 1991—Mark's gone again, didn't come home last night. His girlfriend called about 10:00 P.M., crying. She had found him buying cocaine. My girls sobbed themselves to sleep.

March 27, 1991—Mark's relapsed again. He came in to sleep, about four or five in the morning. He spends the rest of his time drinking and drugging. The counselors tell me I've got to evict him. I can't continue to "enable" him by giving him a safe haven.

March 28, 1991—I went to Mark's room and sat on the edge of his bed. I told him what I had to tell him, and he said he'd be out by April first. I went on to the health club but didn't have much of a workout. I returned to my office and cried.

March 29, 1991—Mark asked to borrow some money for a deposit on a new apartment. I refused, and he grew furious. He cursed. He told me he'd never again ask me for anything. He said he never wanted to talk to us again. He stormed from the room. I sat on the bed and wept.

April 29, 1991—Mark came back yesterday, exactly one month after bolting. He was humble, hurting, pitiful, broken, and determined to get better.

May 11, 1991—I can't continue to live like this, always on edge and full of apprehension about Mark. I see another relapse coming.

July 7, 1991—Mark didn't show up; I have galloping anxiety.

July 9, 1991—Another relapse. When I heard about it, I lay on my office floor in terrible pain. What's wrong with him? What's wrong with me?

On August 31, I found Mark in a seedy apartment, badly depressed and ready to die. "Rob," he slurred, "just look at me. I can't stop. I'm hopeless. I'm a hopeless reject from society. I've lost my job. Lost my friends. I've hurt so many people and broken so many promises.

"Rob," he continued, eyes unfocused, "I've got enough cocaine in this apartment to kill an elephant, and my body won't take much more. It'll only be two or three days. You'll forget about me in a month. I read somewhere that when you die, your friends adjust to it in a month or two. It's just meant to be. Let it be."

After an hour of pleading, I finally choked back my tears and moved toward the door. Turning, I took a last look at him and walked away.

There was nothing more I could do. He would be dead, I knew, within forty-eight hours.

The Pain of Love

Looking back, I see that many of my reactions were appropriate. Portions of my agony were legitimately for Mark. We loved him as part of our family. Our tears were like those of the Savior who wept over Jerusalem. How can you watch another person self-destruct—especially a loved one, especially at close range—without anguish?

Paul wrote of his lost kindred, "I tell the truth in Christ, I am not lying, my conscience also bearing me witness in the Holy Spirit, that I have great sorrow and continual grief in my heart." G. Campbell Morgan said, "Men only pray with prevailing power who do so amid the sobs and sighing of the race."

But too much of my grief was for me. I had become a textbook example of over-involvement. Melody Beattie wrote that those who become over-involved "aren't crazier or sicker than alcoholics, but hurt as much or more. They haven't cornered the market on agony, but they have gone through their pain without the anesthetizing effects of alcohol or other drugs...and the pain that comes from loving someone who's in trouble can be profound."[2]

Somewhere down in my heart, I had needed Mark. He was the brother I didn't have, the son I've never been given. He was siphoned into my soul to fill a hole of unknown origins. I had become dependent on him—on his friendship, his love, and his companionship. Our relationship, which began with his being dependent on me, had turned into my being dependent on him.

It's funny how that can happen.

Beattie continues, "So we become dependent on them. We become dependent on their presence. We become dependent on their need for us. We become dependent on their love. ... A certain amount of emotional dependency is present in most relationships, including the healthiest ones. But many men and women don't just want and need people—they *need* people. Needing people too much can cause problems."

Fallen Lines

My need for Mark caused problems in my pastoral ministry. I became so obsessed, so numbed with pain over Mark, that I wasn't good

2. Melody Beattie, *Codependent No More* (San Francisco: Harper & Row, 1987), p. 5.

for anything or anyone else. I'd grope through each day in a sort of daze, unable to focus, unable to give myself to those who needed me. My study time deteriorated, and I hadn't the energy for even routine administrative duties. I was a basket case at home, unable to provide emotionally for my family.

Late one night it dawned on me that my obsessive pain resulted from violating a basic teaching of Scripture. I was seeking to draw from Mark the emotional support that should have been provided only by other God-ordained sources.

The psalmist wrote, "The lines have fallen to me in pleasant places," and those words assumed new significance that evening. I came to understand that God had drawn a triangle around me, ordaining a trio of friends to meet my deepest needs:

My Master. It's so tempting, as one writer put it, "to impoverish life at its center for the sake of its ever-widening circumference." My drive for an ever-growing ministry had fatigued my center, making me vulnerable; and rather than resting in the Father, I was relying on a rickety brother.

A man's character is often unmasked by observing where he goes to replenish his morale. I decided to view God as my best friend. It may seem irreverent to think of God as a pal, but Abraham was called "God's friend," and the Lord spoke to Moses "face to face, as a man speaks to his friend." Jesus frequently said things like: "The Son of Man is a friend of tax collectors and sinners" and "No longer do I call you servants, but I have called you friends." Most shocking, He said, "Friend, why have you come?" to the greatest traitor in history. I reasoned that if Christ could call Judas His friend, there might be hope for me.

A good friendship involves trust, so I began turning Mark's problems over to the One who can do the impossible. I stopped praying, "Lord, my best friend's killing himself!" Instead, I learned to pray, "Lord, You're my best Friend, so please deal with our buddy Mark."

Some problems we can't solve, despite our best efforts. I shouldn't destroy myself worrying about problems that only God can solve.

My mate. My wife, Katrina, had mourned for Mark, too—we had wept together for him—yet she was baffled by my preoccupation with his condition. I slowly realized that perhaps Mark had been claiming a lot of time and emotional energy that should have gone to her.

We took off for a few days, flew to a resort city, rested, sunned, shopped, and prayed together. I thought of God's wisdom in creating Eve. Alone in his utopia, Adam could soak up emotional strength from many sources—his divinely given occupation, his animal friends, his physical vitality, his lavish environment—but none of those could compare with God's gift of Eve.

Not everyone would agree, but for me, my wife—and only my wife—can be my earthly best friend. For me, seeking deep levels of emotional support and intimacy outside of my marriage is dangerous.

For those without a spouse or an intimate friendship with their spouse, I think of my friend Agnes Frazier. For fifty years she and her husband, Emit, had morning Bible reading and prayer at the breakfast table. On the day he died, she went to bed thinking that she could never again start the day with devotional exercise. But the next morning she bravely sat at the kitchen table and opened her Bible to the spot where she and her husband had quit their reading twenty-four hours before. The verse that stared up at her was "For thy Maker is thy husband."

She smiled and said, "Thank you, Lord."

Me. There is one other person I claim as a best friend. Me.

As Mark's insanity engulfed me, I realized I needed to care for myself, to withdraw for my own protection. F. W. Boreham once wrote, "Very few of us treat ourselves with courtesy. Many a man behaves toward himself as though he and himself had never been introduced. He is at no pains to cultivate his own acquaintance. He never wishes himself a jovial good morning on waking; he never has a good laugh with himself in the course of the day; he never says an encouraging word to himself when things are going badly; he never shakes hands with himself or pats himself on the back when things are going well.

"He simply tolerates himself. He would not get the best out of a horse or a dog if he treated it in such a way; how, then, can he hope, under such impossible conditions, to get the best out of himself?"

How, indeed?

I'm learning to spend more time alone. More time walking. More time secluded. More time talking to myself, saying, "Bless the Lord, O my soul." I'm learning to take trips occasionally by myself, a night now and again in a lodge on the mountainside—just me, my Bible, my journal, a good book, and my walking shoes.

Solitude in moderation deepens the soul and protects me from the seduction of being needed.

Burdened No More

Perhaps God brought Mark into my life to show me secrets of emotional health that I'd unwittingly neglected. God was also at work in Mark—without me.

As I left his dimly lit apartment that bleak afternoon, I left behind the phone number of a trusted counselor. Three days later, Mark called him. That was three years ago, and today Mark is married, sober, and the regional manager of a famous ice cream company.

Do I still worry about his relapsing? All the time. But I continually commit him to God. Just last week, we rendezvoused in Atlanta for a Braves game. He's still my buddy, but I no longer encumber him with the burden of my own emotional health.[3]

PRAYERS FOR A PASTOR'S CLOSET

Spirit of God, Anoint Me

Spirit of power, anoint me for service,
Spirit of holiness, cleanse Thou my heart;
Give to my soul of Thyself a new vision,
And a new measure of power impart.
Fill me with power for service and use me;
Is there not some work my weak hands can do?
Make me a channel of life and of blessing,
And with the Spirit anoint me anew.

—*Elisha A. Hoffman (1904)*

Lord, Use Me to Share Thy Love

My talents, gifts, and graces, Lord, into Thy blessed
hands receive;
And let me live to preach Thy Word, and let me to Thy
glory live;
My every sacred moment spend in publishing the
sinner's Friend.
Enlarge, inflame, and fill my heart with boundless
charity divine,
So shall I all strength exert, and love them with a zeal
like Thine,
And lead them to Thy open side, the sheep for whom
the Shepherd died.

—*Charles Wesley*

3. Rob Morgan's article first appeared in *Leadership Journal*, Winter, 1995.

JULY 17, 2005

SUGGESTED SERMON *Date preached:*

Courage to Confront Sin

By Rev. Michael Easley

Scripture: Nehemiah 13, especially verses 30, 31

Thus I cleansed them of everything pagan. I also assigned duties to the priests and the Levites, each to his service, and to bringing the wood offering and the firstfruits at appointed times. Remember me, O my God, for good! (NKJV)

Introduction: As Christians, we often dismiss or downplay certain sins as if they don't matter. Robertson McQuilkin, when speaking about the victorious Christian life, told the story of a once-godly man who fell into adultery. When asked how it was possible for this man to fall so far, he replied, "He didn't fall; he slid!" We often allow ourselves to slide back into selfish and sinful ways. We must have the courage to confront and overcome sin in our lives and in our church. In our text, we'll read of five areas of sin that crept into Jerusalem. This backsliding occurred perhaps as quickly as two years after Nehemiah's departure.

1. **Sins Regarding Worship (vv. 1–3).** The words, "on this day" (v. 1) refer to a time after Nehemiah returned to Jerusalem to be governor a second time (cf. 13:4–7). The dating of the book suggests he was governor for twelve years (from 444–432 B.C.). The portion of the book of Moses that was read refers to Deuteronomy 23:3–5. The reading of the Law exposed their sins of having Ammonites and Moabites in the assembly. This group refused to join Israel's entry into Canaan and they hired Balaam to curse Israel. (Note: The Ammonites worshiped the Molech by sacrificing children in fire. Archaeological evidence proves that they burned thousands of children. Moabites worshiped Chemosh, to whom they sacrificed children.)

2. **Sins Regarding Evil on the Inside (vv. 4–9).** Nehemiah learned that the high priest Eliashib had welcomed Tobiah into a temple storeroom. Some people cringe at the misuse of the White House for political gain; this was far worse. From the fine print in Nehemiah we learn that Eliashib and Tobiah were closely related by family ties. Tobiah had been the enemy of the Lord's work from the outside; how much damage could he inflict from the inside! Nehemiah recognized this evil and immediately cleansed the room in the temple.

3. **Sins Regarding Failure to Support the Priests and the Temple (vv. 10–14).** A plausible reason why Eliashib housed Tobiah is that the storerooms had been depleted; Israel disobeyed and did not continue the temple contributions of grain, wine, and oil (v. 12). Nehemiah was angry at the Levites who were forsaking the house of God (v. 11). Judah responded by bringing offerings (v. 12) and Nehemiah appointed reliable men (v. 13) to oversee the storehouses. Nehemiah asked God to remember his deeds, not to allow the people's disobedience undo his efforts in reformation.

4. **Sins Regarding the Sabbath (vv. 15–22).** Nehemiah also found the Jews violating the Sabbath. They were working, treading grapes for wine, and engaging in trade with merchants of Tyre. Nehemiah rebuked the people, calling their activity "evil profaning the Sabbath." Nehemiah shut the gates and threatened military actions should the merchants show up again. The second prayer (v. 22b) reveals Nehemiah asking for God's mercy and help.

5. **Sins Regarding Marriages (vv. 23–31).** Back in Nehemiah 10:28–30, the Israelites promised not to allow intermarriage with the nations around them. Nehemiah returned to find illicit marriages with women from Philistines, Ammonites, and Moabites—all of which were forbidden in the Mosaic Law (Ex. 34:12–16; Deut. 7:1–5). The commandment was not due to racism or prejudice, but because every time the Israelites disobeyed this command, they fell into pagan idolatry. Even the priests in Israel were plagued with this sin. Nehemiah prayed that God would judge the high priest's grandson for his evil (v. 29); and prayed again for God to remember and bless Him.

Conclusion: Our culture, our neighbors, and often our church-going friends accept sin as normal. We often overlook so-called small things like a white lie, or a dirty habit. These things grow (James 1:15). We are called to a higher standard as God's people. The courage to confront sin is nothing more and nothing less than what Nehemiah did in these verses: Obey God at His Word. Nehemiah wouldn't accept any less, and neither should we: not in our church, not in our families, and not in our own spiritual lives.

STATS, STORIES, AND MORE

Being Ready for The Master's Return

When you were younger, did you run around your living room, disobeying the rules, and knocking over a lamp? *What will mom do when she gets home?* Remember playing ball too close to the car like your dad warned not to do and throwing that pitch right into his windshield? *Dad will go crazy when he sees this!* We often ignore commands till we break them; suddenly we realize there are consequences. In our passage today, Nehemiah returned to Jerusalem to find the people rebelling against the Lord. He responded with fervor, warning them of God's judgment. Scripture is full of reminders that we will be found out unless we heed the Lord's commands. Adam and Eve faced God Himself in the Garden of Eden when they disobeyed. Moses returned from Mount Sinai to find the Israelites worshiping a golden calf; many were slaughtered in judgment. The Israelites went up to battle and lost because Achan had stolen plunder, which was to go into the Lord's treasury; the Israelites lost soldiers, and Achan lost his family and his life.

Jesus said, "Who then is a faithful and wise servant, whom his master made ruler over his household, to give them food in due season? Blessed is that servant whom his master, when he comes, will find so doing. Assuredly, I say to you that he will make him ruler over all his goods. But if that evil servant says in his heart, 'My master is delaying his coming,' and begins to beat his fellow servants, and to eat and drink with the drunkards, the master of that servant will come on a day when he is not looking for him and at an hour that he is not aware of, and will cut him in two and appoint him his portion with the hypocrites" (Matt. 24:45–51 NKJV).

FOR THE BULLETIN

❁ According to church historian, Philip Schaff, the daily sacrifices in the Jewish Temple ceased on July 17, A.D. 70, as all hands were needed for the defense of Jerusalem. The city, surrounded and besieged by the Romans, was destroyed soon after. ❁ On July 17, A.D. 180, seven men and five women appeared before the Roman proconsul Saturninus in Carthage. Charges against them were read: "Whereas Speratus, Nartzalus, Cittinus, Donata, Vestia, Secunda, and the rest have confessed they live in accordance with the religious rites of the Christians, and, when an opportunity was given them of returning to the usage of the Romans they persevered in their obstinacy, it is our pleasure they should suffer the sword." All twelve were beheaded. ❁ The Council of Ephesus adjourned on July 17, 431. This was the third of seven ecumenical councils of the church and was chiefly noted for its condemnation of Nestorianism. ❁ Martin Luther, 21, entered the Augustinian monastery in Erfurt, German, on July 17, 1505. ❁ Today is the birthday of Isaac Watts, the "Father of English Hymnody." He was born in 1674. It was also on this day 24 years later, in 1698, that he preached his first sermon. ❁ Henry Martyn was an Anglican minister near Cambridge, England, who developed a missionary burden while reading Richard Baxter's *The Saints' Everlasting Rest* and accounts of William Carey's work in India. He was ordained a chaplain with the East India Company and sailed from London on this day in 1805. His preaching and translating were remarkably effective, but he labored in great loneliness and died quite young in 1812.

APPROPRIATE SONGS AND HYMNS

All that Thrills My Soul, Thoro Harris; © 1931 Mrs. Thoro Harris. Renewed 1959 Nazarene Publishing House; Admin. by The Copyright Company.

Be Ye Holy, Walt Harrah; © 1985 Maranatha Praise, Inc.; Admin. by The Copyright Company.

Clean Hands, Pure Heart, John Slick/Mark Gersmehl; © 1986 Paragon Music Corporation; Admin. by Brentwood-Benson Music Publishing, Inc.

Make Me a Servant, Kelly Willard; © 1982 Maranatha! Music/Willing Heart Music; Admin. by Maranatha! Music.

Nothing Between, Charles Albert Tindley; Public Domain.

WORSHIP HELPS

Call to Worship:
I will sing to the LORD as long as I live; I will sing praise to my God while I have my being. May my meditation be sweet to Him; I will be glad in the LORD, (Ps. 104:33, 34 NKJV)

Responsive Reading:

Speaker: Is not My word like a fire?" says the LORD, "And like a hammer that breaks the rock in pieces?" (Jer. 23:29)

All: The words of the LORD are pure words, like silver tried in a furnace of earth, purified seven times. You shall keep them, O LORD, You shall preserve them from this generation forever (Ps. 12:6, 7 NKJV).

Speaker: For as the rain comes down, and the snow from heaven, and do not return there, but water the earth, and make it bring forth and bud, that it may give seed to the sower and bread to the eater, so shall My word be that goes forth from My mouth; it shall not return to Me void, but it shall accomplish what I please, and it shall prosper in the thing for which I sent it (Is. 55:10, 11 NKJV).

All: Your word is a lamp to my feet and a light to my path (Ps. 119:105 NKJV).

Benediction:
When we walk with the Lord in the light of His Word,
What a glory He sheds on our way!
While we do His good will, He abides with us still,
And with all who will trust and obey.
Trust and obey, for there's no other way
To be happy in Jesus, but to trust and obey.

—John H. Sammis

Additional Sermons and Lesson Ideas

Profaning What Is Holy

Date preached:

By Rev. Michael Easley

SCRIPTURE: Nehemiah 13:17–25.

INTRODUCTION: Do you realize when we sin, we are making light of Jesus' sacrifice? When we are tempted, we reject God's blessings to chase after our lusts. The Bible describes this behavior as profanity. Nehemiah used this word (13:17), which means, "to make common that which is sacred." He goes to great lengths to eliminate this problem.

1. Judgment (v. 25). Nehemiah, acting as God's prophet, didn't take Judah's sinful actions lightly. He called God to judge them and even physically assaulted some of them. Nehemiah would do anything to avoid God's judgment falling upon Jerusalem again.
2. Repentance (vv. 25, 26). The prophet didn't stop with a rebuke, but reminded them of sin's dangers and made them take an oath to turn away from this profanity.

CONCLUSION: We must never treat God's holy words or objects as if they are common or unimportant. If we do, judgment comes. God calls us to repent of our sins, not to live with them as if they are natural. God should be superior in our lives. We should say with Paul, "He is before all things, and in him all things hold together" (Col. 1:17; NIV).

Boast in the Cross

Date preached:

Outline by W. Graham Scroggie

SCRIPTURE: Galatians 6:14

INTRODUCTION: What are you most proud of? Is it your children, your sports ability, your mind? Paul turns our attention to what we should glory in above all, the Cross of Jesus Christ.

1. A Historical Fact Is Announced: The Cross of Christ.
2. A Spiritual Experience Is Affirmed: The world has been crucified to us, and we to the world.
3. A Personal Attitude Is Assumed: God forbid that we should boast in anything but the Cross.

CONCLUSION: The attitude we should have is expressed in the hymn "Rock of Ages," "Nothing in my hand I bring, Simply to the cross I cling."

JULY 24, 2005

SUGGESTED SERMON *Date preached:*

Evidences of Genuine Christianity

By Rev. Todd M. Kinde

Scripture: 2 Thessalonians 1:1–5, especially verses 4, 5

We ourselves boast of you among the churches of God for your patience and faith in all your persecutions and tribulations that you endure, which is manifest evidence of the righteous judgment of God, that you may be counted worthy of the kingdom of God. (NKJV)

Introduction: In times when so many things are uncertain and unsure, we desire to have the assurance of a genuine faith in Christ and evidence of the Holy Spirit's work in our lives. We long to sing confidently the classic hymn; "Blessed Assurance Jesus Is Mine." The pastor's heart comes shining through in this thanksgiving section of Paul's second letter to the Thessalonians. Paul enthusiastically gives thanks to God for this congregation and in so doing encourages them with the assurance of their genuine Christianity.

1. **The Evidence of Grace in Your Life (2 Thess. 1:1, 2).** Paul, at the start of his letter and teaching, reminds us that we are in Christ. When the going gets tough, when the struggle for the faith is tenuous, when we suffer for being a Christian, it's all too easy to forget where we are. The daily grind of cares in the world will choke out any remembrance of Christ. To be in Christ is to be a recipient of grace and peace. Grace and peace are found only in God. In His grace, He reaches down to save sinners from eternal condemnation. He is no longer angry with us who are in Christ. Paul's prayer is that we come to know more fully this truth of our relationship with Father God.

2. **The Evidence of Gratitude in Your Life (2 Thess. 1:3a).** Paul says, "We are bound to thank God always for you..." (v. 3). Paul sent Silas and Timothy with the first letter in which he prayed that their faith and love would increase (1 Thess. 3:10, 12). Silas and Timothy returned to Corinth from their mission to Thessalonica and reported of the immediate response of the church to the Word of God and the result of growing faith and love. With the news of revival and repentance in the church at Thessalonica, Paul was perhaps mindful of Psalm 75:1, "We give thanks to You, O God, we give

thanks! For Your wondrous works declare that Your name is near." (NKJV) Giving thanks for the work of Christ in the life of the Church is our Christian duty. Delinquency in this duty is all too easy. We are much more prone to discouragement, emphasizing our weaknesses rather than being thankful and praising God for the progress towards holiness He has accomplished in us.

3. **The Evidence of Growth in Your Life (2 Thess. 1:3b).** Paul is specifically thankful because of the answer to his prayer in the first letter (1 Thess. 3:10, 12) of growing love and faith. Faith, hope, and love form the triad of enduring gifts in the church (1 Cor. 13:13). Love and faithfulness are part of the fruit of the Spirit (Gal. 5:22). Genuine Christianity will demonstrate growing faith and love. Paul recognizes the growth in faith and love because the church has persevered in all the persecutions and trials they are enduring.

4. **The Evidence of Grit in Your Life (2 Thess. 1:4).** This present life is a testing ground of faith. The trials and struggles are to sift us to purify our lives. They also refine us to bring us forth as pure and holy (see 1 Pet. 1:6–7). In one Arab country, a church composed of former Muslims has been established. As a part of their weekly worship they ask one another the question, "How have you been persecuted this week?" They use this opportunity to comfort one another in the struggle and to keep discipline in the church; those who are not being persecuted for faith in Christ in such a culture are probably not living in a manner any different than the world, thus their profession of faith is suspect.

Conclusion: All this, says Paul, is evidence that God's judgment is right and that we are counted worthy of the kingdom of God. The evidences of grace, gratitude, growth, and grit demonstrate the genuineness of our life with Christ. In this, we may have the blessed assurance of our salvation. When we see these fruits increasing in our church and in our lives, we know that we belong to Christ.

STATS, STORIES, AND MORE

Good Fruit

Scripture has a lot to say about the necessity of the Christian producing fruit. Good fruit comes from hearing and understanding God's Word (Matt. 13:23). Producing fruit is proof of true repentance (Luke 3:8) and of our standing with God (Luke 6:44). John the Baptist warned, "And even now the ax is laid to the root of the trees. Therefore every tree which does not bear good fruit is cut down and thrown into the fire" (Matt. 3:10 NKJV). James reminds us that our faith is proven through our good works (James 2:26). Paul reminds us that the Spirit produces fruit through us (Gal. 5:22–25). Jesus gives us the key to producing good fruit, "I am the vine, you are the branches. He who abides in Me, and I in him, bears much fruit; for without Me you can do nothing" (John 15:5 NKJV).

The seventeenth-century minister, Jeremy Taylor was persecuted for his faith. His house was plundered, his family driven out, and his estate confiscated. He wrote: "I am fallen into the hands of publicans and they have taken all from me. What now? They have not taken away my merry countenance, my cheerful spirit, and a good conscience; they have still left me with the providence of God, and all His promises...my hopes of Heaven, and my charity to them, too; and still I sleep and digest, I eat and drink, I read and meditate. And he that hath so many causes of joy, and so great...[should never choose] to sit down upon his little handful of thorns."

FOR THE BULLETIN

❁ The great fire of Rome reportedly began on this day in A.D. 61. Emperor Nero blamed the Christians. ❁ Today is the birthday of Theodore Beza (1519), a close friend and successor of John Calvin in Geneva. ❁ John Newton, Anglican clergyman and hymn writer, was born in London, England, on July 24, 1725. After his mother's death, John alternated between boarding school and the high seas. His life is an incredible story of voyages, dangers, toils, and snares. Finally, on the night of March 9, 1748, John, 23, was jolted awake by a brutal storm that descended too suddenly for the crew to foresee. The next day, in great peril, he cried to the Lord. He eventually became one of England's most celebrated preachers, a great hymnist, and the author of the hymn, "Faith's Review and Expectation"—better known as "Amazing Grace." ❁ Today is also the birthday of Josiah G. Holland (1819), author of the Christmas carol, "There's a Song in the Air." ❁ President U. S. Grant appointed C. I. Scofield, brilliant lawyer and a veteran of the Civil War, as United States Attorney for Kansas. His career was marred by alcoholism until his conversion to Christ at age 36. Scofield then became a Bible student, a pastor and evangelist, a popular Bible teacher, the founder of the Central American Mission, and editor of a famous reference Bible known today as the Scofield Bible. He died on this day in 1921.

APPROPRIATE SONGS AND HYMNS

Candle in the Dark, Rob Bryceson; © 1989 Little Peach Music.

Church of God Elect and Glorious, James E. Seddon/Cyril V. Taylor; © 1982 Hope Publishing Company.

Joy in Serving Jesus, Oswald J. Smith/Bentley D. Ackley; © 1931. Renewed 1959 Word Music, Inc.; Admin. by Word Music Group, Inc.

Salt and Light, Amy Grant/Wes King; © 1992 Age to Age Music/Locally Owned Music, Inc.

To God Be the Glory, Fanny J. Crosby/William H. Doane; Public Domain.

WORSHIP HELPS

Call to Worship:
Father, O Maker of heaven and earth, as we gather in Your glorious presence, make us worthy to stand before You through the sacrifice of Your Son, Jesus Christ, in whose name we pray, Amen.

Scripture Reading:
But the fruit of the Spirit is love, joy, peace, longsuffering, kindness, goodness, faithfulness, gentleness, self-control. Against such there is no law. And those who are Christ's have crucified the flesh with its passions and desires. If we live in the Spirit, let us also walk in the Spirit (Gal. 5:22–25 NKJV).

Kids Talk

Bring two bunches of bananas, one with yellow, ripe bananas, and the other brown and rotting. Gather the children around and hold the two in front of them. "Which of these are good enough to eat?" Allow them to answer and ask them, "What's wrong with the brown ones?" Allow them to answer, "They're rotted," or, "They're gross." Use this opportunity to reply, "You know, we are a lot like these bananas. There are two types of people: some who don't obey God, people who care only for themselves. God sees them like these brown bananas; He doesn't want to use them. We want to be the other type of person, the type that loves and obeys God and our parents. When we live this way, God sees us like ripe fruit, ready to be used and enjoyed. I sure want God to use me, so we should live like He wants us to. Then, we'll be ripe and beautiful in His sight."

Additional Sermons and Lesson Ideas

Noah's News

Date preached:

By Dr. Melvin Worthington

SCRIPTURE: Genesis 6—11

INTRODUCTION: Often when we think of Noah, we think of the flood. We can learn a lot from Noah himself.

1. The Wickedness of the Society (Gen. 6:1–4).
2. The Warning of the Sovereign (Gen. 6:5–13; Heb. 11:7).
3. The Work of the Servant (Gen. 6:13–22). Notice Noah's faith, Noah's fear, Noah's fidelity, and Noah's favor.
4. The Wrath of the Sovereign (Gen. 7:1–24).
5. The Worship of the Servant (Gen. 8:1–22).
6. The Waywardness of the Servant (Gen. 9:1–29). Note the rule, the restitution, the reason, the rainbow, the retrogression.
7. The Witness of the Servant (Gen. 10—11).

CONCLUSION: Noah serves as a lesson in longevity: as a laborer, a light, and a lesson.

Call to Service

Date preached:

By Joshua D. Rowe

SCRIPTURE: Mark 1:16–18

INTRODUCTION: Sometimes we think that God has only called ministers or missionaries into His service. God is calling you and wants to use your gifts in a practical way. Jesus said:

1. Follow Me. Jesus tells the disciples to follow. He doesn't ask us to first understand every theological mystery or to be super-saints. Jesus will teach us as we follow Him.
2. I Will Make You Fishers of Men. Does it seem intimidating to serve the Lord? Is it too high a calling? He wants to use your prior experiences for His service. Perhaps you're a salesman and good with people; He can use you to explain the wonders of His gospel. Maybe you're a doctor; He can use you to heal people physically and spiritually!

CONCLUSION: The Lord is calling you to serve Him wherever you are. He created you and knows your experience. He will teach you as you walk with Him, and He will use the gifts He gave you to further His kingdom.

HELPS FOR THE PASTOR'S FAMILY

Prayers and Promises for Worried Parents

I know families in the parsonage aren't "supposed" to have problems with their kids. I know I'm "supposed" to be an expert on parenting—I even wrote a book about it once! I know I should occasionally preach a sermon to parents.

I do. I'm not. And I can't.

I'm hurting too badly to talk about parenting, and my faith is barely withstanding the onslaught of a troubled prodigal. It's not that I'm feeling guilty or ashamed, and I don't mind people knowing about it in general—in fact, I covet their prayers. It's just so terribly painful. But pain drives me to the Scriptures. There I've noticed that Jesus never turned away distressed parents. He seemed to have a tender heart for them. And while He hasn't answered my prayers as quickly as He answered the father's plea for his demoniac-son in Luke 9, He has given me some verses as shock absorbers for my soul.

He's also given me some great old quotations that have steadied me in rough waters. May I share them with you? There's a fair chance our parsonage isn't the only one containing a troubled child or a worried pastor. So, with apologies for being so open, here are some Post-it® Notes on the wall by my desk:

- I will contend with those who contend with you, and I will save your children.—Isaiah 49:25 (NRSV)
- Call to Me, and I will answer you, and show you great and mighty things, which you do not know.—Jeremiah 33:3 (NKJV)
- When we pray for our children, we are asking God to make His presence a part of their lives and work powerfully in their behalf. That doesn't mean there will always be an immediate response. Sometimes it can take days, weeks, or even years. But our prayers are never lost or meaningless. If we are praying, something is happening, whether we see it or not.—Stormie Omartian
- The prayer of a righteous [parent] is powerful and effective—James 5:16 (NIV, adapted).
- Prayer delights God's ear, it melts His heart, it opens His hand: God cannot deny a praying soul.—Thomas Watson

- Bring the difficulties to God.—Exodus 18:19 (NKJV)
- In our spiritual conflicts, we must look up to heaven for strength; and it is the believing prayer that will be the prevailing prayer.—Matthew Henry
- Our loved ones may spurn our appeals, reject our message, oppose our arguments, despise our persons—but they are helpless against our prayers.—Adapted from J. Sidlow Baxter
- Come on them from above...By intercessory prayer we can hold off Satan from other lives and give the Holy Ghost a chance with them.—Oswald Chambers
- Be careful, keep calm, and don't be afraid. Do not lose heart.—Isaiah 7:4 (NIV)
- Gideon built an altar for worshiping the LORD and called it "The LORD Calms Our Fears."—Judges 6:24 (CEV).

Ruth Bell Graham, who had her own share of suffering in this regard, put it this way: "We mothers must take care of the possible and trust God for the impossible. We are to love, affirm, encourage, teach, listen, and care for the physical needs of the family. We cannot convict of sin, create hunger and thirst after God, or convert. These are miracles, and miracles are not in our department."

Are you worried? Hurting? I know what it's like—and so does your Heavenly Father. Why not put your prodigal on "hold" and deal with your own heart. Come to the Lord for a fresh infusion of faith and courage. Remember, as Amy Carmichael once said, "When you are facing the impossible, you can count on the God of the impossible."[4]

4. For more help, see the editor's book, *Moments for Families with Prodigals,* available in bookstores or on the Internet.

JULY 31, 2005

SUGGESTED SERMON *Date preached:*

The Viciousness of Slander

By Dr. Melvin Worthington

Scripture: Exodus 20:16
You shall not bear false witness against your neighbor. (NKJV)

Introduction: In a world of mud-slinging and tattered self-images, the ninth Commandment guards us from the viciousness of slander. It safeguards honor and a good name. It prohibits defamation and false testimony in court. Our neighbor's good name is guarded by this Commandment, as well as our own name and reputation. This Commandment deals with words rather than works. God gave us the gift of speech, and by this means, we convey thoughts and fellowship with one another. It's a terrible sin to use this gift to smear and damage the reputation of others.

1. **The Admonition in the Text.** The admonition includes the recognition of the importance of the tongue, testimony, and truth. The tongue is a difficult member to tame and it has been the instrument of much slander, perjury, and salacious talk. James 3:6 says, "And the tongue is a fire, a world of iniquity. The tongue is so set among our members that it defiles the whole body, and sets on fire the course of nature, and it is set on fire by hell" (James 3:6 NKJV). We should be on constant guard lest we misuse our tongues. All propensities to lying and untruthfulness in speech are rebuked by this Commandment. It is difficult to over-estimate the value of truth or the importance of being truthful in character and speech.

2. **The Analysis of the Text.** The analysis of the text includes the prohibition, the protection, and the problems of dealing with the false witness. This commandment forbids exaggeration in speech, polite equivocations, flattering compliments, and all classes of slander, backbiting, and imputations of evil where no evil is. Our tongues should be kept from evil speaking, lying, and slandering. There's no such thing as a white lie, for every lie is tarnished by sin. Truth is essential if our society is to exist in harmony and peace. This principle is essential in the worship of God and our walk in society. Lying is satanic, for the devil is the father of lies. Liars belong to the devil's family. God's attitude toward lying is stated clear in

passages such as Colossians 3:9; Revelation 21:8; Proverbs 30:8, and Proverbs 12:19. Truth among people in society is like the bolt in the ship. If nobody told the truth, and people had no confidence in one another, they could not live together in families, communities, or do business.

3. **The Application from the Text.** Social lying, careless lying, believing a lie, exaggeration, living a lie, taking credit for something you did not do and spreading an inaccurate report are ways to violate this Commandment. This is one of the most frequently violated of the Ten Commandments. Every violation of the truth is desecration of the Decalogue and there is no meaner form of rebellion against God and harming one's neighbor than those of lying or creating impressions that are not true in the minds of others. False witness against God plunged the whole human race into sin (Gen. 3). Only those under the power of Satan continue to lie, exaggerate, lead astray, slander, or cast aspersions.

When anyone spoke evil of another in the presence of Russian Czar Peter the Great he would promptly say, "Well, now; but has he not got a bright side? Come tell me what good you know of him." We must remember that it is always easy to splash mud on others rather than help keep them clean.

Conclusion: When the primitive Christians were falsely accused for incest and killing their children, Tertullian wrote a famous apology in their vindication. We should be the brother, friend, and advocate for others, when they are wronged in their good name. God made the tongue to be an instrument of praise. God has set two natural fences to regulate the tongue—the teeth and lips. This Commandment is a third fence to restrain and regulate the tongue. In order to have victory over this terrible sin, we must watch our minds, motives, and mouths. We should pray that God would set a watch before our lips. Perusing the Word of God and prayer will help us overcome this terrible evil, and let us learn to speak as God speaks—speaking the truth in love.

STATS, STORIES, AND MORE

Someone once said . . .

Falsehood is never so false as when it is very nearly true. —G. K. Chesterton

When in doubt, tell the truth. —Mark Twain

A kind word is never lost. It keeps going on and on, from one person to another, until at last it comes back to you again. —Anonymous

A broken bone can heal, but the wound a word opens can fester forever. —Jessamyn West (1902—1984) author

A word from the mouth is like a stone from a sling. —Spanish Proverb

According to polls reported by *USA Today*, Americans lie—and are lied to—much more than we realize. Citing statistics from the book *The Day America Told The Truth*, the newspaper reported that 91% of Americans lie routinely.

36% of those tell dark, important lies
86% lie regularly to parents
75% lie to friends
73% lie to siblings
69% lie to spouses

From the *New York Times Magazine*:

"Everyone tells a little white lie now and then. But a Cornell professor recently claimed to have established the truth of a curious proposition: We fib less frequently when we're online than when we're talking in person. Jeffrey Hancock asked 30 of his undergraduates to record all of their communications—and all of their lies—over the course of a week. When he tallied the results, he found that the students had mishandled the truth in about one-quarter of all face-to-face conversations, and in a whopping 37 percent of phone calls. But when they went into cyberspace, they turned into Boy Scouts: only 1 in 5 instant-messaging chats contained a lie, and barely 14 percent of e-mail messages were dishonest." (From "The Honesty Virus" by Clive Thompson" in *The New York Times Magazine*, March 21, 2004).

FOR THE BULLETIN

❁ Today, July 31, marks the beginning of the ministry of the prophet Ezekiel in 593 B.C., according to Bible commentators. ❁ John Knox was captured in St. Andrews, Scotland, on July 31, 1547, and taken to France where he was held as a galley slave for nineteen months. ❁ John Fawcett was converted as a teenager by listening to George Whitefield. He joined the Baptists and was ordained on July 31, 1765. He began pastoring a poor church in Wainsgate, finding time here and there for writing. His writings spread abroad, and the little church feared they would lose their pastor to a larger place. The call came from London's famous Carter's Lane Church, and the Fawcetts packed their bags for the move. But when the day of departure came, John found himself unable to part from his little flock. Declining the great pulpit, he remained in Wainsgate and out of the experience wrote the hymn, "Bless Be the Tie that Binds." ❁ The great Scottish pastor and hymnist, Horatius Bonar, died on this day in 1889. He began writing hymns for children. His church in Edinburgh sang only the Scottish version of the Psalms, so only the children were allowed to sing his hymns. On one occasion in the adult services, two of his church leaders stormed out in protest when the church attempted to sing one of Bonar's hymns. He wrote "I Heard the Voice of Jesus Say" for his Sunday school children in 1846. ❁ The New American Standard Version of the Bible was published on this day in 1970.

APPROPRIATE SONGS AND HYMNS

Making War in the Heavenlies, George T. Searcy; © 1989 Tourmaline Music.

Whatever Is True, Brian Doerkson/Craig Musseau; © 1991 Mercy/Vineyard Publishing.

Brighten the Corner Where You Are, Ina Duley Ogdon/Charles H. Gabriel; Public Domain.

According to Thy Lovingkindness, Robert C. Savage; © 1958 Singspiration Music; Admin. by Brentwood-Benson Music Publishing, Inc.

Draw Me Closer, Stuart Devane/Glenn Gore; © 1987 Mercy/Vineyard Publishing.

WORSHIP HELPS

Call to Worship:
Rejoice in the LORD, O you righteous! For praise from the upright is beautiful. Praise the LORD with the harp; make melody to Him with an instrument of ten strings. Sing to Him a new song; play skillfully with a shout of joy. For the word of the LORD is right, and all His work is done in truth. He loves righteousness and justice; the earth is full of the goodness of the LORD (Ps. 33:1–5 NKJV).

Offertory Prayer:
O Father in heaven, You have told us that we will reap what we sow. This is true not only in our character, but in our conduct. We want to trust You today with our tithes and offerings, knowing that You are trustworthy to use them for Your kingdom and to continue in Your provision for us. For Your Word says, "He who sows sparingly will also reap sparingly, and he who sows bountifully will also reap bountifully. So let each one give as he purposes in his heart, not grudgingly or of necessity; for God loves a cheerful giver" (2 Cor. 9:6, 7 NKJV). Help us to be cheerful givers today, in Jesus' name. Amen.

Benediction:
May the LORD keep you and be your shade at your right hand. May He preserve you from all evil; He will preserve your soul. May the LORD watch over your coming and going both now and forevermore (adapted from Ps. 121:5–8).

Additional Sermons and Lesson Ideas

God's Guidance

Date preached:

Outline by W. Graham Scroggie

SCRIPTURE: 1 Thessalonians 3:11

INTRODUCTION: We must all consider the unknown path before us.

1. Guidance Is Needed. Choices are presented to us every day, but our outlook on life is limited. We face circumstances over which we have no control. The enemy constantly attempts to hinder us. We must recognize these obstacles and depend upon God for guidance.
2. Guidance Is Promised. The Lord is our shepherd (Ps. 23), guiding us through life's choices and obstacles. Jesus Himself promises to be with us to the end of the age (Matt. 28:20).
3. Guidance Is Conditioned. Before Christ can be our Guide, He must first be our Savior. He said that His sheep hear His voice (John 10:3, 4) and more sheep that must be brought into His pasture (John 10:16). Won't you heed His voice and accept His guidance today?

CONCLUSION: Recognize that you need His guidance and depend upon His promise to guide. Realize also that you must accept Him as Savior and follow Him as your Lord.

The Vineyard of the Lord

Date preached:

By Rev. Peter Grainger

SCRIPTURE: Isaiah 5

INTRODUCTION: Isaiah used a love song about a vineyard to relay the Lord's message to His people. We can learn from the three components of this message:

1. Preparation. The Lord relates His people to a vineyard that He prepared. He asks, "What more could have been done to My vineyard that I have not done?" (v. 4). God is determined to prepare His people according to His will.
2. Expectation. Because the Lord blessed His people so much to prepare them, He asks, "Why then, when I expected it to bring forth good grapes, did it bring forth wild grapes" (v. 4b). The Lord expects His people to produce fruit because of His effort.
3. Condemnation. The Lord reveals that He will punish His people for their disobedience and neglect (vv. 5, 6; 9, 10; 13–16; 24–30).

CONCLUSION: The Lord has blessed us with all we need to live in His will (Eph. 1:3), so let's not disappoint Him who is worthy of a lifetime of service.

AUGUST 7, 2005

SUGGESTED SERMON *Date preached:*

Effective Witnessing

By Dr. Timothy Beougher

Scripture: Romans 10:1–17, especially verse 1
Brethren, my heart's desire and prayer to God for Israel is that they may be saved. (NKJV)

Introduction: Do you have a friend or loved one with whom you want to share the gospel? Maybe its a fellow worker or classmate who needs Jesus, but you just don't know how to be effective? In our passage today, Paul models five principles of an effective witness. Allow God's Word to encourage and challenge you this morning as you seek to reach out to others with God's love.

1. **Comprehend People's Lost Condition (vv. 1–7).** People who live and die without knowing Christ are lost. They are lost now, and they will be lost for all of eternity; that's the straightforward message of the Bible. Paul refers to the Jewish people he has discussed in 9:32, whom he notes pursued righteousness as if it were to be attained by works. Israel's problem was self-righteousness. They wanted to make up their own rules instead of following God's rules. They did not want to accept God's righteousness as a gift of grace; they wanted to earn it by their own human efforts. Thus, they placed themselves under a standard by which they would ultimately be judged and found sadly lacking (v. 5).

Christ gives His righteousness to all who believe (v. 4). Jesus lived a perfect life so we don't have to! That's why Paul notes (vv. 6, 7) that we don't have to somehow get to heaven to find Christ, or to go into the realm of the dead. Salvation is found in simple faith and trust in Jesus Christ. Anyone depending on his or her efforts instead of trusting in God's righteousness is lost.

2. **Demonstrate Compassion for the Lost (v. 1a).** Paul here refers to the Israelites, to his fellow Jews (cf. Rom. 9:2, 3). Remember, Paul was Jewish but realized that Jesus Christ was the only true Savior and so Paul committed his life to Christ. In following Christ, Paul faced persecution from his fellow Jews. They tried to kill him on more than one occasion. How did he respond? Did he say, "They're going to get what's coming to them. They

deserve eternal judgment!" No, Paul demonstrates compassion for the lost, even those who had tried to kill him! The word compassion comes from the Latin *passion*, meaning "to suffer, or to feel," and the prefix *com*, meaning "with." Thus, when we have compassion, we suffer or feel with someone; we should suffer and feel for the lost.

3. **Pray for the Lost (v. 1b).** Why did Paul pray for the lost? Because he understood that only God can change people's hearts. Do you understand that reality? You and I can't change anyone's heart; only God can. God chooses to use our prayers and our witness as part of the means He uses to change people's hearts! Do you have a prayer list for those you know are lost? Do you pray for un-evangelized countries?

4. **Understand the Gospel (vv. 8–13).** The confession "Jesus is Lord" is at the heart of response to the gospel because it combines the twin responses of repentance and faith. Acknowledging Jesus as Lord indicates our acceptance that He is truly God; we place our faith in Him. It also means we remove ourselves from the throne of our life to live for ourselves and enthrone Christ as Lord; we repent of our sin. The confession with the mouth is a natural response to believing in the heart. Verse 12 reminds us that the gospel is universal. Regardless of your background, Jesus Christ saves all who come to Him in genuine repentance and faith. Verse 13 summarizes the gospel, which is by grace through faith.

5. **Share the Gospel (vv. 14–17).** Paul begins a series of rhetorical questions in verse 14. The conclusion of these questions is that the Lord does His work through His people. We must share the gospel! The greatest thing we can do is to be messengers of the Good News. It's a message with a life-changing, worldwide impact, and we are the messengers!

Conclusion: You may say, "I'm not sure I know enough. I'm not sure I would do a very good job in this type of ministry." The bottom line is to begin where you are. If you wait until you have mastered every approach, anticipated every question, read every book, etc., you will never do anything for the lost! You may legitimately feel like there is so much more you could know about sharing your faith. But don't let that stop you from reaching out to others around you right now!

STATS, STORIES, AND MORE

More from Dr. Timothy Beougher:

One July morning, the country's attention was drawn to a western Pennsylvania coal mine where nine miners were trapped 240 feet underground in a cramped, partially flooded mineshaft. CNN and Fox News brought live updates around the clock during the three days of efforts to drill a rescue hole down to the trapped men. Finally, on July 28th, just before 1:00 A.M., the first miner, 43-year-old Randall Fogle was rescued. Over the next two hours the remaining eight miners were brought to the surface to the collective relief of an entire nation. The governor of Pennsylvania noted that over 200 people had been vitally involved in the rescue effort to save the lives of these nine men. Two hundred people dropped what they had been doing to devote themselves to rescuing fellow human beings from certain disaster. If only the church had that kind of urgency and commitment to reach the unbeievers!

Bill Bright's Practice

"Although I have shared Christ personally with many thousands of people through the years, I am a rather reserved person and I do not always find it easy to witness. But I have made this my practice, and I urge you to do the same: Assume that whenever you are alone with another person for more than a few moments you are there by divine appointment to explain to that person the love and forgiveness he can know through faith in Jesus Christ."

FOR THE BULLETIN

✪ Roman Emperor Marcus Trajan died on August 7, 117 at age 65. The Apostolic Father Ignatius of Antioch was martyred under his rule. One of the most interesting documents in early church history is the report of Pliny the Younger to Trajan regarding Christian activities in the empire. ✪ The Council of Pisa concluded on August 7, 1409, having failed to end the "Great Schism" which gave the Catholic world two popes. ✪ Luther was ordered to Rome on August 7, 1518. He wisely refused to comply. ✪ On August 7, 1771, 26-year-old Francis Asbury attended a Methodist Conference in Bristol, England, during which he heard John Wesley say, "Our brethren in America call aloud for help. Who are willing to go over and help them?" Asbury offered himself, and the rest is history. ✪ On Sunday, August 7, 1801, a man wrote to his friend in Baltimore: "My dear friend, I am on my way to one of the greatest meetings of the kind perhaps ever known ... I doubt not but there will be 10,000 people and perhaps 500 wagons. The people encamp on the ground and continue praising God, day and night ..." The man was referring to the famous Cain Ridge Revival, which began that weekend. This camp meeting about twenty miles west of Lexington, Kentucky, was one of the most important religious gatherings in American history and helped trigger the "Second Great Awakening." ✪ On August 7, 1949, the Vatican announced the discovery of bones believed to be those of the apostle Peter.

APPROPRIATE SONGS AND HYMNS

A Charge to Keep I Have, Charles Wesley/Lowell Mason; Public Domain.

Blessed to Be a Blessing, Scott Wesley Brown/Dwight Liles/Niles Borop; © 1988 BMG Songs, Inc./Pamela Kay Music/Niles Borop Music; Admin. by Word Music Group, Inc.

Bold as a Lion, Ron Hamilton; © 1984 Musical Ministries, Inc.; Admin. by Majesty Music, Inc.

Draw Them Near, Lynn De Shazo; © 1992 Integrity's Hosanna! Music.

He Was Not Willing, Lucy R. Meyer; © 1952 Singspiration Music; Admin. by Brentwood-Benson Music Publishing, Inc.

WORSHIP HELPS

Call to Worship:
Let them praise Your great and awesome name—He is holy. Exalt the LORD our God, and worship at His footstool—He is holy (Ps. 99:3, 5).

Welcome:
We're so happy that you took a day out of your busy week to worship with us today. Some people view this day as an added stress: to get the kids up, to drive here, and rush to a crowded restaurant afterwards, but this day was created for our rest. I encourage you to relax here today in the Lord's presence. Allow the Good News you will hear this morning to refresh your heart, to inspire you to service, and renew your passion for your Creator and Savior. Allow all distractions and stresses to fade away while we focus on Him who has it all under His control.

Suggested Scriptures:
Exodus 32:31, 32
Matthew 19:25, 26
Mark 16:15
John 3:36

Offertory Comments:
The *Fort Worth Star Telegram,* in a recent article about the decline in tithing among American churchgoers, quoted a retired Army colonel in Schenectady, New York, named Forest Rittgers, who attends an Episcopalian church and is a committed tither. His comments were very puissant. "I became convinced," he said, "that you don't give God your leftovers, you give Him your firstfruits." We all need to consider this. In terms of our giving and in all our life patterns, are we giving God the leftovers or the firstfruits? He's not very interested in the leftovers, but He has promised incredible blessings on the firstfruits.

Additional Sermons and Lesson Ideas

Overcoming Ambition

Date preached:

By Rev. Todd M. Kinde

SCRIPTURE: James 1:9–11

INTRODUCTION: There are varying degrees of success and failure. Some of us are driven by ambition and others seem to have no ambition at all. A proper view of our humanity will temper our ambitious drives.

1. Recognize the Modesty of Your Humanity (1:9, 10a).
2. Recognize the Mortality of Your Humanity (1:10b, 11a).
3. Recognize the Momentary Nature of Your Humanity (1:11b).

CONCLUSION: Whether we are rich or poor we are told to look to our spiritual identity as the measure of our success. We are to evaluate ourselves by spiritual postures rather than by material possessions.

The Profit of Persecution

Date preached:

By Dr. Melvin Worthington

SCRIPTURE: Revelation 2:8–12

INTRODUCTION: Smyrna is the second church addressed by the Lord Jesus in Revelation (vv. 8–12). It was characterized by tribulation and should be an inspiration to our own church.

1. The Introduction (v. 8). The introduction to this letter includes the pastor, the people, the place, the prerogative, the precept, and the portrait.
2. The Information (v. 9). The information in this letter includes the activity, the affliction, the abasedness, the affluence, and the adversaries.
3. The Instructions (v. 10). They were not to fear the prospects. Christ reminds this church that God foreknows the trials of His people. They were to be faithful to the precepts. Christ predicted that some of them would be imprisoned. He exhorted them, nevertheless, not even to fear death.
4. The Incentive (vv. 10, 11). The incentive includes the crowning (v. 10) and the conquering—Destiny (v. 11).

CONCLUSION: Christians will face suffering and tribulation but they need not fear them. Our present suffering cannot be compared with our coming glory.

CONVERSATIONS IN A PASTOR'S STUDY

The Pastor and Today's Youth Culture

An Interview With Dr. Rick Holland

Explain the unique ministry the Lord has given you now.

I've been in youth ministry for twenty-two years, twelve of those at Grace Community Church with John MacArthur. We have about a thousand collegians who come weekly. I'm director of Student Ministries as well as the College Pastor at Grace Church. I also teach Homiletics at the Master's Seminary. It's a strange combination, but I think those who preach to students ought to be experts and have their theology as tight as a drum. If you're off a little when you're young, the angle says you're going to be off a lot worse later. So we need to be teaching students at the deepest level we can possibly find—not what they can handle, but at the deepest level that we ourselves have discovered.

A lot of people would be surprised that college students could be drawn by expositional preaching.

The Bible is very interesting. When you go verse by verse and unpack the logic the Holy Spirit has frozen in Scripture, it is divine poetry. It flows, it makes sense, it is classical, it connects. Exposition gives the nuances of God's Word and His attributes as you would never do if you just topically picked something here and there to talk about.

Is your application different for students than if you were preaching to an older audience?

Yes and no. The application and illustrations may differ a little, but there are still only three issues of adults and students: Lust of the flesh, lust of the eyes, and pride of life (1 John 2:16). It's just manifested differently in adults than in students, so the application is different but the truth is the same, no matter the age.

Some preachers feel intimidated by a high school or college-age audience. Is that a valid reaction when we look across our pulpit at a bunch of students?

At one level, it's very intimidating because these post-modern young people have been taught to reject anyone who assumes absolute truth or authority. Yet, expositional preaching is the only way to bring them to the knowledge of truth and absolute authority. So once you move beyond the intimidation, it really becomes fun to go after their worldview and show them the biblical worldview. When those are laid alongside one another there is no comparison. Hope, joy, forgiveness are found in the Biblical worldview. Despair, uncertainty, and the fear of death are found in an unbelieving worldview. So to be able to go in the classroom, the dorm room, or the coffee house with these discussions is exhilarating.

Is there a particular reading list you follow to stay current with the youth culture?

Staying current with youth culture is difficult at a lot of levels. First, there are a lot of different youth cultures. They are different in different parts of the country. There are some helpful authors on this, to be sure—Tom Rainer, for example. But what I do to stay in touch with the youth culture is to find out what the students are reading. That's frustrating, too, because today's students are not readers. If you ask the average student how many books he's read this year, he's likely to say, "I've never read a book in my life." They watch television all the time. I don't care much for television, but I have to watch it occasionally to be on the same page with my students.

Are you saying that one of the best ways of keeping current with the culture is to occasionally drop in on their TV viewing habits?

Yes, see what they are watching. It will stun you, but it is very important.

In terms of your personal study habits, you had a tremendous mentor in John MacArthur. But it was a conversation with John's wife that really impressed you, right?

Yes. Mrs. MacArthur said that one morning recently John went up to the study in his house very early, 7:00 or so, and he didn't come down for lunch. Mid-afternoon came, and still no sign of him. Finally she went up to get him because it was dinner time. "Oh," he said when she entered the room. "Is it time for lunch already?" He had been so enthralled in his Bible study he had lost all sense of time. That inspires me. Dr. MacArthur has an unquenchable curiosity about the biblical text like no one I have ever met. I would hope that a lot of that would rub off on me.

AUGUST 14, 2005

SUGGESTED SERMON *Date preached:*

The Remolding Hand of God

By Dr. Woodrow Kroll

Scripture: Jeremiah 18:1–6, especially verse 6
As the clay is in the potter's hand, so are you in My hand. (NKJV)

Introduction: Have you ever heard the term *dumpster diving*? This describes the activity of people who are either thrifty or desperate, making the rounds of garbage cans and dumpsters to salvage items that others have thrown out. Our lives are like items tossed in the garbage. We're ruined and broken. But God can reach down, pluck us out of the garbage, and remold us into something beautiful and useful even after we think we've blown it. I call this the remolding hand of God. God can take your messed-up life in His hand and say to you, "I want to give you another chance." I thank God for a hand like that, because all of us have messed up at some point. All of us have ruined something in our lives. Maybe you've ruined everything. I want to show you several examples Of God's remolding hand from Scripture.

1. **The Wicked King (2 Chr. 33).** Second Chronicles, chapter 33 is the story about a king who was horrible until God got hold of him and changed his life forever. Manasseh was the wickedest king in the history of Judah. He did everything wrong. In fact, it says in verse 9, he made Israel sin more than the nearby pagan nations. God punished Manasseh with imprisonment in Babylon. There he implored the Lord his God, humbled himself, and prayed. God heard his prayer, gave Manasseh a second chance, and brought him back to the kingdom. When you look at the story of Manasseh, you've got to believe in a God of second chances. If you're struggling with the issue of past sin in your life, I offer you a God who has a hand that will remold you just like it remolded and shaped this man.

2. **The Rebellious Preacher (Jon. 1).** Now, let me take you to another story. God calls Jonah as His preacher, but Jonah rebelled, went the wrong way, and sailed into a terrible storm. He was thrown into the ocean and a whale swallowed him. Jonah turned his heart to the Lord and was expelled from the whale. Jonah 3:1 says, "Now the word of the Lord came to Jonah the second time." Listen, God's hand is the kind of hand that can pick you up

from the sandy beach, clean you up, and forgive you for the mistakes you have made and give you another chance to serve Him.

3. **The Ruined Disciple (Matt. 26).** I want you to see one of God's star players who needed another chance. Matthew 26 tells the story of the apostle Peter who denied the Lord. He was the Lord's star player. This proves that any of us can mess up. That's why I'm so glad that in John chapter 21, the Lord Jesus gave Peter another chance. Peter denied the Lord three times. Three times Jesus asked him, "Do you love Me?" Peter went on to become the principle preacher of Christ to the Jewish nation.

4. **The Marred Vessel (Jer. 18).** I want to close today with this passage from Jeremiah 18. This is among the tenderest passages in the Bible. The nation of Israel is represented as clay in the potter's hand. If you're here today in need of God's remaking; If you want God's hand to remold you, reshape your life, redirect you, and make you into something useful for Him; draw comfort from Jeremiah 18. The clay was useless, but the potter picked out the impurities from the clay, put it back on the wheel, and made a useful vessel out it. If a potter can do that with clay, the Lord can do that with you.

Conclusion: Do you need some reshaping today? You need the tender hand of God, like the potter at the wheel, to take the marred clay of your life and remold it; to give it a second chance. God will do that for you. Confess your sin, turn to Him, and let Him shape you into something beautiful.

STATS, STORIES, AND MORE

More from Dr. Woodrow Kroll:

Linda and I were in Florence, Italy, not long ago. There was a huge block of marble. A sculptor had made some mistakes with it and ruined it. So, they set it in the courtyard of the cathedral in Florence. It was there for over 100 years. It was so big, they called it The Giant. Lots of people came by and saw this massive chunk of marble sitting there with grass growing around it. Several came by and took a look to see if they could sculpt something of it. "No," they concluded, "it's been horribly marred by the original sculptor. It just can never be used again."

Ironically, in the year 1505, a young sculptor came by. He looked at the block and said, "I'd like to take a crack at that." So he began to conceive in his mind what he might make of it. He studied carefully the fault lines of the marble and where the other man had ruined it. He worked on it for three years. When he finished, he had a statue that was eighteen feet high, weighing nine tons. Michelangelo took that block of granite and carved The David.

You may think you've blown it so badly that God could never ever again use you. But I want you to look at the hand of God, because the hand of God is a remolding hand. Get a good sense of your sin and apply the principle of 1 John 1:9: "If we confess our sins, He is faithful and just to forgive us our sins and to cleanse us from all unrighteousness." (NKJV)

FOR THE BULLETIN

❁ Today marks the death of the Father of Church History, Eusebius of Caesarea. His *Ecclesiastical History* is our best source about the history of Christianity from the apostolic age to the time of Constantine. ❁ August 14, 1778 also marks the death of British minister and hymnist, Augustus Montague Toplady. By age 12, Toplady was preaching sermons to whoever would listen. At 14, he began writing hymns. At 16, he was converted to Christ while attending a service in a barn. At 22, he was ordained an Anglican priest. As a staunch Calvinist, he despised John Wesley's Arminian theology, saying "I believe him to be the most rancorous hater of the gospel system that ever appeared on this island." In 1776, Augustus wrote an article about God's forgiveness, intending it as a slap at Wesley. He ended his article with an original poem: "Rock of Ages, cleft for me." Augustus Toplady died at age 38, but his poem outlived him and has been called the best-known, best-loved, and most widely useful hymn in the English language. ❁ Today is the birthday (in 1810) of Samuel Sebastian Wesley, grandson of Charles Wesley. He wrote the music for "The Church's One Foundation." ❁ Medical missionary Bill Wallace returned to China on August 14, 1942, and immediately began dispensing medical and spiritual help during the carnage of World War II. Wallace stayed after the Communist takeover, but was arrested on December 19, 1950, on trumped-up espionage charges. When he died from the ordeal, the Communists claimed he had hanged himself; but his body showed no signs of suicide.

APPROPRIATE SONGS AND HYMNS

Onward, Christian Soldiers, Sabine Baring-Gould/Arthur Seymour Sullivan; Public Domain.

Stand Up, Stand Up for Jesus, George Duffield, Jr./George J. Webb; Public Domain.

Holy, Holy, Holy, John B. Dykes/Reginald Heber; Public Domain.

Holy, Holy, Holy, Gary Oliver; © 1991 CMI-HP Publishing, Admin. by Word Music Group, Inc.

Let God Arise, Elizabeth Bacon; © 1970 Sound III, Inc./Universal-MCA Music Admin. by Universal-MCA Music Publishing.

WORSHIP HELPS

Call to Worship:
Therefore, if anyone is in Christ, he is a new creation; old things have passed away; behold, all things have become new. (2 Cor. 5:17 NKJV)

Hymn Story:
"Let Jesus Come Into Your Heart"
One Sunday in 1898, while working at the Methodist Camp Meeting at Mountain Lake Park, New Jersey, Lelia Morris assisted at the altar of the morning service. The subject of the sermon was repentance, and a large number of people came forward to confess their sins. One woman was in obvious spiritual anguish. Lelia went to pray with her. So did song leader, Dr. Henry Gilmour, and the preacher, L. H. Baker. "Just now your doubting give o'er," said Lelia.
"Just now reject Him no more," added Dr. Gilmour.
"Just now throw open the door," said Rev. Baker.
"Let Jesus come into your heart," concluded Lelia. After the service had closed, Lelia took those phrases back to her room and worked them into the hymn, "Let Jesus Come into Your Heart," with its popular chorus: "Just now, your doubtings give o'er; / Just now, reject Him no more; / Just now, throw open the door; / Let Jesus come into your heart."

Benediction:
You, O Lord, have promised to restore our souls, to restore to us the joy of our salvation, to restore us and to revive us again. Lord, we trust You today, for You are the Potter. We are the clay.

Additional Sermons and Lesson Ideas

The Fear of the Lord

Date preached:

By Rev. Peter Grainger

SCRIPTURE: Isaiah 8

INTRODUCTION: In the midst of a national crisis in Judah (see 2 Kin. 16), the Lord declared judgment through Isaiah (vv. 1–4), the consequence of choices made.

1. The Stream or the River (vv. 5–10).
   - A. The Stream (v. 6). The Lord offered security for Jerusalem if they obeyed.
   - B. The River (vv. 7–10). Because Israel rebelled, the Lord warned of punishment from Assyria, his instrument of wrath.
2. The Sanctuary or the Rock (vv. 11–17).
   - A. The Sanctuary (vv. 11–14, 16–17). The Lord offers protection in His presence for those who regard Him as holy.
   - B. The Rock (vv. 14, 15). Because of human obstinacy and rebellion, the disobedient will stumble and fall as if they tripped on a rock.

CONCLUSION: The Lord should be feared and obeyed; disobedience always reaps punishment. Which way will you choose (cf. Rom. 9:30–33; 1 Pet. 2:4–8; Heb. 2:10–13)?

Grace and Glory

Date preached:

By Rev. Charles Haddon Spurgeon

SCRIPTURE: Psalm 84:11

INTRODUCTION: God has two packages for us to open, both gifts given freely.

1. Grace. The Lord may not give gold or gain, but He will give grace. He may send trials, but He will give grace in proportion thereto.
   - A. Sustaining Grace
   - B. Strengthening Grace
   - C. Sanctifying Grace
   - D. Satisfying Grace
2. Glory. What an *and* is in this text! We do not need glory yet, but we shall have it in due order. After we have eaten the bread of grace, we shall drink the wine of glory.

CONCLUSION: These words *grace* and *glory* are enough to make us dance for joy. Grace now and, in a little while, glory forever!

YOUTH SERMON

Why True Love Waits

Date preached:

By Joshua D. Rowe

Scripture: Various

Introduction: True love waits. Is that true? It sounds boring. Sexual abstinence isn't a popular concept. We don't want to wait on anything in our culture. But, I want you to understand that waiting is awesome. Waiting for your husband or wife is not passive; it's very active. It's a challenge, an adventure, and a commitment to a God who deserves everything, and to your future spouse who deserves your purity.

1. **True Love.** Before we dive into our topic of sexual abstinence, I want you to understand one very important thing. You will never have the strength to hold up a commitment to purity until you are totally committed to Jesus Christ as your Lord and Savior. The greatest commandment in Scripture is to "love the LORD your God with all your heart, with all your soul, with all your mind, and with all your strength." Without this commitment, you will never be able to commit yourself to true purity. If you have not made this commitment, I invite you to do so today.

2. **True Love Waits.** Scripture clearly teaches that we shouldn't commit sexual sin, but these passages don't make sense until we understand why sex is an important and wonderful gift from God. That's what I want to focus on. Why wait? Because sex, the way God intended it, is too wonderful to pass up.

   A. **The Lies of Satan and Society.** What do your friends at school think about sex? Do they joke about it? Brag about it? Is casual sex normal? Most teenagers view sex as a goal to attain quickly, not a gift to understand biblically. Some adults tell us we need to wait until we are mature enough or until we understand all the consequences of sex. Some kids are more mature than others, I know. Most of you are aware of the consequences of sex. The real problem is that most of your generation does not have a biblical view of sex.

   B. **The Truth of Scripture.** I know most of you are expecting me to say, "The Bible says sex is bad," or, "You need to just suck it up and wait no matter how hard it may be." But I'm here to tell you that sex is an incredible gift from God, and waiting to have sex is a worthwhile adventure.

(1.) **The Goodness of Sexual Love.** Let's look at Scripture. When God created the world, He said that the light was good (Gen. 1:4); He said the land was good (Gen. 1:10); He said the vegetation was good (Gen. 1:12); He said the solar system was good (Gen. 1:18); He said all ocean creatures and birds were good (Gen. 1:21); He said land animals were good (Gen. 1:25); He said that man was good, along with everything He had made (Gen. 1:31)! God only saw one thing out of all creation that was not good, "It is not good that man should be alone." God saw that man could not emotionally or sexually express himself in a marriage relationship, and it wasn't good. See! God doesn't want you to wait your whole life while you burn with desire. He wants you to have one sexual partner, one spouse to share yourself with. Notice that in all these verses Satan never created anything! All Satan does is twist things. He takes the perfect model of the sexuality God gave us, twists, and perverts it. God gave us this gift of sexual love to be shared in marriage, but Satan lies to us through the media, through friends, and through our own selfishness to twist sex into a self-gratifying sin. We must focus on how wonderful sex really can be if we follow God's model.

(2.) **The Goal of Sexual Love.** Genesis 2:24, 25 tells us, "Therefore a man shall leave his father and mother and be joined to his wife, and they shall become one flesh. And they were both naked, the man and his wife, and were not ashamed." (NKJV) I'm willing to bet that many of you here today are ashamed. Perhaps you've had sex, or sinned through pornography or fantasy, or maybe you have just been too physical with another person; whatever it is, you feel or have felt ashamed.

Imagine being in a marriage relationship, where there is no shame. You can express every physical desire and have a deep, loving, wonderful relationship. You can share your hearts, your goals, your strengths, your weaknesses, your futures, and your bodies together and without shame! God doesn't want to torture you by telling you to wait, but He wants to bless you by keeping you pure for this incredible gift. Sexual sin is like eating too many hamburgers when you are promised a steak dinner. Why do that? Don't spoil your appetite! Don't make yourself ashamed!

C. **The Adventure of Waiting.** So, what do you do in the meantime? There's freedom in waiting. As we read before, sex makes you one flesh with someone else. My advice is to enjoy life now like you won't be able to later so that later you can enjoy life like you can't now. You may never have as much spare time as you do now to enjoy your social life, your hobbies, or your family. In life, we must focus on the gifts God has given us at any particular moment. Now, you have freedom and fun. Later you will be sexually active in marriage. Enjoy each as they come to you. Don't allow Satan to twist the blessings God has given you.

Conclusion: Perhaps you realize that you don't have a true love relationship with Jesus Christ. I invite you to make a commitment today to follow Him. For all of you who do have that relationship, I invite you to make a commitment to remain sexually abstinent until your wedding night.

Closing Prayer: Pray these words in your heart with me, "Lord, I present my body as a living sacrifice, holy, acceptable to You, which is my act of worship to You. I will not be conformed to this world, but I will be transformed by the renewing of my mind, so that I might prove what is that good and acceptable and perfect will of God" (see Rom. 12:1, 2 NKJV).

Quotes for the Pastor's Wall

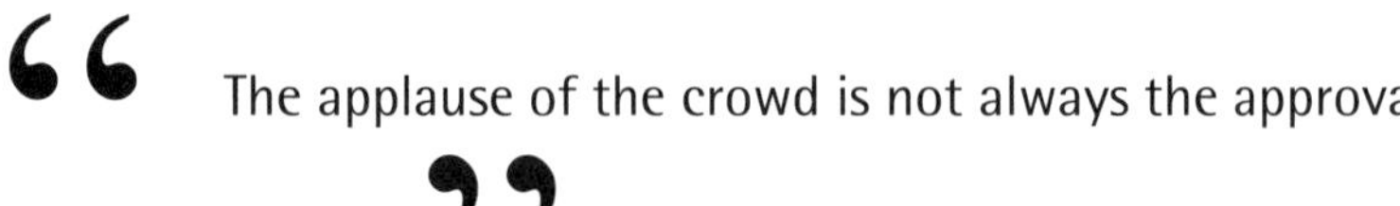

William Culbertson

THOUGHTS FOR THE PASTOR'S SOUL

Why Not Write a Hymn?

While researching for my books *Then Sings My Soul* and *Then Sings My Soul, Book 2,* I noticed that many of our greatest hymns were written by pastors to accompany their weekly sermons. John Newton and Isaac Watts were especially diligent about this. We call Isaac Watts the "Father of English Hymnology," but many people don't realize that he was first and foremost a London pastor.

He preached his first sermon on his twenty-fourth birthday, July 17, 1698, and the following year, he became assistant pastor of London's Mark Lane Church. On March 8, 1702, he became Mark Lane's pastor. Shortly afterward, his health broke. Though only in his twentys, he was already famous throughout England for his sermons, books, and hymns, but the strain of it all was too much for his constitution. He was very short, thin, and weak. When he offered to resign from his pastorate, Mark Lane Church would have none of it. They hired an able assistant, Samuel Price of Wales, and determined to care for their ailing young pastor.

Under the preaching of these two, the old, dying church revived. The building grew too small for the crowds, and a new house of worship was built down the street. Isaac preached when he could, and often wrote hymns to go along with his text.

"Joy to the World," for example, is based on Watts' interpretation of Psalm 98, which says: "Shout joyfully to the LORD, all the earth" (v. 4). As he read Psalm 98, Isaac pondered the real reason for shouting joyfully to the Lord—the Messiah has come to redeem us. The result was a timeless carol that has brightened our Christmases for nearly 300 years.

Several well-known hymns first appeared in Watts' *Psalms of David,* including "O God Our Help in Ages Past" (from Ps. 90), "Joy to the World" (Ps. 98), "Jesus Shall Reign Where'er the Sun," (Ps. 72), and "I'll Praise My Maker," Watts' rendition of Psalm 146.

I'll praise my Maker while I've breath,
And when my voice is lost in death,
Praise shall employ my nobler powers;
My days of praise shall ne'er be past.

The theme of this hymn reflects Isaac's great interest in the afterlife. One of his most popular books was "The World to Come," in which he vividly described the Bible's teaching about heaven, hell, and eternity. He wrote, "Death to a good man is but passing through ... one little dusky room of his Father's house into another that is fair and large, lightsome and glorious, and divinely entertaining."

Then he added this personal note: "Oh, may the rays and splendors of my heavenly apartment shoot far downward and gild the dark entry with such a cheerful beam as to banish every fear when I shall be called to pass through."

It was as he wished. As he lay on his deathbed for three weeks in November of 1748, at age 74, his friends gathered around. Mustering his strength, he exclaimed, "If God should raise me up again, I may finish some more of my papers, or God can make use of me to save a soul, and that will be worth living for. If God has no more service for me to do, through grace I am ready; it is a great mercy to me that I have no manner of fear or dread of death."

He was buried in London's Bunhill Fields, and this epitaph, prepared by him, was placed at his tomb:

Isaac Watts, D.D., pastor of a church of Christ in London.

after fifty years of feeble labours in the Gospel,

interrupted by four years of tiresome sickness,
was at last dismissed to his rest.

2 Corinthians 5:8: Absent from the body, and present with the Lord.

Colossians 3:4: When Christ, who is my life, shall appear,

then shall I also appear with Him in Glory.

Well, I'm no Isaac Watts. Few of us are. But most of us can put together a little rhyme and rhythm. For the last few years, I've occasionally tried this myself. After speaking from a passage, the congregation will sing a stanza from a well-known hymn, then add one or two new stanzas I've composed for the occasion. The people don't know they've just sung a "new" hymn; and though some realize the words seem strangely appropriate to the message, most worshipers don't know their pastor is the culprit. But if my theology, rhyme, and rhythm are reasonably good, the hymn brings the service to an inspiring finish.

During a recent Christmas season, I preached on the names of Christ found in the first chapter of Revelation. For the closing hymn, we chose "Join All the Glorious Names." With apologies to John Newton, I added these two stanzas:

The Babe of Bethlehem, the Faithful Witness, He

Is first and last, was dead, now lives to set us free.

He washed our sins. He is the King, the Lord, the Word,
to Him we sing.

Alpha, Omega He, One like the Son of Man,

Arrayed in light, He reigned before the world began.

He was, and is, and is to come our Glorious Lord, God's only Son.

On another occasion, I preached a Father's Day sermon from the Book of Proverbs. We closed with the moving Irish hymn "Be Thou My Vision," and I wrote a second verse that expressed the truth of the sermon:

Bless thou our children that they may believe.

Help us to guide them Thy Son to receive.

Give us righteous garments, wise souls richly dressed,

That our dear children may forever be blessed.

One couple requested a copy of the words and created an engraving for their child's bedroom. It became their prayer of dedication as parents.

You, too, can write hymns to bless your church. In the earliest days of Christian worship, the inspired psalmists wrote the hymns. In early days of English hymnology, pastors and theologians wrote them. During the era of American gospel songs, they were written by traveling evangelists. Today professional songwriters write much of our Christian music.

None of that is bad. But I think it's time our pastors began once again setting their sermons to verse and leading their churches in praise.

AUGUST 21, 2005

SUGGESTED SERMON *Date preached:*

At His Appearing

By Dr. Melvin Worthington

Scripture: 2 Timothy 4:1–8, especially verses 7, 8
I have fought the good fight, I have finished the race, I have kept the faith. Finally, there is laid up for me the crown of righteousness, which the Lord, the righteous Judge, will give to me on that Day, and not to me only but also to all who have loved His appearing. (NKJV)

Introduction: Life is so much sweeter when we have something to look forward to. The anticipation of the Second Coming of our Lord Jesus Christ gives hope in this wicked world. It is a cleansing, comforting, and compelling hope. As Christians, we are to:

1. **Look for His Appearing (Heb. 9:28).** Looking for the Second Coming of Christ implies anticipation. Notice how the New Testament uses terms such as *watch, ready,* and *wait.* Looking for the Second Coming also implies action. No one knows the day or hour when He will come the second time, but our responsibility is "occupy till He comes." Looking for the Second Coming of Christ implies attitude. We're admonished to patiently wait for His glorious appearing.

2. **Loyal at His Appearing (1 John 2:28).** When Jesus comes the second time, He will bring His reward with Him. It is required of stewards that we be found faithful. We must be steadfast, unmovable, always abounding in the work of the Lord, for we know our labor is not in vain. Titus reminds us that we must be careful to maintain good works. We will all be changed, in a moment, in the twinkling of an eye when the Lord returns, and our loyalty to Christ will be rewarded. Repeatedly in the concluding verses of each of the letters to the seven churches (Rev. 2—3), great and precious promises are given to those who are conquerors and overcomers. Discipline, devotion, and dedication are necessary for stewards who want to be found faithful when the Lord Jesus Christ returns to claim His own.

3. **Labor Till His Appearing (2 Tim. 4:1, 2).** This passage tells us that in light of the One who will judge the living and dead at His appearing, we should

preach the Word. Christ has promised to reward His faithful servants, and the priorities of life are kept in proper focus as we labor for the Lord Jesus. We must work for the night is coming when no man can work. We're to be people with a hand on the plow and an eye on the sky. We must pray that the Lord of the harvest will thrust laborers into the harvest field, and we must be ready to say, "Here am I, send me."

4. **Love for His Appearing (2 Tim. 4:8).** This passage promises a crown of righteousness for all those who have loved His appearing. Paul looked for Christ in his lifetime and eagerly awaited that glorious event. It will be worth it all when we see Christ.

5. **Listen for His Appearing (1 Thess. 4:16).** The Lord Himself will descend from heaven with a shout, with the voice of an archangel, and with the trumpet of God. And the dead in Christ will rise first. We patiently wait for the trumpet of the Lord to sound. What a wonderful sound! What a wonderful day! If we listen carefully, we can hear it in the near future by faith.

6. **Long for His Appearing (Titus 2:11–15; 1 Thess. 1:9, 10).** Just as we long to see our loved ones who have been away, we should long to see the Lord Jesus face-to-face with a far deeper longing. This is the comforting, cleansing, and compelling hope of the Christian in this dark, depraved, and destructive world.

Conclusion: Anticipation of the appearing of our Lord Jesus Christ gives hope to every believer. Our prayer should be that of the apostle John, "He who testifies to these things says, 'Surely I am coming quickly.' Amen. Even so, come, Lord Jesus!" (Rev. 22:20).

When Jesus comes to claim His own,
The living saints and those gone on
Will all as one together rise
To meet the Savior in the skies.
Caught up together in the air
To meet our Lord and Savior there;
With all the saints gone on before
We'll praise His name forever more.

—I. J. Blackwelder

STATS, STORIES, AND MORE

Christians of every generation have longed for Christ to return. *The Didache*, an early document in church history, says: "Let not your lamps be quenched, nor your loins unloosed; but be ready, for you know not the hour in which our Lord will come." St. Cyril wrote in the fourth century: "But let us wait and look for the Lord's coming upon the clouds from heaven. Then shall angelic trumpets sound." Augustine felt the Lord would return somewhere around the year A.D. 1000. In the 1300s, John Wycliffe, studied the signs of the times and concluded that the end of the world and the Second Coming of Christ should be expected immediately. In the sixteenth century, John Calvin preached: "We must hunger after Christ until the dawning of that great day when our Lord will fully manifest the glory of His kingdom." Today His return seems closer than ever.

I've Been Waiting for You

In a little fishing village in Scotland, the people gathered to welcome home a fishing vessel that had been away at sea for days. As the boat neared the shore, the men gazed eagerly toward the dock where a group of their loved ones were waiting. The skipper, looking through his telescope, identified some of the women standing on the shore, saying, "I see Bill's wife. I see Tom's wife. There's David's wife." One man was very anxious because his wife was not there. The boat docked, and he left the boat with a heavy heart and took off toward home, climbing the hill and going up the steps to his house. There was a light in the window. As his opened the door, his wife ran to meet him, saying, "Oh, John, I have been waiting for you." "Yes," he said, "but the other men's wives were watching for them."

FOR THE BULLETIN

❁ Bernard of Clairvaux died on this day, August 21, in 1153, in Clairvaux, France. He was a hymnist as well as the founder and director of monasteries in Europe. Martin Luther called him, "The best monk that ever lived, whom I admire beyond all the rest put together." ❁ In 1503, Giuliano della Rovere was named Pope Julius II. He was a powerful, restless man who tore down the old St. Peter's Cathedral, and, at age 63, descended a long, trembling rope ladder to lay the cornerstone for the new basilica; and he instituted the sale of indulgences to pay for the new edifice, provoking Luther. On August 21, 1511, as he lay unconscious, the cardinals prepared to name his successor, but Julius disappointed them by recovering. ❁ On August 21, 1732, at three in the morning, Count Nickolaus Ludwig von Zinzendorf took two departing missionaries, Leonard Dober and David Nitschmann, in his carriage as far as Brutzen, a distance of fifteen miles. There he laid on them the Lord's blessings and sent them on their way. They traveled by foot a month's journey to Copenhagen and set sail for St. Thomas where they arrived on December 13. Thus began the modern era of Protestant missions. ❁ George Frederick Handel began writing his great "Messiah" on August 21, 1741. ❁ Josef Mohr was ordained as a Roman Catholic priest on August 21, 1815, by the Bishop of Salzburg. He wrote the hymn, "Silent Night." ❁ James Mills Thoburn, Methodist soul-winning missionary to India, departed from Salem, Massachusetts, on April 12, 1859 in a small ship, landing in Calcutta on August 21. Within six months, he was able to preach to the people in their native language.

APPROPRIATE SONGS AND HYMNS

Praise to the Lord, the Almighty, Joachim Neander/Catherine Winkworth; Public Domain.

O for a Faith that Will Not Shrink, William H. Bathurst/Carl G. Glaser; Public Domain.

They that Wait Upon the Lord, Dale Jackson; © 1975 Scripture in Song; Admin. by Integrity Music, Inc.

Surely the Presence of the Lord Is in This Place, Lanny Wolfe; © 1977 Lanny Wolfe Music; Admin. by Gaither Copyright Management.

WORSHIP HELPS

Call to Worship:
And He has on His robe and on His thigh a name written: KING OF KINGS AND LORD OF LORDS. (Rev. 19:16 NKJV)

Scripture Medley:
I am the Alpha and the Omega, the Beginning and the End, says the Lord, who is and who was and who is to come, the Almighty ... Do not be afraid; I am the First and the Last. I am He who lives, and was dead, and behold, I am alive forevermore. Amen. And I have the keys of Hades and of Death. Take heed that no one deceives you. For many will come in My name, saying "I am the Christ," and will deceive many. And you will hear of wars and rumors of wars. See that you are not troubled; for all these things must come to pass ... For nation will rise against nation, and kingdom against kingdom. And there will be famines, pestilences, and earthquakes ... But he who endures to the end shall be saved. And this gospel of the kingdom will be preached in all the world as a witness to all nations, and then the end will come. And behold, I am coming quickly, and My reward is with Me, to give to every one according to his work. I am the Alpha and the Omega, the Beginning and the End, the First and the Last ... I am the Root and the Offspring of David, the Bright and Morning Star." (Rev. 1:8, 17, 18; Matt. 24:4–14; Rev. 22:12, 13, 16.)

Benediction:
Alpha, Omega, beginning and end,
Who is, who was, and who is yet to come—
May grace and peace now upon us descend
From Father, Spirit, and Christ the Son.

—Susan H. Peterson

Additional Sermons and Lesson Ideas

Overcoming Temptation

Date preached:

By Rev. Todd M. Kinde

SCRIPTURE: James 1:12–15

INTRODUCTION: Life comes from God, death comes from sin.

1. God is the Source of Life (1:12).
2. God does not Tempt Us to Sin or Evil (1:13).
3. Desire is the Source of Temptation (1:14).
4. Sin is the Source of Death (1:15).

CONCLUSION: The way out of temptation is to cry out to God Himself. This is what Adam failed to do. Prayer is our safety. Jesus told His disciples to watch and pray that they may not fall into temptation (Matt. 26:40, 41).

Worthy Worship

Date preached:

By Dr. Timothy Beougher

SCRIPTURE: Various

INTRODUCTION: We can take some practical steps from Scripture to deepen our understanding of how to worship.

1. Aspire to Worship (John 4:23, 24).
2. Acknowledge His Presence (Ps. 95:2).
3. Admire His Awesomeness (Heb. 12:28, 29).
4. Admit Your Need (Is. 6:5).
5. Abandon Your Idols (Ex. 20:3–5).
6. Accept His Touch (Mark 8:22).
7. Adopt a Lifestyle of Worship (Rom. 12:1, 2).

CONCLUSION: There's a story of a man who looked down from heaven upon a church singing in their service, but he could hear no sounds. When he asked an angel how this was possible, the angel replied, "Worship without heart is not worship at all."

AUGUST 28, 2005

SUGGESTED SERMON *Date preached:*

When God Crashes the Party

By Dr. Denis Lyle

Scripture: Daniel 5:1–31, especially verse 27
You have been weighed in the balances, and found wanting. (NKJV)

Introduction: Have you ever felt like you were invincible? In adolescents, this this perception is called personal fable, which appears when teenagers drive recklessly or take major risks without much forethought. Maybe you're living in sin now, cheating on your spouse, or stealing from your company, but you feel safe because you think no one will ever know. Belshazzar felt the same way in the impregnable city of Babylon, and yet the very night of one of his biggest parties, the Lord took his life for his sins.

1. **The Tragic Dissipation.** This was a night of royal revelry for Belshazzar and his friends. Some feel this feast was given to boost morale as the enemy was at the gates; others tell us it was to honor one of the Babylonian gods. With rings on their fingers and bracelets on their arms, they were dressed in the finest clothing with opulent jewels. The atmosphere filled with fragrance of perfume. Music, dancing, drinking: it all sounds so up-to-date. Babylonian culture lacked restraint. They overindulged in food, drink, idol worship, sex, etc.

   A. **The Feast Belshazzar Threw.** The feast was marked by intemperance (vv. 1, 5), as the royal party became drunk. The party was full of impropriety: the women mentioned were probably here for the purpose of a sexual orgy (v. 1). We also see impiety: the sacred vessels made by Solomon (see 2 Kin. 20:13) were used for this sinful indulgence of wine; it was blasphemy against the Lord and His sacred things. Idolatry is also clearly displayed: the gods of earthly things are praised (v. 4).

   B. **The Fingers Belshazzar Viewed.** Suddenly, in the same hour (v. 5), the music stopped, the singing ended, the dance floor became silent, the party grinded to a halt. Every eye was riveted on the mysterious fingers writing on the wall. Why did God reveal His judgment in this way? Kings of Babylon were known for writing solemn decrees. Now God reveals to them that He is the true King upon the throne, and He, too, can issue solemn decrees!

C. **The Fear Belshazzar Knew.** The king's countenance changed (v. 6). The jovial, drunken king lost his courage; his knees began to knock (v. 6), and he even cried out loud (v. 7) to bring in interpreters, but no magician or sorcerer could conjure up an explanation.

2. **The Prophetic Revelation.** Leave it to a woman to come up with the best ideas! The queen, having heard all the stories of Daniel's great character and godliness, suggested that he be brought in to interpret the writing on the wall. Daniel responded in two ways:

A. **Daniel Explains History.** Daniel recounted the history of the kings and lays out charges against Belshazzar: he despised the light, not learning from his father's mistakes (v. 22). He desecrated the vessels of the Lord (v. 23), and he defied the Lord by praising dead idols and not glorifying the Lord who held his life (v. 23).

B. **Daniel Reveals Mystery.** The writing on the wall contained a three-fold message from God. Daniel told him that *MENE*, meaning "numbered," revealed that the empire would soon collapse. *TEKEL*, meaning "weighed," meant that Belshazzar had been weighed on God's scales and came up lacking! *PERES*, meaning "divided," implied that God determined to shatter Belshazzar's kingdom and to give it to Medo-Persia.

3. **The Historic Consummation.** Notice how solemn the words are here, "That very night Belshazzar, king of the Chaldeans, was slain" (v. 30). The Medo-Persians devised a scheme: they diverted the water of the Euphrates from its normal channel under the city walls. When the water was shallow enough to be forded, the soldiers entered beneath the city walls through this tunnel (cf. Is. 41:25; 45:1–4).

Conclusion: Looking at your own life, could God come and crash your party at any minute? Are you living in sin, thinking it will never catch up to you? My friends, God is not satisfied until we are completely devoted and obedient to Him. Belshazzar didn't glorify the God that gave him breath, so God took it from Him. How long do we have on this earth? We should choose to glorify, to praise, and to serve the Lord with the lives He has given to us.

STATS, STORIES, AND MORE

More from Dr. Denis Lyle

There's real danger in strong drink. Not only has it a woeful effect on your body and mind but the great evil of intemperance lies in its influence. You do things that you would never do when you are sober. Now almost everywhere we turn today alcohol is prevalent. We cannot read the newspaper, watch TV, or walk on our streets without sensing the power of the enemy in this respect. Wine in Scripture is referred to as "a mocker," "a trouble-maker," and as "a serpent who bites at the last" (Prov. 20:1, 23:20, 23:31, 32 NKJV). In this context, therefore, it's the symbol of stimulation and irresponsible living. No wonder Paul says not to be drunk with wine (Eph. 5:18).

Besides the drink, we should notice the sacred vessels. They were originally made by Solomon (1 Kin. 7:48), shown by Hezekiah (2 Kin. 20:13), and taken by Nebuchadnezzar (2 Chr. 36:10). This king was not content to drink wine to his gods; he wanted to blaspheme the God of the Jews as well. Can you imagine someone coming in on Sunday morning while we are breaking bread, swerving up the aisle, grabbing a cup from the tray, and throwing the wine on the floor? What would we think if he filled it up with a shot of whiskey then turned and shouted to the congregation, "Here's a toast to the devil!" That's what Belshaazar was doing.

Belshaazar had been weighed in God's scales and found wanting! Put the United States on the scales of God and she is found wanting. Put your family on the scales of God and they are found wanting. Only one thing can balance the scales in your life to God's satisfaction and that is the blood of the Lord Jesus!

FOR THE BULLETIN

❁ Aurelius Augustine, a prodigal son who became one of the greatest church leaders in Christian history, died on August 28, 430. ❁ Today is the birthday (in 1796) of William H. Bathurst, Anglican clergyman and hymnist who wrote "O For a Faith that Will Not Shrink." ❁ Ira David Sankey, American evangelist, composer, and hymnist, was born in Lawrence County, Pennsylvania, on this day in 1840. After serving in the Union Army during the Civil War, Ira returned home and became a tax collector. His real love, however, was singing, and he was in demand as a soloist at meetings. His father, hoping he would enter politics, complained, "I am afraid that boy will never amount to anything. All he does is run about the country with a hymnbook under his arm." In 1870, Ira came to the attention of evangelist D. L. Moody, beginning one of the most famous partnerships in evangelistic history. For the next quarter century, Moody and Sankey traveled around the world. Sankey's *Gospel Hymns and Sacred Songs and Solos* sold over fifty million copies. He became his generation's most beloved gospel singer. ❁ Today is the wedding anniversary of D. L. and Emma Moody who were married in 1862. ❁ George Matheson, the great Scottish preacher, died on this day in 1906. Though blind, he preached to great multitudes each Sunday and wrote the hymns "O Love That Wilt Not Let Me Go" and "Make Me a Captive, Lord." ❁ Martin Luther King, Jr. delivered his great "I Have a Dream" Speech on this day in 1963, in Washington D.C.

APPROPRIATE SONGS AND HYMNS

All for Jesus, Mary Dagworthy James; Public Domain.
Clear My Mind, Dan Marks; © 1981 Maranatha! Music.
Every Breath that I Take, Eddie Espinosa; © 1982 Mercy/Vineyard Publishing.
I Am Resolved, Palmer Hartsough/James H. Fillmore; Public Domain.
More Like My Jesus, Charles Kirby; © 1977 Hope Publishing Company.

WORSHIP HELPS

Call to Worship:
Who shall not fear You, O Lord, and glorify Your name? For You alone are holy. For all nations shall come and worship before You, for Your judgments have been manifested. (Rev. 15:4 NKJV)

Offertory Comments:
Our message today reflects upon the story of the ominous "writing on the wall." Belshazzar and his drunken friends decided to use the Lord's holy vessels to indulge themselves at a drunken party. These things had been consecrated to the Lord, but they sinfully desecrated them, which resulted in the ultimate punishment. This reminds us of Joshua 6, when Achan stole from the Lord's treasury and was condemned to death. While these stories warn us against making light of what's dedicated to the Lord, they also reveal an encouraging truth: things that are dedicated to the Lord are precious to Him. You see, the Israelites had handcrafted the vessels of gold in obedience and dedication to the Lord. They devoted the spoils of all of Jericho to the Lord as an offering. The Lord values our sacrifice. Often I hear people criticize churches or charities for misuse of funds, but the Lord is in ultimate control of your resources and how they're used. Give from your heart to the Lord today. Your gifts are precious to Him.

Benediction:
Until the day breaks, and the shadows flee away, come to each of us, O Lord, across the mountains of division. And may grace, mercy, and peace from the Father, the Son, and the Holy Spirit, be with us all forevermore. Amen.

—*W. Graham Scroggie*

Additional Sermons and Lesson Ideas

The Difference in Daniel

Date preached:

By Dr. Denis Lyle

SCRIPTURE: Daniel 5:11–17

INTRODUCTION: What do others say about us when we're not there? Are we different from others because of our faith? When Belshazzar needed someone different from his soothsayers and wise men to interpret the writing on the wall, Daniel was the first resort. Why? Because Daniel was:

1. A Consecrated Man (v. 11). The spirit of "holy gods" was in him. That's the pagan way of noticing the work of God in Daniel's life.
2. An Illuminated Man (v. 12). Filled with God's Spirit, Daniel understood spiritual things.
3. A Separated Man (v. 13). While hundreds of magicians, astrologers, and soothsayers couldn't help the king, the king saw Daniel as separate from this class of Magi.
4. A Liberated Man (vv. 16, 17). When offered a third of the kingdom, Daniel refused. Material things didn't bind him!

CONCLUSION: Do others turn to us for spiritual guidance? Do we make it obvious that God has consecrated, illuminated, separated, and liberated us?

What Bethel Meant

Date preached:

By W. Graham Scroggie

SCRIPTURE: Genesis 28:10–17

INTRODUCTION: The word *Bethel* literally means "house of God." Jacob encountered God at this place, and what he learned changed him. It can change us, too.

1. A Larger World (v. 14). The narrow world Jacob had been living in was tiny in comparison to Bethel under the open sky! This caused him to be more vulnerable.
2. A Clearer Vision (v. 12). A vision of heaven shattered Jacob's earthly view of life. What a different perspective we have on earth when compared with heaven!
3. A Richer Fellowship (v. 12). Jacob felt alone, but saw ascending and descending, the angels, God's ministering spirits!
4. A Nobler Life (v. 15). God promised His presence and His power.
5. A Truer Understanding (vv. 16, 17). Jacob realized that God, while unseen, is ever-present.

CONCLUSION: When faced with God Himself, we understand how great He really is, and how small we really are. Even so, He desires to have a loving relationship with each of us. Won't you respond?

SEPTEMBER 4, 2005

SUGGESTED SERMON *Date preached:*

Staying Moral in an Immoral Age

Scripture: Proverbs 7

Introduction: We live in a sex-saturated society. TV, movies, videos, novels, magazines, billboards, and computer screens bring immorality into our homes and make it appear as the norm. How can God's people remain pure? How can you develop a personal morality strong enough to withstand the seduction of the current age? Today, I'd like to tell you about a man who once saw sex in the city. This man lived long ago, but just like us, he had a window on the world. His window wasn't a television set, but a real window in a real city. This story is found in Proverbs 7. This is a longer passage than I usually read on a Sunday morning, but I think we need to hear the entire chapter.

Scripture Reading: Proverbs 7

Introduction: Sex outside of marriage is a violation of the character and the Laws of God. We don't know if this young man was engaging in premarital or extramarital sex, but Ephesians 5 says, "Among you there must not be even a hint of sexual immorality" (NIV). Sex itself isn't bad; it's a gift of God. But premarital sex, extramarital sex, post-marital sex, and homosexual behavior are perversions of God's plan. The entertainment industry is on a vast evangelistic mission to convince us otherwise, but the devil can never alter the character or standards of a holy God. So, as the writer of Proverbs 7 stood in his window and peered through the lattice, he witnessed a scene with three storylines.

1. **Seduction.** This young man was seduced, presented with temptation so attractive he seemed unable to resist it. Verse 7 calls him a youth, so we would suppose he was full of hormonal energy. Verse 13 says that a woman met him, embraced him, and passionately kissed him. Having ignited this masculine energy, she said, "Let's go to my place." With persuasive words, she seduced him. The devil is in the same business today. He plies his trade by plastering our television shows, movies, and magazines with stimulating sexual images. He does it with men and women who dress immodestly. He does it by getting us involved with a platonic friendship at work. And he does it with the Internet.

2. **Destruction.** The youth paid a high price for his evening of pleasure (vv. 22ff.). We don't know what happened to him. Perhaps he caught a sexually transmitted disease. Perhaps the husband found out and it led to a fight. More likely, the writer was saying that this young man's immorality took him down a road that led him away from God, from holiness, and from eternal life. See Galatians 6:7, 8.

3. **Instruction.** The whole purpose of Proverbs 7 is to instruct, warn, and help us avoid the tragic mistake this youth made. A careful reading of the chapter gives three weapons for staying moral in an immoral age.

   A. **Store Up God's Commandments Within You** (vv. 1–5). See Psalm 119:11 and Matthew 4:1–11. When we fill our minds with the Word, we have ammunition to fend off the devil's attacks.
   B. **Whenever Possible, Avoid the Temptation.** Verse 6 says the youth lacked judgment. How do we know? Because of verse 8: "Passing along the street near her corner; and he took the path to her house." He wasn't just an innocent victim. He was looking to be seduced. He was walking in that direction. What change do you need to make in your lifestyle that will lessen temptation? How can you walk down another street, away from the seducer's neighborhood?
   C. **Make Up Your Mind to Stay Pure.** Verses 24, 25: "Listen ... pay attention ... Do not let your heart turn aside to her ways ..." Determine not to sin in these ways. Set your standards in advance, before you face the temptation.

Conclusion: Compare this young man to two others in the Bible. When faced with a similar temptation, Joseph turned and fled, leaving his cloak in the woman's hands. He realized it is better to lose one's coat than one's character. (See Gen. 39:1–13). The second young man is Jesus Himself. He was tempted in all ways as we are, yet without sin. You and I don't have the strength ourselves to remain victorious. But when Christ, who never sinned, lives within us, He can live His life through us. In Jesus Christ, we can be more than conquerors.

STATS, STORIES, AND MORE

Internet Porn

Paul Strand, Washington correspondent for CBN, reported that everyone is aware it's easy to become addicted to cocaine or heroin, but how about pornography? A group of counselors is warning this addiction may become epidemic. Researchers are finding that when people indulge in porn, they release powerful chemicals in their brain and body. Mark Kastleman, author of *The Drug of the New Millennium*, said, "There are a growing number of therapists and psychologists who are saying that this is as addictive as cocaine." Pornography has always been around, but now it is a widespread crisis. The reason? Blame the Internet, because of what Kastleman calls the three A's: It's accessible, affordable, and anonymous. The anonymity is the key, especially with religious people. They can do it without anyone knowing. You don't stagger around with a hangover the next day or have needle marks in your arms. Roughly, 40 million Americans are sexually involved with the Internet. One man said, "I was a leader in my local church. I worked with youth groups. I served in the community. Yet I had this secret life." Another said "I developed a dual lifestyle. On one hand, we went to church every Sunday ... Yet, on the other hand, I had this addiction." Kastleman says we live in such a stressful time, and religious believers usually don't allow themselves typical stress-relievers like smoking and drinking. But Internet porn is secret. Kastleman said, "Now suddenly you have a little mouse where you hit a button, and instantly you get this flood of brain chemicals. No one knows you're doing it and it's completely affordable or costs nothing at all."

FOR THE BULLETIN

❁ Today is the birthday of Robert Raikes (1735), a newspaper editor in Gloucester, England, who was appalled by conditions he found in the slums of England when he went searching for an employee. He hired teachers to spend Sundays teaching children reading, writing, and the Bible. When the experiment proved successful, he publicized it in his newspaper, giving birth to the movement that later evolved into our Sunday schools. ❁ Today is also the birthday of Marcus Whitman (1802). Marcus and his wife, Narcissa, medical missionaries to the Pacific Northwest, were massacred while attempting to evangelize Native Americans. ❁ Ailing Anglican pastor Henry Lyte preached his last sermon and retired to his home where he wrote the hymn, "Abide with Me," on this day in 1847. He died soon thereafter. ❁ On September 4, 1869, Missionary Hudson Taylor discovered his famous "Exchanged Life." Suffering exhaustion and anxiety, he read a letter from fellow missionary John McCarthy which said the secret to inner victory is "... abiding, not striving nor struggling; looking off to Him, trusting Him for present power." Taylor read those words in little mission station at Chin-kiang and reported, "As I read, I saw it all. I looked to Jesus; and when I saw, oh how the joy flowed." John 15 took center stage in Taylor's life as he realized the joy of abiding in Christ. He later wrote: "As to work, mine was never so plentiful or so difficult; but the weight and strain are now gone ... As I thought of the Vine and the branches, what light the blessed Spirit poured into my soul!"

APPROPRIATE SONGS AND HYMNS

O Lord, You Are My Shepherd, Brian Doerkson; © 1990 Mercy/Vineyard Publishing.

A Heart for God, Dave Hall; © 1991 Dave Hall; Admin. by Worship to the Nations Music.

O to Be Like Thee, Thomas O. Chisholm/William J. Kirkpatrick; Public Domain.

We Praise Thee with Our Minds, Hugh T. McElrath/William J. Reynolds; © 1952, 1964 Broadman Press; Admin. by Genevox Music Group.

Who May Ascend to the Hill of the Lord, Kirk Dearman; © 1989 Maranatha Praise, Inc.; Admin. by The Copyright Company.

WORSHIP HELPS

Call to Worship:
Alleluia! Sing to Jesus! His the scepter, His the throne.
Alleluia! His the triumph, His the victory alone.
—*William C. Dix,* 1867

Scripture Medley on God's Holiness:
The LORD is in His holy temple. Let all the earth keep silence before Him. The four living creatures, each having six wings, were full of eyes around and within. And they do not rest day or night, saying: "Holy, holy, holy, Lord God Almighty, Who was and is and is to come!" The LORD is in His holy temple, the LORD's throne is in heaven; His eyes behold, His eyelids test the sons of men. Who may ascend into the hill of the LORD? Or who may stand in His holy place? He who has clean hands and a pure heart, who has not lifted up his soul to an idol, nor sworn deceitfully. He shall receive blessings from the LORD, and righteousness from the God of his salvation. As obedient children, not conforming yourselves to the former lusts, as in your ignorance; but as He who called you is holy, you also be holy in all your conduct, because it is written, "Be holy, for I am holy." (Hab. 2:20; Rev. 4:8; Ps. 11:4; Ps. 24:3–5; 1 Pet. 1:14–16 NKJV)

Kids Talk

Ask the children which they like best—screen or pages. Show them several screens or pictures of screens—television screens, Palm™ devices, electronic toys, PCs, etc. Then show them several books—children's books, picture books, your Bible. Tell them that screens are all right for some things, but that pages are better—especially the pages of the Bible. Encourage them to read a few minutes every evening at bedtime.

Additional Sermons and Lesson Ideas

Overcoming Deception

Date preached:

By Rev. Todd M. Kinde

SCRIPTURE: James 1:16–27

INTRODUCTION: True satisfaction is found in the Word of God. The antidote to deception is the Word of God.

1. Satisfied with the Word (1:16, 17).
2. Saved by the Word (1:18–21).
3. Servants to the Word (1:22–27a).
4. Sanctified by the Word (1:17b).

CONCLUSION: There is an intense need for bold, vigorous, and systematic teaching of the Scriptures in the church. We have devalued the sufficiency and supremacy of Scripture by looking to programs and promotions, events and experiences, methods and markets to build the church. Christ has said He will build His church and He has determined the means by which He would do so—the Word (John 17:17). The same is true not only for the local church but also for your life.

Common Bond

Date preached:

By Rev. Peter Grainger

SCRIPTURE: Acts 16:25–34

INTRODUCTION: What do we have in common as Christians? We're demographically all over the board, and we have different testimonies of the Lord's work in our lives. We should all, however, share a common bond in a few important areas.

1. We Should Believe (v. 31). We share an unshakable faith in Jesus Christ as our Lord and Savior. This truth is the most essential dimension that should be shared despite denomination.
2. We Should Be Baptized (vv. 32, 33). The believers in the early church were no sooner converted than they were baptized! While this doesn't determine salvation, it's an essential act of obedience.
3. We Should Belong. The text doesn't tell us what happened to these converts, but we can assume they became a part of the Philippian Church. Do you belong to a local body of believers?

CONCLUSION: Our common faith saves us. Our common obedience to God displays our commitment. Our common fellowship proves our faith (John 13:35).

SEPTEMBER 11, 2005

SUGGESTED SERMON *Date preached:*

As We Remember

By Dr. Ed Dobson

Scripture: Various, especially James 4:14
For what is your life? It is even a vapor that appears for a little time and then vanishes away. (NKJV)

Introduction: Where were you when you heard the news of the terrorist attacks on September 11, 2001? We're not likely to forget the circumstances surrounding that day in our lives. As we pause both as a nation and more specifically as a community of believers, I want to share with you three things that we need to keep in mind when we reflect on this tragic event.

1. **Life Is Brief and Uncertain** (James 4:13–17). Most of those who worked in the Trade Towers or the Pentagon woke up that morning, went through their morning routines, and ended up at work as usual. Those who were on the fatal flights that day probably didn't think anything about getting on those planes. However, for many in the Trade Towers, for those on the planes, for those in the Pentagon, this was their last day. Life is brief and so uncertain. James says it's like a vapor that disappears in an instant. We should ask ourselves three questions:

   A. **Am I Ready to Die?** Another way to ask this question is: What have you done with Jesus? The Bible says that God loves you, and that Jesus Christ suffered, died, and shed His blood and rose again so that we could be forgiven and restored to God. Have you ever confessed your sin to God? Have you ever believed and received Jesus Christ as your Savior and Lord? If you have not, I beg you make that decision this morning because life is brief and uncertain. If you have made this decision, what kind of legacy will you leave when you die? Are there people you haven't forgiven? Friends you haven't shared the gospel with?

   B. **Am I Living in Surrender?** James tells us not to tell others our plans, but to qualify every future action in our lives to say, "If the Lord wills, we shall live and do this or that" (James 4:14, 15). One of the biggest struggles in life for Christians is to submit our future to the Lord, but it's the most important struggle to overcome!

C. **Am I Living to the Fullest?** James tells us that knowing the good we should do and refraining from it is sin (v. 17)! While we are still living, we should take every opportunity to serve the Lord. Are you doing this?

2. **God Is Our Only Source of Hope (Ps. 46).** These verses tell us not to fear, but to hope in God during trouble. Reflecting on the events of September 11, we are forced to answer some basic questions like, "Is there a God?" and, "What kind of God would let this happen?" Is this world just chaos, and is tragedy the proof? Is God cruel and uncaring about us? God has revealed Himself through this world and through Scripture, and as Christians, we believe He exists, so why did He allow this to happen? He is not uninvolved or uninformed, as some critics and even scholars might suggest; the Bible teaches that He is ultimately in control. The Lord works through tragedy. Was it not the most horrific tragedy when Jesus Christ, God in human form, was tortured and crucified? Yet, the Lord provided salvation through this tragedy. It's God's job to guide His creation, and ours to hope only in Him.

3. **We Should Be Proactive in Eliminating Hatred and Terrorism (Rom. 1).** You might think I sound like a politician now, but Romans 1:16 tells us that we are not to be ashamed of the gospel because, "it is the power of God to salvation for everyone who believes, for the Jew first and also for the Greek." (NKJV) That includes Osama bin Laden and Saddam Hussein. This doesn't mean we support acts of terror or that we are promoting other religions, but it does mean that even terrorists are fallen, sinful people just like we are without the salvation of Jesus Christ. The gospel is a gospel of peace (Eph. 6:15). We, as believers, have a responsibility to fight darkness, terrorism, and hatred with prayer, fasting, and evangelism. Are you doing your part?

Conclusion: Are you ready to die, to surrender, to live? Is your hope in God or yourself? What are we doing to advance the message of Jesus in our own community and around the world? Our life is vanishing quickly, so make a decision today to surrender your life completely, hoping in Him through tragedy and triumph.

STATS, STORIES, AND MORE

More from Dr. Ed Dobson:

When I was growing up in Ireland and they would make announcements in church, they would say, "Monday night at 8 o'clock we're having a Bible study, the Lord willing." Every announcement was concluded with the words, "the Lord willing." Whatever plans you made, whatever you announced about the future was always surrendered to these words: "the Lord willing." We ought to live every moment of every day in this way.

I went flying with a man in our church. He let me fly the plane a little bit, which is a rather dangerous thing. We were flying along and I was trying to maintain an altitude and follow a specific heading (the heading is on the instruments). I looked up at a compass at the top of the cockpit. The heading I was following was different from the heading on the compass. When I inquired, he said, "Oh, that's simple. When you turn on the communication systems, the radar, and the navigational system, they create all sorts of electrical currents that skew the compass at the top of the cockpit. But if we were to lose all of that equipment or if I were to shut all of it off, the compass would be the true direction."

Life is like that. We turn on all of the extra stuff in life, all of the encumbering junk in our lives skew our true direction. Sometimes God, for reasons beyond logical explanation, interrupts our lives and shuts off all of the current and we discover just how far we have drifted off course. So, this sermon is a mid-course correction.

FOR THE BULLETIN

❁ Today is the anniversary of a major church council in French Christian history. The Council of Agde was held in southern France on September 11, 506, attended by 35 bishops. Among other items of business, the Council looked with jaundiced eye on monasticism among women and forbade the establishing of any additional convents without the bishops' approval. ❁ Henry Hudson discovered Manhattan Island on September 11, 1609. ❁ Today marks the anniversary in 1672 of the ordination of Solomon Stoddard. He served as pastor in Northampton, Massachusetts from 1670 to 1729—nearly sixty years! In 1727, his grandson, Jonathan Edwards, became his co-pastor, and when Stoddard died in 1729, Edwards became the sole pastor. He wrote several books and was an active promoter of revival. Stoddard is one of the most important names in colonial American church history. ❁ John Marriott was baptized on September 11, 1780. He became a prominent British clergyman and hymnist, the author of "Thou Whose Almighty Word." ❁ A. B. Simpson preached his first sermon as pastor of his first church on this day in 1865. He was ordained later in the day and married the next. ❁ On September 11, 1922, the British Mandate of Palestine began. ❁ September 11, 2001, marks the deadliest attack against America by foreign enemies on American soil. Terrorists using three hijacked airliners destroyed the World Trade Center in New York and attacked the Pentagon in Washington. Passengers who subdued terrorists aboard a doomed airliner in Pennsylvania thwarted a fourth attempt.

APPROPRIATE SONGS AND HYMNS

Days of Elijah, Robin Mark; © 1997 Daybreak Music, Ltd.; Admin. by Integrity Music, Inc.

Did You Feel the Mountains Tremble, Martin Smith; © 1994 Curious? Music UK; Admin. by EMI Christian Music Publishing.

Open My Eyes that I May See, Clara H. Scott; Public Domain.

Sanctuary, John W. Thomas/Randy Scruggs; © 1982 Whole Armor Music/Full Armor Publishing; Admin. by The Kruger Organization, Inc.

What If It Were Today?, Lelia N. Morris; Public Domain.

WORSHIP HELPS

Call to Worship:
The LORD also will be a refuge for the oppressed, a refuge in times of trouble. And those who know Your name will put their trust in You; for You, LORD, have not forsaken those who seek You. Sing praises to the LORD, who dwells in Zion! (Ps. 9:9–11 NKJV)

Scripture Reading: Psalm 46 (MSG)
God is a safe place to hide, ready to help when we need him. We stand fearless at the cliff-edge of doom, courageous in sea storm and earthquake, before the rush and roar of oceans, the tremors that shift mountains. Jacob-wrestling God fights for us, GOD of angel armies protects us ... Attention, all! See the marvels of GOD! He plants flowers and trees all over the earth, bans war from pole to pole, breaks all the weapons across his knee. Step out of the traffic! Take a long, loving look at me, your High God, above politics, above everything. Jacob-wrestling God fights for us, GOD of angel armies protects us.

Pastoral Prayer:
In a world of uncertainty, terror, fear, and injustice, we turn to You, O God, for You are our rock, our strength, our refuge, our hope, and our salvation. No act of terror could compare to Your suffering on the Cross for us. You conquered fear and death so that we might live with internal peace and joy despite our circumstances. Guide us now, to be Your shining light, to preach Your gospel of peace until Your triumphant return. We ask in Jesus' name. Amen.

Additional Sermons and Lesson Ideas

Signposts

Date preached:

By Dr. Timothy Beougher

SCRIPTURE: Mark 1:1–8

INTRODUCTION: Our country is full of signposts: road-signs, store signs, advertisements, etc. A signpost points to a destination. John the Baptist was the signpost pointing towards Jesus Christ. This passage highlights three qualities from his life that we need to emulate as we seek to point people to Jesus Christ.

1. Focus On the Problem of Sin and the Possibility of Forgiveness (vv. 4, 5).
2. Follow God Over Social Expectations (v. 6).
3. Faithfully Point Beyond Yourself to Jesus Christ (vv. 7, 8).

CONCLUSION: The key to becoming a signpost that points others towards Christ is to model John the Baptist's philosophy: "He must increase, but I must decrease" (John 3:30 NKJV).

The Vice of Stealing

Date preached:

By Dr. Melvin Worthington

SCRIPTURE: Exodus 20:15

INTRODUCTION: Have you ever had a car broken into? Has money been stolen from your purse or wallet? We feel violated when others steal from us. God spoke the Eighth Commandment to guard our right to our possessions.

1. The Admonition in the Text. This Commandment recognizes the ownership of property and requires the proper use of money. It rebukes stealing in every form—sinful spending, sinful sparing, and simple stealing.
2. The Analysis of the Text. It prohibits both attitudes and acts. This Commandment protects us from the adversary, the alarm, and the anxiety regarding our personal property.
3. The Application from the Text. False pretense in business, fraudulent payments, taking advantage of the ignorant, and stealing are ways this Commandment is violated. The value of this Commandment is for industry, integrity, and intellectual stimulation.

CONCLUSION: We must use that which God has given to us for His glory and human good. This right of ownership of personal property requires that we faithfully use it for the glory of God.

SEPTEMBER 18, 2005

SUGGESTED SERMON *Date preached:*

We've a Story to Yell to the Nations

Scripture: Isaiah 49:1–6; Acts 13:47

Introduction: An old missionary hymn says, "We've a Story to Tell to the Nations." But we're not just to tell them—we're to proclaim the message, to shout it from the rooftops. We've a story to yell to the nations. Isaiah 49 is a messianic chapter. It's all about Jesus Christ. It's a description of His ministry giving us six missionary maxims.

1. **Jesus Christ Was a Missionary (v. 1).** *Listen to me, you islands ... you distant nations* (NIV). The Messiah is speaking. To whom? Distant nations. He isn't speaking just to Israel, but to the islands of the sea and to the continents of the world.

2. **Jesus Christ Was a Missionary Ordained from His Mother's Womb (v. 1).** "Before I was born, the LORD called me; from my birth he has made mention of my name" (NIV). Jesus said, "For this reason I was born and for this I came into the world" (John 18:37 NIV).

3. **Jesus Was a Missionary With a Message (v. 2).** "He has made My mouth like a sharp sword." (NKJV) In Hebrews, we're told that the Word of God is a two-edged sword, piercing to the dividing asunder of soul and spirit ... and is a discerner of the thoughts and intents of the heart. In Revelation 19, as Jesus returns to earth, out of His mouth comes a sharp sword with which to strike down the nations. Warriors in biblical times didn't just need swords for hand-to-hand combat. They needed arrows for enemies that were more distant. Isaiah 49:2 goes on to say: "He made me into a polished arrow and concealed me in His quiver" (NIV).

4. **Jesus Was a Missionary for God's Glory (v. 3).** "In whom I will be glorified." (NKJV) God the Father displayed His splendor in God the Son.

5. **Jesus Was a Missionary Facing Discouragement (v. 4).** This is one of the most remarkable messianic portions in the Bible, for it is the Son's admission that His task seemed thankless.

6. **Jesus Was a Missionary Who Found His Strength in God (v. 5).** "My God shall be my strength." (NKJV)

7. **Jesus Was a Missionary Whose Work Was Greater Than It Seemed (v. 6).** The Father said to Him: "It is too small a thing that You should be My Servant [just for Israel]. I will also give You as a light to the Gentiles, that You should be My salvation to the ends of the earth." (NKJV)

Transition: Keeping this in mind, turn to Acts 13, the first missionary journey of the apostle Paul. In Acts 13, he and Barnabas are set apart and set forth from the church at Antioch (Acts 13:1–3). They traveled on to Pisidian Antioch where he told his listeners that God has commanded him, saying: "I have set you as a light to the Gentiles, that you should be for the salvation to the ends of the earth" (Acts 13:47 NKJV). He quotes Isaiah 49:6!—a messianic passage—applying it to himself! He gives us biblical justification for personalizing this passage about the Messiah's missionary obligation to ourselves. That means:

1. **We Are Missionaries.** We all have a part in the worldwide spread of the gospel. We should all be "world Christians."

2. **We Are Missionaries Ordained from Our Mothers' Wombs.** This helps us find our purpose in life. God is leaving His church on earth a little longer for the evangelization of the nations.

3. **We Are Missionaries with a Message.** We've got a unique gospel that deserves a hearing in the ears of every human being on earth.

4. **We Are Missionaries for God's Glory.** It isn't so we'll make a great name for ourselves or have a lot of fun traveling to exotic locales. It's for His glory alone!

5. **We Are Missionaries Who Will Face Discouragement.** Many times, we seem outnumbered, and our hearts are often cast down because of the resistance we face. But God is building His church, and the gates of hell shall not prevail against it.

6. **We Are Missionaries Who Find Our Strength in God.** We abide in Him, finding strength day by day.

7. **We Are Missionaries Whose Work Is Greater Than It Seems.** Only heaven will reveal the multitudes that will be saved because of our worldwide efforts.

Conclusion: Jesus said, "As the Father has sent Me, I also send you." (John 20:21 NKJV). Jesus Christ is God's missionary to the world, and we're His ambassadors. We've a story to yell to the nations! Are you doing your part?

STATS, STORIES, AND MORE

Missions Stats:

Current population of earth: 6,400,000,000
One-third of the earth's population is under the age of 15.
An estimated 120 million people are presented with the gospel for the first time each year.
At least 2,000 languages still need the Bible translated.

The Progress of the Gospel:

By A.D. 1430, 1% of the earth's population was Christian (1 in 99 after 1,430 years).
By AD 1790, 2% was Christian (One to 49 after 360 years).
By AD 1940, 3% was Christian (One to 32 after 150 years).
By AD 1960, 4% was Christian (One to 24 after 20 years).
By AD 1970, 5% was Christian (One to 19 after 10 years).
By AD 1980, 6% was Christian (One to 16 after 10 years).
By AD 1983, 7% was Christian (One to 13 after 3 years).
By AD 1986, 8% was Christian (One to 11 after 3 years).
By AD 1989, 9% was Christian (One to 10 after 3 years).
By AD 1993, 10% was Christian (One to 9 after 4 years).
By AD 1997, 11% was Christian (One to 8 after 4 years).

FOR THE BULLETIN

❁ Today marks the birth in A.D. 52 of the Roman Emperor and Persecutor of Christians, Marcus Ulpius Trajan. During his reign, the Apostolic Father Ignatius of Antioch was martyred. ❁ Anne Hutchison arrived in Boston on this day in 1634. Born in England the daughter of a minister, she was an enthusiastic Bible teacher, but her teachings resulted in a charge of heresy and she was banished from the Massachusetts Bay colony. She eventually moved to New York; but in 1643, Indians murdered Anne and her large family (except for one daughter). ❁ Today is the birthday, in 1765, of Oliver Holden, composer of the hymn tune CORONATION ("All Hail the Power of Jesus' Name"). His last words are said to have been, "I have some beautiful airs running through my head, if I only had the strength to note them down." ❁ Former inmate Jerry McAuley was the founder of New York's Water Street Mission, a pioneer among American rescue missions. McAuley had been born in Ireland in 1839. His father, a counterfeiter, fled to escape the law, and Jerry never knew him. His mother evidently languished in prison, and his grandmother raised the boy. When she couldn't control him, he was sent to New York where he lived under the docks, drinking, fighting, and stealing from boats. In 1857, he was caught and sent to Sing Sing where he was converted. He devoted himself to rescuing other incorrigibles. Twenty years later on September 18, 1884, the huge Broadway Tabernacle was packed for his funeral, with multitudes flooding surrounding streets.

APPROPRIATE SONGS AND HYMNS

Shout to the North, Martin Smith; © 1995 Curious? Music UK; Admin. by EMI Christian Music Publishing.

Carry the Light, Twila Paris; © 1989 Ariose Music/Mountain Spring Music; Admin. by EMI Christian Music Publishing.

Go Forth, Robert E. Mason; © 1982 Sounds of Vision; Admin. by Integrity Music, Inc.

Send the Light, Charles H. Gabriel; Public Domain.

Share His Love, William J. Reynolds; © 1973 Broadman Press; Admin. by Genevox Music Group.

We Declare Your Name, Paul Baloche/Rita Baloche/Claire Cloninger; © 1995 Integrity's Hosanna! Music/Word Music, Inc./Juniper Landing Music; Admin. by Word Music Group, Inc.

WORSHIP HELPS

Call to Worship:
How shall they hear without a preacher? And how shall they preach unless they are sent? As it is written: "How beautiful are the feet of those who preach the gospel of peace, who bring glad tidings of good things!" Romans 10:14-15

Hymn Story: Send the Light
The author of the missionary hymn, "Send the Light," was Charles Gabriel, who grew up in Iowa, living on a farm until age 17. Even in childhood, he was drawn toward music; and when his Methodist family purchased a small reed organ, he taught himself to play it. With his parents' encouragement, he was leading singing schools by age 16.

He married, but because of his frantic schedule of traveling and teaching music, his marriage failed. In 1887, he moved to California to get a new start, and soon he had remarried. In 1890, he began working at Grace Methodist Episcopal Church in San Francisco. When the Sunday School Superintendent came to him asking for a missionary hymn for Easter Sunday to highlight a Golden Offering, Gabriel wrote "Send the Light." It was sung with enthusiasm that day, March 6, 1890, and a visiting missionary representative who liked the words carried the hymn back to the east coast.

The immediate popularity of "Send the Light" propelled Gabriel to prominence in the hymn-writing community. He had tried once before to support himself by writing hymns, but had failed. Now, he tried again. Within two years, he was in Chicago, devoting his full time to writing and publishing hymns. He wrote many of our favorite gospels songs, but none more popular than: "There's a call comes ringing o'er the restless wave, 'Send the light! Send the light!'"

Additional Sermons and Lesson Ideas

A Simple Message

Date preached:

By Joshua D. Rowe

SCRIPTURE: Mark 1:15

INTRODUCTION: Many of us have thought, "The gospel is too complicated," or, "I wish I could make this simple." While the gospel has a world of implications and will make a world of difference, Jesus made it simple.

1. The Time Is Fulfilled. The long-awaited Savior, who was to fulfill all the prophecies, had finally arrived! Jesus, God Himself did come as a man to solve the problem of sin in the world.
2. Repent. Before we can follow Jesus, we must recognize our sin. We all have sinned (Rom. 3:23), but we can respond to Jesus' calling and, with His help, turn away from our sins.
3. Believe in the Gospel. Jesus came to reconcile us to Himself. God is too holy to accept sinful humans, but Jesus paid the consequence for us. Now, we can simply believe in Him and be saved from our sins.

CONCLUSION: Once we repent and put our faith in Jesus, His Spirit changes us and teaches us. He brings us, little by little, to understand the unfathomable depths of His gospel. However, the message is simple. Now is the time. Turn away from your sins, and follow the Savior!

How to Delight God

Date preached:

SCRIPTURE: Proverbs 15:8

INTRODUCTION: The word *delight* means "a high degree of gratification. Extreme satisfaction. Something that gives great pleasure." What gives that to God? The prayers of a righteous person. That leaves us with four responses.

1. We should delight in prayer. It would give joy to God were we to delight in what delights Him.
2. We should be upright. That's the qualification.
3. We should be faithful in our praying.
4. We should pray in faith, knowing God will answer, for if He delights in our prayers, He will be delighted in answering them.

CONCLUSION: Of all the motivations to pray, none is greater than this. Think of prayer differently. Instead of a duty or drudgery, it's a delight. And not just for you!

TECHNIQUES FOR THE PASTOR'S DELIVERY

Advice on the Voice

By Rev. Charles Haddon Spurgeon

Our first rule with regard to the voice is—do not think too much about it, for recollect the sweetest voice is nothing without something to say, and however well it may be managed, it will be like a well-driven cart with nothing in it.

On the other hand, do not think too little of your voice, for its excellence may greatly conduce to the result that you hope to produce. Exceedingly precious truths may be greatly marred by being delivered in monotonous tones. I once heard a most esteemed minister who mumbled sadly compared to "bumble bee in a pitcher."

When you do pay attention to the voice, *take care not to fall into the habitual and common affectations of the present day*. Scarcely one man in a dozen in the pulpit talks like a man. We only meet with an artificial language and a false tone. This style of speaking is only tolerated in the church because, unfortunately, it is so general there; elsewhere, it would not be endured. A person who has not a natural and true delivery, should not be allowed to occupy the pulpit.

Always speak so as to be heard. I know a man who weighs sixteen stone, and ought to be able to be heard half-a-mile, who is so gracelessly indolent that in his small place of worship you can scarcely hear him in the front of the gallery.

Do not as a rule exert your voice to the utmost in ordinary preaching. Two or three earnest men, now present, are tearing themselves to pieces by needless bawling; their poor lungs are irritated, and their larynx inflamed by boisterous shouting, from which they seem unable to refrain. Now it is all very well to "Cry aloud and spare not," but "Do thyself no harm" is apostolical advice. When persons can hear you with half the amount of voice, it is as well to save the superfluous force for times when it may be wanted. "Waste not, want not" may apply here as well as elsewhere. Be a little economical with that enormous volume of sound. Do not give your hearers head-aches when you mean to give them heart-aches. Adapt your voice to your audience.

Next to the moderation of lung-force, I should place the rule, *modulate your tones*. Alter the key frequently and vary the strain constantly. Let the bass, the treble, and the tenor, take their turn.

The whole day's duty in a church is nothing, in point of labor, compared with the performance of one of Shakespeare's leading characters, nor I should suppose, with any of the very great displays made by our leading statesmen in the Houses of Parliament; and I feel very certain that the disorder, which you designate as "clergyman's sore throat," is attributable generally to the mode of speaking, and not to the length of time or violence of effort that may be employed.

If ministers would speak oftener, their throats and lungs would be less liable to disease. Of this, I am quite sure; it is matter of personal experience and wide observation, and I am confident I am not mistaken. Gentlemen, twice a week preaching is very dangerous, but I have found five or six times healthy, and even twelve or fourteen not excessive.

In everything, be natural. I am myself, by a kind of irresistible influence, drawn to be an imitator, so that a journey to Scotland or Wales will for a week or two materially affect my pronunciation and tone. Strive against it I do, but there it is; and the only cure I know of is to let the mischief die a natural death. Gentlemen, I return to my rule—use your own natural voices. Do not be monkeys, but men; not parrots, but men of originality in all things.

Lastly, I would say with regard to your throats—take care of them. Take care always to clear them well when you are about to speak, but do not be constantly clearing them while you are preaching. A very esteemed brother of my acquaintance always talks in this way: "My dear friends – hem – hem – this is a most – hem – important subject which I have now – hem – hem – to bring before you, and – hem – hem – I have to call upon you to give me – hem – hem – your most serious – hem – attention." Avoid this most zealously.

Others, from want of clearing the throat, talk as if they were choked up, and were just about to expectorate; it were far better to do so at once than to sicken the hearer by repeated unpleasant sounds. Snuffling and sniffing are excusable enough when a man has a cold, but they are extremely unpleasant, and when they become habitual, they ought to be indicted under the Nuisances Act.

If your throats become affected consult a good physician, or if you cannot do this, give what attention you please to the following hint. Never purchase "Cough-no-more Lozenges," or any of the ten thousand emollient compounds. They may serve your turn for a time by removing present uneasiness, but they ruin the throat by their laxative qualities. If you wish to improve your throat, take a good share of pepper—good Cayenne pepper. I always had a little glass of chili vinegar and water just in front of me, a draught of which appeared to give a fresh force to the throat whenever it grew weary and the voice appeared likely to break down.

Condensed from *Lectures to My Students*

SEPTEMBER 25, 2005

SUGGESTED SERMON *Date preached:*

Bringing a Friend to Jesus

By Dr. Timothy Beougher

Scripture: Mark 2:1–17, especially verse 17
Those who are well have no need of a physician, but those who are sick. I did not come to call the righteous, but sinners, to repentance. (NKJV)

Introduction: Have you ever tried to bring a friend to Jesus? It's a difficult task. Relationships can be strained, sacrifices must be made, and the risk of feeling like a failure is a constant deterrent. Our text teaches us that, despite what it may cost, Jesus came to save sinners, and we have a great responsibility to guide them to Him.

1. **Verses 1, 2.** Jesus entered a house in Capernaum and before too long He attracted His usual crowds. Rather than turn them away, He preached the Word to them. The crowd quickly multiplied until no room was left for anyone to squeeze by.

2. **Verses 3, 4.** The house had an external stairway leading to a flat roof. The roof was constructed by laying beams across the tops of the walls, with smaller sticks and reeds forming a patchwork across them. This was covered with some kind of matting and hardened earth, which the men broke through to lower their paralyzed friend into the house.

3. **Verse 5.** Jesus saw their faith and forgave the paralytic's sins. He recognized that this man's physical need was far exceeded by the sickness of his soul.

4. **Verses 6, 7.** The scribes viewed themselves as the guardians of acceptable religious teaching. They took offense at the words of Jesus and His claim that He had the authority to speak as God. To the scribes this was blasphemy; what could be more slanderous than for a man to speak as though He has authority that clearly belongs to God alone?

5. **Verses 8–11.** Jesus challenged their unbelief. The scribes reasoned in their hearts that Jesus could not have the power to forgive sins because

they were convinced Jesus was not God. Jesus exhibited His authority to forgive by healing the man. In a sense, Jesus called their bluff. He acknowledged it was easy to say something one could not verify, so Jesus manifested His authority to forgive by releasing this man from his physical bondage. What was already done in the spiritual realm was now displayed in the physical realm.

6. **Verse 12.** The people were amazed and gave glory to God!

7. **Verses 13–17.** The previous verses show us a model of bringing others to Jesus. In these verses, Jesus is the model of One who reaches out to others. Jesus sought a disciple from among the tax collectors, viewed as one of the most wretched groups of sinners in the culture of that time. Levi followed Him! As it turned out, when Levi invited his Lord to his house, many more tax collectors and sinners showed up. The scribes and Pharisees opposed Jesus' ministry to this sinful segment of society, confronted Him. His response was, "Those who are well have no need of a physician, but those who are sick. I did not come to call the righteous, but sinners, to repentance" (Mark 2:17 NKJV).

Application: These stories teach us about bringing a friend to Jesus. While not every detail in this account can be made synonymous with bringing someone to Christ today, many can be! The person who owned the house in Capernaum allowed his resources to be used; he valued people over his possessions. When we minister to others, whether in our home or in church, we will have to sacrifice. The church is to be a hospital for sinners, not a museum for saints. People matter more than things! The scribes were critical like many of us are when others are unconventional or unorthodox. The friends of the paralytic were deeply concerned about their friend. They had a sense of urgency. Don't we all have friends who need the forgiveness of Jesus? Are we urgent about it? Are we afraid of how others will react, or perhaps of how Jesus will react to our efforts? Jesus did not react harshly to their bold efforts, but compassionately. We tend to think that we must come to Jesus once we are good enough, but as we see through Levi and the other tax collectors, Jesus did not come to call those who think they are righteous, but to call sinners to repentance. What sacrifices have you made to bring others to Jesus? Are you ministering with a sense of urgency, or are you simply criticizing others like the Pharisees? Jesus gave His life to save sinners like us; what are you doing to bring others to Him?

STATS, STORIES, AND MORE

More from Dr. Timothy Beougher:

As a challenge, I'd like to read portions of a letter Jeff West wrote: "You know me. I'm the fellow that takes care of your house when you go on vacation. Sometimes we cook out together on Saturday nights and the kids play in the yard. Our wives are good friends. They drink coffee together, trade recipes, and carpool the children. We are a lot alike, you and me. We want the best for our families. We determine to stand against adversity, to try, to persevere. But sometimes you seem to have more strength than I have.

"On Sunday morning I may be in the yard watering the grass and you drive by with your family, all of you dressed in your Sunday best, and you wave at me. And I wave back knowing where you are going but not why.

"Sometimes it seems that your life is different than mine. Our wives have talked about it, but you and I are scared to mention it. There's a lot about you that I don't know. There's emptiness in my life, a void that I just can't seem to fill, no matter how hard I try. I need desperately to be answered, to be comforted, to know. And I need someone to tell me.

"But we go on; and I don't mention it because some unknown fear prevents me, and you don't mention it because some unknown power binds you. We laugh together; we joke; we share, but not the important things. I'm your neighbor, and I don't know Jesus."

FOR THE BULLETIN

❁ Balboa was the first European to see the Pacific Ocean on September 25, 1512. ❁ Pope Clement VII was upright and intelligent, but unprepared for the hornet's nest of the papacy. When faced with hard decisions, he vacillated. The Venetian ambassador wrote, "The Pope is 48 years old and is a sensible man but slow in decision, which explains his irresolution in action." Clement, finding his treasury bankrupt was chagrined that no Italian banker trusted him. The citizens of Rome decided they didn't like him either. And Clement agonized over his failure to stem Luther's Reformation and to promote reform within his own church. On September 25, 1534, having barely survived his previous misfortunes, he met a miserable death, reportedly from gobbling down a bowl of poisonous mushrooms. ❁ The Peace of Augsburg was formulated on September 25, 1555, officially giving Lutherans religious freedom in Germany. ❁ On September 25, 1643, the Solemn League and Covenant, drawn up by the Scottish General Assembly in London at Westminster Abbey, guaranteeing Presbyterians equal rights with the Anglicans, was submitted to the English Parliament. ❁ September 25, 1714 is the birthday of William Romaine, Anglican evangelical. In addition to his pastoral and preaching ministry, he prepared and published scholarly books for Bible students. In midlife, he came under the influence of evangelist George Whitefield and began preaching with fervor to great crowds. ❁ Today is also the probable birthday, in 1774, of John Chapman aka Johnny Appleseed. ❁ Missionary Luther Rice died on this day in 1836, and evangelist Peter Cartwright died on this day in 1872.

APPROPRIATE SONGS AND HYMNS

Bold as a Lion, Ron Hamilton; © 1984 Musical Ministries; Admin. by Majesty Music, Inc.

Christ for the World We Sing, Samuel Wolcott/Delice De Giardini; © Public Domain.

Fishers of Men, Harry D. Clarke; © 1927. Renewed 1955 Hope Publishing Company.

I Love to Tell the Story; Catherine A. Hankey/William G. Fischer; Public Domain.

Lead Me to Some Soul Today, Wendell P. Loveless/Will H. Houghton; © 1936. Renewed 1964 Hope Publishing Company.

WORSHIP HELPS

Call to Worship:
All Your works shall praise You, O LORD, and Your saints shall bless You. They shall speak of the glory of Your kingdom, and talk of Your power. (Ps. 145:10, 11 NKJV)

Pastoral Prayer:
Our Heavenly Father, You are very good and very great, and we proclaim with the psalmist, "Great is the Lord, and greatly to be praised; and Your greatness is unsearchable." Help us, Lord, to recognize Your glory for ourselves and to express Your goodness to others. Forgive us for treating the gospel like a secret to be hidden instead of an announcement to be heralded. Open our eyes to see You, Oh Lord, and our ears to hear You and our mouths to speak of the glories of Your gospel. Make us fishers of men and women and winners of boys and girls. In Jesus' name. Amen.

Responsive Reading:

Worship Leader: Let the redeemed of the Lord say so, whom He has redeemed from the hand of the enemy.

All: Go home to your friends, and tell them what great things the Lord has done for you, and how He has had compassion on you.

Worship Leader: Go into the highways, and as many as you find, invite.

All: Go therefore and make disciples of all the nations.

Worship Leader: How beautiful upon the mountains are the feet of him who brings good news, who proclaims peace, who brings glad tidings of good things, who proclaims salvation.

All: All that you command us we will do, and wherever you send us we will go.

(Ps. 107:2; Mark 5:19; Matt. 22:9; Matt. 28:19; Is. 52:7; Josh. 1:16 NKJV)

Additional Sermons and Lesson Ideas

Daring Determination

Date preached:

By Dr. Timothy Beougher

SCRIPTURE: Mark 2:1–5

INTRODUCTION: How important is it to you that your friends, family, or loved ones be saved? How committed are you to bringing them to Jesus? The friends of the paralytic in our text display how daring and determined we should be!

1. They Dared to Do the Difficult. These men tried to push through an incredible crowd. Their failure didn't despair them: they burst through the roof to get their friend to Jesus!
2. They Dared to Do the Unorthodox. Many had pushed through the crowd, yelled, or begged Jesus to heal them, but no one had torn through a roof and lowered someone down to Him!
3. They Dared to Do the Costly. When they tore through the roof, they were taking the risk of having to pay for the damage, but their friend's salvation was worth it!

CONCLUSION: For these friends, it didn't matter that it was difficult, or unorthodox, or costly; they were desperate to bring their friend to Jesus. Are you allowing barriers to keep you from attempting to bring another person to Jesus?

Overcoming Prejudice

Date preached:

By Rev. Todd M. Kinde

SCRIPTURE: James 2:1–12

INTRODUCTION: Treating a person with partiality is a sin and evidence of a partial faith.

1. The Situation of Partiality (2:1–7).
2. The Solution of Love (2:8–13).

CONCLUSION: The standard of judgment is the law of liberty (v. 12). It is not an enslaving legalism. Rather, it is a royal law of love (v. 8), which the believer is enabled to keep by the indwelling Holy Spirit (Gal. 5:22, 23). God will judge the sins of prejudice and favoritism.

BAPTISM SERMON

Dead Center

Date preached:

By Rev. Todd M. Kinde

Scripture: 1 Peter 3:13—4:2

Introduction: We all have a tendency to lose direction, wading hopelessly in a sea of activity without real purpose. Perhaps you've been searching, looking for something to keep your life from being meaningless and insignificant. Sooner or later, you'll be disappointed with whatever worldly thing is at the center of your life. The solution is submission to Christ. First Peter 3:13—4:6 describes a life with Christ at dead center. Jesus is Lord of all. As Lord, He is to be the center of your being. In your hearts, you are to set apart Christ as Lord. The term *to set apart* in the Bible means to take something from the periphery and put it in the center.

1. **When Christ Is the Center of Our Being, We Are People of Hope (3:13–17).** Peter reminds us that we who have trusted the Lord Jesus Christ as Savior from our sin and as Lord of our life are blessed. It is true that suffering may accompany the Christian life. Suffering here and now is temporal and should be understood as such. Blessing is eternal and so are our lives in Christ. So, we can function—even amid suffering—with joy. Our hope is in Christ. We need not fear the wrath of God, for we have trusted in His Word. Death and destruction are nothing to us, for the God we serve is able to bring life out of death. Since Christ is central to our being, we will be ready and willing to share of the hope we have in Christ Jesus our Lord, always being ready to give an answer to everyone who asks us about it. Timidity and shyness are pushed away as the hope of Christ comes rushing through our beings and out of our lives. But this will always be done in the character of Christ's submissive spirit—with gentleness and respect. We will speak the truth with love. When Christ is central, we will give the reason for the hope we have in Christ, the hope of eternity with God.

2. **When Christ Is the Center of Our Being, We Are Dead to Sin (3:18–22).** Some of our attitudes need to change. Fear and pride must be eradicated. Because of our sinfulness, the only way to do away with fear and pride is to die to sin and to self. To do this we must identify with the death of Jesus our Lord. Christ suffered in His body. His suffering was to pay what we owed God for our sin and to satisfy the anger of God over our sin. Jesus

was without sin, a perfect person, indeed, God in the flesh. It is only a perfect person who could pay the penalty: the righteous for the unrighteous. Christ suffered and died once for all. It cannot be repeated ever again nor does it need to be. God the Father raised the Son to life anew by the power of the Spirit. The Spirit gives life.

Jesus said, "as it was in the days of Noah, so it will be also in the days of the Son of Man" (Luke 17:26; Matt. 24:37 NKJV). Peter here says that the gospel was preached to the world in the days of Noah before the flood. God waited patiently 120 years while Noah built the ark. During that time, Noah preached with a hammer in his hand (2 Pet. 2:5; Heb. 11:7). This brief statement recalls everything that is in Genesis 6. One hundred and twenty years of preaching resulted in rejection of the message. Eight souls, however, were saved through the floodwater, Noah's family. What about your family? Have you testified of God's salvation to your family?

Peter says this floodwater is a symbol of baptism. It is a baptism not merely of water that washes dirt off your body, but a baptism with Christ. Christ refers to His death as a baptism (Mark 10:32–45; Luke 12:50). When we are converted, we are baptized into Christ's death. We die to sin and self. The ordinance of water baptism is a symbol of that inner regeneration that took place. Paul states in Romans, "How shall we who died to sin live any longer in it? Or do you not know that as many of us as were baptized into Christ Jesus were baptized into His death? Therefore we were buried with Him through baptism into death, that just as Christ was raised from the dead by the glory of the Father, even so we also should walk in newness of life. For if we have been united together in the likeness of His death, certainly we also shall be in the likeness of His resurrection" (Rom. 6:2–5 NKJV).

3. **When Christ Is the Center of Our Being, We Are Alive to God's Will (4:1–2).** Baptism also symbolizes our new life, the power and presence of the Holy Spirit to live that new life through us for the will of God. No longer do the passions of the flesh defeat you. You will not participate in the satisfying of baser desires. Your satisfaction is found in the ultimate desire, the desire for God—the hunger for God. Water baptism testifies to your desire and commitment of exclusive loyalty to the will of God.

Conclusion: Water Baptism is not an option in the Christian life. It is a necessary part of our testimony. When Christ is central to our being, we will have hope, we will die to sin and self, and we will be alive to the will of God. Baptism symbolizes this reality of being dead center with Christ. Will you consider participating in this rite of water baptism? Will you publicly testify that you have died to sin and live for Christ?

OCTOBER 2, 2005

SUGGESTED SERMON *Date preached:*

Divine Direction

By Dr. Denis Lyle

Scripture: 2 Kings 8:1–6, especially verse 6
The king appointed a certain officer for her, saying, "Restore all that was hers, and all the proceeds of the field from the day that she left the land until now." (NKJV)

Introduction: One woman's life-long ambition was to see the Holy Land. Before bed one night, she read some tour brochures and noticed that the airplane she would travel on would be a 747. When she woke up the next morning, her digital clock read, "7:47." She took that as confirmation that her trip was in the will of God. Is that a proper way to determine God's will? How do we know beyond doubt that we're making the decisions God wants us to make? Does He guide today? Our story today sheds some light on the problem of guidance. Three key words seem to unlock the wealth of instruction in this short story.

1. **Guidance.** The woman in this story received guidance from the God of Elisha (v. 1). Elisha had a prior experience with her in chapter four: she attended to his physical needs and he raised her son from the dead (see 2 Kin. 4:1–37). The Lord guided this woman in a personal way. He used Elisha, someone who had previous experience with her, to speak His words directly to her. The Lord was particular in His guidance. He told her to leave home, and gave her a time frame to stay away from the land, which would experience famine. While particular in His guidance, the Lord was still partial in His revelation. He didn't tell her what would happen in those seven years, or exactly where to live. God doesn't tell us every detail of our lives in advance, but He guides us personally and very particularly, but one step at a time so that we might be totally dependent upon Him.

2. **Obedience.** Like her obedient ancestor, this daughter of Abraham went out not knowing where she would go (Heb. 11:8). She obeyed the Word of God that came through the servant of God (2 Kin. 8:2). Notice she obeyed this divine directive in spite of when it came. No evidence of famine existed. She had food, crops, and plenty of water. She also obeyed despite what it cost. She would have to leave her home, her circle of friends, her people (c.f. 2 Kin. 4:13). This woman also obeyed despite whom it crossed.

Her neighbors must have thought her crazy. Why would she leave everything she worked for her entire life because of one command from a prophet? She knew it was the command of God!

3. **Providence.** What do we mean by providence? While the actual word *providence,* does not occur in the Bible, the doctrine does. Providence is the work of God in which He preserves all His creatures, is active in all occurrences in the world, and directs everything to its appointed end.

The woman in this story must have wondered about her home while she was away, what would become of it. She returned to the land after seven years of obedience to have her land restored to her. Not only this, but all the "proceeds of the field from the day she left until now" (v. 6). Imagine having a seven-year leave from work and returning to find that you've been paid as if you had worked! The Lord will bless your obedience!

Conclusion: Divine direction doesn't necessarily mean the answer will be painted across the sky or come to you in a dream. When we have a personal relationship with God, He will personally guide us, especially through His Word. The Lord will work all things out in His providence. Guidance and providence are the Lord's job. He never fails us. Our responsibility is obedience. Perhaps the Lord is calling you to make Him the Lord of your life today. He sent His Son as a sacrifice for your sins, and He wants you to come to know Him. Maybe the Lord is directing you to a new job, to a new ministry, or maybe to make some major changes in your life for Him. The Lord will guide you through the fiercest storms and through the calmest days, simply obey Him and you will be blessed beyond measure.

STATS, STORIES, AND MORE

Chris Rice

The Christian singer/songwriter Chris Rice wrote a song called "The Color Nine" in which he describes his struggle and journey to follow the Lord's direction. He begins the song describing his frustration and misconceptions:

I would take 'No' for an answer, just to know I heard you speak.
And I'm wonderin' why I've never seen the signs they claim they see.
A lot of special revelations meant for everybody but me.
Maybe I don't truly know You, maybe I just simply believe.

Rice ends the song by sharing what he has learned because of this struggle: That the Lord doesn't necessarily speak audibly or tell us every step. Simply following the Lord and depending upon His wisdom is key in our Christian lives:

Now I've never felt the presence, but I know You're always near.
And I've never heard the calling, but somehow You've lead me right here.
So I'm not lookin' for burnin' bushes, or some divine graffiti to appear.
I'm just beggin' You for Your wisdom, and I believe you're puttin' some here.

Dr. F. B. Meyer's Formula for Guidance

One night as F. B. Meyer stood on the deck of a ship approaching land, he wondered how the crew knew when and how to safely steer to the dock. Standing on the bridge and peering through the window, he asked "Captain, how do you know when to turn this ship into that narrow harbor?"

"Do you see those three red lights on the shore?" replied the captain. "When they're all in a straight line I go right in!" Later Meyer said: "When we want to know God's will, there are three things which always occur: the inward impulse, the Word of God, and the trend of circumstances ... Never act until these three things agree."

FOR THE BULLETIN

✽ On October 2, 1187, the Muslim general Saladin captured Jerusalem from the Crusaders. ✽ October 2, 1792 is a red-letter day in this history of Protestant missions. A failure-prone shoemaker named William Carey wrote a book on the obligations of Christians to engage in global missions. He finally nudged his fellow Baptists to adopt this resolution at an associational meeting: "Resolved that a plan be prepared against the next Ministers' meeting at Kettering, for forming a Baptist Society for propagating the gospel among the Heathen." ✽ Five months later, on Tuesday, October 2, 1792, fourteen men huddled in the back-parlor of widow Wallis' house in Kettering and formulated a resolution: "Humbly desirous of making an effort for the propagation of the gospel amongst the Heathen, according to the recommendations of Carey's Enquiry, we unanimously resolve to act in Society together for this purpose; and as, in the divided state of Christendom, each denomination, by exerting itself separately, seems likeliest to accomplish the great end, we name this the Particular Baptist Society for the Propagation of the Gospel among the Heathen." Andrew Fuller passed around his snuffbox with its picture of Paul's conversion on the lid, taking up church history's first collection of pledges for organized, home-supported Protestant missions. ✽ On October 2, 1879, Charles Spurgeon, deeply saddened when his son, Tom, sailed from England to Tasmania for his health and in the Lord's work, spent the night in prayer, gaining the victory over his heartache.

APPROPRIATE SONGS AND HYMNS

Cry of My Heart, Terry Butler; © 1991 Mercy/Vineyard Publishing.

The King of Love My Shepherd Is, Henry W. Baker/John B. Dykes; Public Domain.

A Passion for You, Dave Hollen; © 1992 Mercy/Vineyard Publishing.

Have Your Way, Lord, Wayne Goodine/Geron Davis; © 1996 Paragon Music Corporation/Davishop/Wayne Goodine Music; Admin. by Integrated Copyright Group, Inc.

As High as the Heavens, Don Harris/Martin J. Nystrom; © 1993 Integrity's Hosanna! Music.

WORSHIP HELPS

Call to Worship:
I will bless the LORD at all times; His praise shall continually be in my mouth. My soul shall make its boast in the LORD; the humble shall hear of it and be glad. Oh, magnify the LORD with me, and let us exalt His name together. (Ps. 34:1–3 NKJV)

Offertory Comments:
In his book, *God's Miraculous Plan of Economy*, Jack R. Taylor points out that when Paul wrote that God loves a cheerful giver (2 Cor. 9:7), he used the Greek word *halaros* which sounds almost like its English counterpart *hilarious*. Taylor points out that a cheerful giver is one who really understands the privilege of giving and who knows that it is more blessed to give than to receive. Taylor writes: "But alas, where are the herds of hilarious givers? I think that the species has all but disappeared if there were ever a great crowd of them. If giving is a God-given privilege and is the means of getting into God's providential patter, then we should be happy about it. I keep looking for a church somewhere that takes the offering with exciting expectation during that period which tends to be a dead period filled in by enough music to keep us from sensing the deadness of it. If ever there should be a spontaneous season of praise, it should be during the offering."

Benediction:
Now to the King eternal, immortal, invisible, the only God, be honor and glory forever and ever. Amen. (1 Tim. 1:17 NIV)

Additional Sermons and Lesson Ideas

Enoch's Exit

Date preached:

By Dr. Melvin Worthington

SCRIPTURE: Hebrews 11:5; Genesis 5:21–24.

INTRODUCTION: Enoch was a man who pleased God. The brief record of his life is summed up in a few short words:

1. Enoch's Walk—His Private Life (Gen. 5:24). Enoch not only walked after God he also walked with God. The word walk denotes a devout life, lived in close communion with God. He did this for a period of 365 years.
2. Enoch's Work—His Public Life (Jude 14). Enoch's work includes his method, his message, and his manner.
3. Enoch's Witness—His Pleasing Life (Heb. 11:5, 6; John 8:29). Enoch's witness includes his believing, his behaving, and his blessings.
4. Enoch's Welcome—His Preserved Life (Heb. 11:5; Gen. 5:24). Enoch's welcome includes the disappearance, the departure, and the declaration.

CONCLUSION: Each of us should seek to emulate Enoch's walk, work, witness, and welcome.

More Harm than Good

Date preached:

By Rev. Peter Grainger

SCRIPTURE: 1 Corinthians 11:17–34

INTRODUCTION: How much do you value the Lord's Supper? Are you observing it with respect or neglect? Do you take it with conviction or with carelessness? Paul makes it very clear that proper motives and attitude must accompany the Lord's Supper.

1. The Problem: A Matter of Abuse (vv. 17–27). The rich church members were guilty of:
   - A. Abusing the Poor (vv. 21, 22).
   - B. Abusing the Lord's Supper (vv. 23–26).
   - C. Abusing the Lord (v. 27).
2. The Solution: A Matter of Judgment (vv. 27–34).

CONCLUSION: Jesus initiated The Lord's Supper so that we might reflect and focus on His sacrifice when we remember Him; let us never take this for granted!

OCTOBER 9, 2005

SUGGESTED SERMON *Date preached:*

The Trap of Temptation

By Joshua D. Rowe

Scripture: Joshua 7:1–26, especially verse 12b

I will not be with you anymore unless you destroy whatever among you is devoted to destruction. (NVI)

Introduction: Do you realize that a single sin can potentially ruin your success, your family, a lifetime friendship, or a reputation? Temptations are all around us, waiting to destroy us if we give in (Gen. 4:7). Our passage today teaches how great the consequences of temptation really are, and the necessity of resisting it.

1. **Temptation (v. 1).** Consider the circumstances of Israel: God promised to Abraham to make him a great nation (Gen. 12:2, 3), but a nation must possess land. The Israelites had been roaming in the desert for 40 years because of sin. Finally, Joshua replaced Moses and the new generation arose to conquer their promised land! God was fulfilling His promise, bringing Israel to a great land to become a great nation. However, Achan wanted just a little more (Josh. 7:1). With all these blessings, how could he want more? With all that God has given us, how can we? Temptation causes us to take our focus off of God, His amazing plan, and abundant provision to satisfy our own temporary lust.

   A. **The Test:** God's Command. Israel was given a command. When they overtook Jericho, they were to leave certain spoils for the Lord (Josh. 6:17–19). Achan disobeyed; he stole a sacred robe, some silver, and some gold (vv. 20, 21). This reminds us of Adam and Eve, who were given abundance with one command: to resist one tree, yet they fell. The Spirit convicts us of sin and gives us strength to resist temptation (1 Cor. 10:13), yet we often overlook God's commands to satisfy ourselves.

   B. **The Trap:** Our Desires. James explains, "Let no one say when he is tempted, 'I am tempted by God'; for God cannot be tempted by evil, nor does He Himself tempt anyone. But each one is tempted when he is drawn away by his own desires and enticed" (James 1:13, 14). Achan followed this same pattern, "I saw ... I coveted ... and took ... And there they are, hidden." We must take responsibility, recognizing that our desires caused us to sin. We must never hide like Achan or Adam and Eve. If we fall into the trap of our own lusts, we must not divert responsibility or hide our failure.

2. **The Consequence.** James continues in His explanation of temptation, "Then, when desire has conceived, it gives birth to sin; and sin, when it is full-grown, brings forth death" (James 1:15; c.f. Rom. 6:12 NKJV).

   A. **Shared (vv. 2–5).** One man sinned, yet an entire nation suffered. Israel lost 36 men in battle and, more importantly, they lost the Lord's favor.
   B. **Specific (vv. 14–26).** The Lord not only punished the nation, but also condemned Achan. The Israelites stoned Achan with his entire family and burned their bodies. This suggests the ultimate punishment for sin; eternal separation from God in hell. The harsh reality of hell is a natural result of sin.

3. **Reconciliation.** How do we reconcile if we have been tempted? Achan hid his sin, but God calls us to deal with it.

   A. **Realization (vv. 2–5; 6–12).** Before we can deal with sin, we must realize its presence. Only after Israel lost lives and favor with God did Joshua turn to the Lord for reconciliation. It always costs us to sin. Whether we lose our testimony, our families, our ministry, or our favor with God, our loss is meant to bring us to realize our sin.
   B. **Riddance.** The Lord told Joshua, "I will not be with you anymore unless you destroy whatever among you is devoted to destruction" (v. 12b). When the Israelites found the guilty person, they stoned and killed him. They destroyed all his possessions and killed his family to ensure complete riddance of his evil legacy (vv. 22–26).
   C. **Repentance.** Israel saw the pain and death sin brings. Their riddance of sin marked their personal repentance and dedication to resist temptation. We see and feel the painful effects of sin every day: social injustice, adultery, disease, hatred, etc. Yet, do these things cause us to turn away from sin?

Conclusion: My challenge for you today is to go home and rid yourself of any temptations. Refuse gossiping or getting drunk; throw away the magazines and videos. Whatever it may be, destroy whatever is devoted to destruction. If you have sinned, turn to Jesus Christ who paid the ultimate price of death for us, and commit to resist temptation through His Spirit.

STATS, STORIES, AND MORE

I Took a Walk with Sin

I took a walk with sin one day
I thought I would not fall;
He walked what seemed like miles away
Not bothering me at all.
"What's the harm in walking," I asked
He agreed, and then drew near;
"This walk will not last long," he said,
"I'm scarcely even here."
Then more and more his speech progressed
Of pleasure, of gods, of fun;
Before I could speak "no" or "yes"
I had already begun.
In the end I was alone again
Guilty and hurt, I wept;
But I learned the rule of resisting sin
I must never take the first step.

—Joshua D. Rowe

Someone Once Said . . .

Little sins are not like an inch of candle, which soon expires, but they resemble a trail of powder, which takes the fire until at last the barrels burst asunder.—Rev. William Secker, seventeenth-century British minister

Most of us spend the first six days of each week sowing wild oats; then we go to church on Sunday and pray for a crop failure.—Fred Allen (1894–1956) US comedian

FOR THE BULLETIN

✺ On October 9, 1635, Roger Williams was banished from the Massachusetts Bay Colony for preaching that civil government should not interfere with religious freedom. Being banished, Williams wandered into the wilderness and purchased land from Native Americans where he founded the city of Providence, Rhode Island. ✺ Benjamin Keach, born in 1640, was converted to Christ at 18 and began pastoring ten years later. He served the Horsley Down Baptist Church in Southwark near London. To explain Baptist beliefs to the young, he wrote a primer. The children loved it, but the king didn't. British constables arrested him, and on October 9, 1664, he stood a prisoner in the court of Aylesbury while he was sentenced to prison. He later got into trouble again, this time for publishing a hymnal entitled *Spiritual Melody*. ✺ David Brainerd died at Northampton, Massachusetts, on this day in 1747, from tuberculosis. His diary, published by his father-in-law, Jonathan Edwards, is a classic of American church history. ✺ Today is the birthday of the Methodist leader and missionary, Thomas Coke (1747). ✺ A group of Spanish missionaries settled in Northern California on the site of present-day San Francisco on this day in 1776 and dedicated a mission chapel there. ✺ On October 9, 1845, the Anglican Churchman, John Henry Newman, converted to Roman Catholicism, a move that shook the Church of England to its foundation. Eventually 250 Anglican clergy followed him. Newman is the author of the great hymn, "Lead, Kindly Light."

APPROPRIATE SONGS AND HYMNS

Yield Not to Temptation, Horatio R. Palmer; Public Domain.

At the Name of Jesus, Caroline Maria Noel/Ronn Huff; © 1986 Word Music, Inc.; Admin. by Word Music Group, Inc.

Our Father in Heaven, Frank Hernandez; © 1990 Birdwing Music; Admin. by EMI Christian Music Publishing.

What God Hath Promised, Annie Flint/William M. Runyon; Public Domain.

Sing Hallelujah, Jack Hayford; © 1980 Pilot Point Music; Admin. by The Copyright Company.

WORSHIP HELPS

Call to Worship:

O Father, deign these walls to bless;
Fill with Thy love their emptiness;
And let their door a gateway be
To lead us from ourselves to Thee.
"All Things are Thine"—John G. Whittier / Samuel Webbe; 1872

Scripture Reading Medley:

Jesus was led up by the Spirit into the wilderness to be tempted by the devil. ~ For in that He Himself has suffered, being tempted, He is able to aid those who are tempted ~ Let no one say when he is tempted, "I am tempted by God"; for God cannot be tempted by evil, nor does He Himself tempt anyone. But each one is tempted when he is drawn away by his own desires and enticed. Then, when desire has conceived, it gives birth to sin; and sin, when it is full-grown, brings forth death. Watch and pray, lest you enter into temptation. The spirit indeed is willing, but the flesh is weak. When you pray, say, "Do not lead us into temptation, But deliver us from the evil one." No temptation has overtaken you except such as is common to man; but God is faithful, who will not allow you to be tempted beyond what you are able, but with the temptation will also make the way of escape, that you may be able to bear it. For we do not have a High Priest who cannot sympathize with our weaknesses, but was in all points tempted as we are, yet without sin. Let us therefore come boldly to the throne of grace that we may obtain mercy and find grace to help in time of need. (Matt. 4:1; Heb. 2:18; James 1:13–15; Mark 14:38; Luke 11:2, 4b; 1 Cor. 10:13; Heb. 4:15, 16)

Additional Sermons and Lesson Ideas

Overcoming Idleness

Date preached:

By Rev. Todd M. Kinde

SCRIPTURE: James 2:14–26

INTRODUCTION: Saving faith will manifest itself in a life of obedient actions of love.

1. A Lifeless Faith (2:14–20).
2. A Living Faith (2:21–26).

CONCLUSION: We might think of the body related to the works and the spirit related to faith but James sees it just the opposite. Our faith is the body and the works are the spirit. Works give breath to our words. Works are the spirit of our faith. Works make our faith living and vibrant, real, and meaningful.

We Are His People

Date preached:

Adapted from a sermon by Dr. F. B. Meyer

SCRIPTURE: Psalm 100:3

INTRODUCTION: When we come to Christ, we come under His ownership. We are under Christ's proprietorship. We are His:

1. By Creation. It is He who has made us, and not we ourselves (Ps. 100:3).
2. By Purchase. We were bought with a price (1 Cor. 6:20).
3. By Deed of Gift. Jesus said, "My Father ... has given them to Me" (John 10:29).
4. By Conquest. Our souls have opened to Him their gates, being unable any longer to resist (Ps. 24:7, 8).

CONCLUSION: It is impossible to escape the fact that we are the absolute property of Jesus Christ, Our Lord. The act of consecration, then, consists in the recognition of Christ's absolute proprietorship of our lives. Consecration is simply giving Christ His own and returning stolen property to its rightful owner.

OCTOBER 16, 2005

SUGGESTED SERMON *Date preached:*

The Horror of Hypocrisy

By Dr. Melvin Worthington

Scripture: Revelation 3:1–6, especially verse 1b

... I know your works, that you have a name that you are alive, but you are dead. (NKJV)

Introduction: Sardis is described as a dead church. The church had a reputation that did not reflect reality. It was alive in name only. This was a fickle church. It had a Christian reputation, but was dead. They did not have the life of God in their souls and had not walked consistently before the Lord. The shell was there but the kernel was not. Sardis was the capital city of Lydia and was known as one of the most ancient and famous cities of Asia Minor. The city was noted for its fruit, wool, and the temple of the goddess Cybele, whose worship resembled that of Diana of Ephesus. The Church at Sardis had no conflict with foes within or without, because it had not faithfully witnessed by word or example. The message to Sardis is an unmixed message of rebuke and almost devoid of any word of commendation. The sad condition of this church was due to the sinful surroundings where it was located. It was in the midst of people who practiced the grossest forms of idolatry.

1. **The Inscription (v. 1a).** The inscription includes the angel, the assembly, the area, the authority, the address, and the Almighty. The Almighty has the seven Spirits and the seven stars. He is writing to this dead church in His capacity as judge rather than comforter. He will come upon them possessed with all the power of the Almighty.

2. **The Inventory (vv. 1b, 2b, 4a).** The inventory includes the toil (v. 1b), the testimony (v. 1b), the truth (v. 1b), the test (v. 2b), and the thrill (v. 4a). Christ does not commend this church as a whole but acknowledges they have not defiled their garments. It was a church busy with meetings, promotion, and committees. It had a reputation for being alive, wide-awake, a going, growing church. In spite of its reputation, Sardis had no name with God. It was functioning in the past and living on yesterday's glories and successes. While the church could boast of its large membership, finances, and organizational operation, it lacked quality and reality. This church was untroubled by heresy. A church that has lost its vital force will

not be attacked nor troubled with opposition from without, because it is not worth being attacked. It is lifeless.

3. **The Instruction (vv. 2a, 3a, 6).** The instruction includes the watching, the working, the weighing, and the waiting. The church is exhorted to watch. This is the only solution to its impending ruin. The church is counseled to keep the commands of the gospel. The church is admonished to repent. The church needed to confess its deadness, put away its sin, be filled with the Spirit, and put life and meaning into its works. Without repentance, they could expect sure judgment. They were to be on guard in order that judgment would not catch them unawares.

4. **The Incentive (vv. 3b, 4b, 5).** The incentive includes the sudden coming, the shining clothes, and the successful conquering. As successful conquerors, we will have white raiment, a written record, and a wondrous reception. Christ promises that conquerors will be clothed in white raiment, which reminds us of festivity, victory, purity, and the resurrection body. Conquerors will not have their names blotted out of the Book of Life. Christ will confess them before His Father and the angels.

Conclusion: This letter warns us against the danger of spiritual deadness. It is possible to be orthodox and not have life or to have outward appearances of life and yet be inwardly dead. This letter also sets forth the possibility of professing one thing and being something else. The sin of this church was so deep that it is blessedness only to have been free from it. Sardis was a worldly, impure, and fickle church. The message to this church is the most appalling of all the letters to the seven churches. Christ does not abandon the faithful few. The believers in Sardis who lived pure and separated lives are not ignored. This faithful company was consistent in a city marked by materialism and worldliness. We must remember that God is in the remnant business. Our Lord still works with a few.

STATS, STORIES, AND MORE

Revival Needed

In his book, *Campus Aflame*, J. Edwin Orr described the impact of the Second Great Awakening on American college campuses. "During the last decade of the eighteenth century, the typical Harvard student was atheist. Students at Williams College conducted a mock celebration of Holy Communion. When the Dean at Princeton opened the chapel Bible to read, a pack of playing cards fell out, some radical having cut a rectangle out of each page to fit the pack. Christians were so unpopular that they met in secret and kept their minutes in code .... The last two decades of the eighteenth century were the darkest period, spiritually and morally, in the history of American Christianity."

Then came the awakening. "So far as can be ascertained," writes Orr, "the first of a series of college awakenings occurred as early as 1787. At Hampden Sydney College in Virginia, a few students, none of them an active Christian but all of them concerned about the moral state of the college, met for prayer. They locked themselves in a room, for fear of the other students. One of them said, 'We tried to pray, but such prayer I never heard the like of.' He added, 'We tried to sing, but it was in the most suppressed manner, for we feared the other students.' The ungodly students created a disturbance, and their President came to investigate. He rebuked the rowdies and invited the intercessors to his study for continued prayer. They continued in power, until an awakening was felt at last. Within a short space of time, more than half the number of students professed conversion in a movement that stirred the local churches also."

FOR THE BULLETIN

✲ The artist of the Reformation, Lucas Cranach the Elder, friend of Martin Luther, died on October 16, 1553. ✲ On October 16, 1555, Queen Mary I of England, known as Bloody Mary, had Nicholas Ridley and Hugh Latimer burned at the stake for their Protestant preaching. Latimer's famous quote on the occasion was: "Be of good comfort, Mr. Ridley, and play the man! We shall this day light such a candle by God's grace, in England, as I trust never shall be put out." ✲ Today is also the birthday (1777) of Lorenzo Dow, a powerful but eccentric Methodist preacher from Coventry, Connecticut. His long hair, beard, and peculiar clothing led to his disdainful nickname, "Crazy Dow," but he was zealous in preaching the gospel, especially to Roman Catholics. ✲ The melancholy but faithful Anglican missionary, Henry Martyn, died on this day in 1812 in Tokat, Asia Minor. ✲ The Tremont Hotel opened in Boston on October 16, 1829, being the first modern hotel in American history. ✲ Today marks the death in 1888 of October H. G. Spafford, a Chicago lawyer who wrote the hymn "It Is Well With My Soul" following the deaths of his four daughters at sea. ✲ Cowboy entertainer Stuart Hamblin was converted on October 16, 1949, through the influence of Billy Graham, signaling an extension of the Billy Graham 1949 Los Angeles Crusade. The resulting media attention catapulted the young evangelist to worldwide fame. ✲ Polish Cardinal, Karol Wojtyla, was elected Pope John Paul II on October 16, 1978.

APPROPRIATE SONGS AND HYMNS

Break Me Lord, Steve Jones; © 1988 New Spring Publishing; Admin. by Brentwood-Benson Music Publishing, Inc.

Clean Hands, Pure Heart, John Slick/Mark Gersmehl; © 1986 Paragon Music Corporation; Admin. by Brentwood-Benson Music Publishing, Inc.

Nothing Between, Charles Albert Tindley; Public Domain.

Purify My Heart, Jeff Nelson; © 1993 Maranatha Praise, Inc./Heart Service Music, Inc.; Admin. by Music Services.

The Water of Change, Larry Olson; © 1989 Dakota Road Music.

WORSHIP HELPS

Call to Worship:
Rejoice, ye pure in heart; rejoice give thanks and sing.
Your festal banner wave on high—the cross of Christ, your King.
Rejoice! Rejoice! Rejoice, give thanks, and sing.
—*Edward H. Plumptre*

Reader's Theater (May be adapted as a Responsive Reading)

Reader 1: Do not turn to idols, nor make for yourselves molded gods: I am the LORD your God.

Reader 2: Take heed to yourselves, lest your heart be deceived, and you turn aside and serve other gods and worship them.

Reader 3: Lest the LORD's anger be aroused against you, and He shut up the heavens so that there be no rain.

Reader 1: Come now, and let us reason together, says the LORD. Though your sins are like scarlet, they shall be as white as snow; though they are red like crimson, they shall be as wool.

Reader 3: The LORD will again rejoice over you for good as He rejoiced over your fathers, if you obey the voice of the LORD your God, to keep His commandments and His statutes which are written in this Book of the Law, and if you turn to the LORD your God with all your heart and with all your soul.

Reader 1: The poor shall eat and be satisfied; those who seek Him will praise the LORD ... All the ends of the world shall remember and turn to the LORD, and all the families of the nations shall worship before You.

Reader 2: Turn to the LORD your God and obey His voice (for the LORD your God is a merciful God). (Lev. 19:4; Deut. 11:16, 17; Is. 1:18; Deut. 30:9, 10; Ps. 22:26, 27; Deut. 4:30, 31. NKJV)

Additional Sermons and Lesson Ideas

Four Types of People

Date preached:

By Dr. Timothy Beougher

SCRIPTURE: 1 Corinthians 2:14—3:4

INTRODUCTION: We often classify others as old, young, smart, pretty, women, men, etc. Our focus is usually on the external. Paul puts humans into categories according to their spiritual status.

1. Natural (2:14). This category describes an unbeliever.
2. Spiritual (2:15, 16). Here, Paul defines a mature believer.
3. Infants (3:1, 2a). This description portrays the immature believer.
4. Worldly (3:2b–4). Paul uses this category to describe a carnal believer or an unbeliever who is deceived into a false sense of salvation.

CONCLUSION: In which category do you fall? How can you reach the status of a mature believer?

Epaphras—The Man Who Prayed

Date preached:

By Dr. David Jeremiah

SCRIPTURE: Colossians 1:7 and 4:12

INTRODUCTION: Paul used two phrases to describe Epaphras. In Colossians 1:7 he was Paul's "dear fellow-servant," and in Colossians 4:12, he is described as "a bondservant." We can learn much from him, especially about prayer. He teaches us:

1. To Be Persistent in Our Ministry (Col. 1:7). He was faithful.
2. To Be Precise in Our Communication (Col. 1:8). Paul had never been to Colosse, yet he knew all about the church from Epaphras.
3. To Be Passionate in Our Prayer (Col. 4:12, 13). We are to pray faithfully ("always"), fiercely ("laboring"), fervently ("fervently"), factually ("that they might stand perfect and complete in the will of God").
4. To Be Particular About Our People (Col. 4:13). He was zealous for the Colossians.

CONCLUSION: What would happen if we would all pray for our church as this man prayed for his?

OCTOBER 23, 2005

SUGGESTED SERMON *Date preached:*

The Sanctity of Marriage

By Rev. Peter Grainger

Scripture: Proverbs 5, especially verses 15 and 18b:
Drink water from your own cistern, and running water from your own well ... and rejoice in the wife of your youth.

Introduction: Billboards, magazines, advertisements, movies, soap operas, and talk shows all reflect our culture's changing view on adultery. Adultery is portrayed as an exciting alternative to monogamy, which is more often portrayed as monotony. Nothing could be more diametrically opposed to such thinking and practice than the instruction given in the ancient Book of Proverbs in the Bible, particularly the advice which a father gives to his son. This is not just any father. It is King Solomon of Israel who was reputedly the wisest man who ever lived. Here we see stark contrasts between the fool who walks down "Adultery Avenue," which leads to a frustrating dead end, versus the wise man who walks along the "Fidelity Freeway," which leads to fulfillment and life.

1. **Adultery: A Dead End (vv. 3–14).** "You shall not commit adultery" is the seventh of the Ten Commandments given by God (Ex. 20:14). The reason the prohibition is made is that human beings are prone to disobey it. We see some benefit in doing so, which we temporarily believe outweighs the risk of any negative consequences.

   A. **The Temptation (vv. 1–3).** The goal is not money or goods but sexual satisfaction from someone else's wife or husband. The Book of Proverbs consistently portrays the woman as the person who offers this and the man who is tempted to take it. This in part reflects the realities of ancient society and the unequal status of women. Perhaps it also reflects the different psychological make-up of the sexes in which men are far more susceptible to the temptation of instant sexual gratification (though this is disputed by some). Whatever the case, both men and women are vulnerable to the sin of adultery. Proverbs depicts the woman as the seductress and the man as the intended victim (c.f. Prov. 7:22, 23). The author does not deny her attractiveness of speech or body, comparing her lips to honey and her mouth to smooth oil, but he reveals the true peril of this type of relationship.

B. **The Consequences (vv. 4–14).** God set up the institution of marriage for one man and one woman monogamously, not to be separated (Matt. 19:4–6). Committing adultery tears apart what God joined together, damaging both parts of the whole. Even worse, adultery is a sin against God. Adultery is not the unforgivable sin as we see through David (2 Sam. 11, 12), but the story of David also teaches us that consequences will occur. Our verses in Proverbs warn that everything could be taken from an adulterer: his honor (v. 9), his time (v. 9), his wealth (v. 10), and his body (v. 11). They also warn that an adulterer will live with constant regret (vv. 12–14).

2. **Fidelity: A Refreshing Spring (vv. 15–20).** These verses use the language of water: drawn from a cistern, running water from a well (fed by a spring). Water of course was the most valuable and essential commodity in the ancient world for sustenance, refreshment, and satisfaction. The water here is a metaphor, a picture for sexual satisfaction, given and received in an intimate relationship. This satisfaction is not to be shared with others but only within the exclusive relationship of a man and woman, a husband a wife. Solomon instructs men to "rejoice with the wife of your youth" (v. 18), not to trade her in for a newer model. Wives are not cars but people, made like us in the image of God and given generously by him to complement what we lack. Thus, we are also to be "enraptured with her love" (v. 19). The word translated "captivated" is translated as "intoxicated, exhilarated, invigorated, infatuated, or ravished," hardly bland or boring. This relationship of the deepest intimacy comes closest to the ultimate intimacy for which we were made, with God Himself (Eph. 5:31, 32).

Conclusion: The Proverb concludes to remind us that God is always watching us and will always react to our sin (vv. 21–23). Whether you're married or not, we're all susceptible to lust, which Jesus tells us is equal to adultery in our heart (Matt. 5:28), we must surrender ourselves to God and His plan for marriage. When we simply obey, our marriages and especially our relationship with God will be blessed.

STATS, STORIES, AND MORE

More from Rev. Peter Grainger:

When Bertrand Russell, the British philosopher met and fell in love with Alys Pearsall Smith, a practicing Quaker, it was with great reluctance that he agreed to her demands that he should marry her in 1894 saying the "having to advertise the most intimate thing imaginable is loathsome to me."

All he had done, in his view, was to choose Alys as his sexual mate, the marriage being no more than a public announcement of the deed. In his book, *Is Modern Marriage a Failure?* he declared that the best one could hope for, for both men and women, was serial monogamy for the sake of raising children, with freedom to pursue sexual fulfillment wherever one could find it. He certainly practiced what he preached for Alys was the first of his four wives and many mistresses. His amoral views were so shocking in his day that in 1940 a United States court disqualified him from holding a professorship in New York.

Today his views are the norm, if not in theory, then certainly in practice in most Western societies. According to the Office of National Statistics, the number of people getting married in Britain has fallen below the 300,000 mark, a staggering drop of 25% in a decade. Four in ten marriages end in the divorce courts and by the year 2025 divorces are set to outnumber marriages. Nowadays more than 70% of women cohabit before marriage (compared with 5% in the 1950s) and men are staying single longer. If trends continue, by 2010 some 60% of men between the ages of 25 and 40 will be bachelors.

FOR THE BULLETIN

❁ According to the now-discredited calculations of Archbishop James Ussher, the heavens and the earth were created on October 23, 4004 B.C. Ussher's chronology was published in 1650. ❁ On this day in 1576, Jacob Arminius enrolled in the University of Leiden. ❁ James Hannington, British missionary to Africa, was seized by warriors of the lawless Mwanga tribe and held in miserable conditions. On October 23, 1885, he wrote in his diary, "I woke full of pain and weak. I don't see how I can stand all this, yet I don't want to give in." One week later, he was killed. ❁ Among Christianity's greatest treasures is the *Codex Alexandrinus*, a manuscript of the Greek Bible written in the early 400s. It contains virtually the entire Bible, along with the Apocrypha, some hymns, and two letters written by Clement, Bishop of Rome. It was housed in the British Royal Library, which caught fire on October 23, 1731. The alarm was given, and an eyewitness told of the learned Dr. Bentley "in nightgown and great wig" fleeing the building with the Codex Alexandrinus under his arm. The disastrous fire drew public attention to the plight of the Royal Library, and a generation later, it found a home in the newly founded British Museum where today the Codex Alexandrinus is securely displayed. ❁ October 23, 1915, 25,000 women marched through New York City, demanding the right to vote.

APPROPRIATE SONGS AND HYMNS

Wonder of Wonders Here Revealed, Jane Parker Huber/William Boyd; © 1980 Jane Parker Huber; Admin. by Westminster John Knox Press.

When Love Is Found, Brian Wren; © 1983 Hope Publishing Company.

In Our Households, Heavenly Father, Marie J. Post/Dale Grotenhuis; © 1987 CRC Publications.

A Christian Home; Barbara Hart/Jean Sibelius © 1965, 1986 Singspiration Music; Admin. by Brentwood-Benson Music Publishing, Inc.

Cherish the Moment, Ron Hamilton; © 1990 Majesty Music, Inc.

WORSHIP HELPS

Call to Worship:
These walls we to Thy honor raise;
Long may they echo with Thy praise;
And Thou, descending, fill the place
With choicest tokens of Thy grace.
"And Will the Great Eternal God"

—Phillip Doddridge / Edward Miller, 1790

Pastoral Prayer:
Heavenly Father, we bless You today. We say with the ancient apostle: "Blessed be the God and Father of our Lord Jesus Christ, who according to His abundant mercy has begotten us again in a living hope through the resurrection of Jesus Christ from the dead, into an inheritance incorruptible and undefiled and that does not fade away, reserved in heaven for you who are kept by the power of God through faith ready for salvation to be revealed in the last time." Fix our thoughts, O Lord, on You. Fix our hearts on heaven. Strengthen our faith, and give grace to any here that are facing trials and tribulations in their lives. We look to You, Lord, and trust in Your almighty hand. In Jesus' name. Amen.

Kids Talk

Talk to the children about thanking God for their food. Use the old poem by hymnist Maltbie D. Babcock:

Back of the loaf is the snowy flour
And back of the flour the mill,
And back of the mill is the wheat and the shower,
And the sun and the Father's will.

Additional Sermons and Lesson Ideas

True Commitment

Date preached:

By Joshua D. Rowe

SCRIPTURE: Mark 1:32–39

INTRODUCTION: What does it mean to be committed to ministry? What elements are most important to be effective? Jesus models the crucial elements to having a true commitment to ministry. He was committed to:

1. People (vv. 32–34). These verses tell us the sun had already set; it was late, and the whole city gathered to be healed by Jesus. Jesus stayed up late because He was committed to people.
2. Prayer (vv. 35–37). After a long night of ministry, Jesus still got up long before the sun came up again to pray! Jesus got up early because He was committed to prayer.
3. Purpose (vv. 38, 39). He was having effective ministry there, so why would He move to the next town? It was His purpose! Jesus kept preaching because He was committed to His purpose.

CONCLUSION: Do you passionately and sacrificially minister to people? Are you sustained by a consistent prayer life? Are you using your spiritual gifts to carry out God's purpose for you?

The Judgment Day

Date preached:

By Dr. R. A. Torrey

SCRIPTURE: Acts 17:31

INTRODUCTION: Two events in the future are certain, the coming of Christ for His people, and the coming of a Judgment Day for the world. Notice this about the judgment:

1. The Certainty of It (John 5:22, 23)
2. The Universality of It. He will judge the world.
3. The Basis of It. It will be a judgment of what we have done in the body (2 Cor. 5:10), the secret things we have done (Rom. 2:16), and what we have done with Christ (John 3:18, 19).
4. Who Will Sit as Judge.
5. The Issue Will Be Eternal.

CONCLUSION: There's a great day coming! Are you ready for the Judgment Day?

CLASSICS FOR THE PASTOR'S LIBRARY

Eusebius: The Church History

"A classic is a book that has never finished saying what it has to say," wrote Italo Calvino.

The Church History of Eusebius fits that category, and I've spent many a happy hour learning things I'd never before known about Christ, the apostles, the early church, and the expansion of Christianity in the first centuries.

The title, "Father of Church History," could have gone to Luke, who wrote two historical works in the first century; or to Hegesippus, the second-century church historian. But Luke's books are included in Scripture, and Hegesippus' works are no longer extant except as quoted by Eusebius and other ancients. So the title "Father of Church History" goes to Eusebius who, in the third century, composed a fascinating record of the first 300 years of the gospel.

Eusebius was born in Palestine in the 260s, and was mentored by a learned church leader in Caesarea named Pamphilus, who was slain for his faith in A.D. 310. Eusebius later became Bishop of Caesarea, but he was first and foremost a scholar, a historian, and an author. His best-known work, *The Church History,* traces the story of Christianity from the birth of Christ to A.D. 324.

It isn't a perfect book. Eusebius was neither inspired nor infallible. He tended to view the early church from the institutional perspective of the fourth century. He quoted laborious sections from other writers, and he didn't always corroborate his sources. He was overly harsh with the Jews, and he idealized the Emperor Constantine. He displayed greater interest in the Eastern Church than in the Western.

But I couldn't put his book down.

Here's what you'll discover in Eusebius:

- An account of the life of Christ with details not found in the Gospel. I didn't realize, for example, that Barnabus was thought to have been one of the seventy, as was Sosthenes (1 Cor. 1:1), and Matthias, who took Judas' place.
- A sensational record of alleged correspondence between Jesus Christ of Nazareth and King Abgar, discovered in the vaults on ancient Edessa.
- A statue of Jesus in the north of Israel. Eusebuis wrote: "This statue, they say, resembled the features of Jesus and was still extant in my own

time: I saw it with my own eyes when I stayed in the city." The statue, which was destroyed by Emperor Maximin Daia shortly after A.D. 305, commemorated the healing of the woman with the hemorrhage in Mark 5. According to Eusebius, she was from Caesarea Philippi.

- An account of Jesus' half-brother James, who, following the Lord's Resurrection, became the leader of the Church of Jerusalem. Eusebius tells us that his knees became as callused as a camel's due to his prayer life. We also have a dramatic account of his martyrdom at the temple in Jerusalem.
- A story about the great-grandsons of Joseph and Mary (the grand-nephews of Jesus), whose Christian witness helped end the Domitian persecution.
- Accounts of the original apostles later in life.
- The vivid story of Polycarp, 86, disciple of the apostle John, who faced Roman troops with both courage and eloquence.

It was Eusebuis' accounts of the Roman persecutions that most moved me. He did for the Roman era what John Foxe was later to do for the times of (Bloody) Mary I of England. That is, he composed a record of martyrs whose stories would horrify and inspire the generations of Christians who follow. Listen to this passage:

> *Others died fastened to trees: they bent down their strongest branches by machines, fastened one of the martyr's legs to each, and then let the branches fly back to their natural position, instantly tearing apart the limbs of their victims. This went on not for a few days but for some whole years. Sometimes ten or more, at times more than twenty were put to death, or thirty, or almost sixty; at other times a hundred men, women, and little children were condemned to a variety of punishments and killed in a single day. I myself saw some of these mass executions by decapitation or fire, a slaughter that dulled the murderous axe until it wore out and broke in pieces, while the executioners grew so tired they had to work in shifts.*

If you'd like to dip into some of these stories, try the new translation (with commentary) of Eusebius by Dr. Paul L. Maier, professor of ancient history at Western Michigan University. In the preface, Dr. Maier explains that he endeavored to give us the text as it would have been had Eusebius had a good editor.

OCTOBER 30, 2005

REFORMATION SUNDAY SUGGESTED SERMON *Date preached:*

I Am Not Ashamed

Scripture: Romans 1:1–17, especially verse 16
I am not ashamed of the gospel of Christ. (NKJV)

Introduction: Today is Reformation Sunday, the anniversary of the day (October 31, 1517) when Martin Luther nailed his Ninety-Five Theses to the Cathedral door in Wittenberg, Germany. His action sprang from his theology. In 1514, Luther had been studying the letter of Romans in his office, and as he worked his way through the first chapter, he came to verses 16 and 17. He began seeing a great truth of Scripture that had been lost to many in the church of that day: Keeping of the law cannot save us; not by observing of the sacraments or by trying to live a good life. We can never be declared righteous in God's sight by our own efforts. We are saved by grace through faith—declared righteous in God's sight by the merits of Christ alone: "I am not ashamed of the gospel of Christ, for it is the power of God to salvation for everyone who believes ... for in it the righteousness of God is revealed from faith to faith; as it is written, 'The just shall live by faith.'" Today I'd like for us to study this same passage of Scripture, the prologue of Romans, and glean some insight.

1. **Respond to Your Calling (vv. 1–7).** The first paragraph of Paul's prologue tells us we're called to be conveyers of the gospel. He uses the word *call* four times. He goes on to say that through Christ he has received "grace and apostleship to call people from among all the Gentiles to the obedience that comes from faith" (NIV). Then he says: "... among whom you also are the called of Jesus Christ; to all who are in Rome, beloved of God, called to be saints." We are called; we are called to call others; we are the called of Jesus Christ; we are called to be saints (Rom. 1:6, 7 NKJV). It's as though the Lord is leaning over the balustrades of heaven, calling down to you and me, saying, "Hey, you! Hey you over there. Go tell those people. I have someone for you to tell! That's your assignment." You never know when God may use you to plant a life-changing seed in someone's heart, for that's our calling.

2. **Pray and Plan for Open Doors (vv. 8–15).** We need to be intentional about our witnessing, praying for open doors. Paul was strategic. From about

A.D. 47 to A.D. 57, he evangelized the eastern half of the Roman Empire during three great missionary tours. As he finished his last tour in Acts 20, he stopped in Corinth where, for three months, he rested in the villa of a friend named Gaius, and there he planned his next move. He dreamed of evangelizing the western half of the Empire. He devised a plan to go to Rome, and from there, to Spain. In Corinth, he composed the Book of Romans and sent it on its way. He was praying for open doors. He was asking God to send him to Rome, to Spain, to the West. He was pleading for more opportunities to share the gospel. What does this mean to us? If you've never shared Christ with another, let me suggest this prayer: "Lord, show me an open door. Lord, open my eyes to the person you want me to evangelize. Lord, give me a soul to do this." Pray for open doors. Make it an earnest, daily prayer. Begin thinking strategically. Begin planning. Who can I reach? Who can I win? How can I go about it?

3. **Share the Gospel Without Shame (vv. 14–17).** It would have been easy for Christians in first-century Rome to feel embarrassed about the gospel, because they were such a strange little group. Just a few years later, in fact, Emperor Nero blamed them with burning down the city of Rome and they would be viciously persecuted. But Paul said, "It doesn't matter what others think. I am a debtor. I have an obligation. I owe it to my Lord and to the world around me to share the gospel; and I am not ashamed of the gospel of Christ because it is the power of God for everyone who believes."

Conclusion: So respond to your calling, plan and pray for opportunities to share the gospel without embarrassment. Be proud of the Lord; Boast in Him; Brag about Him; Tell others of Him. You never know what's going to happen when you share the gospel.

STATS, STORIES, AND MORE

F. F. Bruce once said, ""There's no telling what may happen when people begin to study the Epistle to the Romans." Here are three examples:

Aurelius Augustine was born in North Africa in the fourth century. His father was a pagan, but his mother, Monica, was a devout Christian. Augustine became an immoral young adult who joined a cult and broke his mother's heart. Monica prayed for him ceaselessly; and one day in Milan, Italy, as Augustine sat in a friend's garden he heard a child singing, "Take up and read!" He opened the Bible and read from Romans 13. By the time he finished the sentence, he later said, he was converted. He went on to become one of the greatest leaders of the early church.

In the late fifteenth century, a Catholic monk in Germany named Martin Luther tried to find inner peace. He did everything possible to fulfill the requirements of his Augustinian order, yet he was a tormented man. His mentor, Johann von Staupitz, sent Luther to Wittenberg to teach the Book of Romans at the university. As Luther came to Romans 1:16, 17, his eyes were opened and he became a transformed man.

John Wesley was a miserable failure as he sat in a Moravian meetinghouse on Aldersgate Street in London listening to the reading of Luther's preface of the Book of Romans. But that night, Wesley's heart was strangely warmed and he was transformed into a great force of revival in this world.

FOR THE BULLETIN

❁ On October 30, 451, the Bishop of Constantinople was given equality with the Bishop of Rome, becoming the Patriarch of the Eastern Church. ❁ October 30, 1451 marks the birthday of Christopher Columbus. ❁ Lutheranism was made the official religion in Denmark on this day in 1536 by edict of Christian III. ❁ October 30, 1735 is the birthday of John Adams, second President of the United States. ❁ The Wesley Chapel on John Street in New York City was formally dedicated on October 30, 1768, making it the first Methodist Church building in America. ❁ Missionary to Hawaii, Hiram Bingham, was born on October 30, 1789. Bingham, a Vermont native, graduated from Middlebury College and Andover Theological Seminary and was sent by the American Board as one of their first missionaries to Hawaii. This area was chosen because of the death of a young man named Obookiah, a native of Hawaii, who had deeply affected the Christians there, including Bingham. From 1819 to 1849, Bingham was stationed in Honolulu and became the pastor of the first church there. ❁ Today is also the birthday of Feodor Mikhailovich Dostoevski, Russian novelist, born in 1821. Bob Jones Sr. was also born today, in 1883. He became an American fundamentalist preacher best known for starting a college named for him for the purpose of training ministers and promoting conservative theology and values. ❁ October 30, 1895 the Luther League of America was organized. ❁ On October 30, 1938, radio actor Orson Welles panicked the nation with his broadcast of "War of the Worlds."

APPROPRIATE SONGS AND HYMNS

Be Bold and Be Strong, Martin J. Nystrom; © 1990 Integrity's Hosanna! Music.
Carry the Torch, David Baroni/Lynn Keesecker; © 1985 Dayspring Music Inc./Manna Music, Inc.; Admin. by Manna Music, Inc.
Go, Chris Christensen; © 1994 Integrity's Hosanna! Music; Admin. by Integrity Music, Inc.
Lift High the Cross, George William Kitchin/Michael Robert Newbolt/Sydney Hugo Nicholson; © 1974, 1992 Hope Publishing Company.
Only Trust Him, John H. Stockton; Public Domain.

WORSHIP HELPS

Call to Worship:
For I am not ashamed of the gospel of Christ, for it is the power of God to salvation for everyone who believes, for the Jew first and also for the Greek. For in it the righteousness of God is revealed from faith to faith; as it is written, "The just shall live by faith" (Rom. 1:16, 17 NKJV).

Hymn Story: "A Mighty Fortress"
Martin Luther was a great reformer, but he was also a musician, having been born in an area of Germany known for its music. In his little Thuringian village, Martin grew up listening to his mother sing. He joined a boys' choir and became proficient with the flute (recorder). When the Protestant Reformation began, Luther determined to restore worship to the German Church. He worked with skilled musicians to create new music for Christians, to be sung in the vernacular. He helped revive congregational singing and wrote a number of hymns.
In the forward of a book, Luther once wrote: "Next to the Word of God, the noble art of music is the greatest treasure in the world. It controls our thoughts, minds, hearts, and spirits ... A person who ... does not regard music as a marvelous creation of God ... does not deserve to be called a human being; he should be permitted to hear nothing but the braying of asses and the grunting of hogs." Luther's most famous hymn is "Ein' feste Burg ist unser Gott,"—"A Mighty Fortress is Our God." Based on Psalm 46, it reflects Luther's awareness of our intense struggle with Satan. In difficulty and danger, Luther would often resort to this song, saying to his associate, "Come, Philip, let us sing the 46th Psalm."

Additional Sermons and Lesson Ideas

Overcoming Talkativeness

Date preached:

By Rev. Todd M. Kinde

SCRIPTURE: James 3:1–12

INTRODUCTION: The tongue that professes faith should prove to be consistent in all speech.

1. The Power of the Tongue (3:1–4).
2. The Pride of the Tongue (3:5–7).
3. The Poison of the Tongue (3:8–12).

CONCLUSION: James uses a set of parables (v. 12) to help us with our tongue. What we need is a change of our nature. We need to be made into a new person by the regenerating work of the Holy Spirit that will yield the fruit of the Spirit, including self-control.

Sinfulness of Selfishness

Date preached:

By Dr. Melvin Worthington

SCRIPTURE: Exodus 20:17

INTRODUCTION: How often do we try to keep up with the Joneses? God gives a clear commandment not to covet.

1. The Admonition in the Text. The admonition includes the call, the condemnation, the control, and the character.
2. The Analysis of the Text. The analysis includes the obsession, the objects, the objective, and the obligation.
3. The Application from the Text. The application includes the cases, the curse, and the counsel.

CONCLUSION: Covetousness is a very serious sin. It lurks within the heart of every human being. We must learn to be content with what God has given us, with His allotment of Divine providence. We must not repine or complain because of God's dealings nor envy the lot or possessions of others (Ps. 37; Phil. 4:11, 12). Our attitude should be one of satisfaction with what we have (present), security in our hope (prospect), and strength through hardships (persecution).

HEROES FOR THE PASTOR'S HEART

The English Reformers

Many people think the English Reformation occurred in sixteenth-century England because the Pope wouldn't grant a divorce to King Henry VIII, resulting in Henry's breaking relations with Rome.

That isn't entirely true. While King Henry did suspend relations with Rome and declare himself head of the Church of England, he still believed Catholic doctrine and observed Catholic rituals. He just wanted Catholicism without the pope.

The real English Reformation is better credited to a scholar at Cambridge University named Thomas Bilney who embraced Reformation truth after reading Erasmus's Greek New Testament.

Bilney, a quiet scholar at Cambridge University, had acquired a Greek New Testament from the famous scholar Erasmus. While pouring over it, he was deeply stirred by one verse of Scripture, 1 Timothy 1:15: "Christ Jesus came into the world to save sinners!"

"This one sentence," he later wrote, "through God's instruction and inward working, did so exhilarate my heart, which before was wounded with the guilt of my sins, that immediately I found wonderful comfort and quietness in my soul. My bruised bones leaped for joy."

Bilney wanted to share his conversion with others, but this was Reformation truth, and despite King Henry's problems with the pope, the Reformation had not yet stirred England. Teachers such as Luther—and teachings like justification by grace through faith—were being fiercely attacked by English churchmen like the young, but powerful and influential, Hugh Latimer.

Bilney listened to young Latimer rail against the Reformation, he prayed an unusual prayer, saying: "O God, I am but 'little Bilney,' and shall never do any great thing for Thee. But give me the soul of that man, Hugh Latimer, and what wonders *he* shall do in Thy most holy name."

One day, breathing a prayer, Bilney pulled Latimer aside, and told him, "Oh, sir, for God's sake, hear my confession." It was a ploy, for as Latimer sat and listened, Bilney spoke Erasmus's Greek New Testament and he shared what had happened to him through it. Reaching into his sleeve, he drew out the precious book, and it opened to a passage heavily underlined, 1 Timothy 1:15.

As Latimer read those words, his eyes were opened, and he himself saw the pure and simple truth of the gospel, that Jesus Christ came into the world to save sinners. The effect on Latimer was reminiscent of the conversion of Saul of Tarsus. Tears poured down his cheeks, and in that moment he, too, was born again.

Soon Latimer was preaching the faith he had once labored to destroy. As a result, he fell from favor during Henry's reign and spent time in the Tower of London. When the more Protestant-leaning King Edward VI came to the throne, Latimer was released for ministry; but when Edward died, Latimer was among those caught and condemned by officials of Queen Mary.

On October 16, 1555, he and Nicholas Ridley were tied back-to-back to the stake in Oxford and set aflame. "Be of good comfort, Mr. Ridley," Latimer cried in words that still echo through Christian history. "Play the man! We shall this day light such a candle, by God's grace, in England, as I trust shall never be put out."

Because of the courage of "Little Bilney" and his great disciple, Hugh Latimer, the Reformation fires swept over England and, in time, to America.

And the flames leaped up, but the blinding smoke
Could not the soul of Hugh Latimer choke;
For, said he, "Brother Ridley, be of good cheer,
A candle in England is lighted here,
Which by the grace of God shall never go out!" —
And that speech in whispers was echoed about —
Latimer's Light shall never go out,
However the winds may blow it about.
Latimer's Light can come to stay
Till the trump of a coming judging day.

** Poem taken from *A Frank Boreham Treasury*, complied by Peter F. Gunther (Chicago: Moody Press, 1984), p. 11.

—*Frank Borham* (1871–1959)

NOVEMBER 6, 2005

SUGGESTED SERMON *Date preached:*

The Adventure of Faith

By Dr. Timothy Beougher

Scripture: Exodus 14:10–22, especially verse 15
Then the LORD said to Moses, "Why are you crying out to Me? Tell the sons of Israel to go forward" (NKJV).

Introduction: Faith is an adventure, a way of life that involves interactive steps and crucial decisions. Faith often begins with a vision or revelation from God. It usually induces excitement and enthusiasm. However, obstacles will arise to test our faith, often leading to doubt and fear. The key question today is: What will our response be, to go forward, to stay still, or to fall back? Let's look at these responses in more detail.

1. **Let's Go Back (vv. 10–12).** In Exodus 12—13 we read of God's provision for the Israelites. Following the Feast of the Passover and the death of all the Egyptians' first-born children, the Egyptians begged the Israelites to leave. The Israelites not only were allowed to leave, the Egyptians gave them silver and gold to take with them. After this, who could doubt God's providential care? Adventures of faith always start exciting. Then comes an obstacle and we begin to doubt God's leading. Pharaoh and his army were that obstacle (Ex. 14:10). Israel was afraid because they focused on the Egyptians instead of on the Lord. When we fear, we focus on circumstances instead of on God and the vision He has given us. The Israelites retreated to their "fond" memories of Egypt (Ex. 14:11, 12), the place of their former slavery! Has God called you to do something? Have you allowed fear to cloud your vision? Don't go back.

2. **Let's Stand Still (vv. 13, 14).** When a challenge to faith comes, some don't say, "Let's go back," they instead say, "Let's stand still." They halt in the present. In the midst of opportunity, they become paralyzed. Standing still is the right thing to do at times. That is what Moses challenged the people to do (vv. 13, 14). There is a time to pray and reflect but there is also a time to act. Moses said, "Stand still." God is going to say, "Go forward." Moses knew it wasn't right to go back, but he didn't yet have the faith to go forward. It is never enough to stand still where we are, to be apathetic.

Churches do not ever really stand still; they either make progress or they fall backward. Christians do not stand still; they either grow or they decline in their spiritual life. We must not stand still when God says to go forward!

3. **Let's Go Forward (vv. 15–22).** In the adventure of faith, there's a time to pray and reflect but also a time to act: "And the LORD said to Moses, 'Why do you cry to Me? Tell the children of Israel to go forward'" (Ex. 14:15). Going forward involves risk. God asked the Israelites to go ahead by faith, not by sight. God also calls us to walk by faith, not by sight. This doesn't mean we do something crazy, but it does mean we need to trust God. Sight says, "We can't do it; we don't have the resources." Faith says, "We can do it; God has the resources." Faith always stretches us beyond where we are. If you can see every step of the way, it is not really faith, it is sight. We go forward for three reasons:

   A. **God's Glory Is Displayed (v. 18).** The words of verse 18 make clear that the Lord will be glorified when we move forward, "Then the Egyptians shall know that I am the LORD, when I have gained honor for Myself over Pharaoh, his chariots, and his horsemen."
   B. **God's Protection Is Displayed (vv. 19, 20).** The pillar of cloud that had been in front of them to guide them, now moved behind them to protect them from the enemy. God gave them a supernatural protection between them and their enemies.
   C. **God's Power Is Displayed (vv. 21, 22).** Moses lifted his rod and the very sea divided to provide dry land for the Israelites to walk through!

Conclusion: Has God been leading you to take a personal step of faith? But have you allowed fear to stop you in your tracks? Perhaps you need to take a step of faith to trust Christ for the first time to save you from your sins and grant you a new life in Him. Whatever the case may be, the Lord is calling us to go forward in faith despite what obstacles may be in the way. The Lord who called you is responsible to provide the way; you're simply responsible to obey.

STATS, STORIES, AND MORE

More from Dr. Timothy Beougher:

In spite of all He had done for the Israelites, in spite of all the plagues He had brought upon Egypt, they didn't believe that God could handle this situation. They should have been singing "Onward Christian Soldiers," but instead they were reflecting this parody:

Backward Christian soldiers, fleeing from the fight.
With the cross of Jesus, clearly out of sight.
Christ our rightful Master, stands against the foe,
But forward into battle, we're chicken to go.
Like a mighty tortoise moves the church of God;
Brothers we are treading, where we've always trod.
We are much divided, many bodies we.
Having different doctrines, not much charity.
Crowns and thrones may perish, kingdoms rise and wane
But the Church of Jesus, hidden does remain.
Gates of hell should never, against that Church prevail.
We have Christ's own promise, but think that it will fail.
Sit here, then, ye people—join our useless throng;
Blend with ours, your voices, in a feeble song.
Blessings, ease, and comfort, ask from Christ the King.
With our faithless thinking, we won't do a thing.

Gladys Aylward, missionary to China for more than 50 years, was forced to flee when the Japanese invaded Yangcheng. She took with her more than 100 orphans, seeking to lead them out of the war zone to safety. One night she despaired of ever reaching safety. A 13-year-old girl reminded her of the story of Moses and the Israelites crossing the Red Sea. "But I am not Moses," Gladys protested. "Of course you aren't," the girl said, "But Jehovah is still God."

FOR THE BULLETIN

✽ Today is the birthday of Benjamin Hall Kennedy (1804), who translated into English the great German hymn, "Ask Ye What Great Thing I Know." ✽ Liberia, black Africa's first independent state, was established in the early 1800s through the efforts of the American Colonization Society, an organization devoted to repatriating American ex-slaves in colonies along the African coast. The first missionary of the Methodist Episcopal Church, Melville Beveridge Cox, left America for Liberia aboard the *Jupiter* on November 6, 1832. He wrote, "I know I cannot live long in Africa, but I hope to live long enough to get there; and if it please God that my bones shall lie in an African grave, I shall have established such a bond between Africa and the church at home as shall not be broken until Africa be redeemed." To students of Connecticut's Wesleyan University, he said, "Let a thousand fall before Africa be given up." Disembarking at Monrovia on March 7, 1833, he threw himself into the work, but died less than four months later. ✽ American evangelist, Billy Sunday, died on this day in 1935. He was at a relative's house in bed, with his wife answering correspondence nearby. Calling to her, Billy said, "I'm getting dizzy, Ma!" He leaned forward, and slumped back on his pillow, sighing deeply. And he was gone. ✽ On November 6, 1977, the Barnes Lake Dam burst in Toccoa Falls, Georgia, killing 38 students and instructors at Toccoa Falls College.

APPROPRIATE SONGS AND HYMNS

Yes, Lord, I Believe, Paul Baloche/Ed Kerr; © 1994 Integrity's Hosanna! Music; Admin. by Integrity Music Group, Inc.

We've Come This Far By Faith, Albert A. Goodson; © 1963 Manna Music, Inc.

Stand and See, Bill Batstone/Phil Kristenson; © 1994 Maranatha Praise, Inc.; Admin. by The Copyright Company.

Lead Me to the Father, Craig Musseau; © 1998 Mercy/Vineyard Publishing.

All that I Need, Dan Marks; © 1992 Maranatha Praise, Inc.; Admin. by The Copyright Company.

WORSHIP HELPS

Call to Worship:
Trust in Him at all times, you people;
Pour out your heart before Him;
God is a refuge for us.
(Ps. 62:7 NKJV)

Scripture Reading:
Now faith is the substance of things hoped for, the evidence of things not seen. For by it the elders obtained a good testimony. By faith we understand that the worlds were framed by the word of God, so that the things which are seen were not made of things which are visible. By faith Abel offered to God a more excellent sacrifice than Cain, through which he obtained witness that he was righteous, God testifying of his gifts; and through it he being dead still speaks. By faith Enoch was taken away so that he did not see death, "and was not found, because God had taken him"; for before he was taken he had this testimony that he pleased God. But without faith it is impossible to please Him, for he who comes to God must believe that He is, and that He is a rewarder of those who diligently seek Him (Heb. 11:1–6 NKJV).

Kids Talk

Sing with the children the little song, "The B-I-B-L-E," and afterward ask the children what it means "to stand up on the Word of God." Let them suggest answers. Tell them that the members of one family (that of the Dutch Christian, Corrie Ten Boom), would actually write out Bible promises and place them in their shoes. When they became discouraged or disheartened, they would ask each other, "What is in your shoe?" They were literally standing on the promises of God.

Additional Sermons and Lesson Ideas

The Peril of Procrastination

Date preached:

By Rev. Peter Grainger

SCRIPTURE: Various Proverbs

INTRODUCTION: Is your life hectic? Does work keep piling up? We often react to stress by putting things off. It's a way to take control, when in fact, we are losing it. The Book of Proverbs brings out three truths concerning procrastinators or sluggards.

1. The Character of the Sluggard.
   A. Laziness (Prov. 6:9–10; 12:27; 19:24; 22:13; 26:13).
   B. Restlessness (Prov. 13:4; 21:25–26).
   C. Helplessness (Prov. 15:19).
   D. Uselessness (Prov. 10:26; 18:9).
2. The Consequences for the Sluggard (Prov. 6:9–11; 24:30–34; 26:16).
3. The Challenge to the Sluggard. Maybe you're thinking "I'm not lazy, I never get to sleep," or "I work all the time." Many of us are selective sluggards; we choose what to invest our time in while neglecting what really matters. Scripture's challenge to all of us is to commit our time to the Lord; live and work diligently as His servant.

CONCLUSION: As the old hymn says, "Shake off dull sloth and joyfully rise / to pay thy morning sacrifice."

Christ Is

Date preached:

By Rev. Charles H. Spurgeon

SCRIPTURE: Colossians 3:4

INTRODUCTION: What is Christ to us?

1. He is the Source of Life (Eph. 2:1).
2. He is the Substance of Life (Col. 3:4).
3. He is the Sustenance of Life (John 6:50).
4. He is the Solace of Life (Ps. 63:3).

CONCLUSION: Oh, how safe, how honored, how happy are Christians, since Christ is their life!

NOVEMBER 13, 2005

SUGGESTED SERMON *Date preached:*

A Home with a Difference

By Dr. Denis Lyle

Scripture: 2 Kings 4:8–17, especially verse 10
Let us make a small upper room on the wall; and let us put a bed for him there, and a table and a chair and a lampstand; so it will be, whenever he comes to us, he can turn in there.

Introduction: Our Scripture today features a well-heeled middle class couple, who seem to have everything: a large house, a secure income, a happy marriage, and all of their material needs met. Their home is an example to us; we should always use our blessings to bless others. Let's look at some of the characteristics of this "Home with a Difference."

1. **A Holiness Known by this Home (vv. 8–10).** Geographically, Shunem was in the North of Israel in the Valley of Esdraelon. It was between Samaria and Carmel along a road that Elisha was accustomed to traveling. A notable woman would stop him as he passed, urging him to eat (v. 8). She went to much trouble to be hospitable because she knew he was a holy man of God (v. 9). She did not designate him as a nice man, a popular, or brilliant, or successful man of God; she was touched with the godliness of his life in a time of moral depravity. We note this about Elisha:

   A. **His Godly Life Was Distinctive.** How did she perceive the prophet's holiness? Did she find him at prayer? Did she see him immersed in the Word? Was it his conversation and conduct? She could certainly see God in the prophet somehow. Do people at school, home, or work perceive that we are holy men and women of God? Do our conversation and conduct measure up?

   B. **His Godly Life Was Impressive.** This woman was impressed enough to have her husband build him a separate room in her house! As Christians, we are constantly under the scrutiny of others: do they see Christ in us?

   C. **His Godly Life Was Extensive.** Stopping by this house time and time again, Elisha must have had an incredible impact, a consistency about his holiness that impressed this woman. Are we living consistently holy lifestyles, or do we simply put on a mask when at church or among Christians?

2. **A Helpfulness That Was Found in This Home (vv. 8–10).** Scripture describes this woman as "notable," which can be translated as "wealthy." Instead of hoarding her wealth, she freely gave to this man of God.

   A. **She Provided for Him Practically.** Notice that she didn't attempt to impress him with her wealth, but simply provided him with food and shelter (vv. 8–10). She was committed to the ministry of hospitality, not to entertaining him. This ministry should be characteristic of us (see 1 Tim. 3:2; Titus 1:8; 1 Pet. 4:9).
   B. **She Provided for Him Regularly.** This was no fleeting mood of kindness, which suddenly came upon her and suddenly disappeared. This was a commitment. We should share such a commitment.
   C. **She Provided for Him Spiritually.** Along with meeting his practical needs, many suggest that the room had spiritual significance: the bed represents his spiritual rest, the table, his spiritual food, the stool represents communion, and the candlestick represents testimony. Perhaps this is the case, but either way, the room certainly provided a solitary place for his prayer and meditation.

3. **A Happiness That Was Brought to This Home (vv. 11–17).** When Elisha inquired of what he could do in return for her, she responded saying, "I dwell among my own people" (v. 13). In other words, "Thanks but I have all I need." She was content! Elisha found out that she lacked one thing, the sunshine of a child's presence and the music of a child's voice.

   A. **Her Service Was Noticed.** This woman didn't have ulterior motives; she didn't want to brag to others about her ministry or to have Elisha give her any special treatment. The Lord urged Elisha to go the extra mile in finding out how he could bless her (v. 14). He noticed her generosity and humility. Is this the way we minister to others, or do we attempt to be flashy or to get something out of it for ourselves (see Luke 17:10).
   B. **Her Service Was Rewarded.** Verse 17 tells us, "... the woman conceived, and bore a son." Remember Jesus' words, "He who receives a prophet in the name of a prophet shall receive a prophet's reward" (Matt. 10:41a NKJV). God rewards genuine hospitality (see also Heb. 13:2).

Conclusion: Is your home filled with holiness, hospitality, and happiness? We will only achieve these things if all the possessions, even our very homes and lives, are completely surrendered to the Lord's service.

STATS, STORIES, AND MORE

More from Dr. Denis Lyle:

Many years ago, a man left the American continent and went away for several years. When he left, he was an unknown: no one knew that this man really existed or that he really lived. After being away from America for several years, he returned. Upon his return, he was greeted with a cheering crowd and was given a hero's welcome. This man had not fought a battle and won a great victory: this man had not made a tremendous discovery that had brought great benefit and aid to people: this man had written a simple song. In the song were these words, "Be it ever so humble, there's no place like home." In the words which this man had been inspired to pen, he expressed the feeling of the hearts of many people about the home and the importance of the home. Some years ago, a preacher visited an old feudal castle in England. The castle was so old that one of its towers dated back to the fifteenth century. At breakfast, the minister noticed high overhead a massive beam that spanned the grand old hall. The beam bore this inscription: "That house shall be preserved and never shall decay, where Almighty God is worshiped day by day." What a testimony concerning the home! When you pray together as a family, are active in a church together, serve God together, and make the Lord the determining factor in every decision, you're establishing a solid foundation for your home.

FOR THE BULLETIN

✽ Today is the birthday of St. Augustine. Historian Philip Schaff wrote, "Aurelius Augustinus, born on the 13th of November, 354, at Tagaste, an unimportant village of the fertile province Numidia in North Africa, not far from Hippo Regius, inherited from his heathen father, Patricius, a passionate sensibility, from his Christian mother, Monica the deep yearning towards God so grandly pressed in his sentence: 'Thou hast made us for Thee, and our heart is restless till it rests in Thee.'" ✽ Jacobus Arminius, professor at the University of Leiden, toned down some of the sharper points of Calvinism, especially those articulated by Theodore Beza. The controversy became so acute that the Dutch national assembly asked both sides to submit their positions in writing. Arminius died before responding, but a war of pamphlets, books, and sermons so divided Holland that the national assembly convened the Synod of Dort, which began November 13, 1618. From the beginning, the Synod regarded the followers of Arminius as heretics, and on January 14, 1619, the Arminians were condemned. All 200 Arminian pastors in Holland were thrown from office, and any who would not be silent were banished from the country. The decisions at the Council of Dort became the basis for the Reformed Faith. ✽ Today is the anniversary of Charles and Elizabeth Finney, who were married on November 13, 1848. ✽ Edward Mote, an English cabinetmaker, died on this day in 1874. He is the author of the hymn, "My Hope Is Built on Nothing Less."

APPROPRIATE SONGS AND HYMNS

A Man with a Perfect Heart, Jack Hayford; © 1995 Annamarie Music; Admin. by Maranatha! Music.

As for Me, Dan Marks; © 1982 Maranatha! Music.

Holy God Make Me Holy, Bob Kilpatrick; © 1985 Bob Kilpatrick Music; Admin. by The Lorenze Corporation.

Pure and Holy, Mike Hudson/Bob Farnsworth; © 1985 Straightway Music/Hummingbird Unaffiliated Catalog; Admin. by Unaffiliated Admin.

To Thee We Ascribe Glory, Kirk Dearman; © 1984, 1988 Celebrant Music.

WORSHIP HELPS

Call to Worship:
I will sing aloud of Your mercy in the morning ...
To You, O my Strength, I will sing praises;
For God is my defense,
My God of mercy.
(Ps. 59:16, 17 NKJV).

Pastoral Prayer:
Thank you, Lord, for our church, our community, our homes, and our leaders. You have told us that Your house is to be a house of prayer for all nations. You've told us that prayers and petitions should be made for all in authority over us. So, we pray today for our President, our Governor, and the Mayor of our city. We pray for our city council and for the school board members in our area. We need wise leaders, O Lord—men and women who will demonstrate and exercise that wisdom that comes from above. Bless our land and our homes with peace. We pray in Jesus' name. Amen.

Offertory Moment:
In his book, *The Tithe: Challenge or Legalism?* Douglas W. Johnson talks about giving as a life-pattern for Christians. Some people, he suggests, simply give as the spirit moves them. Johnson wrote, "Giving is a discipline, not just a few random contributions generated by emotional highs. A life rooted in Christian values is disciplined. It moves toward a goal and follows a purpose. Unless a person is disciplined in every part of life—including giving—there will be no discernible pattern and few worthwhile contributions from that life."

Additional Sermons and Lesson Ideas

Overcoming Envy

Date preached:

By Rev. Todd M. Kinde

SCRIPTURE: James 3:13–18

INTRODUCTION: The source of envy is a fallen understanding of true wisdom.

1. A Definition of Wisdom (3:13).
2. A Demonic Wisdom (3:14–16).
3. A Divine Wisdom (3:17, 18).

CONCLUSION: The harvest of this divine wisdom is righteousness. The climate for growing righteousness is not bitterness or competitiveness but peace. The great peacemaker is Jesus who has borne our guilt and punishment so that by grace through faith we might avoid the wrath and curse of God. This is peace. The Cross is God's wisdom in Christ. The Cross is God's peace in Christ. The Cross is God's salvation in Christ.

The Creator's Character

Date preached:

By Dr. Melvin Worthington

SCRIPTURE: 1 John 1:1–10

INTRODUCTION: How would you describe God the Creator? In the epistle of 1 John, we have an excellent description; John declares that God is Light and there is no darkness in Him. By nature, God is pure, holy, righteous, and just.

1. The Manifestation of Life (1 John 1:1–3). These verses set forth the eternal Son as the Creator, the earthly sojourn in the first coming, the enjoyable supping in fellowship, and the ending summary or completion.
2. The Motivation of the Letter (1 John 1:4). The purpose for writing the letter is that the joy of the readers might be full.
3. The Magnification of Light (I John 1:5–10). These verses note the message, the mistake, and the miracle.

CONCLUSION: Christianity is based on the fact man is sinful and needs a savior. Without admitting this fact, one cannot be a Christian. John reminds us that only Christ Himself is sinless and perfect, which makes Him alone worthy of our faith.

NOVEMBER 20, 2005

SUGGESTED SERMON *Date preached:*

The Perfect Church

By Rev. Peter Grainger

Scripture: 1 Corinthians 1:1–9, especially verse 4.
I thank my God always concerning you for the grace of God which was given to you by Christ Jesus. (NKJV)

Introduction: What's your idea of the perfect church? Does that mean perfect members, a huge congregation, or excellent choir? From Paul's perspective, the perfect church is the church in Christ. We need to remember that the church of Corinth was plagued with problems, but Paul focuses on God's work despite those problems. Three things exist in the Corinthian church, and in every church of God.

1. **Called by God (vv. 1–3).** Notice the repeated use of the word *call* in Paul's opening greeting. He begins by describing himself as "called to be an apostle of Jesus Christ" (v. 1). Paul says he is an apostle, a messenger of Jesus Christ. Paul once hated Jesus Christ and did all he could to suppress and persecute Christians until Jesus Himself literally stopped him in his tracks and set his life on a new course. He was called by Jesus to be an apostle (see Acts 9:1–22). Paul also uses *called* to describe those in the Corinthian church, who were "called to be saints, with all who in every place call on the name of Jesus Christ our Lord, both theirs and ours" (1 Cor. 1:2). This includes all Christians, everywhere. Christians are those who call on the name of Jesus Christ as their Lord and Savior as a response to His call. Is the Lord calling you, convicting you of sin, or showing you His love? Won't you respond to His call? The greeting to the church from Paul follows; he expresses God's grace (unmerited favor and love) and God's peace (well-being and wholeness which God the Father has given to His children). If you enjoy these privileges and belong to Christ, then you also share them with other Christians, people from all over the world.

2. **Enriched by God (vv. 4–7).** God will complete His will: to build His church. God has provided His people, the members of His church, with all the resources they need. Despite all the problems in the church at Corinth, Paul surprises us by saying that he gives thanks to God that they have

been enriched in everything and come short in no gift. Remember that many of the problems in the church in Corinth were centered on the use (or abuse) of spiritual gifts! Paul knew the problem was not the gifts, but misuse of them, so he is thankful for the gifts themselves which are of God. Instead of complaining about the church and what we lack, we should rejoice and give thanks that God has given His church all that we need. Paul mentions two broad areas of the Lord's gifts: speaking gifts, which focus on speaking truth, and knowledge gifts, which focus on explaining truth (v. 6). These gifts are evidence or confirmation that the Corinthians are genuine Christians (v. 6). So, if you are a genuine Christian, God has gifted you.

What gifts has God given you? How are you using them? Having focused on the past (called by God), and the present (enriched by God), Paul then turns to the future:

3. **Kept by God (vv. 8, 9).** Verse 7 ends with these words: "eagerly waiting for the revelation of our Lord Jesus Christ." The Corinthian Christians have every spiritual gift they need but they have not yet arrived at perfection because Christ has not yet returned. The gifts they received needed to be used so that the church could function and live as God intends in preparation for Christ's return. But, looking at the church in Corinth, let alone the church in our day and ourselves personally, we wonder if we will ever be ready for the return of Christ. If this were dependent on us, there would be no hope.

Once again, Paul shifts the focus from the church to God the Father and to Jesus with a note of future assurance, "Who will also confirm you to the end, that you may be blameless in the day of our Lord Jesus Christ. God is faithful, by whom you were called into the fellowship of His Son, Jesus Christ our Lord" (vv. 8, 9 NKJV).

Conclusion: If Paul could have such confidence about God's ability and commitment to the church in Corinth, surely we should have such confidence about our church and even about ourselves. Since God has called us into fellowship with His Son Jesus Christ our Lord, He has gifted us with all we need and will hold us firm until the end. Our confidence is not in ourselves but in God.

STATS, STORIES, AND MORE

More from Rev. Peter Grainger:

To understand 1 Corinthians, we can look at the historical and geographical context of the book. Five times larger than Athens, Corinth wasn't nearly as historical or popular. The Romans had razed the original ancient city of some two hundred years before as a punishment for leading a rebellion against the Empire. Julius Caesar had re-established it as a Roman colony a hundred years later. Now Corinth was just over a hundred years old with a large cosmopolitan population of a quarter to three quarters of a million people. Two thirds of the people were slaves. The rest were a mobile mixture of sailors, who used Corinth's two ports from which a worldwide trade flourished, businessmen, and government officials.

People flocked to Corinth from the four corners of the Empire. Fortune hunters came to get rich quick and pleasure-seekers came to spend money on a holiday from morality. Professionalism and every form of quackery and cheating degraded the Isthmian Games, second only to the Olympics and hosted every two years by Corinth.

The church, started by Paul who first preached the gospel to this city, had become as bad as its culture. The church was plagued with sexual immorality and worldly sins. To rebuke, correct, encourage, and admonish the church, Paul wrote the letter of 1 Corinthians.

FOR THE BULLETIN

❁ On November 20, 1541, the great Reformer, John Calvin, at age 32, established a theocratic government at Geneva, leading to that city's central role in the growing Reformation movement. ❁ November 20, 1847 marks the death of pastor/hymnist Henry Lyte (See Worship Helps). ❁ On November 20, 1849, missionary/explorer David Livingstone sailed for South Africa. ❁ On this day in 1850, the blind poet, Fanny Crosby, 31, attended a revival service at John Street Methodist Church in New York. "After a prayer was offered," she recalled, "they began to sing the grand old consecration hymn, 'Alas! And Did My Savior Bleed?' and when they reached the third line of the fifth stanza, 'Here, Lord, I give myself away,' my very soul was flooded with celestial light." This marked the date of assurance for her of her salvation. She went on to write thousands of hymns and gospel songs, including "Rescue the Perishing," "Blessed Assurance," and "Safe in the Arms of Jesus." She became the third best-known evangelical figure in America during her lifetime, the others being D. L. Moody and Ira Sankey. In addition to writing hymns, she was well known for her sermons and for her work at rescue missions. ❁ On November 20, 1872, Annie Sherwood Hawks' hymn, "I Need Thee Every Hour," was first sung at a National Baptist Sunday School Convention in Cincinnati. ❁ A significant weekly Sunday event began on this day in 1947. It was the debut of the Sunday political program, Meet the Press, on the National Broadcasting Network.

APPROPRIATE SONGS AND HYMNS

We Are Called to Be God's People, Thomas Jackson/Franz Joseph Haydn; © 1975 Broadman Press; Admin. by Genevox Music Group.

A Glorious Church, Ralph Hudson; Public Domain.

Community of Christ, Shirley Erena Murray; © 1992 Hope Publishing Company.

He Reigns on High, Steve Young; © 1984 Zionsong Music.

O Church of God United, Frederick B. Morley; © 1954. Renewed 1982 The Hymn Society of Hope Publishing Company; Admin. by Hope Publishing Company.

WORSHIP HELPS

Call to Worship:
Be with us, gracious Lord, today;
This house we dedicate to Thee;
O hear Thy servants as they pray,
And let Thine ear attentive be!
—*Charles D. Bell* (1818–1898)

Hymn Story: "Abide With Me"
On Sunday, September 4, 1847, Pastor Henry Lyte, 54, entered his pulpit with difficulty and preached what was to be his last sermon. He had planned a therapeutic holiday in Italy. That afternoon he walked along the coast in pensive prayer then retired to his room, emerging an hour later with a written copy of "Abide With Me." Some accounts indicate he wrote the poem during that hour; others say that he discovered it in the bottom of his desk as he packed for his trip to Italy, and that it had been written a quarter century earlier. Probably both stories are true. It is likely that, finding sketches of a poem he had previously started, he prayerfully revised and completed it that evening. Shortly afterward, Henry departed for Italy. Stopping in Avignon, France, he again revised "Abide With Me" and posted it to his wife. Arriving on the French Riviera, he checked into the Hotel de Angleterre in Nice, and there on November 20, 1847, his lungs finally gave out. Another English clergyman, a Rev. Manning of Chichester, who happened to be staying in the same hotel, attended him during his final hours. Henry's last words were, "Peace! Joy!" When news of his death reached Brixham, the fishermen of the village asked Henry's son-in-law, also a minister, to hold a memorial service. It was on this occasion that "Abide With Me" was first sung.

Additional Sermons and Lesson Ideas

A Third Opinion

Date preached:

By Dr. Timothy Beougher

SCRIPTURE: Mark 3:20–35

INTRODUCTION: Someone has said that life's greatest question is found in Mark 8:21, when Jesus asks the disciples, "Who do you say that I am?" People answer that question is a variety of ways. How we answer determines our eternal destiny!

1. The First Opinion: Jesus is a Madman (vv. 20, 21).
2. The Second Opinion: Jesus is a Demoniac (vv. 22–30).
3. A Third Opinion: Jesus is the Son of God (Mark 8:29; Rom. 9:5).

CONCLUSION: It's impossible to accept Jesus as only a good moral teacher, for He claimed to be God and must either have been telling the truth, lying, or have been crazy. What's your opinion? Will you mock Him as a madman? Reject Him as a demoniac? Or exalt Him and follow Him as your Lord?

Overwhelmed

Date preached:

SCRIPTURE: Psalm 61:2

INTRODUCTION: Feeling overwhelmed?

1. Overwhelmed with Fear (Ps. 55:5)
2. Overwhelmed with Depression (Ps. 77:3)
3. Overwhelmed with Foes (Ps. 124:4)
4. Overwhelmed with Trouble (Ps. 142:3)
5. Overwhelmed with Distress (Ps. 143:4)

CONCLUSION: "From the end of the earth I will cry to You, when my heart is overwhelmed; Lead me to the rock that is higher than I" (Ps. 61:2).

THANKSGIVING SERMON

Thanksgiving Truths

Date preached:

By Dr. Melvin Worthington

Scripture: Psalm 100; 145 (NKJV).

Introduction: Thanksgiving is the day when we pause to reflect, remember, and respect the abundant blessings that God has bestowed upon us. Millions will use this special day, which has been appointed as Thanksgiving Day, as a day of indulgence, intemperance, and ingratitude, not respecting their Creator, conscience, or country. Thanksgiving is the act of rendering praise and thanksgiving; this praise and thanksgiving may take the form of private prayer or public proclamation as one articulates his appreciation for the blessings he enjoys. Thanksgiving is more than a day; it should be the disposition which all Christians should display every day, the attitude which should daily characterize those who are disciplined and devoted disciples of Christ.

1. **Christians Thank God for His Goodness (Jer. 33:11).** God's goodness leads men to repentance (Rom. 2:4). Thankfulness for God's goodness is always in order. The Psalms abound with references to God's goodness.

2. **Christians Thank God for His Greatness (Ps. 48:1; 145:3; 147:5).** David declared God's greatness when he said, "Great is the LORD, and greatly to be praised in the city of our God, in His holy mountain" (Ps. 48:1). In Psalm 145:3, God's greatness is described by the words "Great is the LORD, and greatly to be praised; and His greatness is unsearchable" (NKJV). Psalm 147:5 declares, "Great is our LORD, and mighty in power; His understanding is infinite" (NKJV). The greatness of God's person, power, and provisions should bring praise and thanksgiving from the heart of the Christian. Are you?

3. **Christians Thank God for His Grace (1 Cor. 1:4).** Grace is defined as unmerited or undeserved favor. Grace cannot be earned, but it can be experienced and enjoyed. Christians live by God's grace, learn by God's grace, labor by God's grace, look for His coming by grace, and manifest loyalty by God's grace. Believers are saved, schooled, sanctified, secured, and satisfied by God's grace. The truth of God's grace should cause praise and thanksgiving.

4. **Christians Thank God for His Gospel (2 Cor. 8:18).** The gospel is God's Good News regarding the salvation provided for sinful people. In this verse, Paul gives an example of a brother whose praise is in the gospel. Paul elsewhere acknowledges preaching the gospel that is the power of God to salvation for all who believe (Rom. 1:16). He is assured of the power of the gospel to change the lives of all who believe. The gospel, which brings the news of salvation for fallen mankind, should provoke thankfulness and praise for every Christian.

5. **Christians Thank God for His Guidance (Ps. 67:4 NIV).** We have no reason to fret or worry, for the Lord guides the nations! The writer of Proverbs declares, "Trust in the LORD with all your heart, and lean not on your own understanding; in all your ways acknowledge Him, and He shall direct your paths" (Prov. 3:5, 6). David declared "The steps of a good man are ordered by the LORD, and He delights in his way" (Ps. 37:23 NKJV). The Christian can be assured of and should be thankful for the Lord's personal, practical, positive, and providential guidance.

6. **Christians Thank God for His Government (Is. 9:6).** Jesus once said to Martha, "You are worried and troubled about many things" (Luke 10:41 NKJV). How often we are the same! We should trust rather than toil. Isaiah prophesied about Jesus, that the government would rest on His shoulders (Is. 9:6). The providence and sovereignty of God in the affairs of men are comforting truths. We can be assured "that all things work together for good to those who love God, to those who are called according to His purpose" (Rom. 8:28 NKJV). The entire Book of Daniel suggests that God's hand superintends the affairs of men. The grand pillars of God's providence, which support the universe, should provoke thanksgiving and praise.

7. **Christians Thank God for His Gifts (2 Cor. 9:13).** Here, Paul gives thanks to God for a gift so incredible, that only He could be the true author of it. The Lord has given us salvation. He gave His Son to pay our sin debt. He has given us His Spirit. He has given us the gifts of the Spirit. The gifts that God has bestowed on His children are cause for thanksgiving and praise.

8. **Christians Thank God for His Gospel Preachers (2 Cor. 9:13).** Throughout the course of time, God has called individuals to declare His message. God has always had a person to do His bidding: Noah, Abraham, Moses,

Daniel, Joseph, Peter, Paul, and many others, perhaps even you. Our hearts should be filled with thanksgiving and praises for those who have faithfully answered God's call to articulate God's Word.

Conclusion: Thanksgiving truths commence with God, continue with God, and consummate in God. The psalmist expressed it succinctly when he declared, "Make a joyful shout to the LORD, all you lands! Serve the LORD with gladness; come before His presence with singing. Know that the LORD, He is God; It is He who has made us, and not we ourselves; we are His people and the sheep of His pasture. Enter into His gates with thanksgiving, and into His courts with praise. Be thankful to Him, and bless His name. For the LORD is good; His mercy is everlasting, and His truth endures to all generations" (Ps. 100 NKJV).

CLASSICS FOR THE PASTOR'S LIBRARY

The Kneeling Christian

The best seventy-five-cent investment I've ever made was for an old hardbound copy of *The Kneeling Christian.* I found it in a used bookstore in Florida. It was marked $1.50, and I would have paid ten times that for it; but the owner glanced at it, shrugged, and said, "You can have it for 75 cents." The months that followed, as it happened, were awfully stressful, and *The Kneeling Christian* became my constant comfort and friend. I consider it the greatest classic on prayer in my library.

We know little about the background of this book because its author, Albert Ernest Richardson, didn't even want us to know his name. He wrote several books under the pseudonym "An Unknown Christian," and it was only with the help of my friend, researcher Chuck Sherrill and his contacts at the British Library, that I uncovered his name. *The Kneeling Christian* has since been reprinted in many languages by many publishing houses. It is now available for free downloading on several Internet sites, and is available in paperback from HarperCollins Publishers. The twelve short chapters deal with subjects like:

- God's Great Need

- Almost Incredible Promises
- How Shall I Pray?
- Must I Agonize?
- Does God Always Answer Prayer?

One of the first insights to meet us in *The Kneeling Christian* is the observation that in the Upper Room passages of John 13–16, Jesus invites us seven times to ask for anything in His name: "Six times over, almost in the same breath, our Savior commands us to ask whatsoever we will. This is the greatest—the most wonderful—promise ever made. Yet, most practically ignore it. We have often spent time in reflecting on our Lord's seven words from the Cross, [but] have we ever spent one hour in meditating upon our Savior's sevenfold invitation to pray."

Here are two other quotes to whet your appetite:

- We can accomplish far more by our prayers than by our work. Prayer is omnipotent; it can do anything God can do! When we pray God works. All fruitfulness in service is the outcome of prayer—of the worker's prayers, or of those who are holding up holy hands on his behalf.
- There is no doubt whatever that the devil opposes our approach to God in prayer, and does all he can to prevent the prayer of faith. His chief way of hindering us is to try to fill our minds with the thought of our needs, so that they shall not be occupied with thoughts of God, our loving Father, to whom we pray. He wants us to think more of the gift than of the Giver. The Holy Spirit leads us to pray for a brother. We get as far as "O God, bless my brother"—and away go our thoughts to the brother, and his affairs, and his difficulties, his hopes and his fears, and away goes prayer! How hard the devil makes it for us to concentrate our thoughts upon God! This is why we urge people to get a realization of the glory of God, and the power of God, and the presence of God, before offering up any petition.

If you can find a copy of *The Kneeling Christian,* grab it and read it slowly, a page or two each day during your devotions. It will turn you into its title.

NOVEMBER 27, 2005

SUGGESTED SERMON *Date preached:*

Requirements for Service

By Dr. Denis Lyle

Scripture: 2 Kings 2:1–18, especially verse 14
He took the mantle of Elijah that fell from him and struck the waters and said, "Where is the LORD, the God of Elijah?" And when he also had struck the waters, they were divided here and there; and Elisha crossed over (NASB).

Introduction: Our text for today brings up a very relevant question: what are the requirements for serving the Lord? Elijah was ready to be with the Lord, having reached maturity, while Elisha was just blossoming out. Three requirements for service shine through for us in our passage:

1. **The Recognition of Elijah's God.** Notice Elisha's words, "Where is the LORD, the God of Elijah?" (v. 14). This is not a cry of despair or unbelief. It is the cry of dependence, which rises from the depths of Elisha's soul. Right at the beginning of his public ministry, Elisha calls on the name of the Lord for he was so conscious of his own unfitness for the task that God had called him to do. Elijah had been translated to a higher sphere of service, but the God of Elijah had not left the world. Elisha's task depended not on the reputation of Elijah, but on the resources of the living God! Elisha recognized that the God of Elijah was His God also.

2. **The Reception of Elijah's Spirit.** The only possession Elijah left behind was his mantle. The mantle is more than a piece of clothing. It's part of the very personality of the prophet. Elijah's mantle has spiritual significance. It was the symbol of spiritual power (v. 15) and reminds us of the Holy Spirit. (see John 15:26, 27; Acts 1:8). Elisha proved himself through:

   A. **The Test of Loyalty.** What was the purpose of this long walk that took them from Gilgal to Jordan via Bethel and Jericho (vv. 2–6)? Why did Elijah say three times to Elisha, "Stay here please" (vv. 2, 4, 6)? Did he want privacy? Did he wish to spare Elisha the pain of parting? Possibly, but more probably it was to test Elisha's resolve, loyalty, and fidelity. God entrusts His Spirit to those who give their lives to Jesus. Are you loyal to go wherever He leads?

B. **The Test of Loneliness.** I wonder was there a little hint of jealousy from the other prophets, "Do you know the LORD will take away your master from over you today?" (v. 3). Perhaps they were implying that Elisha's greatness would be shrunk when he no longer lived under Elijah's shadow. Elisha surely felt alone. Ministry can be a lonely place, filled with opposition, criticism, and pain. Despite all of this, we must be committed to receive and obey the Spirit.

C. **The Test of Love.** In verse 9, it sounds as if Elijah was giving his associate a blank check. What would Elisha write in the box? What was his heart really set upon? What did he desire above all? When Elisha asked for a double portion of Elijah's spirit, he was asking that he might be equipped to fully represent his ascended master. He did not want to be a sensation, he wanted to be a servant. Would you pass this test? What is your heart really set upon? What would you write in the box? Do you long to have spiritual power in your ministry?

3. **The Revelation of Elijah's Power.** Following the example of Elijah, Elisha turned to the Jordan and struck its waters with the mantle. In his hand it became an instrument of power. Would anyone question our need for the power of the Holy Spirit today? Our lives are often barren, many churches dead, our service often ineffective; we desperately need the power of the Holy Spirit. We need His Spirit in our personal walk as we grow closer to the Savior. We need Him in our public service as we preach the gospel and serve others for His sake.

Conclusion: So, "Where is the LORD, the God of Elijah" (v. 14)? Elijah was gone, but his God is still here. Elisha realized this and we must as well! Are you available to God? Will you allow Him to take you, cleanse you, fill you, and use you to His glory?

STATS, STORIES, AND MORE

Revival Power

Jonathan Edwards preached "Sinners in the Hands of an Angry God"—the most famous sermon in American history—on Sunday, July 8, 1741, while ministering in Enfield, Connecticut. A group of women had spent the previous night praying for revival. When Edwards rose to speak, he announced that his text was Deuteronomy 32:35, "Their foot shall slide in due time." The hellfire and brimstone approach of the sermon was somewhat a departure for Edwards. Of his 1,000 written sermons, less than a dozen are of this type. Edwards neither gestured nor raised his voice. He spoke softly and simply, warning the unconverted that they were dangling over hell like a spider over the fire. "O sinner! consider the fearful danger. The unconverted are now walking over the pit of hell on a rotten covering, and there are innumerable places in this covering so weak that it will not bear their weight, and these places are not seen."

Edwards' voice was lost amid cries and commotion from the crowd. He paused, appealing for calm. Then he concluded: "Let everyone that is out of Christ, now awake and fly from the wrath to come. The wrath of Almighty God is now undoubtedly hanging over a great part of this congregation. Let every one fly out of Sodom."

People held to pews and posts, feeling they were sliding into hell. Others shook uncontrollably and rolled on the floor. Throughout the night cries of men and women were heard throughout the village, begging God to save them. Five hundred were converted that evening, sparking a revival that swept thousands into the kingdom.

FOR THE BULLETIN

❁ A dark day for Christendom occurred on November 27, 1095, when Pope Urban II in France announced the First Crusade at the Council of Clermont. He wanted to free the Holy Land from Muslim control and secure access for Christian pilgrims. As Urban proclaimed the cause, the crowd roared back, "God wills it! God wills it!" Shortly thereafter, the first European armies departed to war. ❁ Adelaide Pollard was born on this day in Iowa in 1862. At one time, Adelaide felt that God was calling her to Africa as a missionary. To her intense disappointment, she was unable to raise her financial support. Heartsick, Adelaide, attended a prayer meeting. That night an elderly woman prayed, "It doesn't matter what you bring into our lives, Lord. Just have your own way with us." That phrase rushed into Adelaide's heart, and the verses began shaping in her mind, and by bedtime she had written out the hymn, "Have Thine Own Way." ❁ Today is the birthday (1874) of the Zionist leader, Chaim Weizmann. ❁ Earnest Presswood, Canadian missionary in Borneo, was successful in his work, though at a cost. His wife died while suffering a miscarriage, and Ernie buried her in a coffin made with timbers from the house they were building on the island. His service was disrupted between 1940 and 1945 by war in the South Pacific, and for five years, Ernie wondered and worried about his suffering flock. On November 27, 1945, when he returned, he found the graves of many Christians, but the church in Borneo was triumphant. By now, Ernie was old beyond his 38 years, and he died three months later of pneumonia after a rafting accident—having planted a church and reaped a harvest that thrives to this day.

APPROPRIATE SONGS AND HYMNS

Abba Father, Cecilie Hobson; © 1978 Celebration.

God Is in the House, Darlene Zschech/Russell Fragar; © 1995 Darlene Zschech/Russell Fragar; Admin. by Integrity Music, Inc.

Have I Done My Best for Jesus, Ensign Edwin Young/Harry Stors; © 1924. Renewed Harry N. Stors; Admin. Brentwood-Benson Music Publishing.

Man of the Spirit, Bill Batstone; © 1993 Maranatha Praise, Inc.; Admin. by The Copyright Company.

Where He Leads Me, E.W. Blandy/John S. Norris; Public Domain.

WORSHIP HELPS

Call to Worship:
Blessed is the Lord God of Israel,
For He has visited and redeemed His people.
(Luke 1:68 NKJV).

Advent Reading:
Today is the first Sunday of Advent, and when we think of Christ, we think not only of Bethlehem but also of Nazareth and Galilee. The Coming Messiah, proclaimed the ancient prophets, would hail from the lands of Zebulun and Naphtali, by the way of the sea, beyond the Jordan, from Galilee of the Gentiles. There the carpenter Joseph lived. There the tender Mary raised her sons. There the Son of Man preached on the hillsides, walked on the waters, and proclaimed His love to the hungering multitudes. Of this place Isaiah wrote: "The people who walked in darkness have seen a great light; those who dwelt in the land of the shadow of death, upon them a light has shined" (Is. 9:2 NKJV).

Scripture Reading Medley:
Be kindly affectionate to one another with brotherly love, in honor giving preference to one another; not lagging in diligence, fervent in spirit, serving the LORD. Serve the LORD with gladness; come before His presence with singing. And whatever you do, do it heartily, as to the Lord and not to men, knowing that from the Lord you will receive the reward of the inheritance; for you serve the Lord Christ. As each one has received a gift, minister to one another, as good stewards of the manifold grace of God. If anyone speaks, let him speak as the oracles of God. If anyone ministers, let him do it as with the ability which God supplies, that in all things God may be glorified through Jesus Christ, to whom belong the glory and the dominion forever and ever. Amen. (Rom. 12:10, 11; Ps. 100:2; Col. 3:23, 24; 1 Pet. 4:10, 11 NKJV).

Additional Sermons and Lesson Ideas

An Ambassador

Date preached:

By Dr. Melvin Worthington

SCRIPTURE: 2 Corinthians 5:20; Ephesians 6:20

INTRODUCTION: No finer term describes the Christian than *ambassador.*

1. The Term Defined. Two elements included in the definition are messenger and interpreter. An ambassador is an official representative of a king or government (Is. 30:4; 2 Chr. 3:31; 2 Chr. 35:21; Is. 33:7). The term is used in a figurative sense in the New Testament (Eph. 6:20; 2 Cor. 5:20). Christians are official representatives of Christ, commissioned by Christ, their sovereign Lord, with the ministry and message of reconciliation.
2. The Traits Disclosed. The traits include the ambassador's appointment, authority, allegiance, agenda, adaptability, accountability, arena, and assignment. As ambassadors, Christians must do the work that Christ would do if He were present.
3. The Thorough Development. God educates and elevates His ambassadors. Moses, Joseph, Daniel and Paul illustrate this principle. God evaluates His ambassadors. The three Hebrew boys in Daniel 3 illustrate this principle.

CONCLUSION: Are you doing God's work? Are you worthy of being called His ambassador?

Exuberant Praise

Date preached:

SCRIPTURE: Psalm 150

INTRODUCTION: How are you feeling right now? Weary? Tired? Worried? How about thankful? Worshipful? Look at Psalm 150 for a dose of praise.

1. Where to Praise God (v. 1)
2. Why to Praise God (v. 2)
3. How to Praise God (vv. 3–5)
4. Who Should Praise God (v. 6)

CONCLUSION: Do you have breath? Then praise the Lord!

TECHNIQUES FOR THE PASTOR'S DELIVERY

Using Notes in Preaching

By R. W. Dale

About the comparative advantages of preaching from a manuscript and preaching extemporaneously, I have some difficulty in speaking. It seems to me that the overwhelming weight of the argument is on the side of extemporaneous preaching; but I have very rarely the courage to go into the pulpit without carrying with me the notes of my sermon, and occasionally I read every sentence from the first to the last. The contrast between my theory of preaching and my practice is in this respect very glaring.

It is not every man that appears in the pulpit without his manuscript who is an extemporaneous preacher. In Scotland and in France, where the people regard the "paper" with horror, it is a common practice for ministers to write their sermons and learn them by heart—clause after clause, sentence after sentence, paragraph after paragraph. Some men, without any attempt to learn what they have written, reproduce it with hardly a variation of a single phrase. I have heard of eminent preachers who are able to compose and to retain in their memory long discourses without putting pen to paper. None of these are extemporaneous preachers.

On the other hand it is not necessary, in order to preach extemporaneously, that we should choose our text as we go into the pulpit, and say what happens to come first. M. Coquerel puts it admirably when he says that the extemporaneous preacher "knows what he is going to say, but does not know how he will say it."

It must be conceded that in sermons in which clearness and precise accuracy in the statement of truth are of special importance, the man who reads is likely to have a great advantage. Language is a difficult instrument to master, and even the ablest speakers and those who have had the longest practice cannot always command at the moment the simplest and most transparent expression of their thought. This is especially true when they are dealing with unfamiliar lines of speculation. The written sermon is also likely to be most successful in the clear and orderly development of an elaborate argument.

Nor is it fair to say that those who read their sermons show a distrust of the aid of the Holy Spirit. Our self-distrust, our dependence upon divine teaching and aid, may be just as perfect when we are writing as when we are speaking. I do not accept the superstition that implies that the Spirit of God is with us in the pulpit and not in the study.

It is not true that read sermons are always dry and dull, or that extemporaneous sermons are necessarily vivacious and vigorous. Dr. Chalmers was accustomed to read every syllable, and yet he preached with a fire and a passion that created great excitement and produced the deepest impression. How weak, how dreary, an extemporaneous preacher may be, we all know. But few of us have Dr. Chalmer's strong and impetuous nature. Unless there is extraordinary force in the preacher, the manuscript somehow comes between him and the congregation.

The extemporaneous preacher will also be likely to have an advantage in his style. It is true that he can hardly be accurate. But what the extemporaneous speaker loses in accuracy, he may more than gain in ease, directness, and vigor. He will escape the formality and the bookishness of manner which are the snare of most writers, and which are intolerable to all listeners; and in the generous heat which comes from direct contact with his audience, he may achieve boldness both of thought and expression which are rarely achieved at the desk.

In speaking extemporaneously, we watch the faces of the people, and we often discover that statements which seemed to ourselves perfectly clear require repeating, illustrating, and expanding.

I admit that the question cannot be determined peremptorily; that there are advantages on the side of preaching from a full manuscript, as well as advantages on the side of preaching from the briefest notes, or from no notes at all. Very much depends on the preacher, very much depends on the character of the congregation. But I say again that, on the whole, I am clear that the practice of reading our sermons lessens the interest and impairs the power of preaching.

(Excerpted from Lecture 6, "Extemporaneous Preaching and Style," from *The Yale Lectures on Preaching*, 1877–78 by R. W. Dale)

DECEMBER 4, 2005

SUGGESTED SERMON *Date preached:*

How Should We Then Give?

By Dr. Timothy Beougher

Scripture: 2 Corinthians 8:1–13, especially verse 9
For you know the grace of our Lord Jesus Christ, that though He was rich, yet for your sakes He became poor, that you through His poverty might become rich (NKJV).

Introduction: Here at the beginning of Advent, we want to consider the subject of giving—one very appropriate for the Christmas season. Jesus is God's great Christmas gift to us, the Magi brought gifts to Him, and we all exchange gifts with each other. In our text today, the apostle Paul focuses on giving. He's referring to what we commonly call stewardship, and as we will see, the emphasis of the Bible is not on money but on principles. The big question today is, "How does the Lord want us to give?" Paul points out the Macedonian believers (Philippians, Thessalonians, and Bereans) are perfect examples of how Christians should give.

1. **Gratefully (v. 1).** The motive for giving in the New Testament is the grace of God, God's abundant goodness (cf. vv. 6, 7, 9, 19, and 9:8). Christian giving flows from the heart, an expression of gratitude for what Christ has done for us. We love because He first loved us and we give because He first gave to us; true giving always originates with the grace of God. We see from Scripture that people can give with the wrong motives, in order to be seen and recognized by others (Matt. 6:1, 2). Others may give attempting to earn favor with God. We can't earn favor with God, we can only accept His grace through Jesus Christ. A sure mark of a heart that has been touched by the grace of God is this: it counts giving a privilege.

2. **Sacrificially (v. 2).** The Macedonian believers had not simply gone through hard times. The text says they experienced, a great trial of affliction, and, deep poverty. The Greek word for *deep poverty* describes a beggar who has absolutely nothing to his name. We're not exactly sure what caused their poverty or affliction, but their circumstances did not prevent them from giving. In fact, they gave generously! They didn't use their difficult circumstances as an excuse for not giving. They didn't have much to give, but they still gave sacrificially. It's the attitude, not the amount that makes the

difference to God. The principle this passage teaches us is that God is not looking for equal gifts, but equal sacrifice (cf. Mark 12:41–44).

3. **Eagerly (vv. 3, 4).** Have you ever heard anyone beg that an offering be taken so they could have the privilege of giving? That's what these Christians did! They were "freely willing" (v. 3). Their motivation to give came from eagerness inside of them, not from external pressure. Giving that stems from coercion or guilt is not giving God's way (2 Cor. 9:7). The Macedonians' giving was voluntary and spontaneous. It flowed from grace, not from guilt.

4. **Spiritually (v. 5).** The most important thing about giving is not that you give your money but that you give yourselves to the Lord (see Rom. 12:1, 2). God is more interested in possessing our heart than our possessions. If we give ourselves to God, we will not have a problem giving of our possessions, for then we will understand that God owns it all anyway.

5. **Motivated by Love (vv. 7–9).** Paul wanted to be sure the Corinthians understood that he was not ordering them to give. He was contrasting the attitude of the Corinthian church with the attitude of the churches of Macedonia. The Macedonians were following the example of Christ, who gave from a heart of love. Paul is challenging the Corinthians to prove their love for Christ and for others by sharing in the offering. Paul is not twisting their arms or applying pressure, but he reminds them that giving flows out of a heart that has been touched by the love and the grace of God. He uses the example of Christ, who became poor for our sakes, that He we might become rich (v. 9). Jesus was rich in His person, for He Himself is God. He was rich in His possessions, for He could point to anything in the world and say, "That's mine." He was rich in His position as the King of kings and Lord of lords. He was rich in His power, for nothing is too difficult for Him! Despite all these riches, He became poor because, "God so loved the world that He gave His only begotten Son" (John 3:16 NKJV). How much more should we give out of our love for Him!

Conclusion: Someone once said, "You can give without loving, but you cannot love without giving." Does your giving reflect your gratefulness, your eagerness, and your love? Do you give spiritually and sacrificially? We should never neglect the privilege of giving back to the One who gave Himself for us.

STATS, STORIES, AND MORE

More from Dr. Timothy Beougher:

Larry Burkett, writing in the August 1999 issue of "Commission" magazine, noted: "Having enough money isn't the problem. The problem is where and how we spend it. Over the last 15 years, our recreational spending has gone up 400 percent and our interest on debt had gone up 500 percent. But our giving has gone up only 4 percent."

One Sunday, the pastor of a small church announced a special offering. One usher, as he passed the offering plate, overheard a man say, "I guess I could give $10 and not feel it." The usher replied, "Why don't you give $20 and feel it?" It's only when we feel it that we are truly giving sacrificially.

Ray Stedman, long-time pastor at Peninsula Bible Church in Palo Alto, California, maintained: "If God has not done anything for you, then, for goodness' sake, do not give Him a dime. But if He has, then pour it out according to the measure you have received."

At a carnival, a strong man stood on a stoop in front of a crowd. He squeezed a lemon until every drop of juice was out of it. He challenged the crowd: for a price of $1 they could attempt to squeeze another drop from the lemon. They would be paid $1,000 for every drop they could squeeze out. Man after man tried: a body builder, an ironworker, a farmer, a lumberjack, but not one could squeeze out a drop. Then a small, frail-looking man stepped forward and took the challenge. The crowd was laughing and poking fun at him. He quietly took the lemon and squeezed out three drops. The carnival strong man paid him $3,000 and asked him the secret of his amazing strength. He replied, "I happen to be the treasurer at a church. That lemon was easy compared to squeezing money out of reluctant church members!"

FOR THE BULLETIN

❁ On December 4, 1093, Anselm was consecrated archbishop of Canterbury. He is considered one of the greatest theologians of the eleventh century. He stoutly defended the right of the church to operate independently of the English monarch, a position that led to his being banished. ❁ The Council of Trent, the Roman Catholic Council overseeing the Counter Reformation, dissolved on this day in 1563. It had lasted eighteen years, meeting in 25 sessions as it responded to the growing Protestant Movement and to charges of corruption in the official church. ❁ Today is the birthday (1584) of the Massachusetts Bay pastor, John Cotton, the "Father of New England Congregationalism". ❁ John Nisbet, Scottish Covenanter, was hanged in Edinburgh on December 4, 1685. When told he would be executed on the coming Friday, Nisbet said: "O for Friday! O for Friday! O Lord, give patience to wait Thy appointed time!" ❁ On this day in 1742, a gentleman called on John Wesley and offered him a piece of land for the opening of his orphan house in Newcastle-on-Tyne. Wesley bought the land for thirty pounds and shortly thereafter laid the cornerstone for the building. It became a center for preaching the gospel and for meeting the physical and spiritual needs of people. Part of the building was also used as a hospital. ❁ The International Bible Society was founded in New York City on this day in 1809.

APPROPRIATE SONGS AND HYMNS

Because I Have Been Given Much, Grace Noll Crowell/Phillip Landgrave; © 1975 Broadman Press; Admin. by Genevox Music Group.

God Whose Giving Knows No End, Robert Edwards Franz Joseph Haydn; © 1961. Renewed 1989 The Hymn Society of Hope Publishing Company; Admin. by Hope Publishing Company.

Make Me a Captive Lord, George Matheson/George J. Elvey; © Public Domain.

We Give Thee But Thine Own, William H. How/Lowell Mason/George J. Webb; Public Domain.

Come, Come Ye Saints, Avis B. Christiansen/William Clayton; © 1966 Hope Publishing Company.

WORSHIP HELPS

Call to Worship:
For God so loved the world that He gave His only begotten Son, that whoever believes in Him should not perish but have everlasting life. (John 3:16 NKJV)

Advent Reading:
Today is the second Sunday of Advent, a time for celebrating anew God becoming a man and living among us. Jesus, the God-Man! Jesus, the King of kings! Jesus the Only Begotten! Jesus, the One who came into the world to bring life and light to every soul under the sun. Though Jesus hailed from a small Judean town, His presence towers over empires. Though born in the darkness of a cave, He is the light of the world. May those who seek Him see Him; and may those who see Him make His message known; and may those who hear it marvel at the news.

Offertory Comment:
In his book, *Giving God's Way*, John MacArthur makes this comment on 1 Corinthians 16:2 ("On the first day of the week let each one of you lay something aside, storing up as he may prosper, that there be no collections when I come"): "Giving is to be done systematically, proportionately, faithfully, as you purpose in your heart. The Greek word translated *purpose* means "to choose beforehand." You are to plan, pray, prepare—and not to give haphazardly."

Benediction:
Thank you, O Lord Jesus, for Your indescribable gift. For though You were rich, yet You became poor that we, through Your poverty, might be rich!

Additional Sermons and Lesson Ideas

Overcoming Division

Date preached:

By Rev. Todd M. Kinde

SCRIPTURE: James 4:1–12

INTRODUCTION: Do you ever feel like you're all alone? Relationships always have problems, or God seems so distant? Division is overcome by understanding our proper position before God.

1. Division with One another (4:1–3)
2. Division with God (4:4–6)
3. Drawing Near to God (4:7–10)
4. Drawing Near to One Another (4:11, 12)

CONCLUSION: We are to speak the truth in love. We are to love one another. To speak harshly is to break God's law and gives the devil a foothold to work division among us.

Wrong on Two Counts

Date preached:

By Rev. Peter Grainger

SCRIPTURE: Malachi 2:17—3:5

INTRODUCTION: We often mistake God's grace for apathy, His love for weakness. The Israelites made this mistake; they were wrong on two counts:

1. The Lord's Character (2:17).
   A. Their Error. They mistook the Lord's patience for impotence.
   B. The Result. They lived how they pleased.
   C. The Consequence. The Lord was wearied and judged them.
2. The Lord's Coming (3:1–5). The Lord reveals that He will come not to bless, but to judge His people. He uses illustrations of a launderer's soap and a refiner's fire to emphasize this point.

CONCLUSION: How do you view the Lord? As an apathetic figure, or as a Holy God who demands for His people to live in obedience to Him?

HYMNS FOR THE PASTOR'S PEOPLE

What Child Is This?

What child is this, who laid to rest,
on Mary's lap is sleeping?
Whom angels greet with anthems sweet,
while shepherds watch are keeping?
This, this is Christ the King,
whom shepherds guard and angels sing;
Haste, haste to bring Him laud,
the Babe, the Son of Mary.
Why lies He in such mean estate,
where ox and ass are feeding?
Good Christian, fear; for sinners here
the silent Word is pleading.
Nails, spear, shall pierce Him thro',
the cross be borne, for me, for you.
Hail, hail the Word made flesh,
the Babe, the Son of Mary.
So bring Him incense, gold, and myrrh;
come peasant, king to own Him.
The King of kings, salvation brings;
let loving hearts enthrone Him.
Raise, raise the song on high;
the virgin sings her lullaby.
Joy, joy for Christ is born,
the Babe, the Son of Mary.

This hymn story is by Robert J. Morgan, *Then Sings My Soul, Book Two,* a collection of stories about 150 favorite hymns, which is being released by Nelson Reference & Electronic Publishing in September, 2004.

What Child Is This?

When the angels had gone away from them into heaven, . . . the shepherds said to one another, "Let us now go to Bethlehem" Luke 2:15

Feelings of sadness come over me whenever I hear this deeply moving carol. It is, after all, set in the key of E minor, the "saddest of all keys." Yet triumphant joy dispels the sadness as we exclaim: "This, this is Christ the King, whom shepherds guard and angels sing."

The melancholic melody is a famous old British tune called "Greensleeves," originally a ballad about a man pining for his lost love, the fair Lady Greensleeves. Tradition says it was composed by King Henry VIII for Anne Boleyn. That's unlikely, but we do know that Henry's daughter, Queen Elizabeth I, danced to the tune.

Shakespeare referred to it twice in his play, *The Merry Wives of Windsor*. In Act V, for example, Falstaff said, "Let the sky rain potatoes; let it thunder to the tune of 'Green Sleeves.'"

It was licensed to two different printers in 1580, and soon thereafter was being used with religious texts. Its first association with Christmas came in 1642, in a book titled *New Christmas Carols*, in which it was used with the poem "The Old Year Now Away Has Fled." The last verse says: *Come, give's more liquor when I doe call, / I'll drink to each one in this hall . . . And God send us a happy new yeare!*

For nearly 150 years, however, "Greensleeves" has been most identified with "What Child Is This?" The words of this carol are taken from a longer poem written by an insurance agent named William Chatterton Dix, born in Bristol, England, in 1837. His father was a surgeon who wanted his son to follow his footsteps. But having no interest in medicine, William left Bristol Grammar School, moved to Glasgow, and sold insurance.

His greatest love was his prose and poetry for Christ. He wrote two devotional books, a book for children, and scores of hymns, two of which remain popular Christmas carols: "What Child Is This?" and "As with Gladness Men of Old."

All of Dix's hymns should be more widely sung today, for they are masterpieces of poetry, filled with rich scriptural truth.

DECEMBER 11, 2005

SUGGESTED SERMON *Date preached:*

Master in the Manger

Adapted from a message by Frances Ridley Havergal

Scripture: Luke 5:5

But Simon answered and said to Him, "Master, we have toiled all night and caught nothing; nevertheless at Your word I will let down the net" (NKJV).

Introduction: It's so easy, during the Christmas season, to visualize Jesus Christ as the lowly child in the manger, surrounded by sheep and cattle, sleeping peacefully on a bed of hay; and to forget that lying there in that rugged feed bin is the King of the Ages, the God of Time and Space, and the Master of the Universe. The word *master* has fallen out of use, perhaps because of its deplorable connotations from the era of American slavery. But, it is a biblical word that we should use regarding the Christ Child. He bids us call Him Master. "Ye call me Master and Lord," Jesus said in John 13:13 (KJV), "and ye say well; for so I am." The word *Master* occurs 54 times in the gospels (NKJV) and was one of Peter's favorite ways of addressing Christ:

Master, we have toiled all night—Luke 5:5
Master, Master, we are perishing!—Luke 8:24
Master, the multitudes throng and press you—Luke 8:45
Master, it is good for us to be here—Luke 9:33

What does this word imply? It calls forth the whole attitude of the soul towards our beloved Lord.

1. **Love.** For forty-three years, at one minute after midnight on Christmas Eve, Bert Holloway of Cambridge, England has handed his wife, Ethel a love letter. The gift is a tradition that they started when they were married. Mrs. Holloway says she treasures all the love letters from her husband.

During this Christmas season, find new ways of expressing your undying love to the Master. Christmas is a time when we should express our love for God, because He has expressed His love for us in the gift of His Son. We love Him because He first loved us. We are dazzled when we glimpse His love—the love that sent Him from Heaven's portals to Earth's woes—and we are overwhelmed with our unworthiness of it. Our eyes fill and our heart heaves. Sometimes the tide rises too high for verbal prayer or praise and we have to be silent in love—the very silence being an echo of the eternal depth of calmness of His exceeding great love. Only one word does not interrupt the still music of such a moment—*Master.*

2. **Adoration.** Breathing of His name is all we can do to express the unexplainable recognition of His glory. Already He is admired in all them that believe with the admiration of astonishment. "We praise You, we bless You, we worship You, we glorify You, and we give thanks to You for Your great glory." We are saying all that when we but utter that single word *Master.*

3. **Allegiance.** The true utterance of the word *Master* is the very oath of allegiance. We cannot, must not, dare not, will not henceforth serve two masters nor many masters.

4. **Confidence.** We have found one whom we can trust implicitly, and rest upon entirely. We have put our lives into His hand. We have burned the bridge behind us, because we are quite sure He is the captain of our salvation. We have entered His service forever. We have given our allegiance unreservedly, because we confide in Him unreservedly. There is no question about it. We know whom we have believed, and therefore we say, "Master!"

5. **Obedience.** All is a mockery without this. Not only our lips, but our lives must say, "Master!" And by His grace, we shall say it; the name shall be emblazoned on every page of our lives. This is the test, the fruit, and the manifestation of love. But, oh, how sweet to know that as we pledge our obedience to Him, so He enables us to obey by His grace and Spirit in our lives.

Conclusion: Jesus Christ is the Master in the manger. He demands and deserves—and shall have—our love, adoration, allegiance, confidence, and obedience this holiday season and always. Jesus warned about trying to serve two masters (Matt. 6:24). Come today and say to the Master: "Take my life and let it be consecrated, Lord, to Thee."

STATS, STORIES, AND MORE

More from Frances Ridley Havergal:

Jesus, Master, Whose I am,
Purchased Thine alone to be,
By Thy blood, O spotless Lamb,
Shed so willingly for me,
Let my heart be all Thine own,
Let me live for Thee alone.
Other lords have long held sway;
Now Thy Name alone to bear,
Thy dear voice alone obey,
Is my daily, hourly prayer;
Whom have I in heaven but Thee?
Nothing else my joy can be.
Jesus, Master, Whom I serve,
Though so feebly and so ill,
Strengthen hand and heart and nerve
All Thy bidding to fulfill;
Open Thou mine eyes to see
All the work Thou hast for me.
Jesus, Master, I am Thine;
Keep me faithful, keep me near;
Let Thy presence in me shine
All my homeward way to cheer,
Jesus, at Thy feet I fall,
O be Thou my all in all.

FOR THE BULLETIN

❁ On December 11, 1475, Giovani de Medici was born. He became Pope Leo X in 1513 and was Luther's archenemy and the pope who excommunicated him. ❁ On December 11, 1518, the Swiss Reformer, Ulrich Zwingli, was installed as pastor of the Old Minster Church in Zurich, where he served for thirteen years before dying on the battlefield. He shocked and pleased the congregation by announcing that he would break a thousand years of tradition by abandoning the church liturgy and the weekly prescribed readings as a basis for his sermons. Instead, he would teach verse-by-verse through the New Testament. ❁ Today is the birthday, in 1792, of Joseph Mohr, of Salzburg, Austria. As priest of Saint Nicholas Church in Oberndorf, Austria, he wrote the words to "Stille Nacht" ("Silent Night"). ❁ The American evangelist, John R. Rice, was born on December 11, 1895. ❁ On June 13-14, 1972, Portuguese security police arrested hundreds of people in Mozambique. Among them were about twenty members of the Presbyterian Church, including its president, Rev. Zedequias Manganhela. Their crime was insisting on the autonomy of the Presbyterian Church. Several months later, Rev. Manganhela, 60, died in prison. The official report claimed he had committed suicide on December 11, 1972, following six months of isolation and interrogation by the security police. No one who knew him believed the official story.

APPROPRIATE SONGS AND HYMNS

O Come, O Come Emmanuel, John M. Neale/Henry S. Coffin/Thomas Helmore; Public Domain.

O Come Messiah, Come Again, Vann Trapp/Thomas Helmore; © 1983 Word Music, Inc.; Admin. by Word Music Group.

Joy to the World, Isaac Watts/George Frederick Handel; Public Domain.

Child of Love, Tina English; © 1976 Word Music, Inc.; Admin. by Word Music Group, Inc.

Lord, Come This Christmas, Andy Park; © 1990 Mercy/Vineyard Publishing.

WORSHIP HELPS

Call to Worship:
Awake, my soul, awake, my tongue,
My glory wake and sing,
And celebrate the holy birth,
The birth of Israel's King!
—*Benjamin Keach*, 1700

Scripture Reading:
Now Mary arose in those days and went to the hill country with haste, to a city of Judah, and entered the house of Zacharias and greeted Elizabeth. And it happened, when Elizabeth heard the greeting of Mary, that the babe leaped in her womb; and Elizabeth was filled with the Holy Spirit. Then she spoke out with a loud voice and said, "Blessed are you among women, and blessed is the fruit of your womb! But why is this granted to me, that the mother of my Lord should come to me? For indeed, as soon as the voice of your greeting sounded in my ears, the babe leaped in my womb for joy. Blessed is she who believed, for there will be a fulfillment of those things which were told her from the Lord" (Luke 1:39–45 NKJV).

Advent Reading:
As we light this Advent Candle on the third Sunday of the season, we proclaim: Glory to Christ who is the highest; Glory to Christ who stooped the lowest; Glory to Christ who loves the deepest. Glory to Jesus the Christ, Son of Adam, Son of Abraham, Son of David, Son of Joseph, Son of God. Glory to the King of Kings, the King of Righteousness, the King of the Jews, the King of the Ages, the Prince of Peace. Glory to the Master, the Messiah, the Man of Sorrows, the Maker of Heaven and Earth.

Additional Sermons and Lesson Ideas

The Danger of Division

Date preached:

By Dr. Timothy Beougher

SCRIPTURE: 1 Corinthians 1:10–17

INTRODUCTION: In an age of such diversity, in a country with so many people from so many places, it's no wonder our churches have divisions. Paul, in 1 Corinthians, addresses this problem.

1. Report of Division (vv. 10, 11)
2. Reasons for Division (vv. 11, 12)
3. Response to Division (v. 10)
4. Remedy for Division (vv. 13–17)
   A. Focus on Christ (v. 13)
   B. Focus on the Gospel (vv. 14–17)

CONCLUSION: The danger of division is lurking everywhere: in every disagreement or grudge. We must focus on Jesus, who came to save the lost. The gospel brings us together as brothers and sisters in Christ; are we living out this truth?

What Christ Means to Me

Date preached:

Adapted from a message by Dr. W. H. Griffith Thomas

SCRIPTURE: Matthew 1:20

INTRODUCTION: Conceived by the Holy Spirit, Christ came to earth for you and me. He used four phrases to sum up all He means to us.

1. Come to Me (Matt. 11:28). We come to Him as Savior.
2. Learn of Me (Matt. 11:29). We learn of Him as Teacher.
3. Follow Me (Matt. 4:19). We follow Him as Master.
4. Abide in Me (John 15:4). We abide in Him as our life.

CONCLUSION: Are you coming, learning, following, and abiding? Then you've got the Christmas spirit.

DECEMBER 18, 2005

SUGGESTED SERMON *Date preached:*

The Triune We Worship

By Dr. Melvin Worthington

Scripture: Exodus 20:1–3, especially verse 3
You shall have no other gods before Me.

Introduction: As we draw near to Christmas, we should draw near to the Savior. During all the singing, shopping, and stress, we should take time to reflect and worship. Commercialism can easily consume our attention, becoming, frankly, a god to us. This Christmas season, I want us to focus on God. The First Commandment forbids the worship of false gods. It addresses whom we are to worship and it guards the unity of God.

1. **The Admonition in the Text.** The exclusiveness of worship is disclosed. The essence of worship is described. The Eternal we worship is denoted. The essential of worship is declared. This asserts the reality of God. It assumes that God is. It further stresses the unity of God against polytheism. The Triune God is the only God to be worshiped. This Commandment not only forbids all idolatry in thought, word, and deed, but also enjoins us to love, fear, serve, and cleave to the Lord. It allows no compromise. The person mentioned in Exodus 20:1, 2, the Lord, is to be the only object of worship. The Commandment prohibits the worship of any god other than the Lord. He is unique. His people were therefore not to add the worship of false gods to their worship of the Lord. This Commandment sets forth who we are to worship.

2. **The Analysis of the Text.**

   A. **The injunction.** We must recognize God as the true God. This remains a perpetual, practical, and personal obligation.
   B. **The inevitable.** Men become like that which they worship (Rom. 1). There can be no adequate gods substituted for the true God.
   C. **The ignorance.** It is terrible to see professing Christians worshiping demons through spiritism, clairvoyance, palmistry, and related occultism (Deut. 18:9–22). Our concept of God must be intelligent and sincere. We must know who He is. This implies knowledge of His attributes.

God has two kinds of attributes—moral and non-moral. His moral attributes include His omnipresence, omniscience, omnipotence, and immutability. His non-moral attributes include justice, mercy, grace, truth, and righteousness. One's recognition of God as our God involves a constant sense of His presence, of His majesty, of His goodness, and of His providence as well as our dependence on Him and our responsibility and obligation to Him.

3. **The Application from the Text.** In applying this text, we note our deity, devotion, duty, and danger. The duty enjoined in this Commandment is the highest duty of man. The foundation of all morality is the duty man owes to God. The sin against this Commandment is in giving glory and honor to any creature that is due to God only. The Commandment against idolatry was no sooner given than it was broken. This was true in the erecting of the golden calf. When one becomes a Christian, he or she is faced with this eternal truth of the sovereignty of God; that God demands first place in one's life.

The apostle John exhorts Christians to keep themselves from idols (I John 5:21). The command to abstain from idolatry is needed no less today than it was in Moses' day. The application of this Commandment and all the others deal not only with outward actions but inward motives. Hence, there may be idolatry without idols in the vulgar sense and without worshiping demons in any form. Whosoever seeks happiness in the creature rather than the Creator violates this Commandment. We should ask ourselves two questions: (1) Who is my god? and (2) To what is my life devoted?

Conclusion: Whom do we worship? What am I devoted to? If the answer indicates anything that puts God in the background, we are guilty of idolatry. The Old Testament reminds us that our loving Lord and Savior, Jesus, is the same God who commands us to worship Him alone, and the same Spirit that lives within us to make us holy. Let's direct our worship to our Triune God this Christmas!

STATS, STORIES, AND MORE

Someone once said ...

The incarnation is in itself an unfathomable mystery, but it makes sense of everything else that the New Testament contains—J. I. Packer

The hinge of history is on the door of a Bethlehem stable—Ralph W. Sockman, nineteenth-century Methodist pastor

Let us not flutter too high, but remain by the manger and the swaddling cloths of Christ, "in whom dwelleth all the fullness of the Godhead bodily."—Martin Luther

Apart from [the doctrine of the Trinity], doctrines such as the deity of Christ, the incarnation, the personality of the Holy Spirit, regeneration, justification, sanctification, the meaning of the crucifixion, and the resurrection cannot be understood—Dr. Loraine Boettner

The Ocean in a Hole

W. A. Criswell, in a sermon on the Trinity, said, "In reading the life of Augustine, I note that one day when he was walking along the seashore, he saw a little boy digging a trench in the sand. He walked over to the lad and asked him what he was doing. The little fellow replied, 'Sir, I am making a trench.' 'Why are you doing it?' asked Augustine. The little lad replied, 'I am going to empty the sea into my trench.' The great thinker, the greatest of the Latin Fathers, continued his walk and mused: 'So the lad thinks that he is going to empty the sea into the little trench he has made in the sand. Sometimes we are like that. We propose to encompass the infinitude of God in the small limits of our mind.'"

FOR THE BULLETIN

❁ According to records compiled by John Foxe, a British Protestant named John Philpot was burned at the stake on December 18, 1555. When the death sentence was announced, Philpot replied, "I am ready; God grant me strength and a joyful resurrection." At the stake, he said, "Shall I disdain to suffer at this stake, seeing my Redeemer did not refuse to suffer a most vile death upon the cross for me?" Then in the midst of the fiery flames, he yielded his soul into the hands of Almighty God. ❁ Today is the birthday of Charles Wesley (1707), co-founder of Methodism with his brother, John, and the composer of some of Christendom's greatest hymns, including the Christmas carols, "Come, Thou Long-Expected Jesus," and "Hark! The Herald Angels Sing." ❁ The first Sunday newspaper in America made its appearance on this day in 1796, *The Baltimore Monitor*. ❁ Emory University of Atlanta, Georgia, was chartered on this day in 1834. ❁ Today is the birthday of Congregational preacher, Layman Abbott, born in 1835; and of Francis Thompson, author of the poem, "The Hound of Heaven," who was born in 1859. ❁ Charles Spurgeon preached for the first time at London's Park Street Church to about eighty people on December 18, 1853. ❁ The Thirteenth Amendment to the Constitution abolished slavery in the United States on December 18, 1865. ❁ Today marks the conversion of the great Indian Christian, Sundar Singh, who received Christ as Savior on December 18, 1904, at the age of fifteen.

APPROPRIATE SONGS AND HYMNS

Heart of Worship, Matt Redman; © 1997 Kingsway's/Thankyou Music; Admin. by EMI Christian Music Publishing.

Come, Thou Long Expected Jesus, Charles Wesley/Rowland H. Prichard; Public Domain.

Crown Him, Chris Machen; © 1991 Desert North Music/Word Music, Inc.; Admin. by Word Music Group, Inc.

Emmanuel Has Come, Don Moen; © 1996 Integrity's Hosanna! Music.

I'll Give My Heart, Chris Christensen; © 1984 Integrity's Hosanna! Music.

WORSHIP HELPS

Call to Worship:
To Him be glory in the church by Christ Jesus to all generations, forever and ever. Amen. (Eph. 3:21 NKJV).

Hymn Story:
Today is the birthday of Charles Wesley, author of "Come, Thou Long Expected Jesus," and "Hark! The Herald Angels Sing." How many hymns did Wesley compose? No one has been able to count them. In all, Charles wrote over 9,000 literary texts of one kind or another, but not all of them should be classified as hymns. Experts put the number somewhere between 3,000 and 6,000.

Advent Reading:
And so it was that while they were there the days were accomplished that she should be delivered. And she brought forth her firstborn son and wrapped Him in swaddling cloths and laid him in the manger; because there was no room for them in the inn. Imagine! No room for the Baby Jesus. No room in Bethlehem. No room in public places for the manger. No room in department store windows for the Nativity. No room in the classrooms for the holy songs of Christmas. No room in the courthouse for the Ruler of the Ages. No room for Him during the rush of holiday madness.

There is room here, dear Jesus—room in our home, room in our church; room in our hearts. On this fourth Sunday of Advent, we light a candle with the simple prayer of the olden poet who said: "O come to my heart, Lord Jesus, there is room in my heart for Thee."

Benediction:
May the blessings of God the Father, God the Son, and God the Holy Spirit attend to your hours this day, and may the Triune God brighten your days this week. In Jesus' name. Amen.

Additional Sermons and Lesson Ideas

Overcoming Greed

Date preached:

By Rev. Todd M. Kinde

SCRIPTURE: James 4:13—5:6

INTRODUCTION: Two major sins are addressed in this section of James: planning without calculating God in the equation, and pleasure-seeking to the abuse of others.

1. Vanishing Plans (4:13–16).
2. Vanishing Opportunities (4:17).
3. Vanishing Pleasures (5:1–6).

CONCLUSION: A true disciple of Jesus has no attachment to wealth and pleasures. When a wealthy believer sees a need, she will give to help meet the need (Matt. 19:21, 22; Prov. 29:7). In all your planning, are you planning for the return of Christ?

The Call of the Lord

Date preached:

By Rev. Peter Grainger

SCRIPTURE: Isaiah 6

INTRODUCTION: Have you ever felt inferior because someone so important was in the room with you? Imagine being confronted by the God of creation! How should you respond to His presence? Isaiah was in this very position.

1. Desolation (vv. 1–7). Isaiah realized his human sinfulness in the presence of divine holiness. He immediately confessed, "I am undone ... I am a man of unclean lips" (v. 5). The Lord cleansed Him, as He will cleanse us when we confess (1 John 1:9).
2. Dedication (vv. 8–10). Isaiah immediately volunteered to be the Lord's servant. The Lord calls for messengers who have been cleansed (2 Tim. 2:20, 21) and commissioned (John 20:21).
3. Decimation (vv. 11–13). The Lord then speaks words of judgment concerning Israel; they will be desolated and exiled. His promise, however, is to restore them when they have learned (Is. 11:1–9).

CONCLUSION: The Lord is in this place. He is calling you to confess your sin and to answer His call to service. The gospel is salvation from coming judgment: a message not easily received, but we are called to preach it. Will you answer His call?

HYMNS FOR THE PASTOR'S PEOPLE

I Heard the Bells on Christmas Day

I heard the bells on Christmas day
Their old familiar carols play,
And wild and sweet the words repeat,
Of peace on earth, goodwill to men.

And thought how, as the day had come,
The belfries of all Christendom
Had rolled along th'unbroken song
Of peace on earth, goodwill to men.

And in despair I bowed my head:
"There is no peace on earth," I said,
"For hate is strong, and mocks the song
Of peace on earth, goodwill to men."

Then pealed the bells more loud and deep:
"God is not dead, nor doth He sleep;
The wrong shall fail, the right prevail,
With peace on earth, goodwill to men."

Till ringing, singing on its way,
The world revolved from night to day,
A voice, a chime, a chant sublime,
Of peace on earth, goodwill to men!

This hymn story is by Robert J. Morgan, *Then Sings My Soul, Book Two*, a collection of stories about 150 favorite hymns, which is being released by Nelson Reference & Electronic Publishing in September, 2004.

I Heard the Bells on Christmas Day

Behold, He who keeps Israel shall neither slumber nor sleep (Ps. 121:4 NKJV).

The famous Longfellow brothers were born and raised in Portland, Maine, in the 1800s. Henry Wadsworth was born in 1807, and younger brother Samuel arrived in 1819. Henry became a Harvard professor of literature and one of America's greatest writers, and Samuel became a Unitarian minister and a hymnist.

While Henry was publishing his books, however, dark clouds were gathering over his life and over all America. In 1861, his wife tragically died when her dress caught fire in their home in Cambridge, Massachusetts. That same year, the Civil War broke out, tearing the nation apart. Two years later, during the fiercest days of the conflict, Henry's son, Charley, seventeen, ran away from home and hopped aboard a train to join President Lincoln's army.

Charley proved a brave and popular soldier. He saw action at the Battle of Chancellorsville in 1863, but in early June he contracted typhoid fever and malaria and was sent home to recover. He missed the Battle of Gettysburg, but by August, Charley was well enough to return to the field. On November 27, during the battle of New Hope Church in Virginia, he was shot through the left shoulder. The bullet nicked his spine and came close to paralyzing him. He was carried into the church and later taken to Washington to recuperate.

Receiving the news on December 1, 1863, Henry left immediately for Washington. He found his son well enough to travel and they headed back to Cambridge, arriving home on December 8. For weeks Henry sat by his son's bedside, slowly nursing his boy back to health.

On Christmas Day, December 25, 1863, Henry gave vent to his feelings in this plaintive carol that can only be understood against the backdrop of war. Two stanzas now omitted from most hymnals speak of the cannons thundering in the South and of hatred tearing apart "the hearth-stones of a continent." The poet feels like dropping his head in despair, but then he hears the Christmas bells. Their triumphant pealing reminds him that "God is not dead, nor doth He sleep."

The Sunday school children of the Unitarian Church of the Disciples in Boston first sang this song during that year's Christmas celebration. How wonderful that such a song should emerge from the bloody clouds of the War Between the States.

DECEMBER 25, 2005

SUGGESTED SERMON *Date preached:*

How to Celebrate Christmas

By Dr. David Jeremiah

Scripture: Luke 2:1–20

Introduction: During this season of shopping and entertaining, let's remember why Christmas is celebrated in the first place. We decorate our homes, send out cards, visit friends, buy presents, and go caroling. Some celebrate a portion of Christmas Day watching football games. For some, it's a time for drinking and partying. But this is a holiday to honor the fact that God sent His Son to be born in a manger and to become our Savior. As Christians, we should celebrate in a unique way. I'd like to suggest four responses to the birthday of Christ based on today's passage.

1. **By Witnessing About Christ (v. 17).** The shepherds "made widely known the saying which was told them concerning this Child." We're to make Him known to those around us and help them understand that He came as a Savior. There are many opportunities available during Christmas. We can witness through the cards we send out. We witness by how we decorate our homes. We witness through the seasonal music we sing. And we witness by inviting people to attend church services with us. Many will come at this season of the year that would never darken our doors otherwise. Be intentional about sharing Christ this Christmas.

2. **By Wondering at Christ (v. 18).** Those who heard the shepherds wondered at the things told them. I was reminded this week of a word seldom used today: *muse*. It means sit back, meditate, and think. The word *amuse* adds the negative prefix which means "to not muse." Amusements are those things that keep us from thinking seriously about anything. Christmas is a wonderful time for amusement, yet when those in Luke 2 heard about Jesus they mused on Him. Think about it! Here is a story of purity wrapped up in the birth of a Child born to a young mother. Here is joy amidst seeming tragedy. Here is a great announcement to a lowly group of shepherds. Here is a Baby born to die. Here is a King born in stable to poor parents, yet was God manifest in flesh. G. Campbell Morgan wrote, "In the presence of such a holy miracle, there can be no fitting attitude of the human

intellect save that of acceptance of the truth without any attempt to explain the mystery."

3. **By Waiting Before Christ (v. 19).** We also celebrate Christmas by waiting before Christ, even as Mary pondered all these things in her heart. You say, "Isn't that what you were just saying?" Well, the word *ponder* is even more intense than *wonder*. It means to delve beneath the surface and to contemplate, trying to understand. Mary pondered and treasured them up. She committed them to memory. She was a woman who thought deeply about what was happening in her life. It's easy to become so busy between Thanksgiving and Christmas that we don't spend time in personal Bible study and prayer. We can let the outward celebrations of the holiday take us away from the one thing that could mean the most to us as Christians. We have to make time for waiting before God.

4. **By Worshiping Christ (v. 20).** The shepherds returned, glorifying and praising God. I believe Christmas affords tremendous opportunities for glorifying God as we sing our wonderful carols, as we pray personally, quietly praise Him, and publicly worship. Oh, to celebrate Christmas as Christians, we've got to take a step back from the busyness of the season and the materialism of the world and focus on Him!

Conclusion: Years ago in a European country, a christening took place for a baby who had been born to royalty. As the guests arrived, a servant met them at the door and took their wraps. Eventually someone asked, "Where's the baby?" The nurse was sent to fetch him, but she couldn't find him. Finally, a guest recalled having seen the baby in the bed where the coats had been placed. The parents were horrified to find there the lifeless form of their son who had been smothered under the pile of coats. What irony. The real purpose of the gathering had been forgotten and the one to be honored was killed. I wonder if that isn't true for many at this time of year. Jesus is our celebration. He is our Honored One. He is our King. This year let's honor Him by witnessing, wondering, waiting before Him and worshiping Him!

STATS, STORIES, AND MORE

More from Dr. David Jeremiah:

Here is the Ancient of Days becoming a baby in Bethlehem. Here is the one who thunders in the heavens crying in a cradle. Here is Him to gives to all their meat in due season, feeding at His mother's breast. Here is the one who made all flesh, now becoming flesh Himself. Here is the One who could summon legions of angels, wrapped in an infant's clothing. Here is the mighty God, now a helpless child. Do you ever just stop and think about that? No wonder one of the old divines said, "I can scarce get passed His cradle in my wondering, to wonder at His cross."

Several years ago, I was preaching in Chicago during the Christmas season. One evening, as I walked down the street, I got caught up in the Christmas spirit. I heard the bells of the Salvation Army ringing out their need for money. I heard carols coming from the various PA systems. People were bustling amid Christmas lights. I don't know how to explain the emotion, but it just seemed that I just wanted to scream out, "Oh God, thank you for letting me be alive. I just am so excited to be alive right now." Have you ever experienced anything like that? As we contemplate the wonder of who Jesus is and what He did to come down here in His love for us, we ought to be so full of thanksgiving and praise we can hardly contain it.

FOR THE BULLETIN

❁ The birth of Christ began to be commemorated and celebrated yearly on December 25, 337. ❁ On December 25, 390, the Emperor Theodosius performed public penance under the influence of Bishop Ambrose for having massacred 7,000 people in Thessalonica. He later died in Ambrose's arms. ❁ On December 25, 496, Clovis, King of the Franks, was baptized with his army of 3,000, the first of many mass conversions that occurred during the Middle Ages, leading to the christianizing of Europe. ❁ On December 25, 800, Charlemagne, kneeling at the altar of St. Peter's, was impulsively crowned supreme ruler of the western world by Pope Leo III. ❁ On December 25, 1066, William the Conqueror became the first British monarch to be crowned in Westminster Abby. ❁ On December 25, 1075, Pope Gregory VII was kidnapped while saying Mass. ❁ On December 25, 1223, St. Francis of Assisi assembled the first living Nativity scene in known Christian history, in Greccio, Italy. ❁ On December 25, 1752, Philip Embury was converted. "The Lord shone into my soul by a glimpse of His redeeming love," he wrote. Embury later boarded the "Methodist Mayflower" for America and became the first to plant Methodism in the colonies. ❁ On December 25, 1776, George Washington led his troops across the Delaware River for a surprise attack. ❁ On December 25, 1923, during the presidency of Calvin Coolidge, the first electrically lit Christmas tree appeared in the White House.

APPROPRIATE SONGS AND HYMNS

I Heard the Bells on Christmas Day, Henry W. Longfellow/Jean Baptiste Calkin; Public Domain.

O Come All Ye Faithful, John Francis Wade/Frederick Oakeley; Public Domain.

Ring the Bells, Dan Burgess; © 1993 Dan Burgess Music Company; Admin. by Maranatha! Music.

Thou Didst Leave Thy Throne, Emily E.S. Elliott/Timothy Richard Matthews; Public Domain.

Love Has Come, Ken Bible; © 1996 Integrity's Hosanna! Music; Admin. by Integrity Music Group, Inc.

WORSHIP HELPS

Call to Worship:
Do not be afraid, for behold, I bring you good tidings of great joy which will be to all people. For there is born to you this day in the city of David a Savior, who is Christ the Lord. (Luke 2:10, 11 NKJV)

Prayer:
Lord Jesus, this is Your birthday. We celebrate Your coming into this world. And though we enjoy the trappings that are around us at this season, we will not forget to focus our attention on You and to give thanks daily that You cared enough about us to respond to the love of Your Father and come to be born and to die on the Cross for our sins.—Dr. David Jeremiah

Word of Welcome:
Some people talk about the difficulties of ministering to CEO's—those who attend church on "Christmas and Easter Only." We're glad you're here in any case, and we want you to worship with us today—and next Sunday as well. Plan now to begin the New Year in church. Plan to make it a new habit in your life and for your family. You are always welcome here.

Advent Reading:
Praise Him, O you servants of the LORD! You who stand in the house of the LORD; in the courts of the house of our God, praise the LORD, for the LORD is good; Sing praises to His name, for it is pleasant; Praise the LORD! Praise the LORD from the heavens! Praise Him in the heights! Praise Him, all His angels! Praise Him, all His hosts! Praise Him, sun and moon! Praise Him, all you stars of light! Let them all say: "Glory to God in the Highest and on earth peace, goodwill toward men."
(Ps. 135:1–3; 148:1–3; Luke 2:14 NKJV)

Additional Sermons and Lesson Ideas

A Carol Sermon

Date preached:

SCRIPTURE: Luke 1:47

INTRODUCTION: "Good Christian Men, Rejoice!" is an ancient Latin carol, translated by John M. Neale in 1853. The word *men*, of course, is a generic word. We might use the informal word *folks*. Notice these phrases in the three stanzas.

1. "Give ye heed to what we say: Jesus Christ is born today." That's the reality of His birth.
2. "Now ye hear of endless bliss: Jesus Christ was born for this." That's the reason of His birth.
3. "Now ye need not fear the grave: Jesus Christ was born to save." That's the result of His birth.

CONCLUSION: This is the day the Lord has made! Let us rejoice!

What Is Christmas?

Date preached:

By Dr. David Jeremiah

SCRIPTURE: Hebrews 2: 9–18

INTRODUCTION: At this season of the year, the greatest emotion any of us can have is that of wonder. Here are some of the things we wonder about.

1. Who Was Born? (v. 9). "But we see Jesus." This Jesus is the Word, the Son of God.
2. Where Did He Come From? (v. 9). We understand from Hebrews 2 that He did not begin in Bethlehem. This passage teaches He was made in the flesh, for He already existed.
3. Why Did He Come?
   A. He came to destroy Satan's power (v. 14).
   B. He came to die for everyone (v. 14).
   C. He came to deliver us from the fear of death (v. 15).
   D. He came to demonstrate His love for you (v. 18).
   E. He came down so we could go up (v. 17).

CONCLUSION: I want to ask you this question: Have you ever received His gift?

WEDDING SERMON

Suitable for a Second Marriage

By Rev. Todd M. Kinde

Scripture: Ephesians 5:25–27

Introduction: As we gather for this ceremony we recognize we are coming to a Christian wedding. It is not like what the world performs. Its foundation is Christ Jesus our Lord, and that foundation supports a different kind of home. The truth of Christ's love for His bride, the church, works into our daily situations and relationships. Marriage becomes a spiritual covenant between two people in the presence of Christ Himself. These two people stand before us to make such a covenant. They come to this new relationship with eyes open acknowledging the hard work demanded in committing to exclusive love and loyalty.

Marriage is certainly for our pleasure, enjoyment, and companionship. Marriage, however, is the work of the living Triune God revealing Himself to humankind. The union between man and woman in marriage is more than sociological or biological. It is theological. The intimacy a man and woman share in marriage is an example, an object lesson, teaching us about an even greater intimacy that Christ has with His bride, the church.

Understanding this dynamic, Paul addresses the husband in verse 25, charging him to love his wife. Similarly, Paul addresses the wife in verse 33, charging her to respect her husband. We see mutual interplay between husband and wife to love and respect one another within the covenant of marriage. What is the nature of this love and respect that has been renewed, rediscovered, and rekindled in the hearts of these two people today?

1. **Love Gives (Eph. 5:25).** As Christ loved the church and gave Himself up for her, so we love and give of ourselves in marriage. This kind of love is unconditional and unselfish. It loves for better or worse, for richer or poorer, in sickness and in health. This love chases after the one who is hurting and weak. This love gives when the other is not able to give. This love is concerned about pleasing the other. There are no strings attached to this love. This love has given up all rights to self and flows freely in gracious generosity. Love gives special gifts. Not necessarily expensive gifts or many gifts but small, thoughtful tokens of love and respect. Love gives in serving one

another. Love gives in exclusive time together. Love gives in a gentle touch. Love gives in tender words.

2. **Love Cleanses (Eph. 5:26).** As Christ sanctifies and cleanses the church, so love and respect within marriage cleanse and purify. The bride and the groom have been preparing themselves for this ceremony. They have taken time washing, shaving, gargling, and perfuming, dressing in a beautiful gown and dapper tuxedo. Because they love one another they clean up for one other.

But the cleansing is more than what we see on the surface. An inner spiritual cleansing has occurred and will continue throughout this new relationship. Verse 25 tells us that Jesus cleanses His bride, the church, through the washing of the Word. Have you thought about the Scriptures in that way? When you come to read the Scriptures you are in actuality soaking in a spiritual bath.

In a marriage relationship, any marriage relationship, we come with some residue that needs to be washed. The Word of God makes us new. The joy a husband and wife share is to come daily to the Word of God and apply the sponge of His love to the areas in our spirit that need cleansed. Love is unconditional and accepts us as we are but true love loves deeply enough not to leave us as we are.

3. **Love Exalts (Eph. 5:27).** As Christ will exalt His bride, the church, to present her pure and holy so, too, love and respect within marriage will lift and exalt one another. Christ prepares His church to present her to Himself in the royal sanctuary. He lifts her from her humble place and exalts her. He will lift us to His royal dwelling. Love that gives and cleanses, also exalts. In another place Paul says, "Therefore comfort each other and edify one another, just as you also are doing" (1 Thess. 5:11 NKJV). To be loved and to love is a great lifting experience. A husband and wife in love free each other to greater heights of fulfillment and strength. Walk together climbing the hills of life as you gently encourage one another to the exalted height of true love and fellowship.

Conclusion: It is this kind of love that has been rediscovered here today. Love that gives, cleanses and exalts. We cannot do this in and of ourselves. We must be changed by the power of God through faith in Christ who gave Himself for us. Then God takes residence in us. Then you find the life, love, and respect you are seeking. We become the temple of God and by the controlling and enabling of His Holy Spirit we can love, honor, and cherish from this day forward and forever.

WEDDING SERMON

The Marks of Discipleship in a Marriage

Dear friends and family, we have gathered here today to witness the uniting of two lives into union: one home and one family. Marriage is an exclusive friendship and a unique relationship, set apart and sanctified by God in Scripture and in history. It was designed by the Almighty and unveiled in the Garden of Eden when, in God's benevolent wisdom, He created a man and a woman, individually suited to meet the needs of the other, and thus brought together as husband and wife.

In the years since, marriage has brought joy and fulfillment to millions of people through hundreds of generations; but marriage is only truly joyous and fulfilling if certain elements are present from the beginning. Today I want to take a moment to give you three items that are necessary in a happy and honorable home. These three items, according to John's Gospel, qualify you to be the disciples of our Lord.

1. **The First Is a Bible.** John 8:31 says, "If you abide in My word, you are My disciples indeed" (NKJV). In an enduring marriage, each of the partners needs a relationship with God through Jesus Christ, one that is daily and constant, and one that exhibits unbroken fellowship with Christ in His Word. Both of you need to read God's Word together, even if only a few verses every day. Psalm 119:105 says, "Your word is a lamp to my feet and a light to my path" (NKJV). A few verses later (v. 111), we read, "Your testimonies [referring to the Scriptures] I have taken as a heritage forever, for they are the rejoicing of my heart."

I'd like to suggest you establish the heritage of the Holy Scriptures in your home, beginning or ending the day, every day, by reading at least a small portion of God's Word together. It symbolizes the presence of Christ in your home, and it serves as an acknowledgement of your constant need for His guidance and care. As you read the Bible and pray jointly, you are laying a spiritual foundation for your marriage that is unassailable and unfailing.

2. **The Second Item Is a Basin.** I'm referring to the account of John 13 when the twelve disciples were arguing among themselves and our Lord took a basin and towel and washed their feet. He told us we should do the same. He was referring to the performing of humble acts of service one for the

other. Near the end of that story, in John 13:35, Jesus said, "By this all will know that you are My disciples, if you have love for one another" (NKJV).

Love isn't merely a matter of romantic feelings and mellow moods. It's the continual relegating of our own needs to second place and putting the other person first. It's the constant exhibition of humble acts of service toward the other.

All of us are self-centered by nature, and in a marriage this shows up by our desire to have our own way. Like the twelve disciples, we get our feelings hurt and argue about who will be first. But Jesus is among us as the servant. It's hard to destroy a marriage in which the partners are emulating His example, looking for ways—large and small—in which they can serve the other with humility and love.

3. **The Third Item Is a Burden.** Jesus said in John 15:8, "By this My Father is glorified, that you bear much fruit; so you will be My disciples" (NKJV).

God doesn't bless us just to bless us. He blesses us to make us a blessing, and He gives us a burden for what He wants us to do. He brings us together in a marriage, not just to enrich our lives but also to make us partners in ministry. Jesus told us to work, for the night is coming. He told us to go, for the world is perishing. He told us to love, for the world is hurting. God has a plan for your marriage, to use you to further His kingdom and to strengthen His church. So, I encourage you to be about Your Master's business. Find a joint ministry for Him and be found faithful in serving Him with all your heart, bearing much fruit for His kingdom.

Conclusion: Take up the Bible, the basin, and the burden. As you do, you will be our Lord's disciples, and your home will glow with His presence and I can assure you that God will add a fourth element to your marriage—blessing. For blessed is the husband and the wife who continue in God's Word, who love each other with Christ's love, and who bear much fruit in His field of labor. Happy are the people who are in such a state; happy are the people whose God is the LORD! (Ps. 144:15 NKJV).

If you then, ____________ and ______________ are ready to enter into this blessing by the exchanging of vows, will you please join your right hands.

(To the groom): ____________, will you repeat after me: By the grace of God, I take you, ____________ (bride's name), as my wedded wife, to have and to hold from this day forward. Leaving all others, I promise before God and our assembled friends and family to be devoted only to you. I am ready to share with you God's Word, to experience with you Christ's love, and join with you in the life and labor He gives us from this time forth.

(To the bride): ___________, will you repeat after me: By the grace of God, I take you, ____________ (groom's name), as my wedded husband, to have and to hold from this day forward. I promise before God and our assembled friends to be devoted only to you. I am ready to share with you God's Word, to experience with you Christ's love, and join with you in the life and labor He gives us from this time forth.

Then you are each given to the other in the indivisible bonds of matrimony for as long as you both shall live. May God bless this union with His presence, His promises, His power, His peace, and His permanence.

The wedding ring is a sign and seal of this union. It tells all who see it that you have entered into an intimate and exclusive relationship with the other. The gold in the rings speaks of the richness of your love, the shape of the ring speaks of the unending nature of your marriage, and the visibility of the ring speaks of your joy and pride in belonging to the other.

(To the groom): _______________, will you place the ring on your bride's finger? And _________________ (bride's name), will you place the ring on your groom's finger? As you do so, I pronounce on you the ancient blessing of the priests of old: The LORD bless you and keep you; the LORD make His face shine upon you, and be gracious to you; the LORD lift up His countenance upon you, and give you peace" (Num. 6:24–26 NKJV).

(Prayer)
And now, by the authority vested in me, I pronounce you husband and wife.
________________ (groom), you may now kiss your bride.
Ladies and Gentlemen, it is my pleasure to present to you __________ and ________________.

WEDDING SERMON

The Meaning of Love

Dear friends, we have gathered today to unite __________ and __________ in the loving bonds of matrimony. There is a word uttered in every wedding and whispered by every couple. It's a term the youngest child can write with crayon, yet so deep that only God's stylus can engrave it on our hearts. It's a concept as vast as the universe yet small enough to deposit in the humblest home. It's the largest, broadest, deepest word in the world. It's the theme of a thousand songs, the topic of a million letters, and the subject of countless sermons. This word occurs 544 times in the Bible and is described as the infinite attribute of our everlasting God. It's talked about more than it's practiced and its over-use has overtaxed its meaning.

This is the word: love. We talk about falling in love, being in love, staying in love, making love, and loving one another with all our hearts. Our prayers, poems, and promises are all centered in love as, with great emotional sincerity, we say to each other, "I love you with all my heart." Or as Elizabeth Barrett Browning put it:

How do I love thee? Let me count the ways.
I love thee to the depth and breadth and height
My soul can reach, when feeling out of sight
For the ends of my Being and ideal Grace.
I love thee to the level of everyday's
Most quiet need, by sun and candlelight.
I love thee freely, as men strive for Right;
I love thee purely, as they turn from Praise.
I love thee with the passion put to use
In my old griefs, and with my childhood's faith.
I love thee with a love I seemed to lose
With my lost saints—I love thee with the breath,
Smiles, tears, of all my life! And, if God choose,
I shall but love thee better after death.

Notice the poet said: "I love thee to the level of everyday's most quiet need, by sun and candlelight." In other words, love isn't just a fleeting feeling of passion or a fickle emotion that flickers with the candlelight then vanishes. It is a God-given persistent attitude of putting the needs of the other person before your own. It is meeting the unspoken everyday needs of the other person both day and night. It is not naive happiness but never-ending humility.

Love is more than glowing moonlight, soft music, or tender impulses. It is a tough choice that requires hard work and constant attentiveness. Here's a paraphrase the way the apostle Paul put it in 1 Corinthians 13:

> *No matter what I say, what I believe, and what I do,*
> *I'm bankrupt without love.*
> *Love never gives up.*
> *Love cares more for others than for self.*
> *Love doesn't want what it doesn't have.*
> *Love doesn't strut,*
> *Doesn't have a swelled head,*
> *Doesn't force itself on others,*
> *Isn't always "me first,"*
> *Doesn't fly off the handle,*
> *Doesn't keep score of the sins of others,*
> *Doesn't revel when others grovel,*
> *Takes pleasure in the flowering of truth,*
> *Puts up with anything,*
> *Always looks for the best,*
> *Never looks back,*
> *But keeps going to the end.*
> *Love never dies.*
> (1 Cor. 13:3–8 MSG)

This is a unique brand of love shed abroad by the Holy Spirit in the hearts and lives of earnest followers of Jesus Christ. We don't inherit that kind of love from our parents and we can't learn it from a book or movie. It is the fruit of the Holy Spirit. The Bible teaches that it flows like a river into and out of the hearts of godly men and women. The apostle John said, "Beloved, let us love one another, for love is of God; and everyone who loves is born of God and knows God. He who does not love does not know God, for God is love. In this the love of God was manifested toward us, that God has sent His only begotten Son into the world, that we might live through Him. In this is love, not that we loved God, but that He loved us and sent His son to be the propitiation for our sins. Beloved, if God so loved us, we also ought to love one another" (1 John 4:7–11 NKJV).

And so, ______________ and ______________, I urge you to put Christ first in your lives, let His Spirit work in your hearts, and let the love of God rule your marriage and govern your home. Stay close to Him in personal prayer, Bible study, and faithful church involvement. Belong to Him first and foremost, and then you may belong to one another in Him.

If you then, ____________ and ______________ are ready to enter into this relationship of love and loyalty by the exchanging of vows, will you please join your right hands.

(To the groom): ___________, will you repeat after me: In taking the woman I hold by the right hand to be my wedded wife before God and these witnesses, I promise to love her with the love of Christ, and, leaving all others, remain always true to her from this time forth and forever.

(To the bride): ___________, will you repeat after me: In taking the man I hold by the right hand to be my wedded husband before God and these witnesses, I promise to love him with the love of Christ, and, leaving all others, remain always true to him from this time forth and forever.

(Minister): Then you are each given to the other in the indivisible bonds of matrimony for richer or poorer, in poverty and in wealth, in sickness and in health, for as long as you both shall live.

Quotes for the Pastor's Wall

"Veni, vedi, velcro"

(I came, I saw, I stuck around)

Anonymous

FUNERAL SERMON

GENERAL

Caught Up Together in the Clouds

By Joshua D. Rowe

Today we have gathered in memory of ______________________________.
Personal Comments

Scripture: 1 Thessalonians 4:13–18, especially verse 17

Introduction: In this time when we feel such heartache, pain, and loss, Scripure offers so much comfort, encouragement, and victory. It seems that, in writing to the Thessalonian believers, Paul knew of some church members who had recently lost loved ones. To those who were hurting and grieving, he offered reasons to hope.

1. **A Different Reaction (v. 13).** Paul specifically addressed those in the church who have lost friends, family, or loved ones. He says we should react to death differently than those who have no hope. Two things to keep in mind:

   A. **Our Mourning Is Natural.** Paul isn't saying we should not be sad when our loved ones die. Psalm 116:15 is often translated, "Precious in the sight of the Lord is the death of His godly ones." The Hebrew word for *precious* refers often to precious stones or possessions; it can also be translated "costly, expensive." The Lord does His work on earth through His people, so doesn't it make sense that their death is costly? He knows our loss because He experiences it with us! Do you remember the story about Lazarus' death? Jesus knew He would raise Lazarus from the dead (John 11:4), but when he saw the sad faces, approached the sealed tomb, and felt the loss of a loved one, Jesus wept (John 11:35). We know that departed believers will be resurrected, but being apart from them causes natural pain and grief.

   B. **Our Rejoicing Is Supernatural.** Paul explains that we are to react differently than those who have no hope. Although we mourn and grieve, the Lord is with us through it all. As believers, we have comfort and hope in the future: we know that our departed loved ones who were fellow believers are now with the Lord (2 Cor. 5:8); Scripture even calls them blessed:

"And I heard a voice from heaven, saying, 'Write, "Blessed are the dead who die in the Lord from now on!" 'Yes,' says the Spirit, 'so that they may rest from their labors, for their deeds follow with them'" (Rev. 14:13 NKJV).

2. **An Important Reality (vv. 14–17).** Paul reminds us that if we believe in the gospel, we also believe in the Second Coming of Christ! No topic is more comforting to us in our loss than that of the resurrection; it's the true hope that only we as Christians have. The scene he describes causes us to pause in our grief and anticipate the future:

   A. **The Privilege of Deceased Saints (vv. 14, 15).** When Christ returns, He will bring the deceased believers with Him! While we grieve their loss, surely they rejoice and anticipate the day when they will be the first to see the resurrected Christ return for His people.
   B. **The Triumphant Return of Christ (v. 16).** We are told that, "The Lord Himself will descend from heaven with a shout, with the voice of the archangel and with the trumpet of God, and the dead in Christ will rise first" (v. 16). When Christ comes for the second time, it will not be in a manger, wrapped in swaddling cloths, announced by a single star to wise men or by an angel to shepherds, but He will come wrapped in glory and splendor with an earth-shaking shout of the archangel, and with the trumpet of God Himself! And who will be the first to see these things? The dead in Christ will see it.
   C. **The Triumphant Reunion (v. 17).** After the deceased saints are resurrected to be with Christ in His glory, "then we who are alive and remain will be caught up together with them in the clouds to meet the Lord in the air, and so we shall always be with the Lord" (v. 17). We will be reunited with our fellow believers whom we have lost, and all together, we will be united with Christ in all His glory for the rest of eternity!

Conclusion: Today we are naturally grieved. But we also have reason for great comfort. I encourage you to put a bookmark in 1 Thessalonians 4. When you feel the deepest pain, you can read this passage. Surely, this will engage you in the deepest anticipation of Christ's return. Paul said about these verses, "Therefore comfort one another with these words" (v. 18). As we leave today, let's remind each other in our grief that our friend will be one of the first to see the magnificent return of the Savior, Jesus Christ; we'll meet our friend later, together in the clouds.

FUNERAL SERMON

Especially for a Youth or Child

It Is Well with the Child

By Rev. Richard Sharpe Jr.

Today we have gathered in honor and memory of ________________________.

Personal Comments:

Scripture: 2 Kings 4:8–37, especially verse 26

Introduction: Some years ago we had a set of twins born into our family. One of them had health problems, so after a few weeks of keeping our child in the hospital, the doctor sent him home with us, giving us danger signs to watch for. Unfortunately, the doctor told us to watch for the wrong signs; our son died after only five weeks on this earth. It was hard to lose our son but we also knew that the Lord had a reason for his death. In the town where I was ministering was a fire department; its members responded to the emergency call regarding our son. They came well equipped to save lives, but they didn't have the equipment to save our son. Everything they had was for an adult. I remember their shock as they stood in our kitchen, unable to help our son. Our son proved to be a witness to the members of the fire department, to their need for the Lord. God has a purpose for everyone coming into this world. Even if it is a short life, there is a reason. In 2 Kings 4 we find a comforting story about the death of a beloved child:

1. **A Mother's Wish (vv. 14–16).** Elisha was a man of God who traveled the country to spread the Word of the Lord. He needed places to stay in these travels. One particular couple was quite generous, giving him a room to sleep in. This couple had no children. The prophet wanted to do something for the couple and they wanted a child: At first, the woman thought Elisha was lying about something that meant so much to her. She knew him to be a man of God but didn't think even God could give her a child at that time in her life.

2. **A Mother's Joy (v. 17).** This woman did have a son as Elisha predicted. Imagine her joy! Imagine how happy his father was to have a hand in the field and a son to be proud of. Things seemed to be going so well until one day the child's head started hurting and he was taken into the house with his mother.

3. **A Mother's Sorrow (vv. 18–21).** Not only did her son fall sick but also he died. This mother who had so much joy now was beside herself. Gathering her courage, she went to see the man of God, seeking his help (vv. 22ff.).

4. **A Mother's Hope (vv. 30–37).** The woman got the prophet's attention and brought him back to the house. The servant, Gehazi, couldn't do anything for the boy except confirm that the child was dead. Elisha attempted to revive the child, but was unsuccessful the first time; listen to the story as it reaches its climax and conclusion:

"He went in therefore, shut the door behind the two of them, and prayed to the Lord. And he went up and lay on the child, and put his mouth on his mouth, his eyes on his eyes, and his hands on his hands; and he stretched himself out on the child, and the flesh of the child became warm. He returned and walked back and forth in the house, and again went up and stretched himself out on him; then the child sneezed seven times, and the child opened his eyes." The son was restored to his mother. It is great to see a child brought back to life.

So, why does this story have a happy ending, when the beloved child whose body lies here today was not so fortunate? I'm here to share with you the hope that God offers through Jesus Christ. There is a day coming when this child, all his/her friends, and loved ones can be reunited with each other. Death does not end life, it begins it. Eternity is in front of us. The Lord is just and righteous to deal with our children; the question is, how will we respond to Him?

Conclusion: This child's parents or loved ones have a choice to make. Accept Jesus Christ as your Savior and join this child in heaven. Do you know Christ as your Savior? John 3:16 says: "For God so loved the world that He gave His only begotten Son, that whoever believes in Him should not perish but have everlasting life." Do you believe? Have you turned from your sins and asked Christ to come into your life? You can do this today. Even in the face of such difficulty, God offers hope through Jesus Christ. Trust in Him and in the promises given to you through the Bible; give Him your heart and let Him ease your pain.

FUNERAL SERMON

Especially for a Non-Christian

Choices

By Rev. Richard Sharpe Jr.

Today we have gathered in honor and memory of ____________________.

Personal Comments

Scripture: Luke 16:19–31 (NASB)

Introduction: This life is full of choices. Experts tell us we make over a hundred decisions each day. We decide what time to get up, what clothes to wear for the day, which way to drive to work or even whether to go to work. The choices are always before us. We never face a day without choices. Well, today we have a choice to make. The choice is where we will spend eternity. Some of us have made that choice, but others don't want to think about it. One day that choice will be final. As we gather in honor of our friend, we're faced with an important question: Where will we spend eternity when we leave this earth?

1. **Two Men.** We read in the Gospel of Luke about two men. Some call this a parable. In it we are given a vivid account of two types of people.

   A. **The First Was a Rich Man.** "There was a certain rich man who was clothed in purple and fine linen and fared sumptuously every day" (v. 19). Here we learn some things about this man: he was rich, wore fine clothes, and lived in luxury. This man had everything money could buy. He had taken hold of life and lived it to the hilt. He had no worries from a human perspective. Everyone would like to live this way. We often wish we could do anything we wanted and go wherever we desired without worrying about the cost. Here was that person. He did it his way.

   B. **The Second Man Was Lazarus.** He was "full of sores ... desiring to be fed with the crumbs which fell from the rich man's table. Moreover the dogs came and licked his sores" (vv. 20, 21). Lazarus was a beggar with no place to live except the street. His only friends were dogs, and dogs were his only medical help. He had nothing. He was disdained and friendless. Christ told this story to let people know there are two types of individuals in the world. This beggar trusted in God for help and comfort.

2. **Two Choices.** Not only did these men differ in their lifestyle, they also differed in their personal choices. All of us have the same choices to make.

   A. **Lazarus.** "So it was that the beggar died, and was carried by the angels to Abraham's bosom" (v. 22). The beggar had no known burial, but he was carried by angels to this place of comfort, also referred to as Abraham's bosom. We learn later that this is a place called paradise (Luke 23:43). Paradise, or Abraham's bosom, is a place for those who believe in Jesus Christ to save them from the punishment of sin and give their lives to Him as Lord. Lazarus made this choice.
   B. **The Rich Man.** "And the rich man also died and was buried. In Hades he lifted up his eyes, being in torment, and saw Abraham far away and Lazarus in his bosom. And he cried out and said, 'Father Abraham, have mercy on me, and send Lazarus so that he may dip the tip of his finger in water and cool off my tongue, for I am in agony in this flame.' But Abraham said, 'Child, remember that during your life you received your good things, and likewise Lazarus bad things; but now he is being comforted here, and you are in agony. And besides all this, between us and you there is a great chasm fixed, so that those who wish to come over from here to you will not be able, and that none may cross over from there to us'" (Luke 16:22–26 NASB).

The rich man had a funeral, was buried, and found himself in a place called Hades or hell, a place of torment. While he was there, the rich man wanted mercy; he quickly learned that after death there is no mercy. He also learned from Abraham that the Bible is the only source of learning about life after death. Most of all, he learned that the choices made in life affect our eternal future. The rich man made the wrong choice; he ignored the Scripture that directs us to Jesus Christ!

Conclusion: Each one here today has a choice to make concerning eternity. We can choose to believe in Christ, following Him as Lord or we can live for ourselves with no hope for the future. If you choose Jesus Christ, then you must confess your sin and believe in the gospel of Christ. This gospel tells us that Christ died on the Cross for our sins, was buried, and rose from the dead. If you want more information regarding this way of life, please see me after the service.

The other choice is to go your own way and live as if this life was all that matters. Once this choice is made, you'll have to live with it for all eternity. The question to consider, as we are faced with the reality of life and death, is what choice will you make?

FUNERAL SERMON

For a Suicide Victim

Only One Unpardonable Sin

By Rev. Richard Sharpe Jr.

Today we have gathered in honor and memory of ____________________.

Personal Comments

Scripture: John 3:9–21; 10:25–30

Introduction: One of the problems we have with this type of tragedy is we are unsure what the Bible teaches about suicide. Some believe that if someone takes his/her own life they will never go to heaven. This leaves family and friends in serious doubt and pain. The Bible is clear about the problem of sin in our world. There is only one way to get into heaven—through our Lord Jesus Christ. He died on the Cross for the sins of the world. In this time of sorrow, we must ask very important questions:

1. **Was Our Loved One a Child of the King?** The Bible tells us in John 3:16, "For God so loved the world that He gave His only begotten Son, that whoever believes in Him should not perish but have everlasting life." So, anyone who asks Christ to come into his or her heart has everlasting life with the Father. Many people go to church, give their money, and do good deeds but have never made a commitment to Christ. They think their good works will get them into heaven. This simply isn't so. But as they realize that God can give them hope, they begin looking for answers in Him.

Jesus often met with religious folks during His lifetime on earth. In one instance, He talked with a man named Nicodemus. This man was a teacher of the Jewish religion who came to Jesus by night. He asked questions. Jesus told Him what it really means to be born again spiritually: "Whoever believes in [Jesus] should not perish but have eternal life" (John 3:15). Romans 10:9, 10 tells us, "If you confess with your mouth the Lord Jesus and believe in your heart that God has raised Him from the dead, you will be saved. For with the heart one believes unto righteousness, and with the mouth confession is made unto salvation." If we want to be born of the Spirit, we have to confess and believe. We need to confess that we are people who have sinned. We have to admit that we are outcasts in the sight of God. We have to admit that we can't save ourselves. We have to believe that Jesus died on the Cross for our sins and that He was raised from the dead to give us eternal life in heaven. If we confess and believe, we have eternal life. The King will accept us into His kingdom of heaven.

2. **Was Our Loved One Condemned by the King?** Let's return to John chapter three. In verse 18 we read: "He who believes in Him is not condemned; but he who does not believe is condemned already, because he has not believed in the name of the only begotten Son of God" (NKJV). Here we see that belief in Christ takes condemnation away from an individual. Only not believing condemns someone—nothing else can. John 3:36 tells us that those who do not believe in Him must endure God's wrath.

3. **Can Anyone or Anything Take a Believer Out of the Father's Hand?** We have to ask, "Is my loved one someone who had accepted Christ as his/her personal Savior?" Only two people know the answer to this question: our loved one and God. We have to leave our loved one in the hands of a holy and just God. Remember John 10:28, 29: "And I give them eternal life, and they shall never perish; neither shall anyone snatch them out of My hand. My Father, who has given them to Me, is greater than all; and no one is able to snatch them out of My Father's hand" (NKJV). Once someone enters the family of God he will never leave, no matter what happens in this life.

Conclusion: In such a time of great sorrow and distress, we can trust God with our loved one. The question that remains with us is: Have we accepted Christ as our personal Savior so we can join our loved ones in heaven? I encourage you to confess and believe in the Lord Jesus Christ. There is only one thing that will keep us out of heaven, that is to not believe in the Lord Jesus Christ. Here in the midst of death, we are given an opportunity for eternal life!

Prayer: Lord, take these words of our Lord Jesus and bless them to our hearts: "Let not your heart be troubled; you believe in God, believe also in Me. In My Father's house are many mansions; if it were not so, I would have told you. I go to prepare a place for you. And if I go and prepare a place for you, I will come again and receive you to Myself; that where I am, there you may be also" (John 14:1–3 NKJV).

Special Services Registry

The forms on the following pages are designed to be duplicated and used repeatedly as neeeded. Most copy machines will allow you to enlarge them to fill a full page if desired. Since they also are included in the CD-ROM in the back of the book, you may use that digital file to customize the forms to fit your specific needs.

Sermons Preached

Date	Text	Title/Subject

Sermons Preached

Date	Text	Title/Subject

Marriages Log

Date	Bride	Groom

Funerals Log

Date	Name of Deceased	Scripture Used

Baptisms / Confirmations

Date	Name	Notes

Baby Dedication Registration

Infant's Name: ______________________________

Significance of Given Names: ______________________________

Date of Birth: ______________________________

Parents' Names: ______________________________

____

Siblings: ______________________________

____

____

____

Maternal Grandparents: ______________________________

Paternal Grandparents: ______________________________

Life Verse: ______________________________

Date of Dedication: ______________________________

Wedding Registration

Date of Wedding: ______________________________

Location of Wedding: ______________________________

Bride: ______________________________

Religious Affiliation: ______________________________

Bride's Parents: ______________________________

Groom: ______________________________

Religious Affiliation: ______________________________

Groom's Parents: ______________________________

Ceremony to be Planned by Minister: __________ by Couple: __________

Other Minister(s) Assisting: ______________________________

Maid/Matron of Honor: ______________________________

Best Man: ______________________________

Wedding Planner: ______________________________

Date of Rehearsal: ______________________________

Reception Open to All Wedding Guests: ______ By Invitation Only: ______

Location of Reception: ______________________________

Wedding Photos to be Taken:__________ During Ceremony

__________ After Ceremony

Other ______________________________

Date of Counseling: ______________________________

Date of Registration: ______________________________

Funeral Registration

Name of Deceased: ______________________________

Age: ______________________________

Religious Affiliation: ______________________________

Survivors:

Spouse: ______________________________

Parents: ______________________________

Children: ______________________________

Siblings: ______________________________

Grandchildren: ______________________________

Date of Death: ______________________________

Time and Place of Visitation: ______________________________

Date of Funeral or Memorial Service: ______________________________

Funeral Home Responsible: ______________________________

Location of Funeral or Memorial Service: ______________________________

Scripture Used: ______________ Hymns Used: ______________

Eulogy by: ______________________________

Other Minister(s) Assisting: ______________________________

Pallbearers: ______________________________

Date of Interment: ______________ Place of Interment: ______________

Graveside Service: _______Yes No _______

Subject Index

Scripture Index

1. **Minimum System Requirements**

Computer/Processor
- Intel Pentium III or AMD Athlon with CD-ROM Drive

Operating System
- Windows 98 SE, Window ME, Windows 2000, or Windows XP including all Windows Updates

Memory
- 128MB RAM

Hard Drive Space
- 250 MB Minimum

Screen Resolution
- 800x600 or Higher

2. **Contact Information**

Technical Support
Email: nelsoncdtech@thomasnelson.con
Web: www.nelsonreference.com
Phone: (615) 902-2440
Fax: (615) 902-2450

SOFTWARE LICENSE AGREEMENT